I'm stubborn as those garbage bags
that time cannot decay,

I'm junk but I'm still holding up
this little wild bouquet.

— Leonard Cohen, "Democracy"

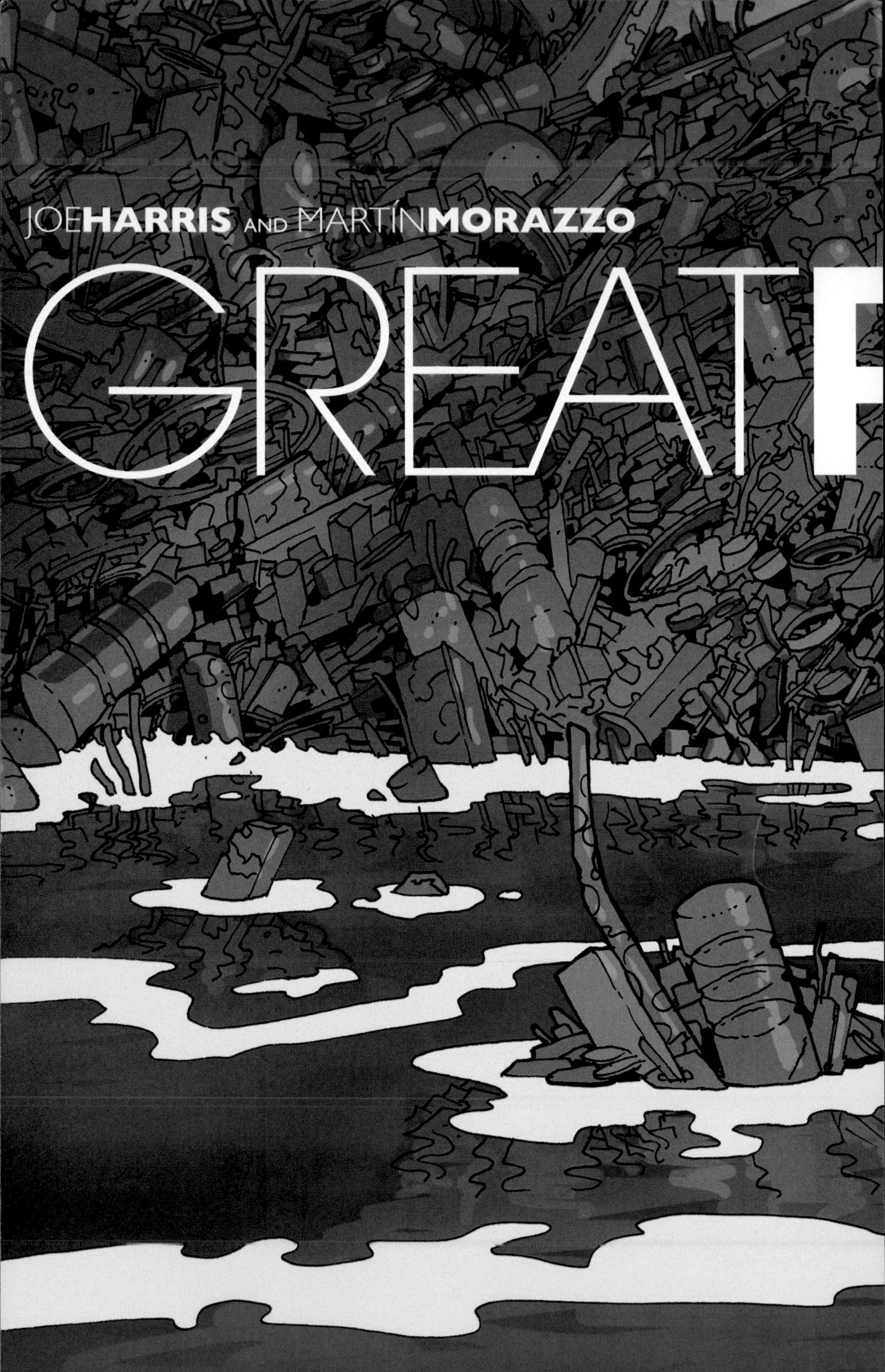
JOE HARRIS AND MARTÍN MORAZZO
GREAT

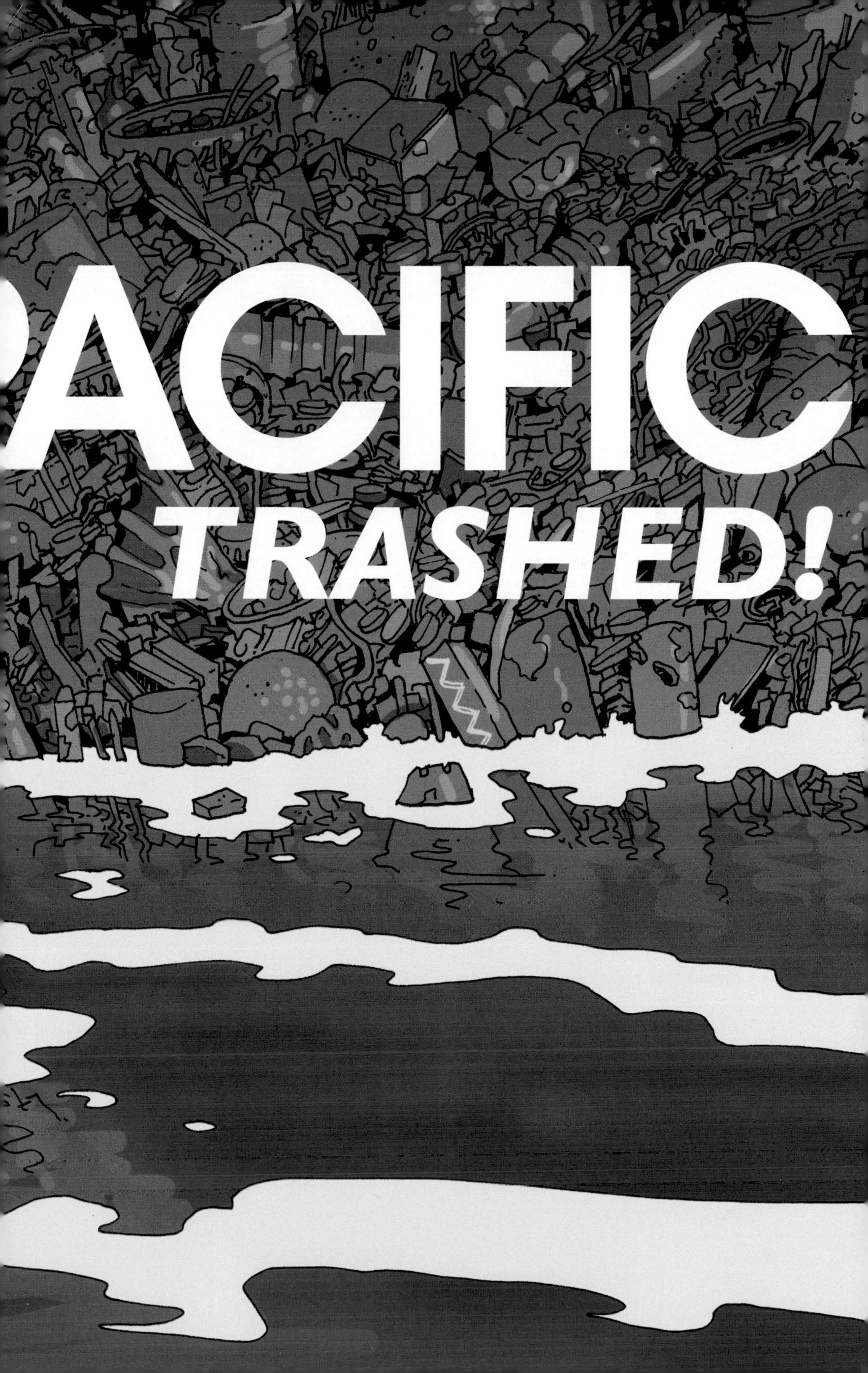
PACIFIC
TRASHED!

CREATED BY
JOE**HARRIS** AND
MARTÍN**MORAZZO**

WRITTEN BY
JOE**HARRIS**

ART BY
MARTÍN**MORAZZO**

COLORS BY
TIZA **STUDIO**

LETTERS BY
DOUGLAS E. **SHERWOOD**

DESIGN BY SEAN**DOVE**
EDITED BY SHAWNA**GORE**

WWW. GREATPACIFICCOMICS.COM
WWW.IMAGECOMICS.COM

PUBLISHED BY IMAGE COMICS, INC.

This book collects issues **1-6** of the
Image Comics series **GREAT PACIFIC**

First edition May 2013
ISBN — 978-1-60706-684-2

Great Pacific™: Trashed! 2013. Published by Image Comics. © and
™ 2013 Joe Harris. Names, characters, places, and incidents fea-
tured in this publication either are the product of the author's
imagination or are used fictitiously. Any resemblance to actual per-
sons (living or dead) events, institutions, or locales, without satiric
intent, is coincidental. Printed in the U.S.A. For information regard-
ing the CPSIA on this printed material call: 203-595-3636 and
provide reference # RICH – 484911.

For Foreign Licensing Inquiries:
foreignlicensing@imagecomics.com

CHAPTER**ONE**

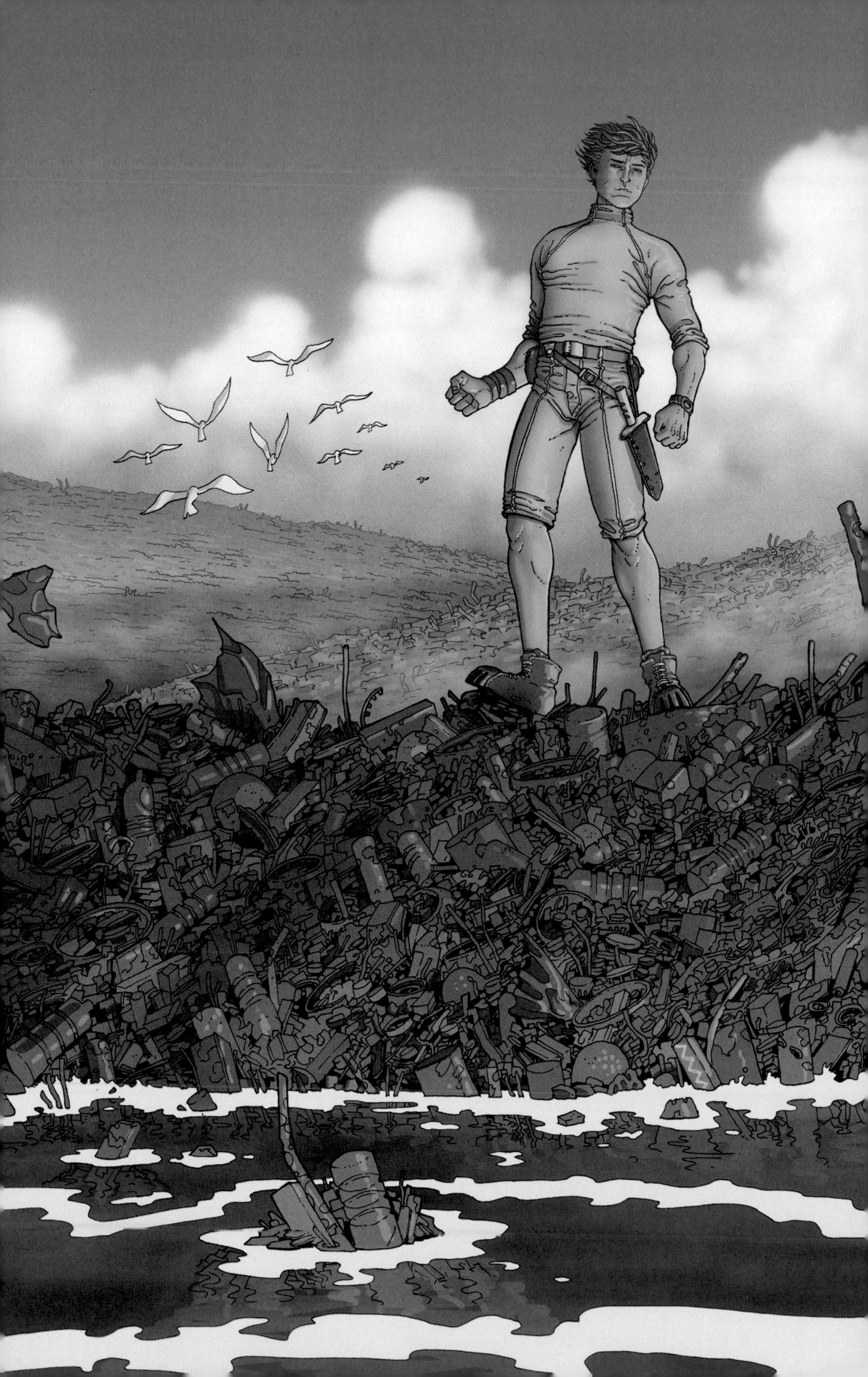

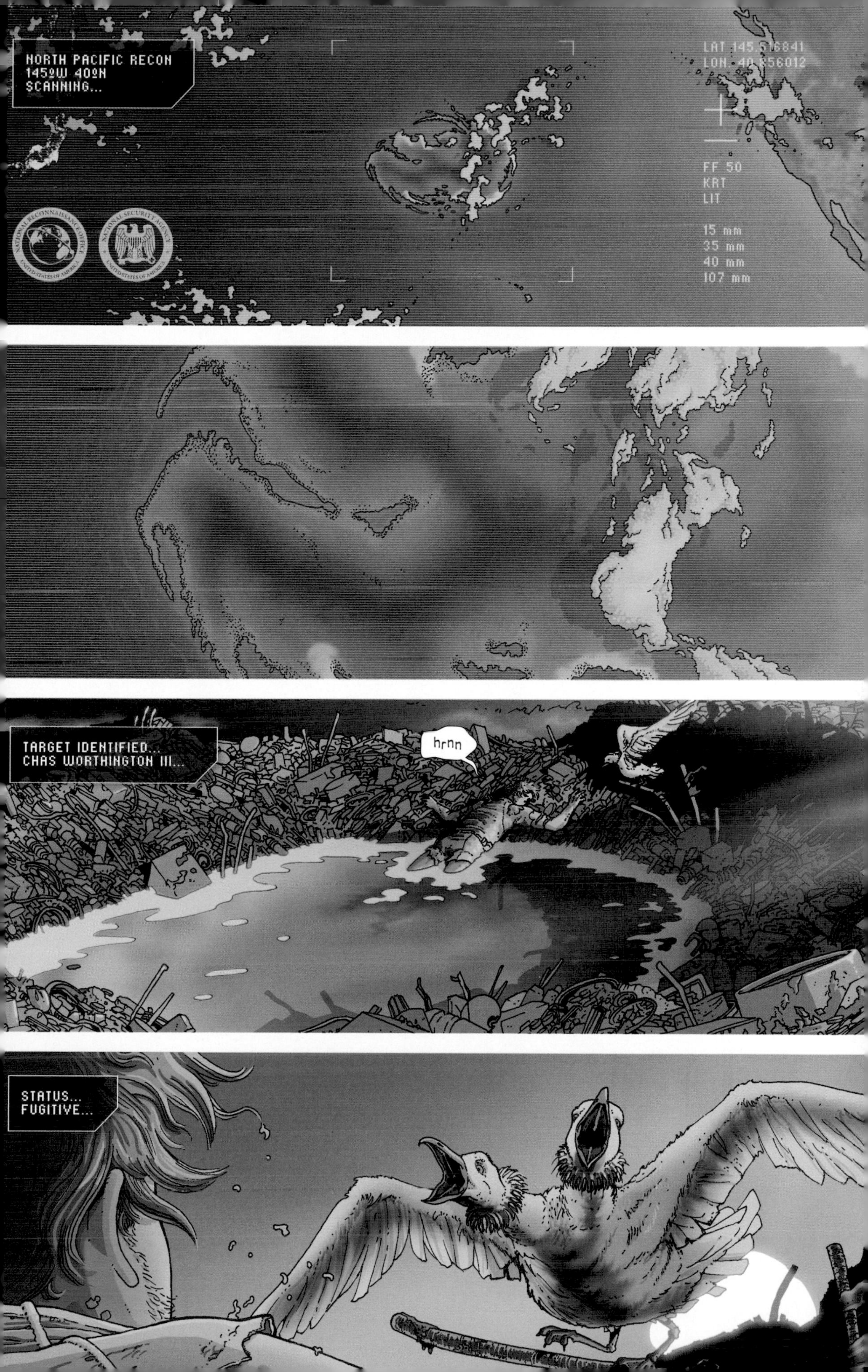
NORTH PACIFIC RECON
145ºW 40ºN
SCANNING...
LAT 145.516841
LON 40.856012
FF 50
KRT
LIT
15 mm
35 mm
40 mm
107 mm
TARGET IDENTIFIED...
CHAS WORTHINGTON III...
hrnn
STATUS...
FUGITIVE...

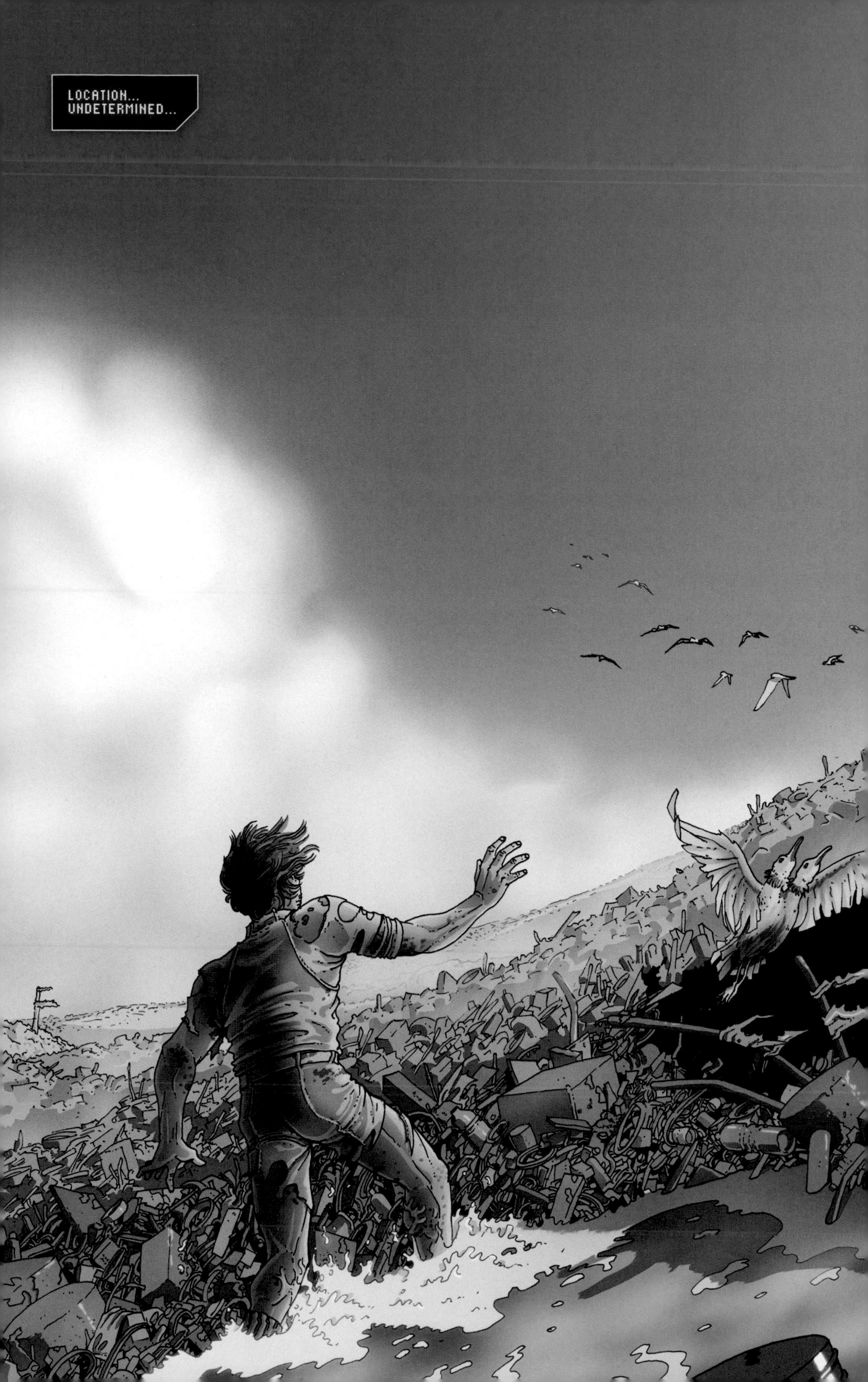
LOCATION...
UNDETERMINED...

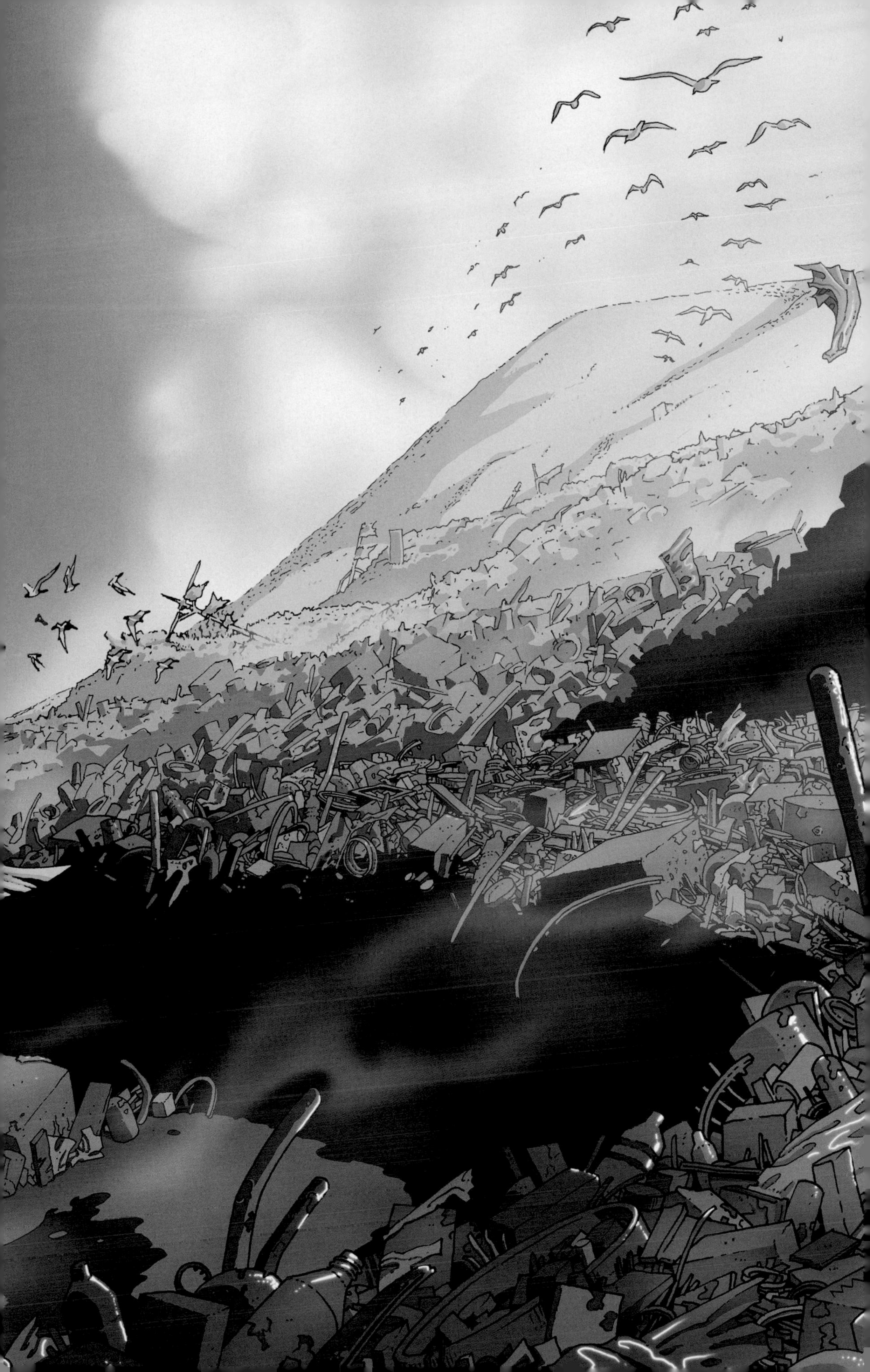

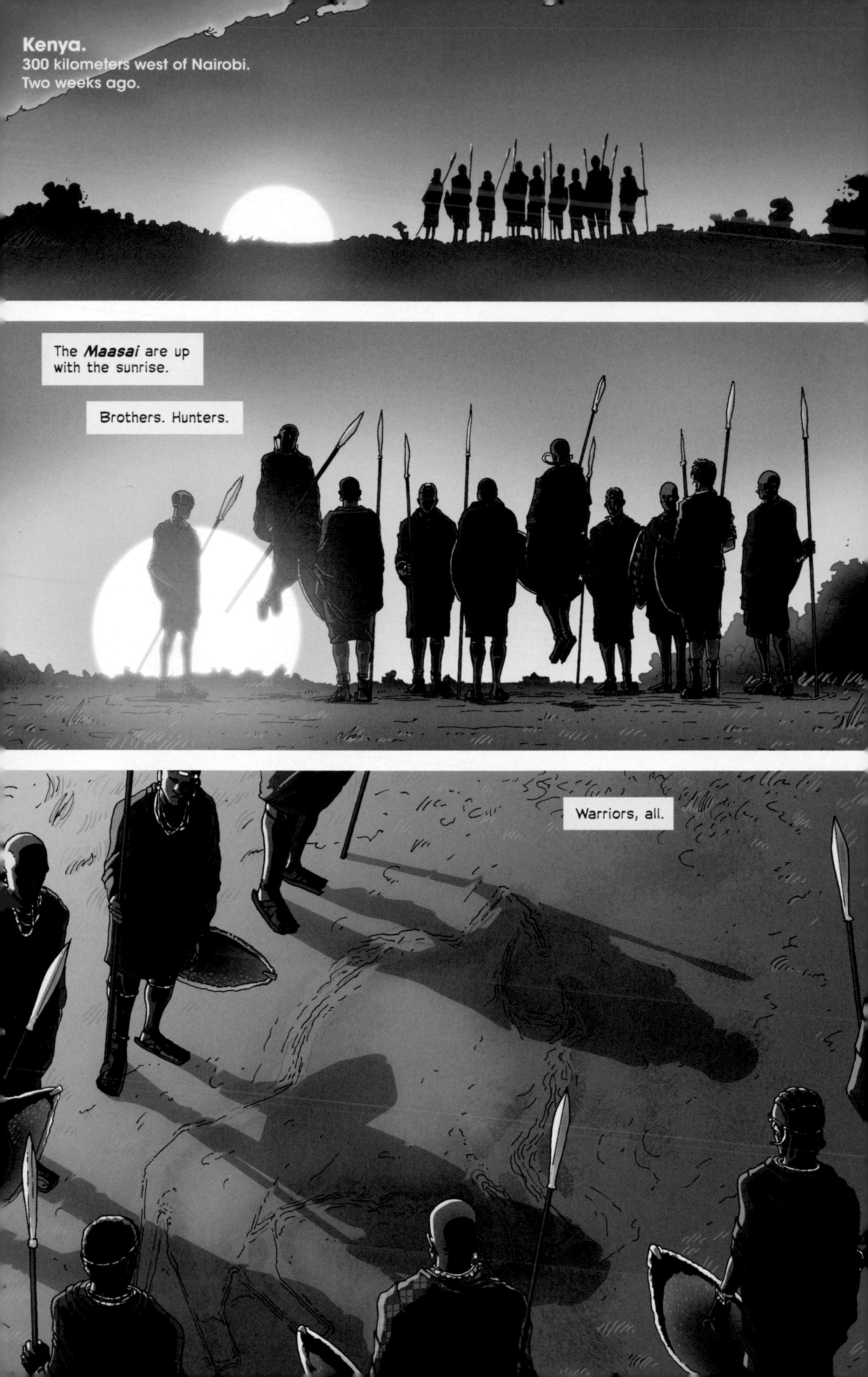
Kenya.
300 kilometers west of Nairobi.
Two weeks ago.
The *Maasai* are up with the sunrise.
Brothers. Hunters.
Warriors, all.

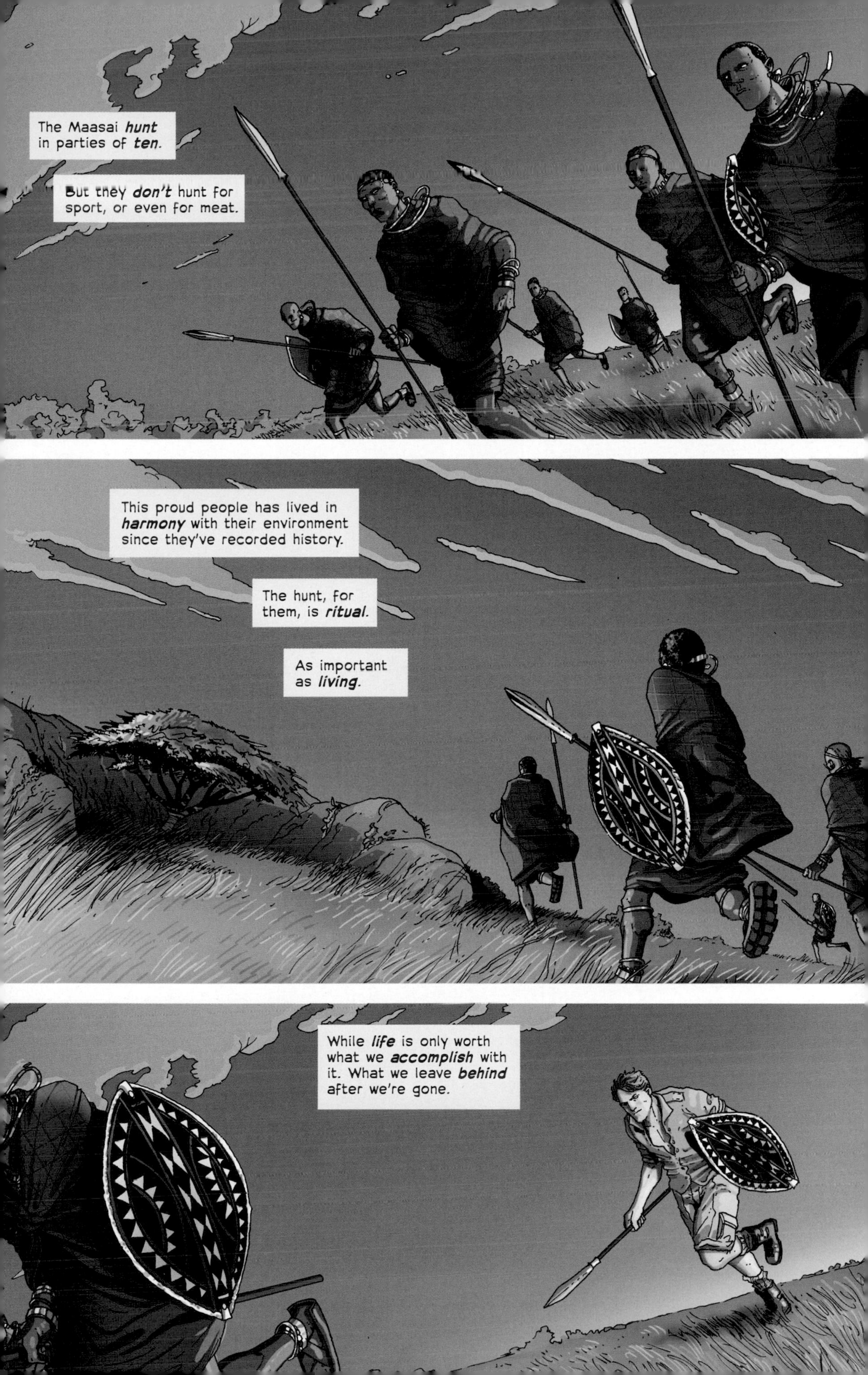
The Maasai *hunt* in parties of *ten*.
But they *don't* hunt for sport, or even for meat.
This proud people has lived in *harmony* with their environment since they've recorded history.
The hunt, for them, is *ritual*.
As important as *living*.
While *life* is only worth what we *accomplish* with it. What we leave *behind* after we're gone.

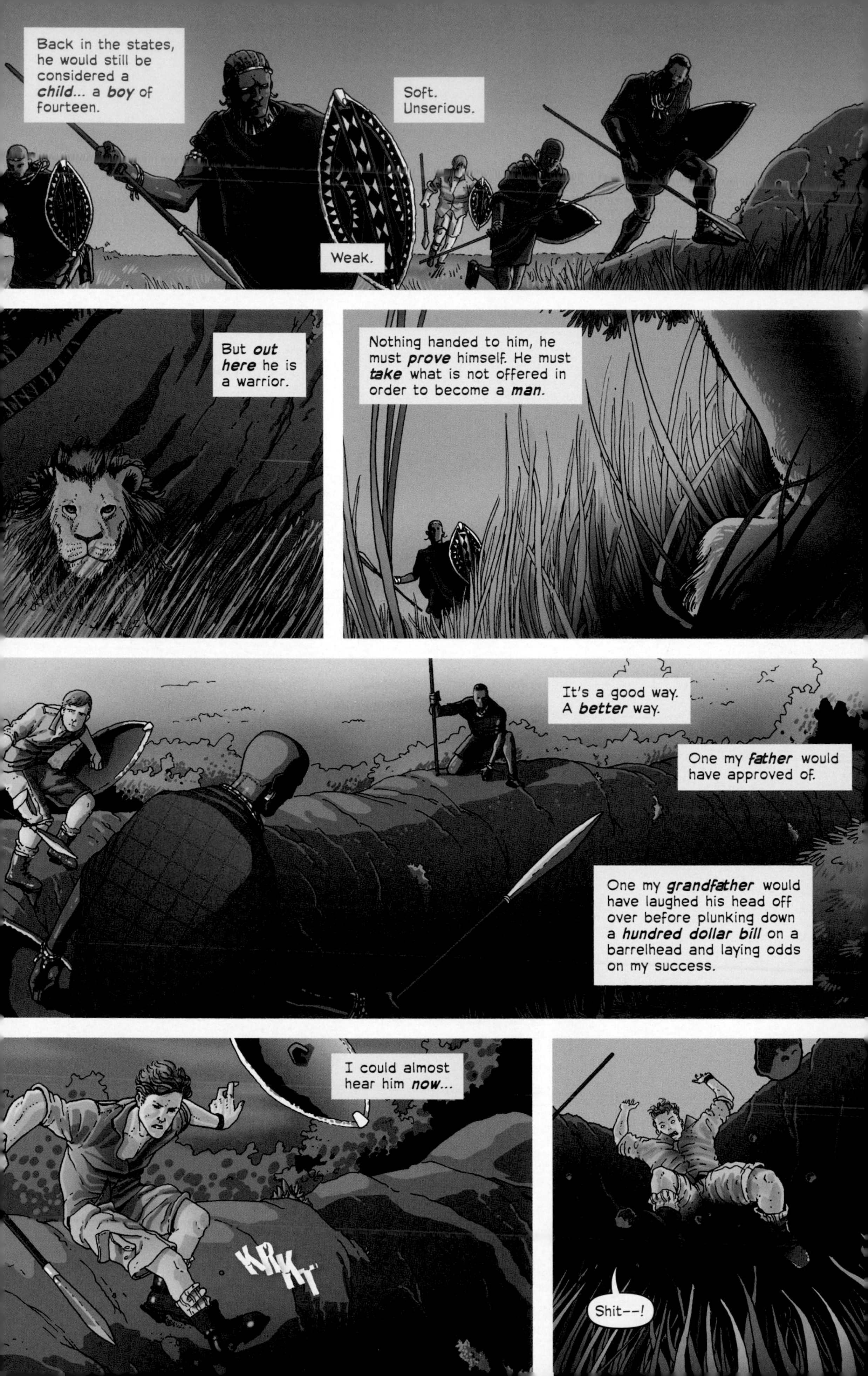

Back in the states, he would still be considered a *child*... a *boy* of fourteen.
Soft. Unserious.
Weak.
But *out here* he is a warrior.
Nothing handed to him, he must *prove* himself. He must *take* what is not offered in order to become a *man*.
It's a good way. A *better* way.
One my *father* would have approved of.
One my *grandfather* would have laughed his head off over before plunking down a *hundred dollar bill* on a barrelhead and laying odds on my success.
I could almost hear him *now*...
KRKKT
Shit--!

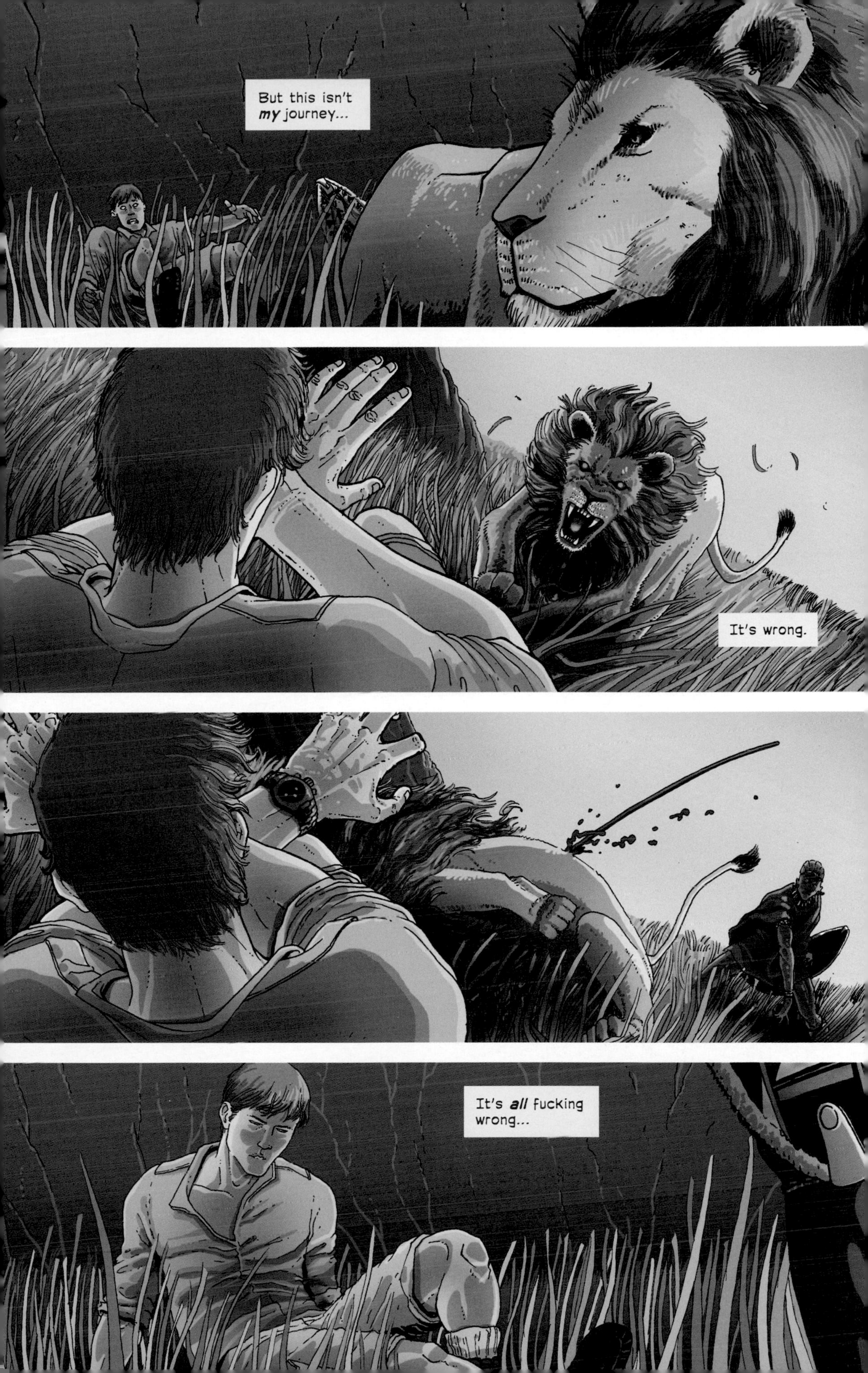
But this isn't *my* journey...
It's wrong.
It's *all* fucking wrong...

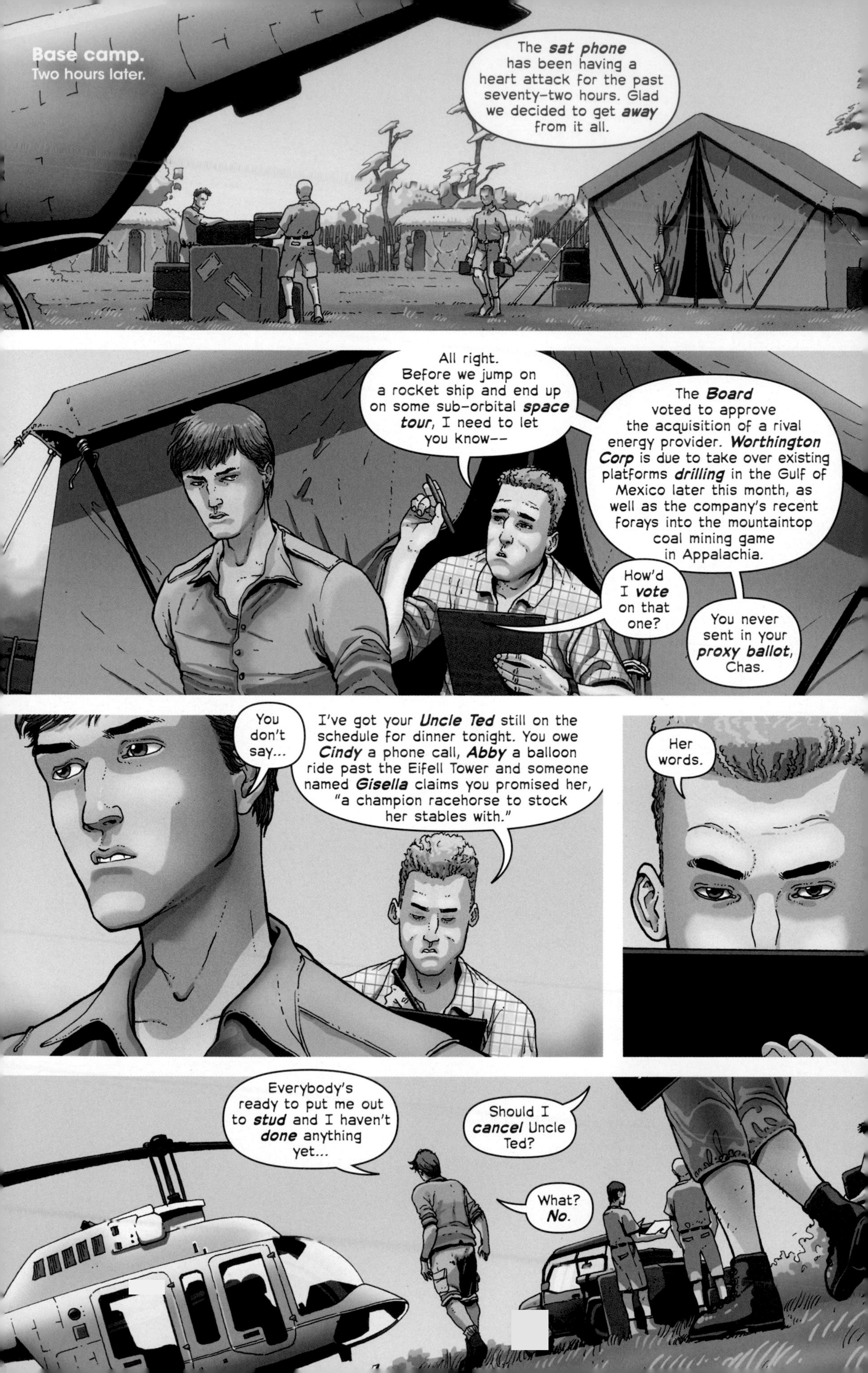
Base camp.
Two hours later.
The sat phone has been having a heart attack for the past seventy-two hours. Glad we decided to get away from it all.
All right. Before we jump on a rocket ship and end up on some sub-orbital space tour, I need to let you know--
The Board voted to approve the acquisition of a rival energy provider. Worthington Corp is due to take over existing platforms drilling in the Gulf of Mexico later this month, as well as the company's recent forays into the mountaintop coal mining game in Appalachia.
How'd I vote on that one?
You never sent in your proxy ballot, Chas.
You don't say...
I've got your Uncle Ted still on the schedule for dinner tonight. You owe Cindy a phone call, Abby a balloon ride past the Eifell Tower and someone named Gisella claims you promised her, "a champion racehorse to stock her stables with."
Her words.
Everybody's ready to put me out to stud and I haven't done anything yet...
Should I cancel Uncle Ted?
What? No.

I'm supposedly the *heir* to everything the great *Worthington* name has built for itself. Cancel Paris.

Ted is *family*.

Oh, one more thing...

We got some strange email from the *Center For Environmental Studies* in *Oslo*. They say you ordered some data on something called...

The *Pacific Gyre*..?

I'll take care of that, Alex.

Well... what *is* it?

Mister Chas! Mister Chas!

For your help with *irrigation systems* and for stocking our *medical clinic* with supplies...

We extend to you a *gift*.

Oh... wow.

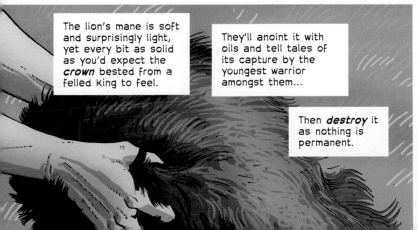

The lion's mane is soft and surprisingly light, yet every bit as solid as you'd expect the *crown* bested from a felled king to feel.

They'll anoint it with oils and tell tales of its capture by the youngest warrior amongst them...

Then *destroy* it as nothing is permanent.

This is *most* generous... but I *cannot* accept it.

I am sorry.

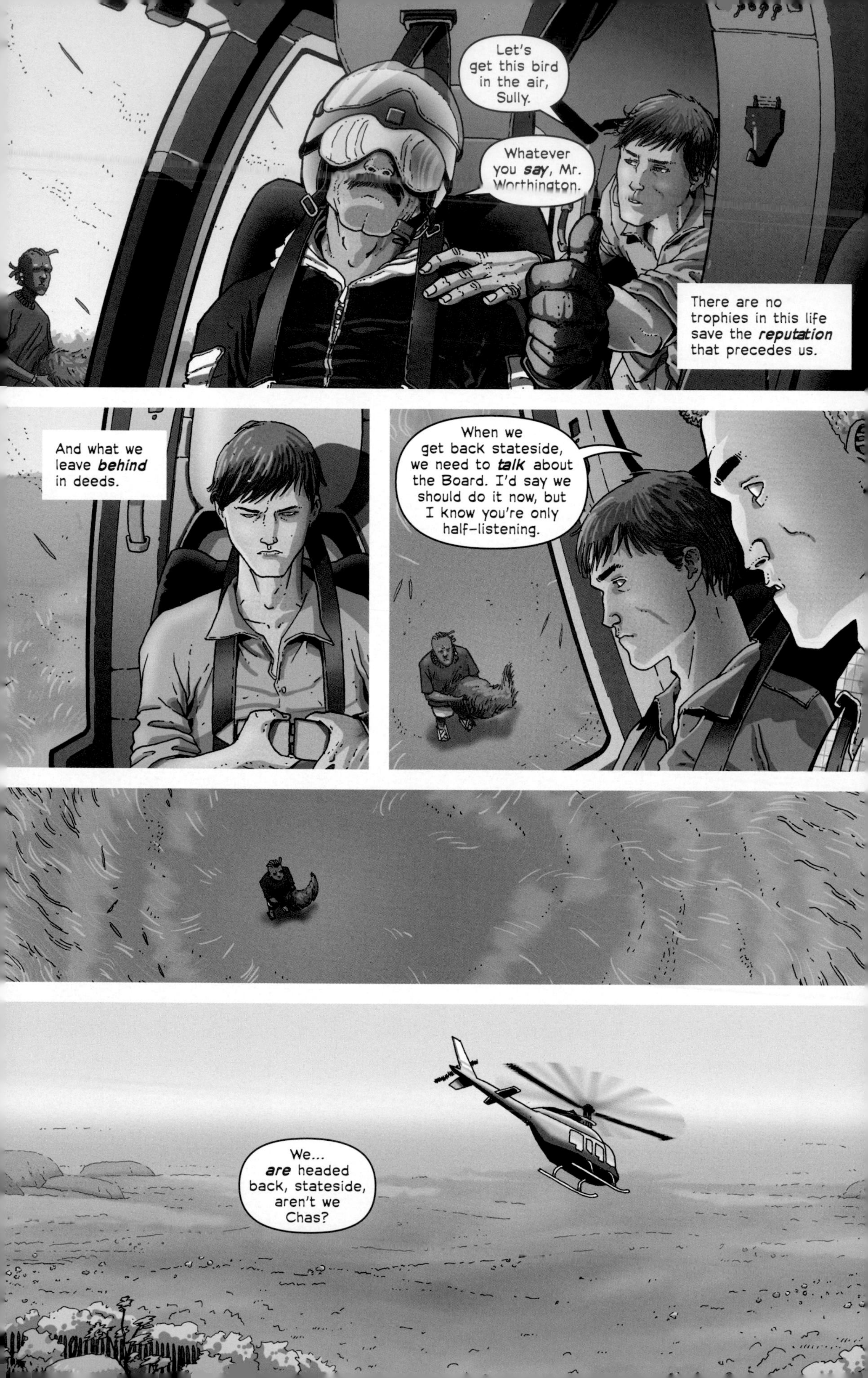
Let's get this bird in the air, Sully.
Whatever you *say*, Mr. Worthington.
There are no trophies in this life save the *reputation* that precedes us.
And what we leave *behind* in deeds.
When we get back stateside, we need to *talk* about the Board. I'd say we should do it now, but I know you're only half-listening.
We... *are* headed back, stateside, aren't we Chas?

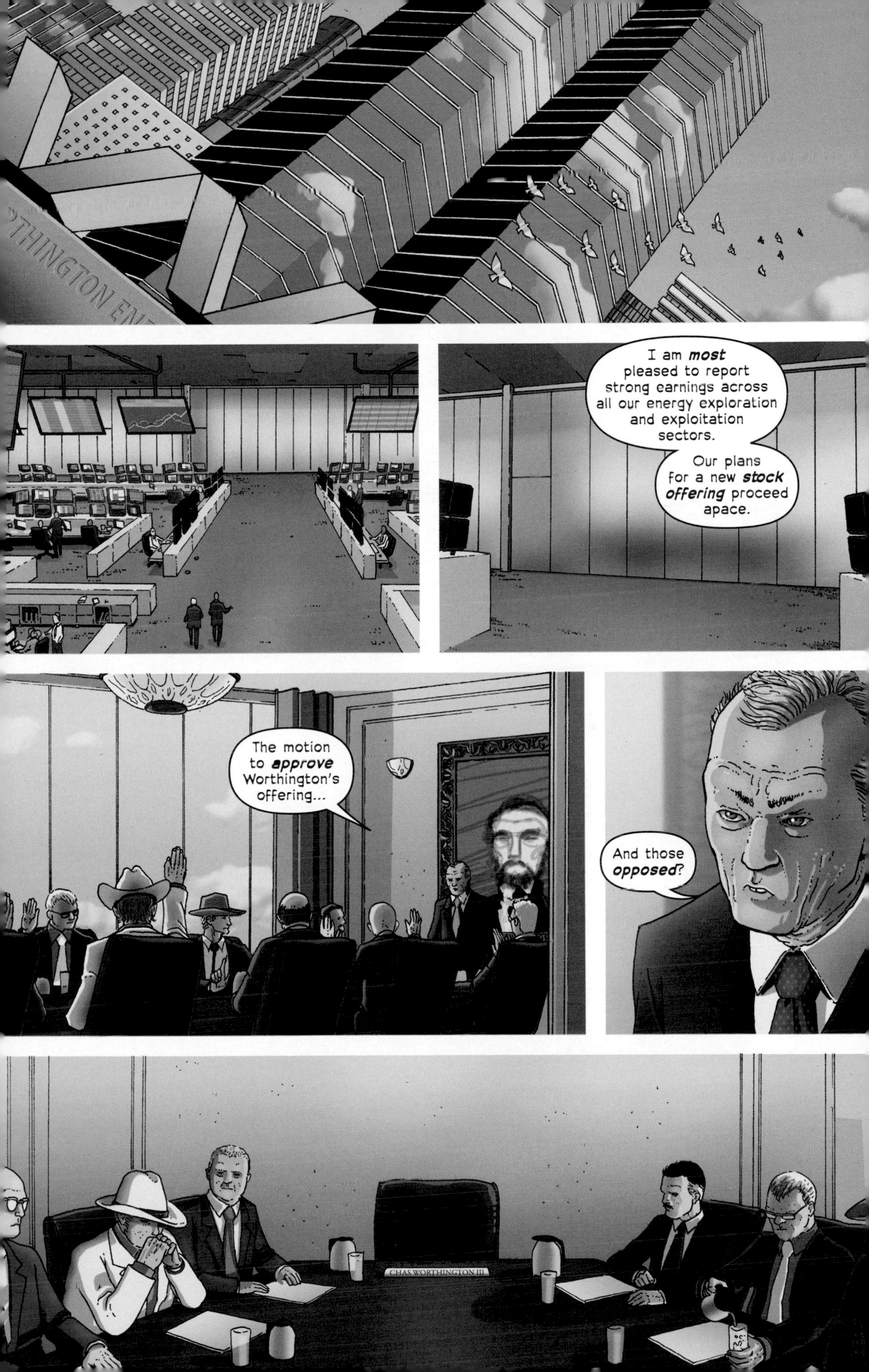

THINGTON ENE
I am *most* pleased to report strong earnings across all our energy exploration and exploitation sectors.
Our plans for a new *stock offering* proceed apace.
The motion to *approve* Worthington's offering...
And those *opposed*?
CHAS WORTHINGTON III

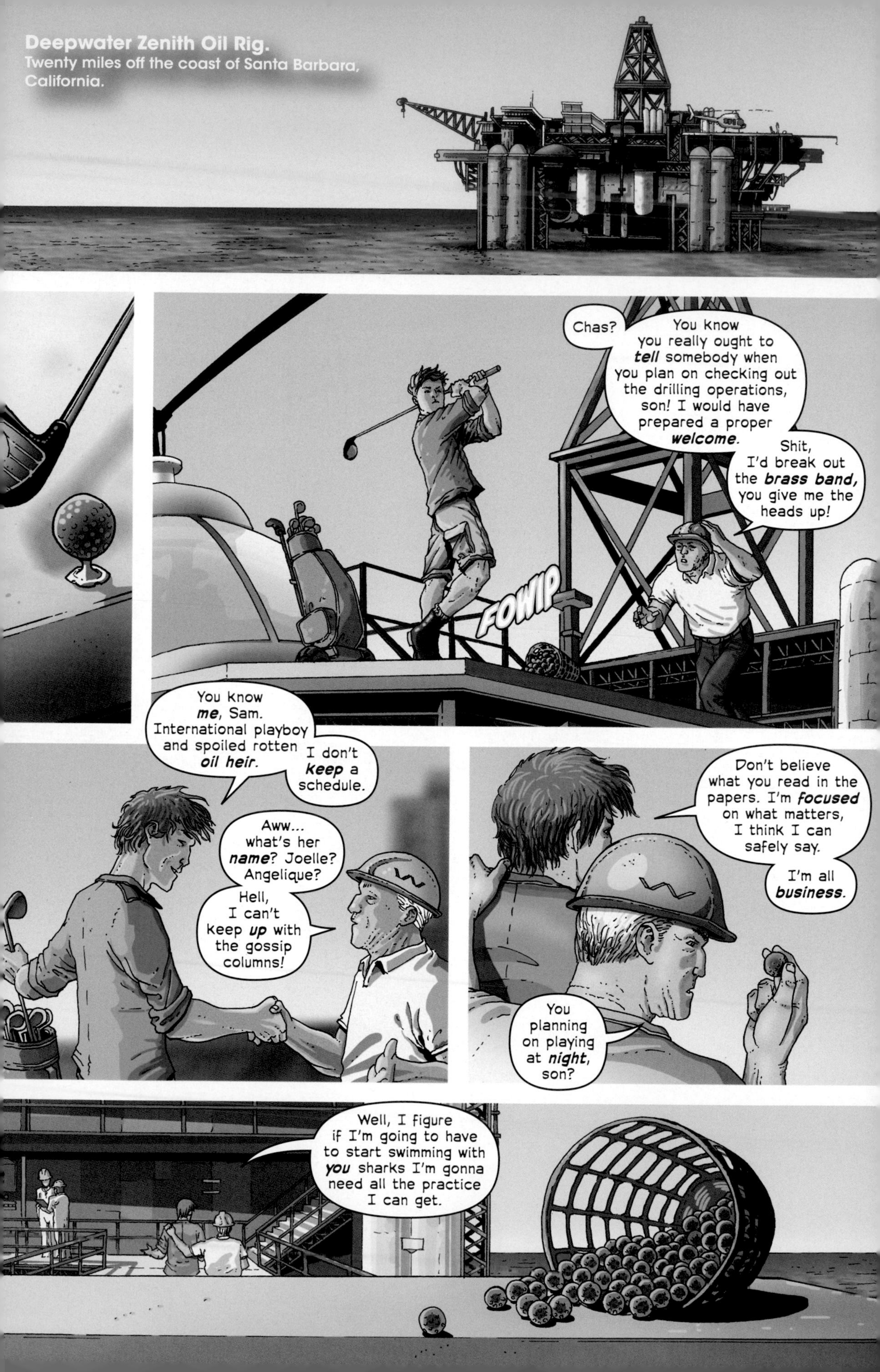

Deepwater Zenith Oil Rig.
Twenty miles off the coast of Santa Barbara, California.
Chas?
You know you really ought to tell somebody when you plan on checking out the drilling operations, son! I would have prepared a proper welcome.
Shit, I'd break out the brass band, you give me the heads up!
FOWIP
You know me, Sam. International playboy and spoiled rotten oil heir.
I don't keep a schedule.
Aww... what's her name? Joelle? Angelique?
Hell, I can't keep up with the gossip columns!
Don't believe what you read in the papers. I'm focused on what matters, I think I can safely say.
I'm all business.
You planning on playing at night, son?
Well, I figure if I'm going to have to start swimming with you sharks I'm gonna need all the practice I can get.

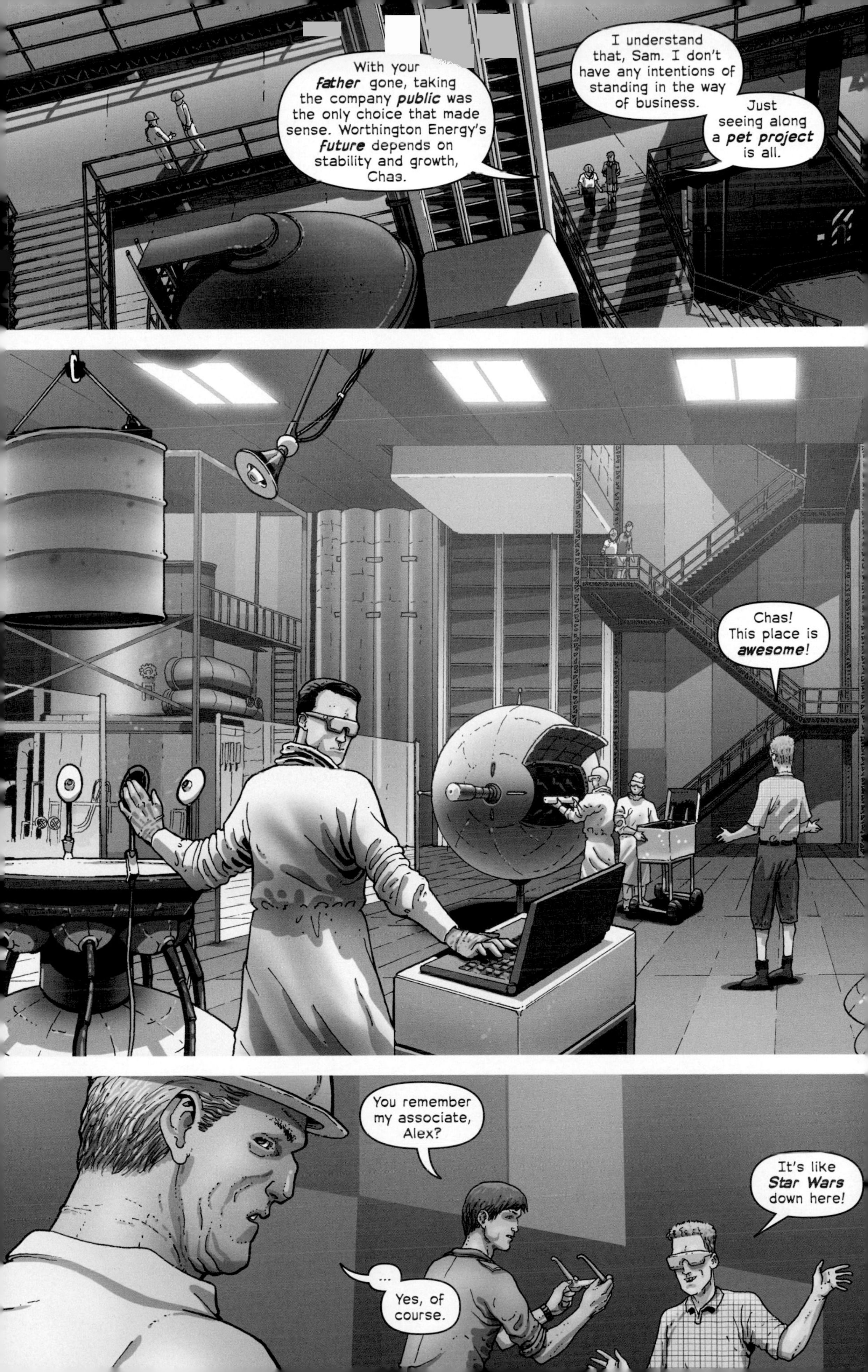
With your *father* gone, taking the company *public* was the only choice that made sense. Worthington Energy's *future* depends on stability and growth, Chas.
I understand that, Sam. I don't have any intentions of standing in the way of business.
Just seeing along a *pet project* is all.
Chas! This place is *awesome*!
You remember my associate, Alex?
... Yes, of course.
It's like *Star Wars* down here!

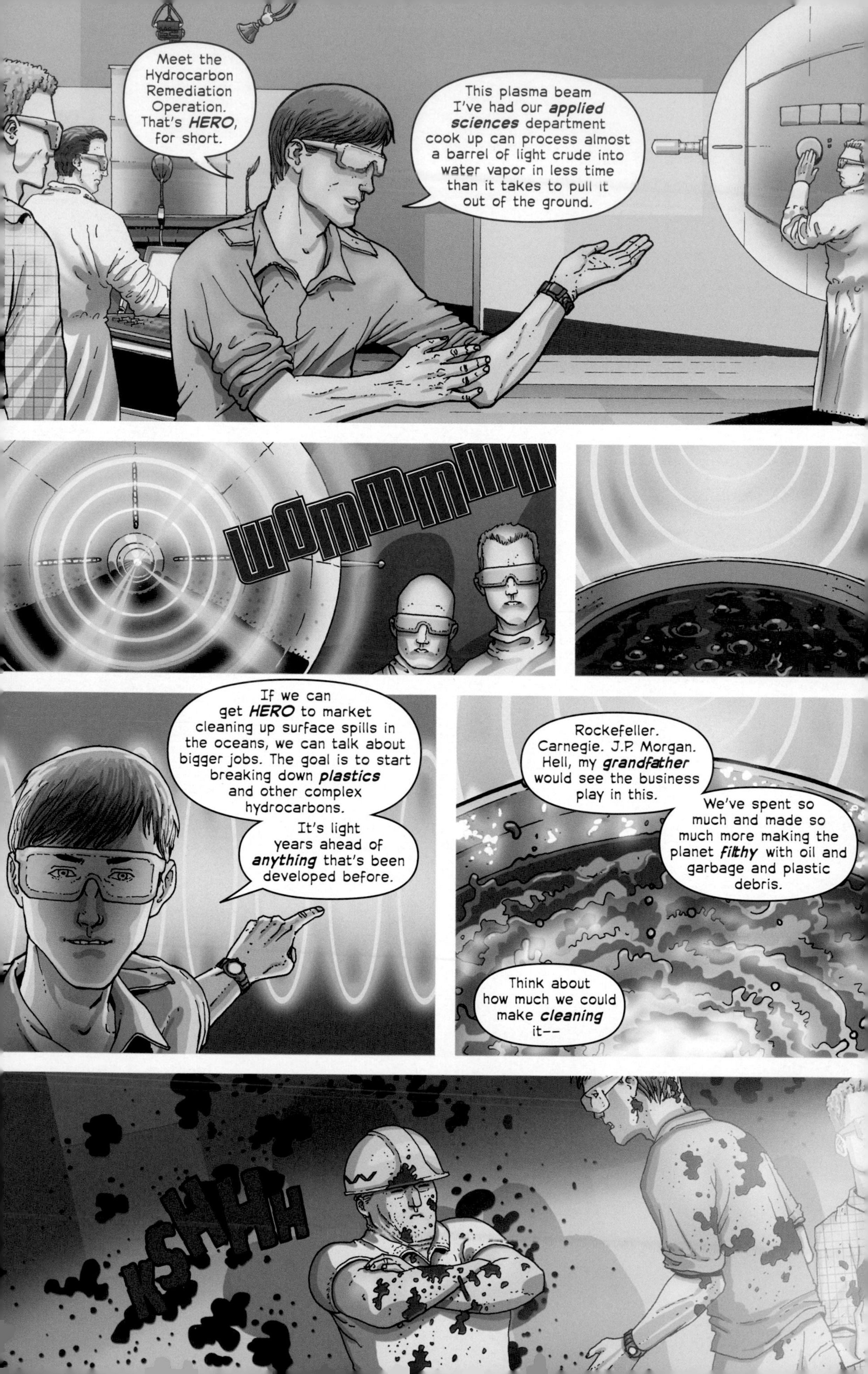
Meet the Hydrocarbon Remediation Operation. That's HERO, for short.
This plasma beam I've had our applied sciences department cook up can process almost a barrel of light crude into water vapor in less time than it takes to pull it out of the ground.
WOMMMMM
If we can get HERO to market cleaning up surface spills in the oceans, we can talk about bigger jobs. The goal is to start breaking down plastics and other complex hydrocarbons.
It's light years ahead of anything that's been developed before.
Rockefeller. Carnegie. J.P. Morgan. Hell, my grandfather would see the business play in this.
We've spent so much and made so much more making the planet filthy with oil and garbage and plastic debris.
Think about how much we could make cleaning it--
KSHHH

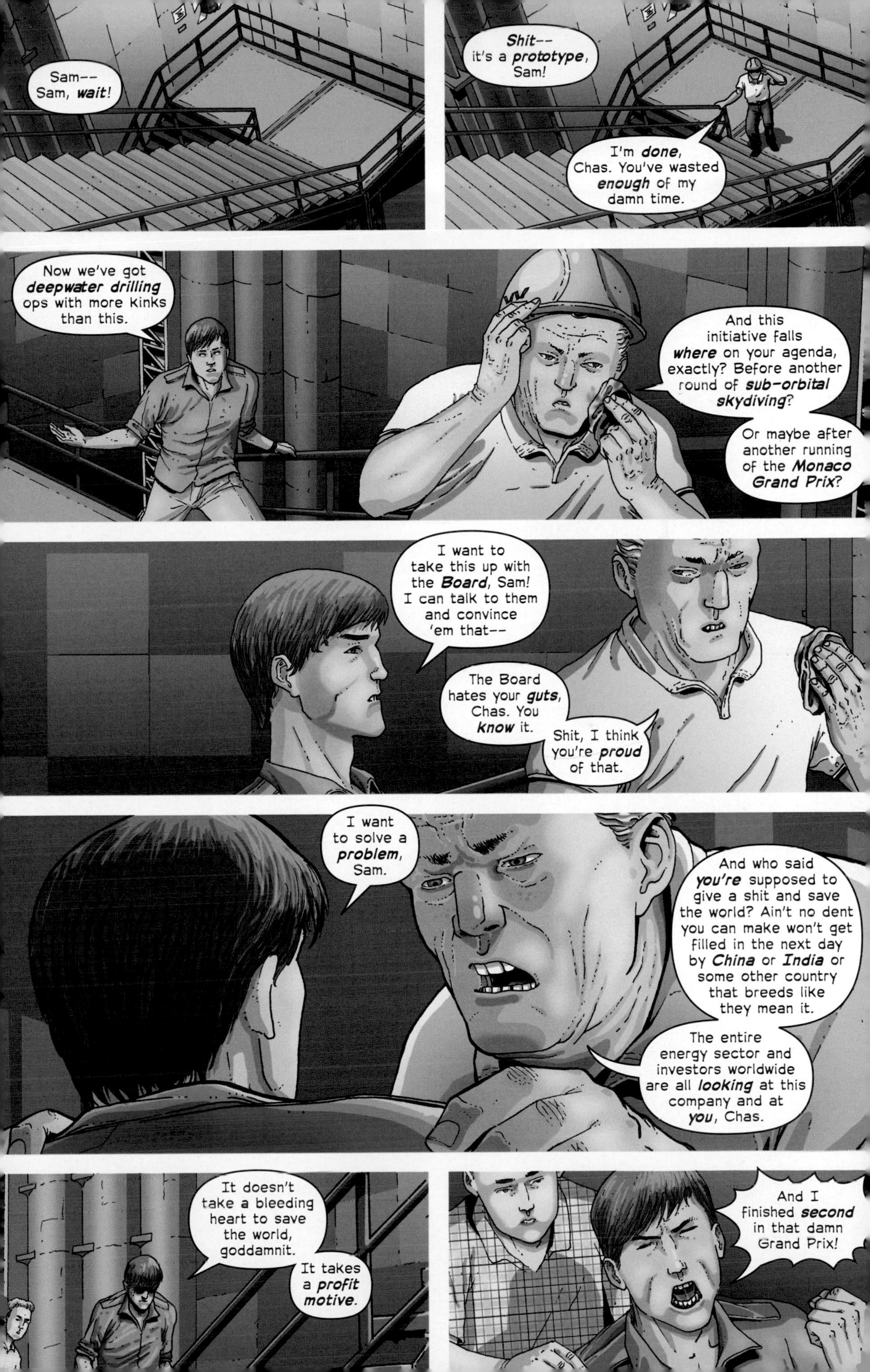
Sam--
Sam, *wait*!
Shit--
it's a *prototype*,
Sam!
I'm *done*,
Chas. You've wasted
enough of my
damn time.
Now we've got
deepwater drilling
ops with more kinks
than this.
And this
initiative falls
where on your agenda,
exactly? Before another
round of *sub-orbital*
skydiving?
Or maybe after
another running
of the *Monaco*
Grand Prix?
I want to
take this up with
the *Board*, Sam!
I can talk to them
and convince
'em that--
The Board
hates your *guts*,
Chas. You
know it.
Shit, I think
you're *proud*
of that.
I want
to solve a
problem,
Sam.
And who said
you're supposed to
give a shit and save
the world? Ain't no dent
you can make won't get
filled in the next day
by *China* or *India* or
some other country
that breeds like
they mean it.
The entire
energy sector and
investors worldwide
are all *looking* at this
company and at
you, Chas.
It doesn't
take a bleeding
heart to save
the world,
goddamnit.
It takes
a *profit*
motive.
And I
finished *second*
in that damn
Grand Prix!

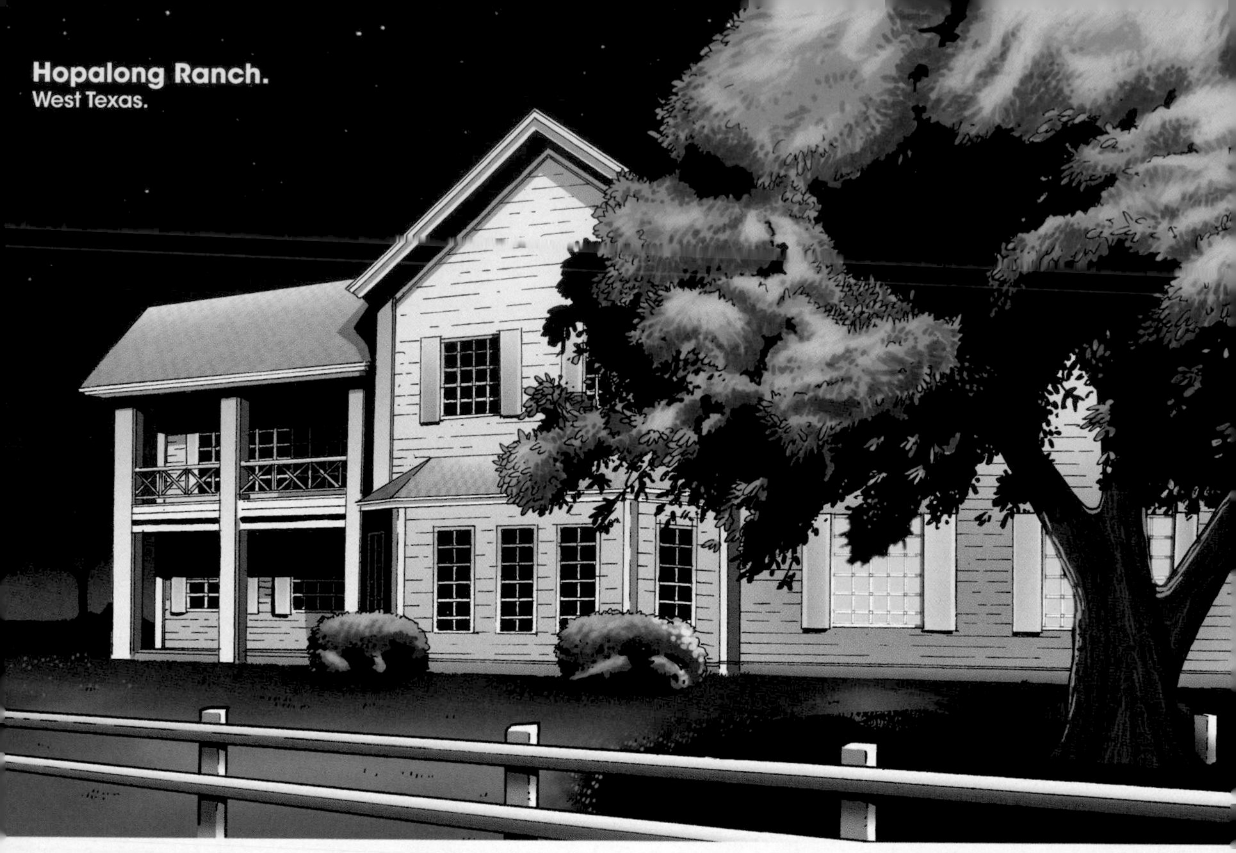
Hopalong Ranch.
West Texas.

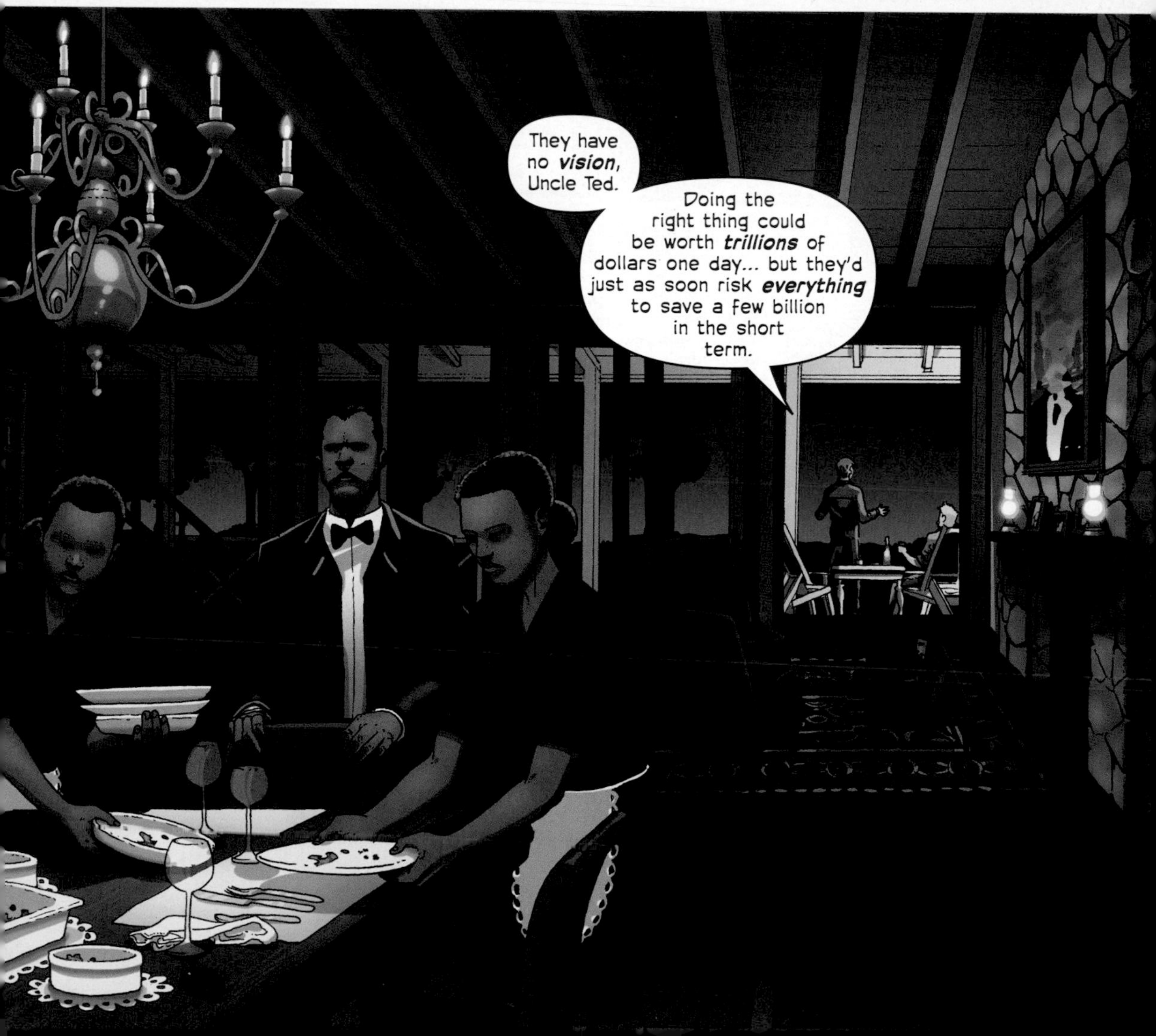
They have no ***vision***, Uncle Ted.
Doing the right thing could be worth ***trillions*** of dollars one day... but they'd just as soon risk ***everything*** to save a few billion in the short term.

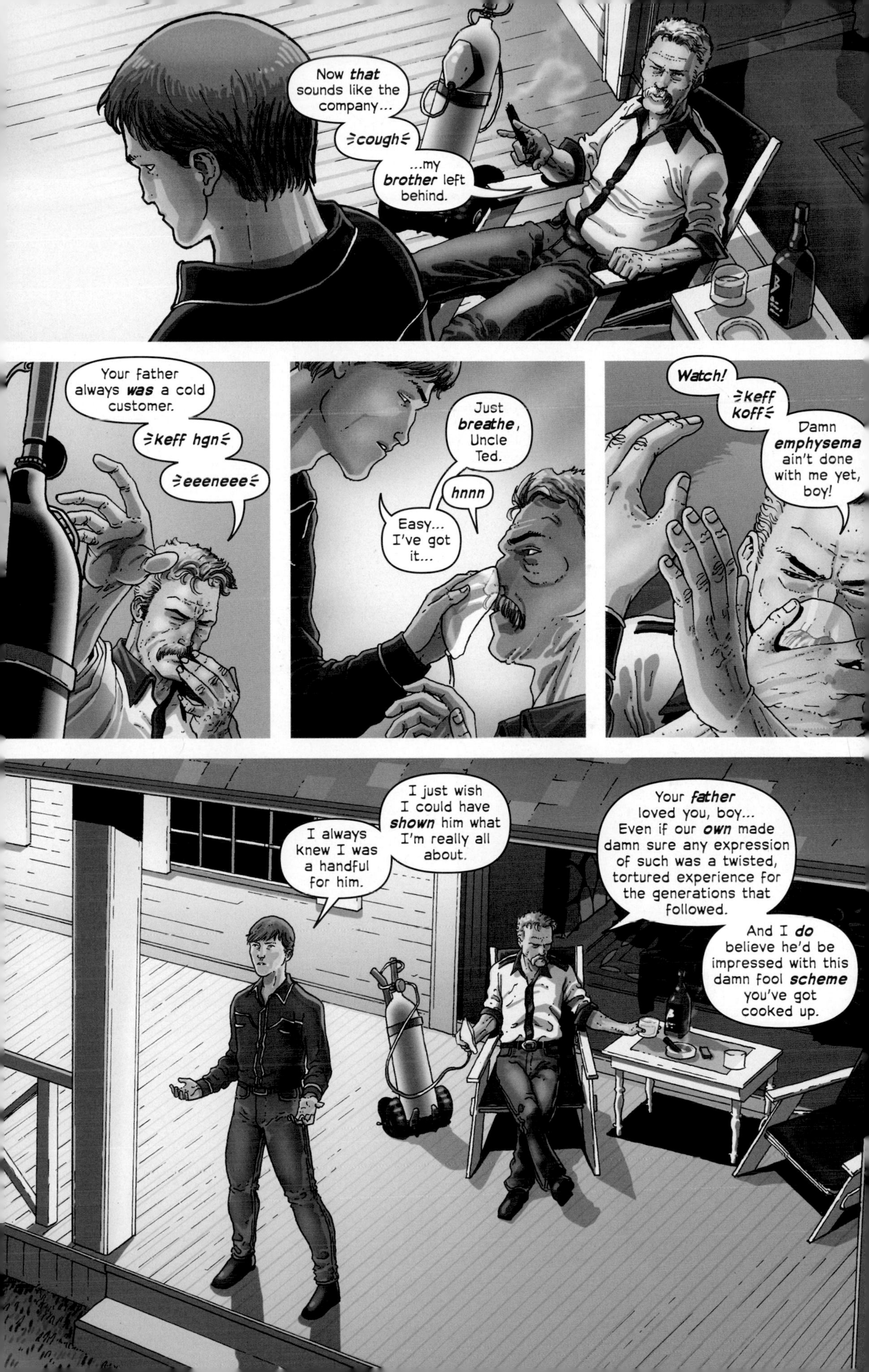

Now *that* sounds like the company...
≥*cough*≤
...my *brother* left behind.
Your father always *was* a cold customer.
≥*keff hgn*≤
≥*eeeneee*≤
Just *breathe*, Uncle Ted.
hnnn
Easy... I've got it...
Watch!
≥*keff koff*≤
Damn *emphysema* ain't done with me yet, boy!
I always knew I was a handful for him.
I just wish I could have *shown* him what I'm really all about.
Your *father* loved you, boy... Even if our *own* made damn sure any expression of such was a twisted, tortured experience for the generations that followed.
And I *do* believe he'd be impressed with this damn fool *scheme* you've got cooked up.

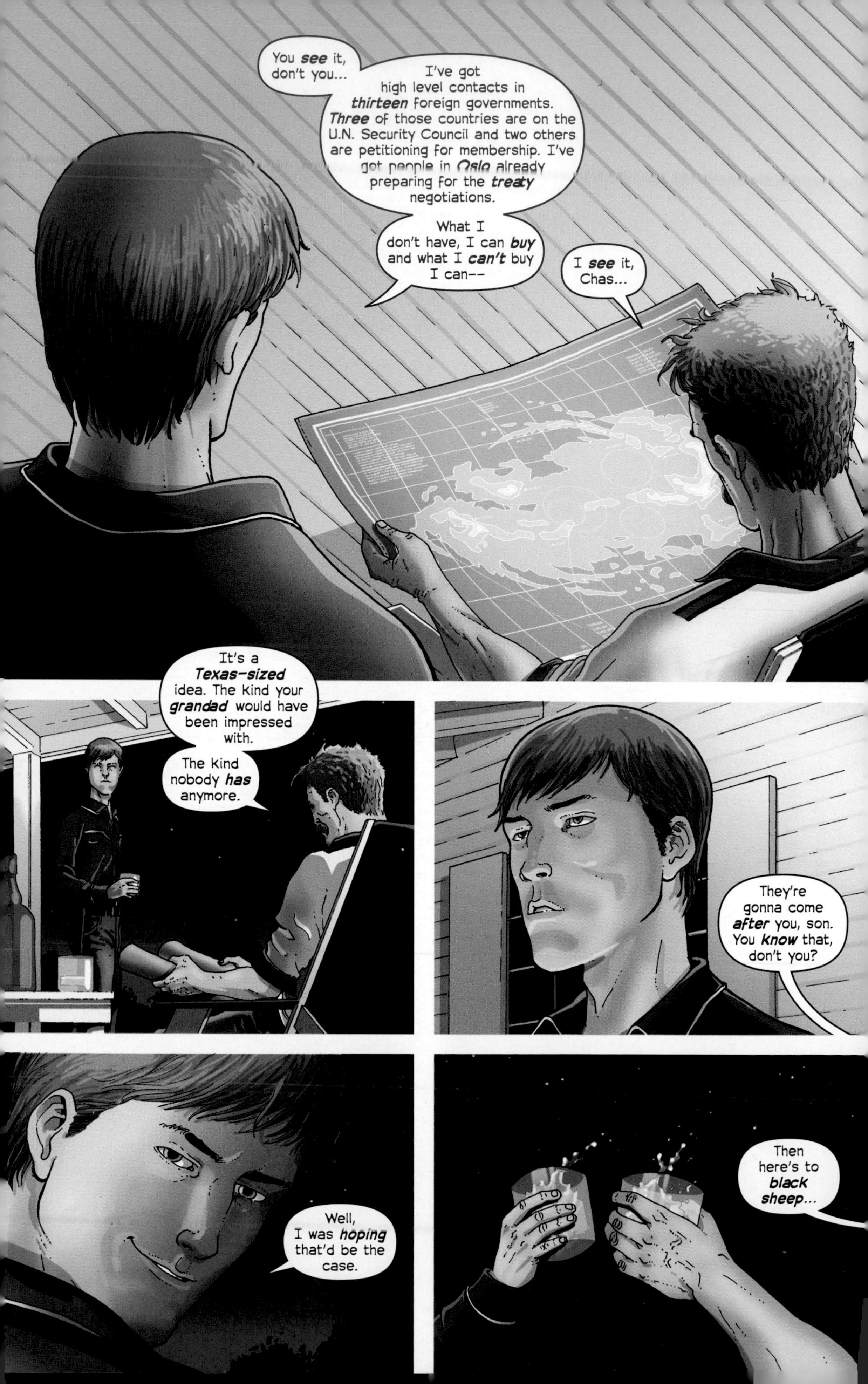
You see it, don't you...
I've got high level contacts in thirteen foreign governments. Three of those countries are on the U.N. Security Council and two others are petitioning for membership. I've got people in Oslo already preparing for the treaty negotiations.
What I don't have, I can buy and what I can't buy I can--
I see it, Chas...
It's a Texas-sized idea. The kind your grandad would have been impressed with.
The kind nobody has anymore.
They're gonna come after you, son. You know that, don't you?
Well, I was hoping that'd be the case.
Then here's to black sheep...

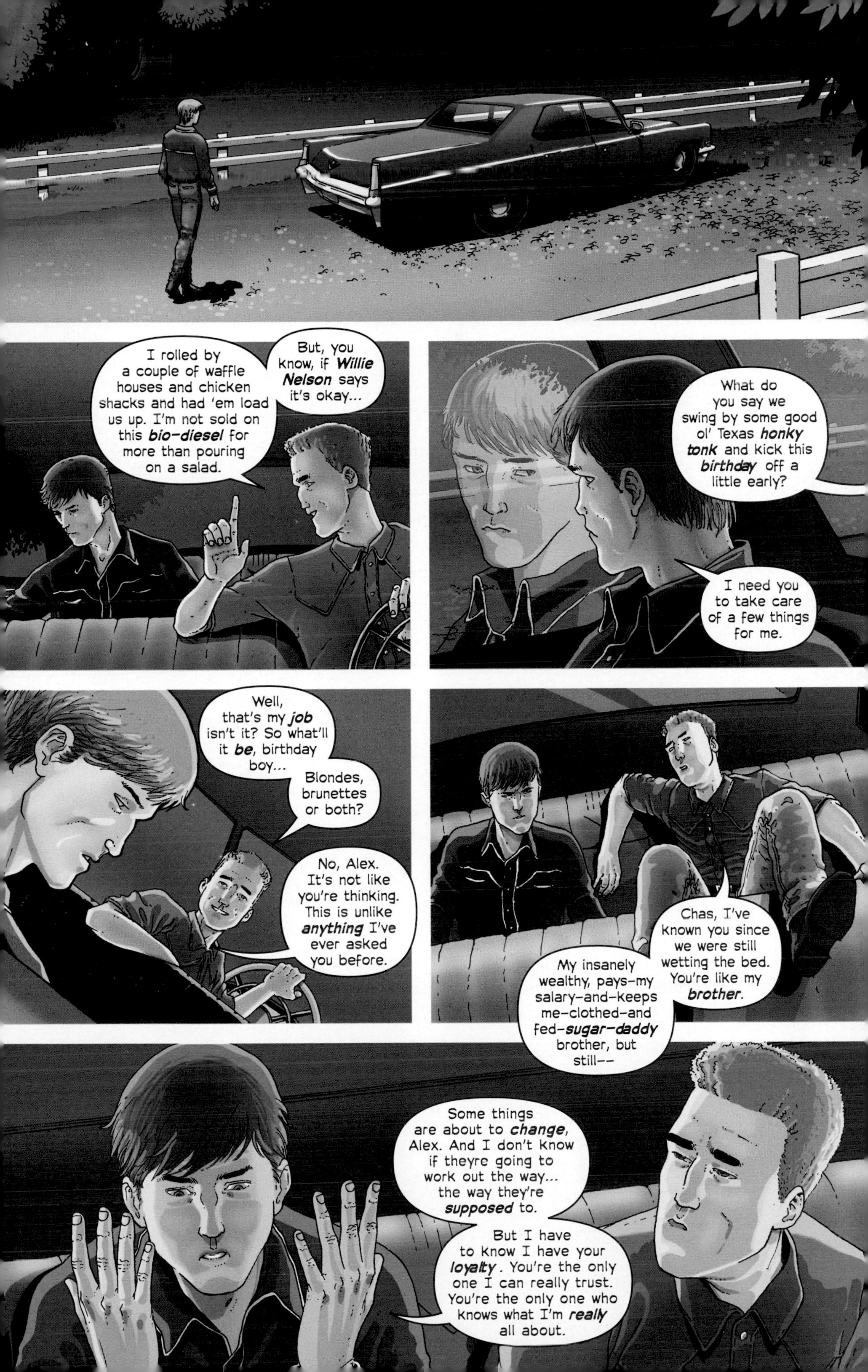
I rolled by a couple of waffle houses and chicken shacks and had 'em load us up. I'm not sold on this *bio-diesel* for more than pouring on a salad.
But, you know, if *Willie Nelson* says it's okay...
What do you say we swing by some good ol' Texas *honky tonk* and kick this *birthday* off a little early?
I need you to take care of a few things for me.
Well, that's my *job* isn't it? So what'll it *be*, birthday boy...
Blondes, brunettes or both?
No, Alex. It's not like you're thinking. This is unlike *anything* I've ever asked you before.
Chas, I've known you since we were still wetting the bed. You're like my *brother*.
My insanely wealthy, pays-my salary-and-keeps me-clothed-and fed-*sugar-daddy* brother, but still--
Some things are about to *change*, Alex. And I don't know if theyre going to work out the way... the way they're *supposed* to.
But I have to know I have your *loyalty*. You're the only one I can really trust. You're the only one who knows what I'm *really* all about.

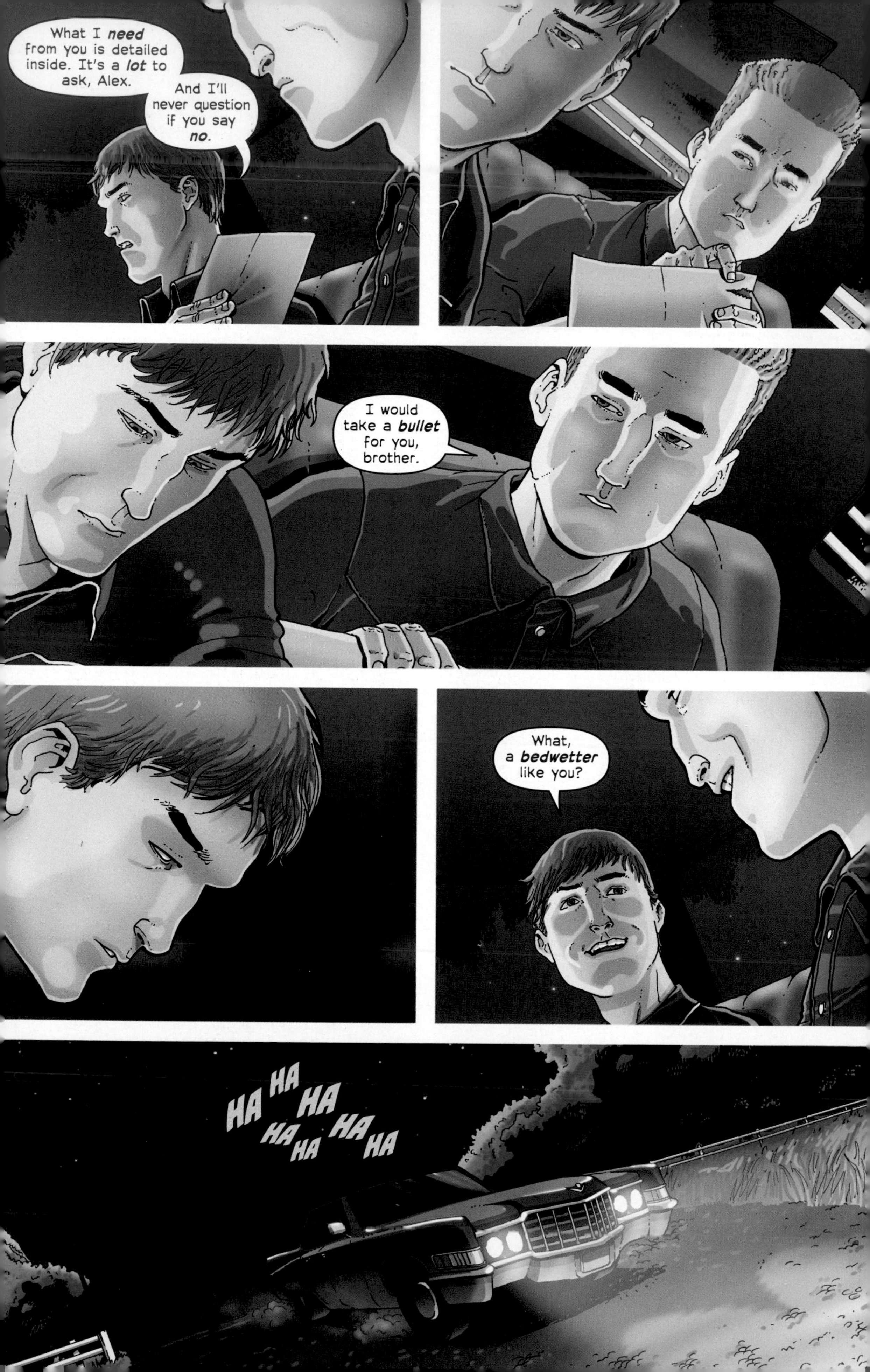
What I *need* from you is detailed inside. It's a *lot* to ask, Alex.
And I'll never question if you say *no*.
I would take a *bullet* for you, brother.
What, a *bedwetter* like you?
HA HA HA HA HA HA HA HA

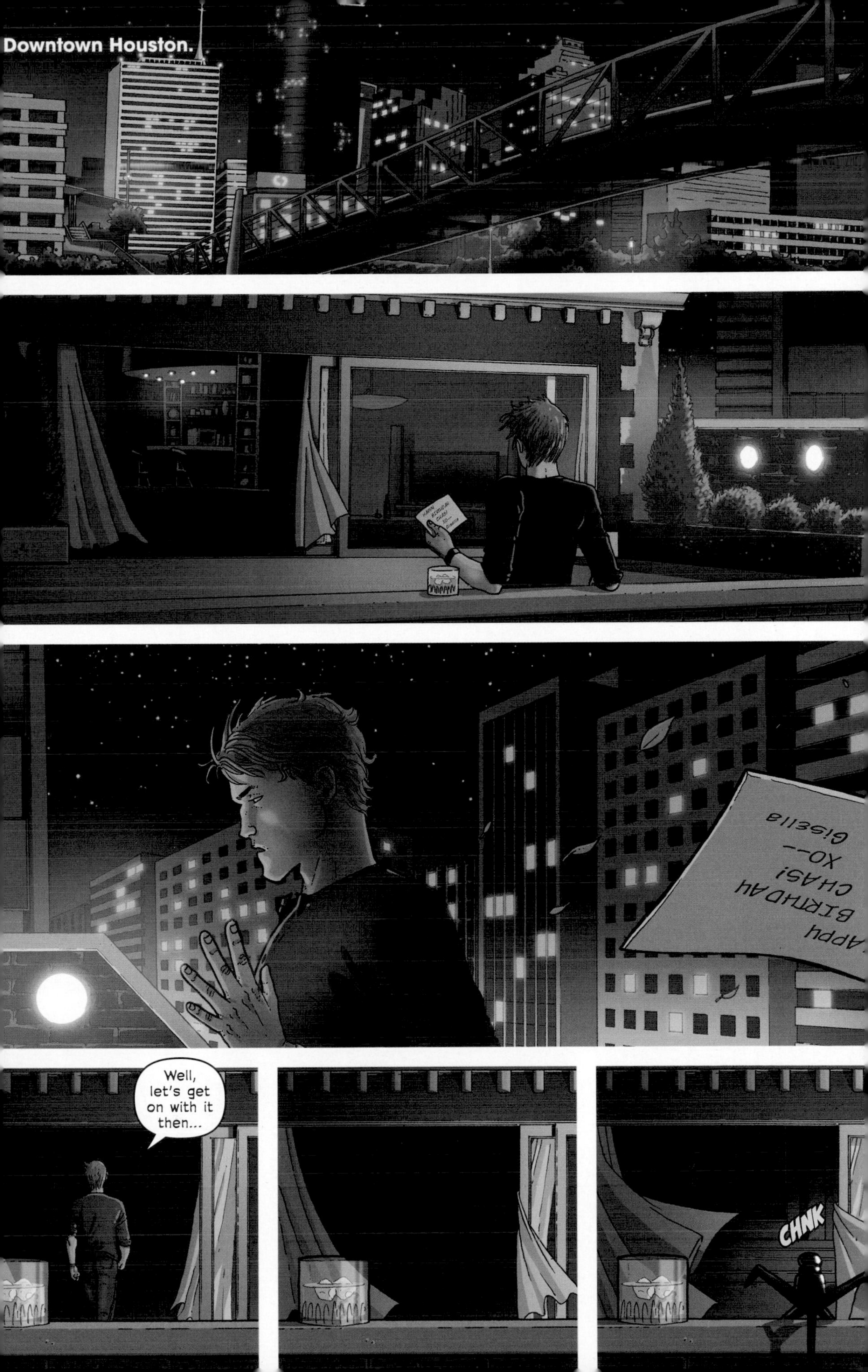
Downtown Houston.
APPY BIRTHDAY CHAS! XO-- Gisella
Well, let's get on with it then...
CHNK

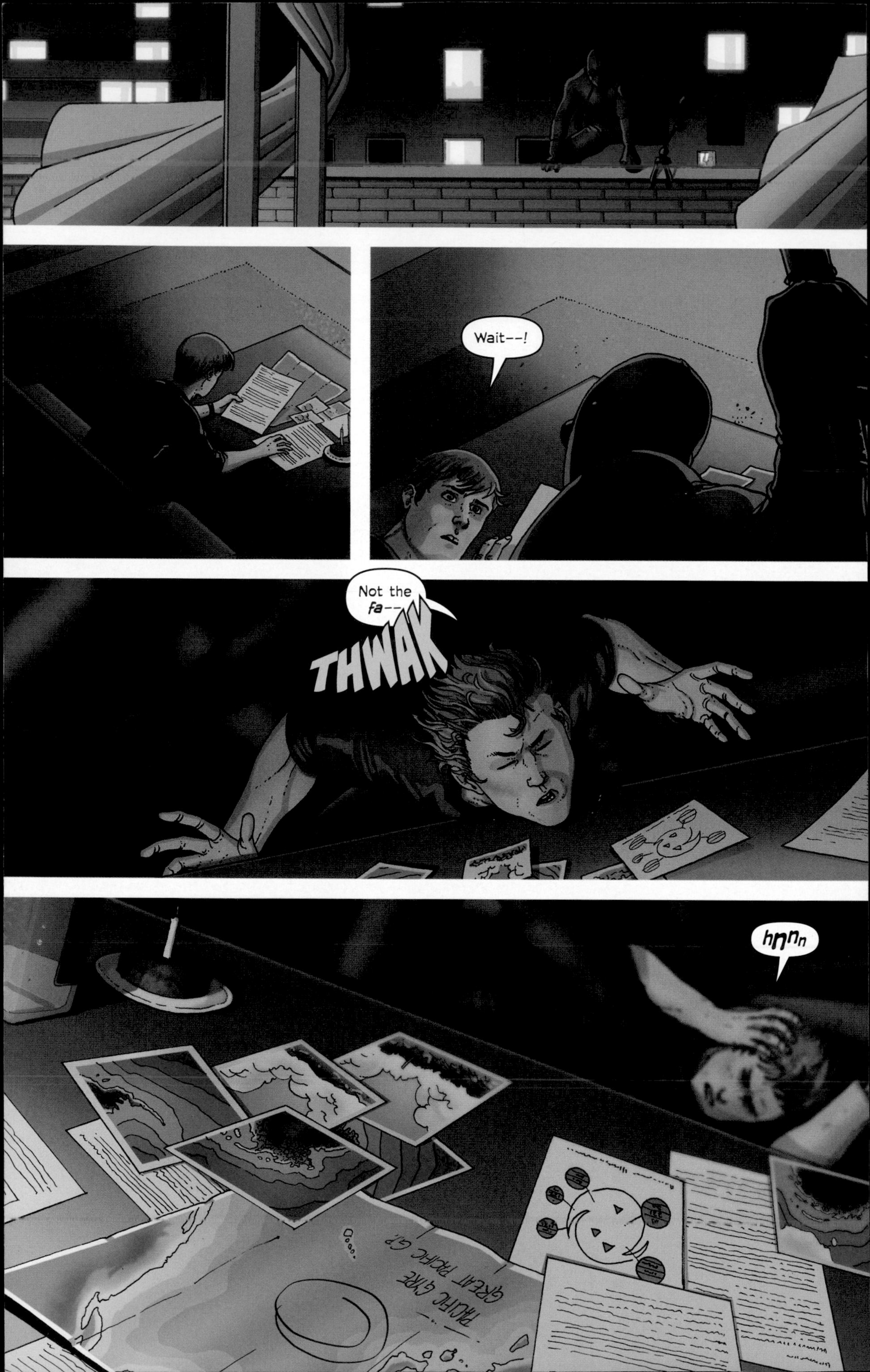
Wait--!
Not the fa--
THWAK
hnnn
PACIFIC GYRE
GREAT PACIFIC G.P.

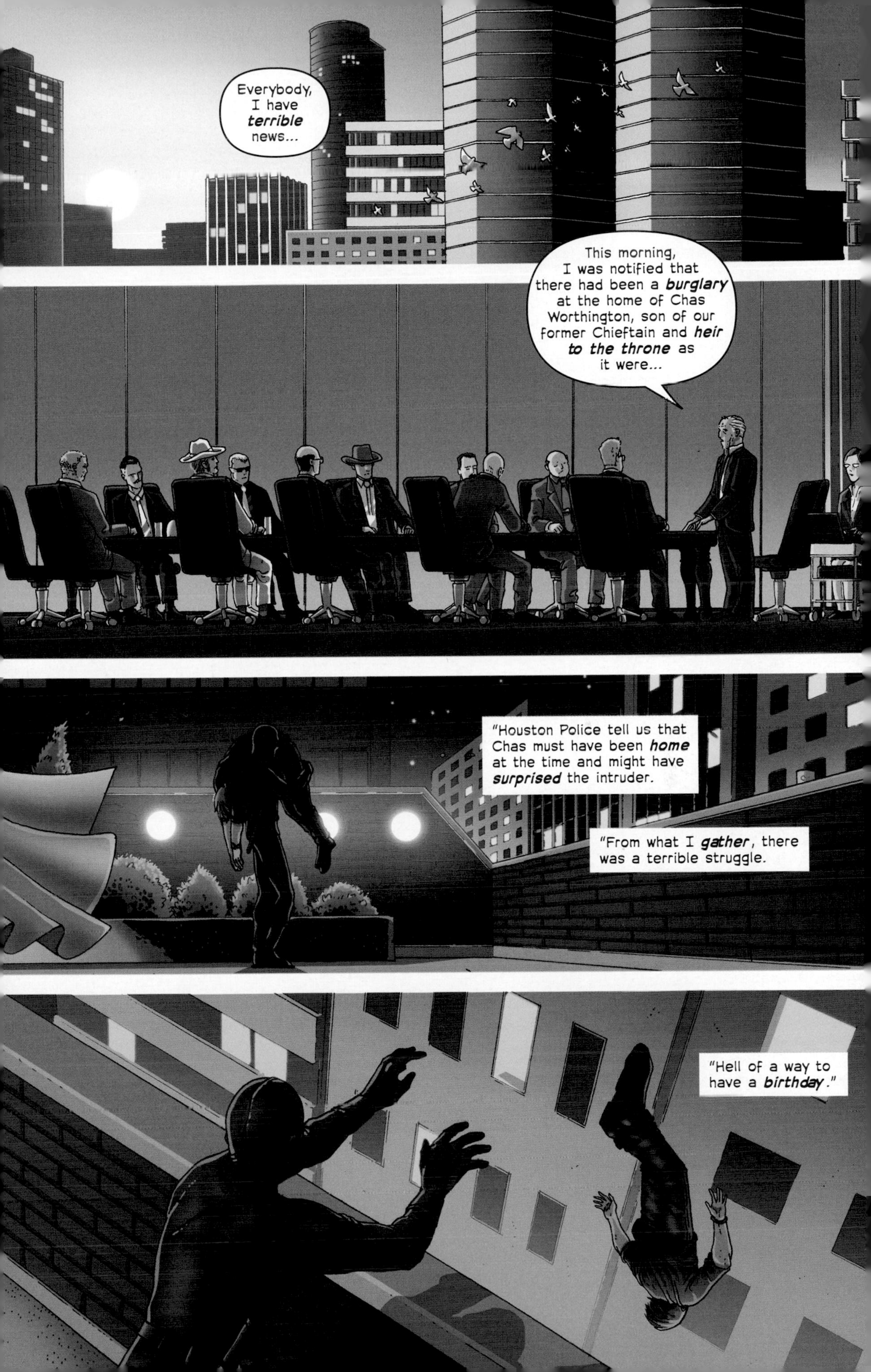
Everybody, I have *terrible* news...
This morning, I was notified that there had been a *burglary* at the home of Chas Worthington, son of our former Chieftain and *heir to the throne* as it were...
"Houston Police tell us that Chas must have been *home* at the time and might have *surprised* the intruder.
"From what I *gather*, there was a terrible struggle.
"Hell of a way to have a *birthday*."

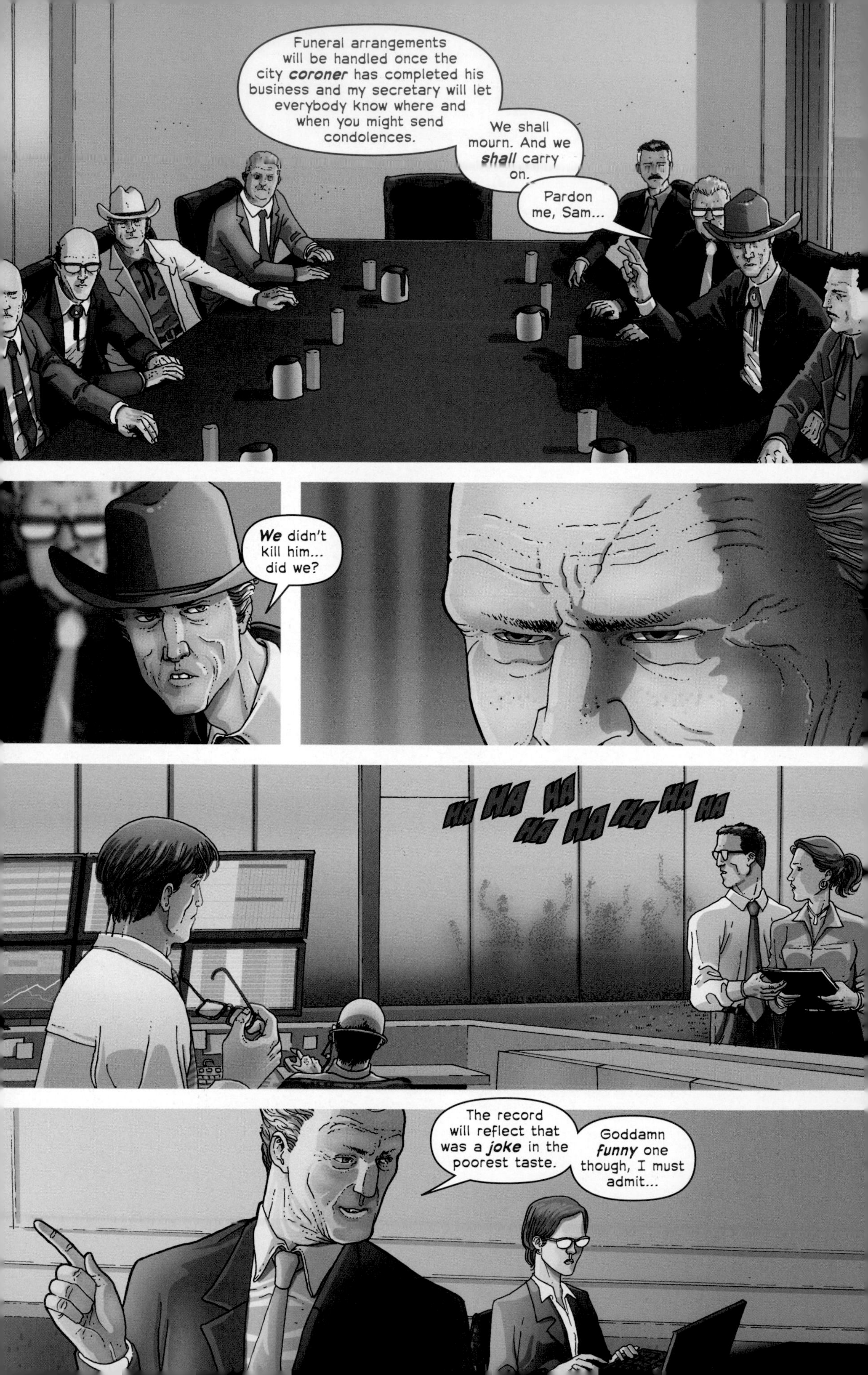
Funeral arrangements will be handled once the city *coroner* has completed his business and my secretary will let everybody know where and when you might send condolences.
We shall mourn. And we *shall* carry on.
Pardon me, Sam...
We didn't kill him... did we?
HA HA HA HA HA HA HA HA
The record will reflect that was a *joke* in the poorest taste.
Goddamn *funny* one though, I must admit...

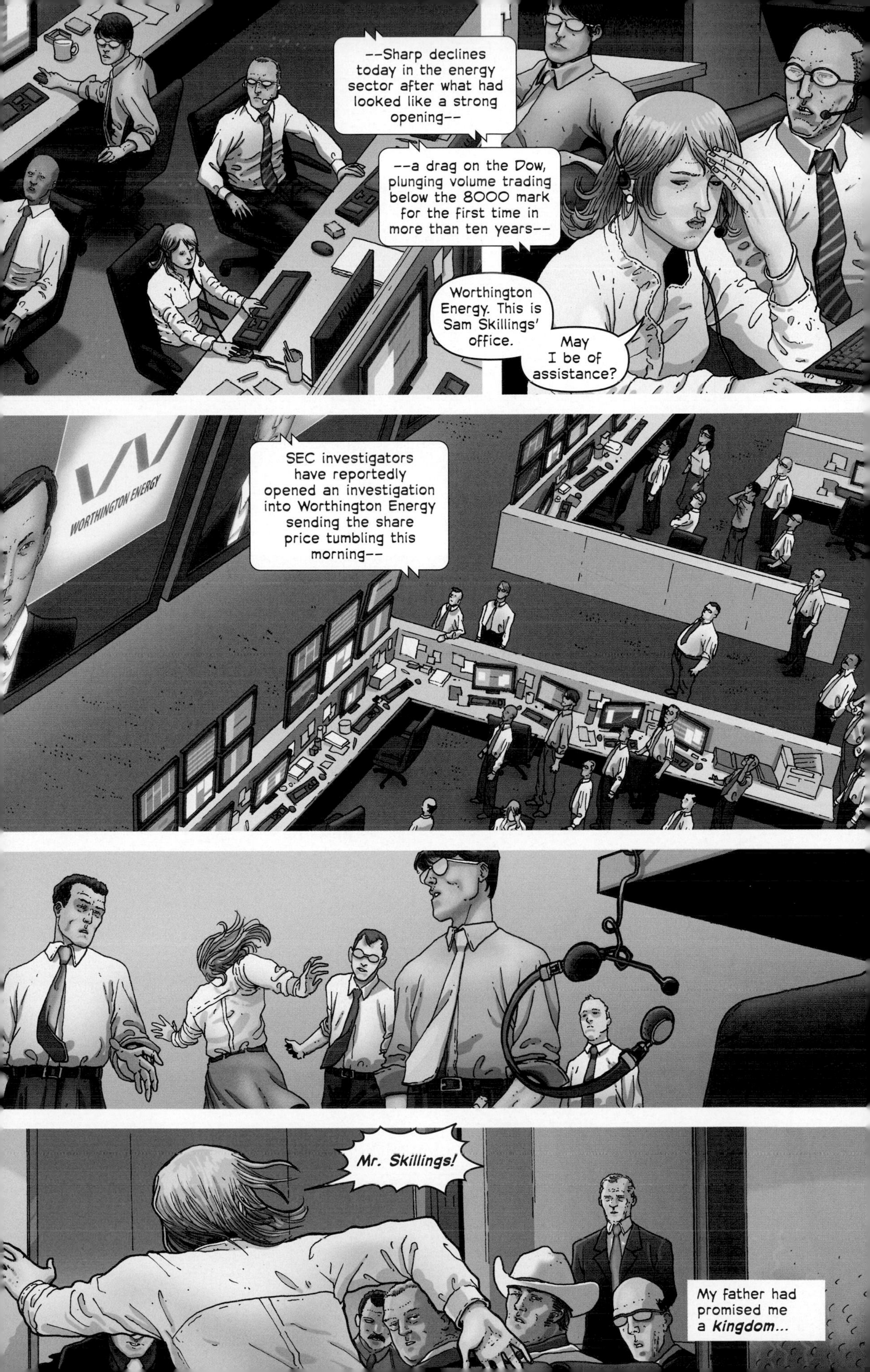
--Sharp declines today in the energy sector after what had looked like a strong opening--
--a drag on the Dow, plunging volume trading below the 8000 mark for the first time in more than ten years--
Worthington Energy. This is Sam Skillings' office.
May I be of assistance?
WORTHINGTON ENERGY
SEC investigators have reportedly opened an investigation into Worthington Energy sending the share price tumbling this morning--
Mr. Skillings!
My father had promised me a *kingdom*...

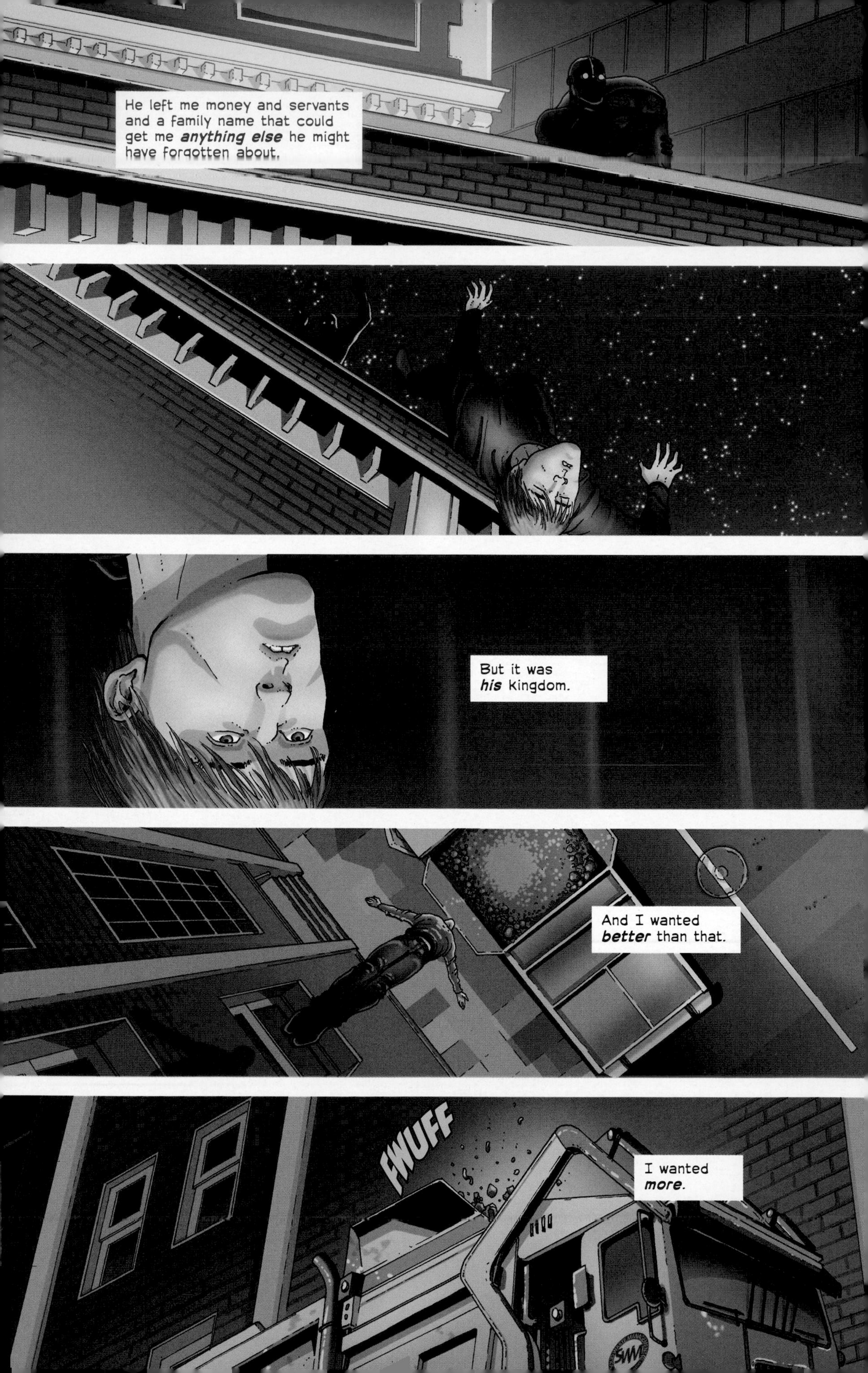
He left me money and servants and a family name that could get me *anything else* he might have forgotten about.
But it was *his* kingdom.
And I wanted *better* than that.
FWUFF
I wanted *more*.

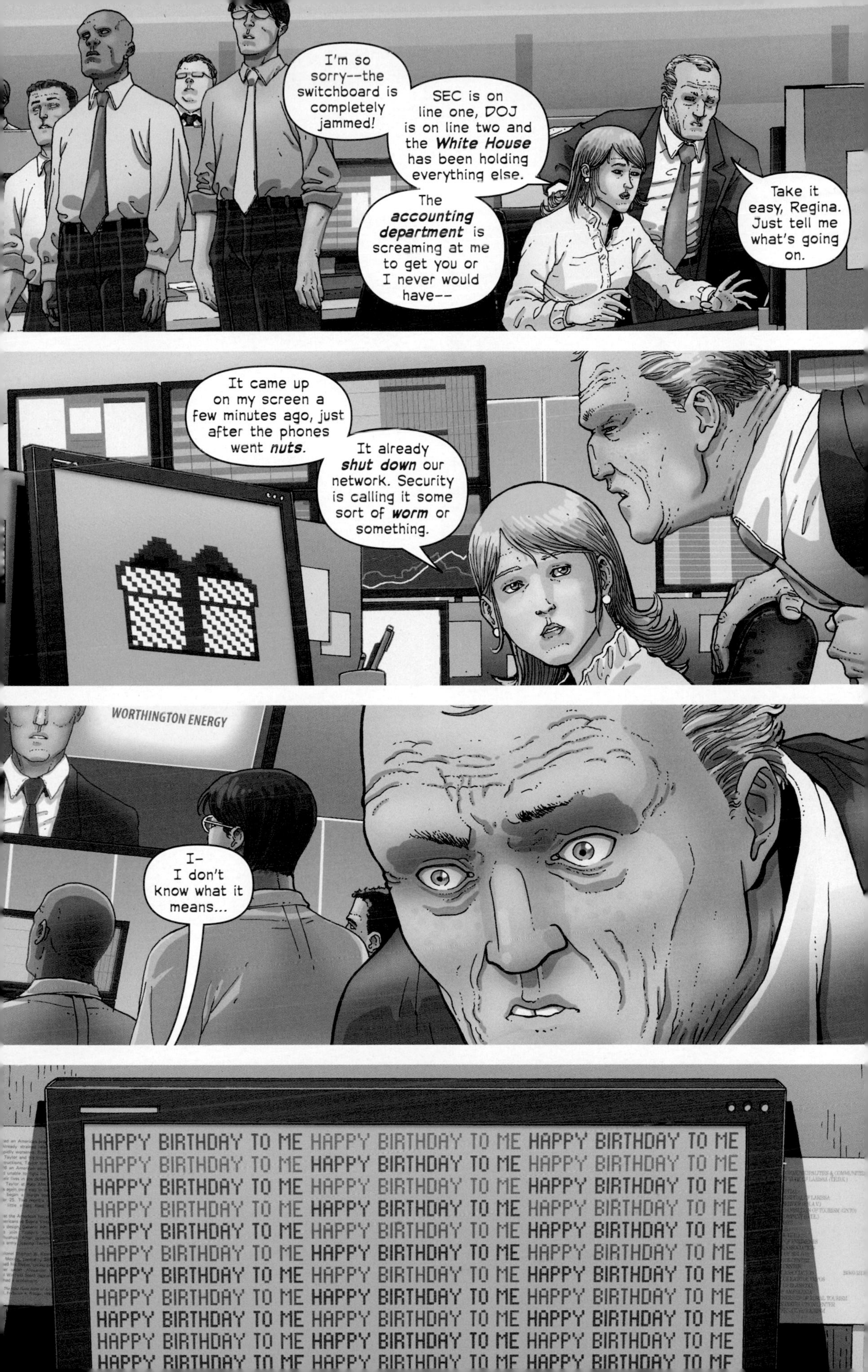
I'm so sorry--the switchboard is completely jammed!
SEC is on line one, DOJ is on line two and the *White House* has been holding everything else.
The *accounting department* is screaming at me to get you or I never would have--
Take it easy, Regina. Just tell me what's going on.
It came up on my screen a few minutes ago, just after the phones went *nuts*.
It already *shut down* our network. Security is calling it some sort of *worm* or something.
WORTHINGTON ENERGY
I- I don't know what it means...
HAPPY BIRTHDAY TO ME HAPPY BIRTHDAY TO ME HAPPY BIRTHDAY TO ME
HAPPY BIRTHDAY TO ME HAPPY BIRTHDAY TO ME HAPPY BIRTHDAY TO ME
HAPPY BIRTHDAY TO ME HAPPY BIRTHDAY TO ME HAPPY BIRTHDAY TO ME
HAPPY BIRTHDAY TO ME HAPPY BIRTHDAY TO ME HAPPY BIRTHDAY TO ME
HAPPY BIRTHDAY TO ME HAPPY BIRTHDAY TO ME HAPPY BIRTHDAY TO ME
HAPPY BIRTHDAY TO ME HAPPY BIRTHDAY TO ME HAPPY BIRTHDAY TO ME
HAPPY BIRTHDAY TO ME HAPPY BIRTHDAY TO ME HAPPY BIRTHDAY TO ME
HAPPY BIRTHDAY TO ME HAPPY BIRTHDAY TO ME HAPPY BIRTHDAY TO ME
HAPPY BIRTHDAY TO ME HAPPY BIRTHDAY TO ME HAPPY BIRTHDAY TO ME
HAPPY BIRTHDAY TO ME HAPPY BIRTHDAY TO ME HAPPY BIRTHDAY TO ME

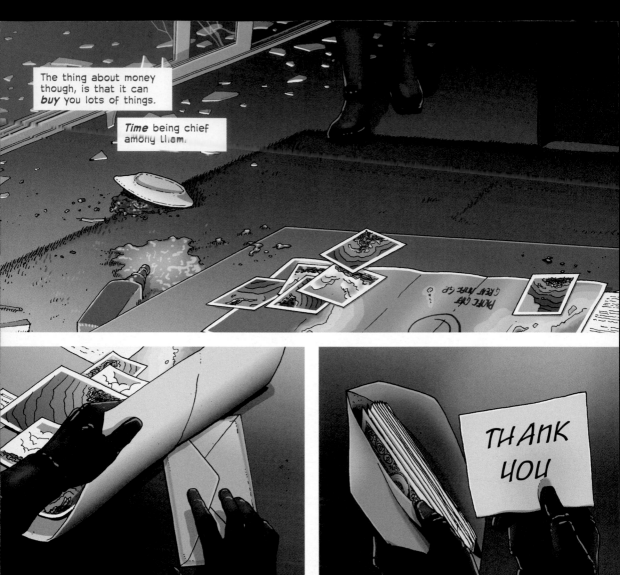

The thing about money though, is that it can *buy* you lots of things.

Time being chief among them.

THANK YOU

My father left me everything I could possibly want...

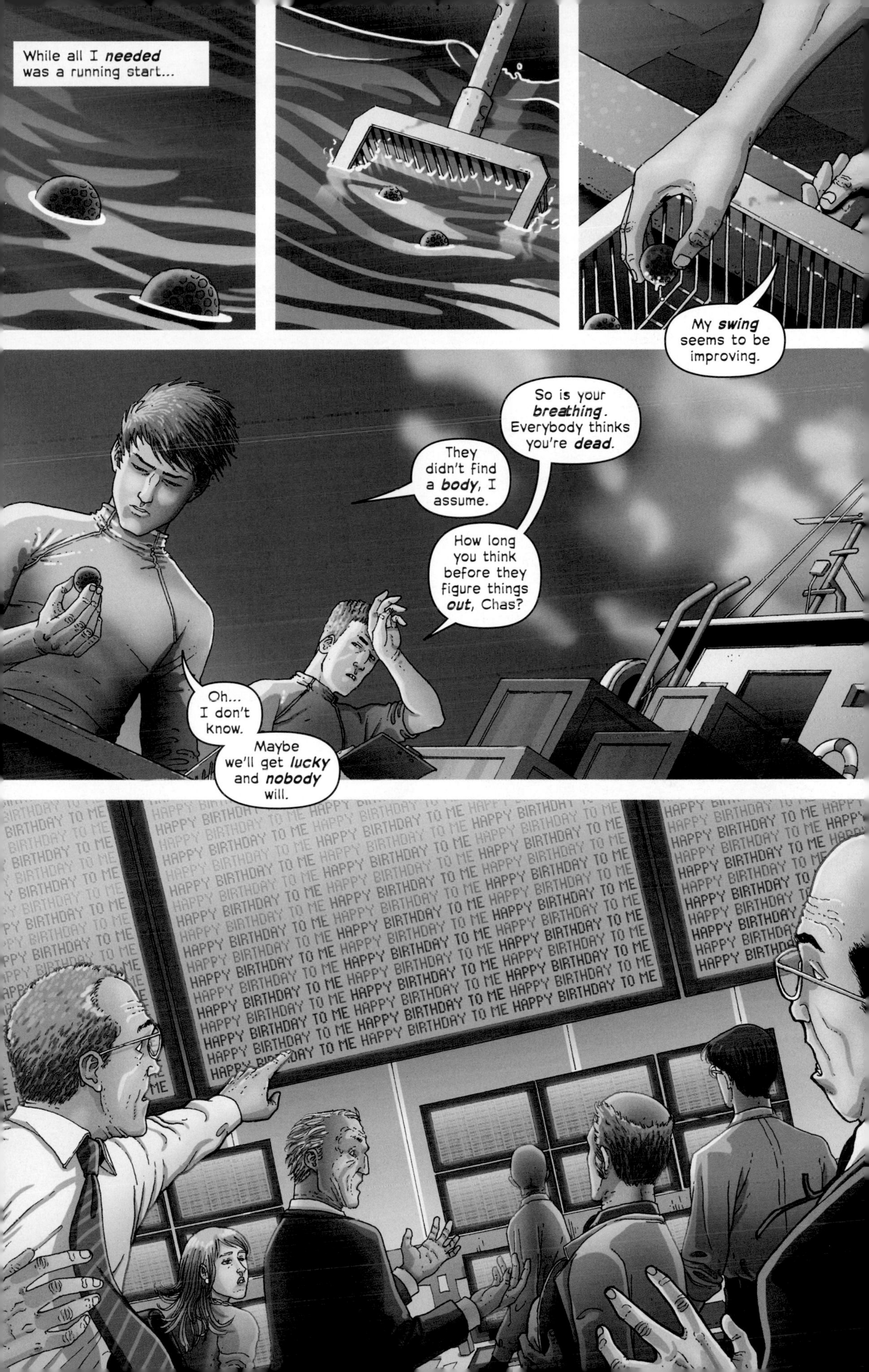
While all I *needed* was a running start...
My *swing* seems to be improving.
So is your *breathing*. Everybody thinks you're *dead*.
They didn't find a *body*, I assume.
How long you think before they figure things *out*, Chas?
Oh... I don't know.
Maybe we'll get *lucky* and *nobody* will.
HAPPY BIRTHDAY TO ME

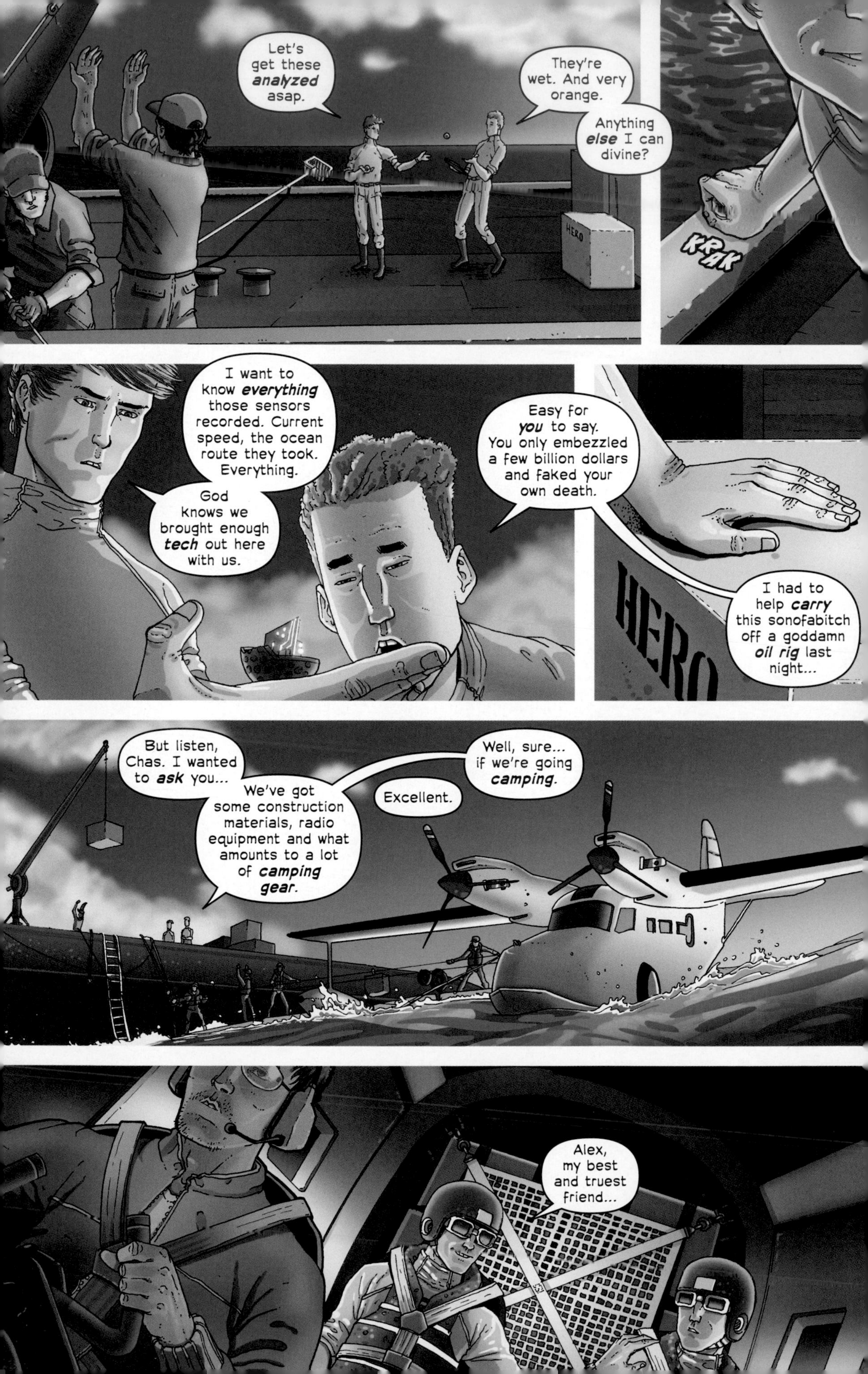

Let's get these *analyzed* asap.
They're wet. And very orange.
Anything *else* I can divine?
KRAK
I want to know *everything* those sensors recorded. Current speed, the ocean route they took. Everything.
God knows we brought enough *tech* out here with us.
Easy for *you* to say. You only embezzled a few billion dollars and faked your own death.
HERO
I had to help *carry* this sonofabitch off a goddamn *oil rig* last night...
But listen, Chas. I wanted to *ask* you...
We've got some construction materials, radio equipment and what amounts to a lot of *camping gear*.
Excellent.
Well, sure... if we're going *camping*.
Alex, my best and truest friend...

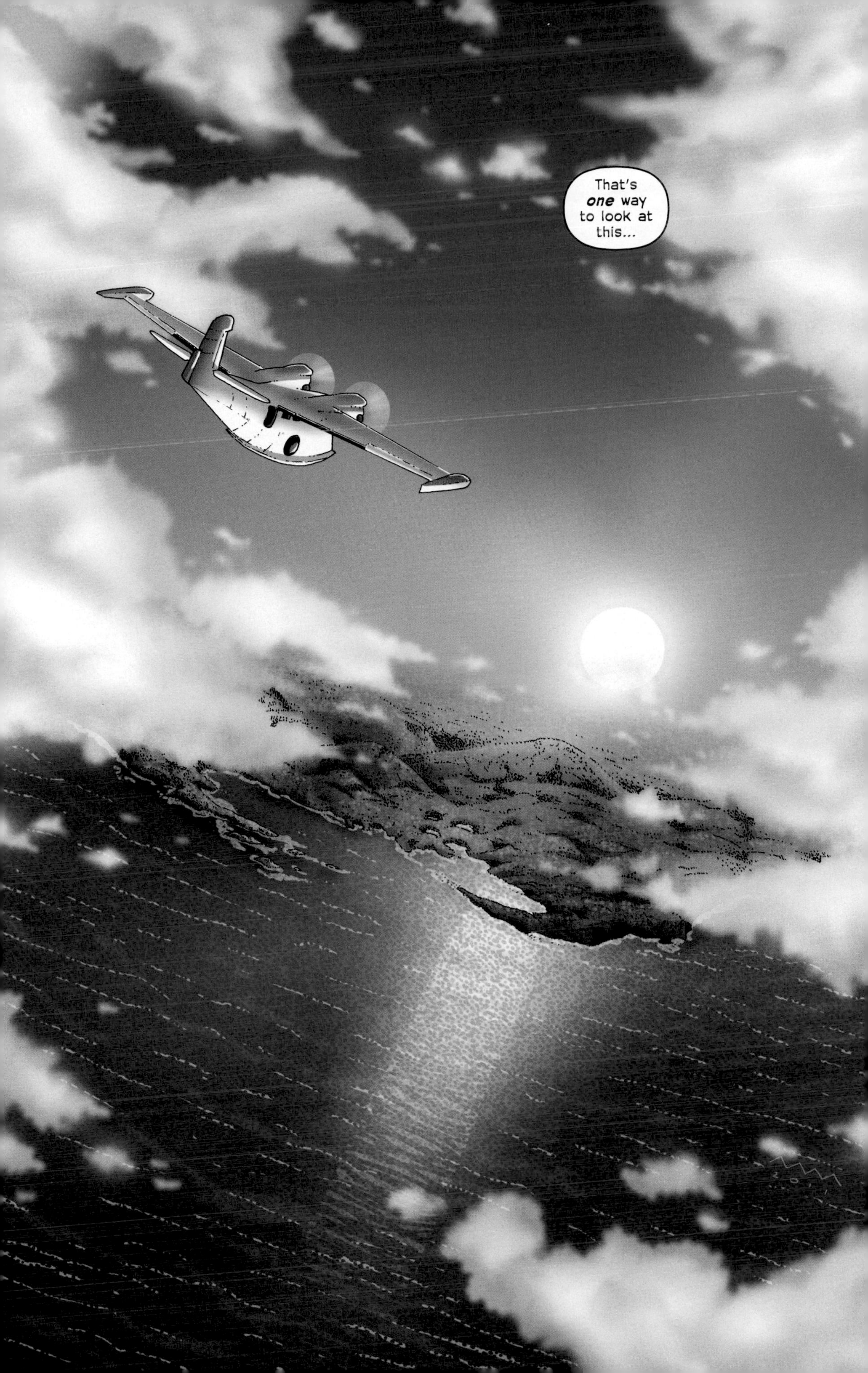
That's *one* way to look at this...

CHAPTER**TWO**

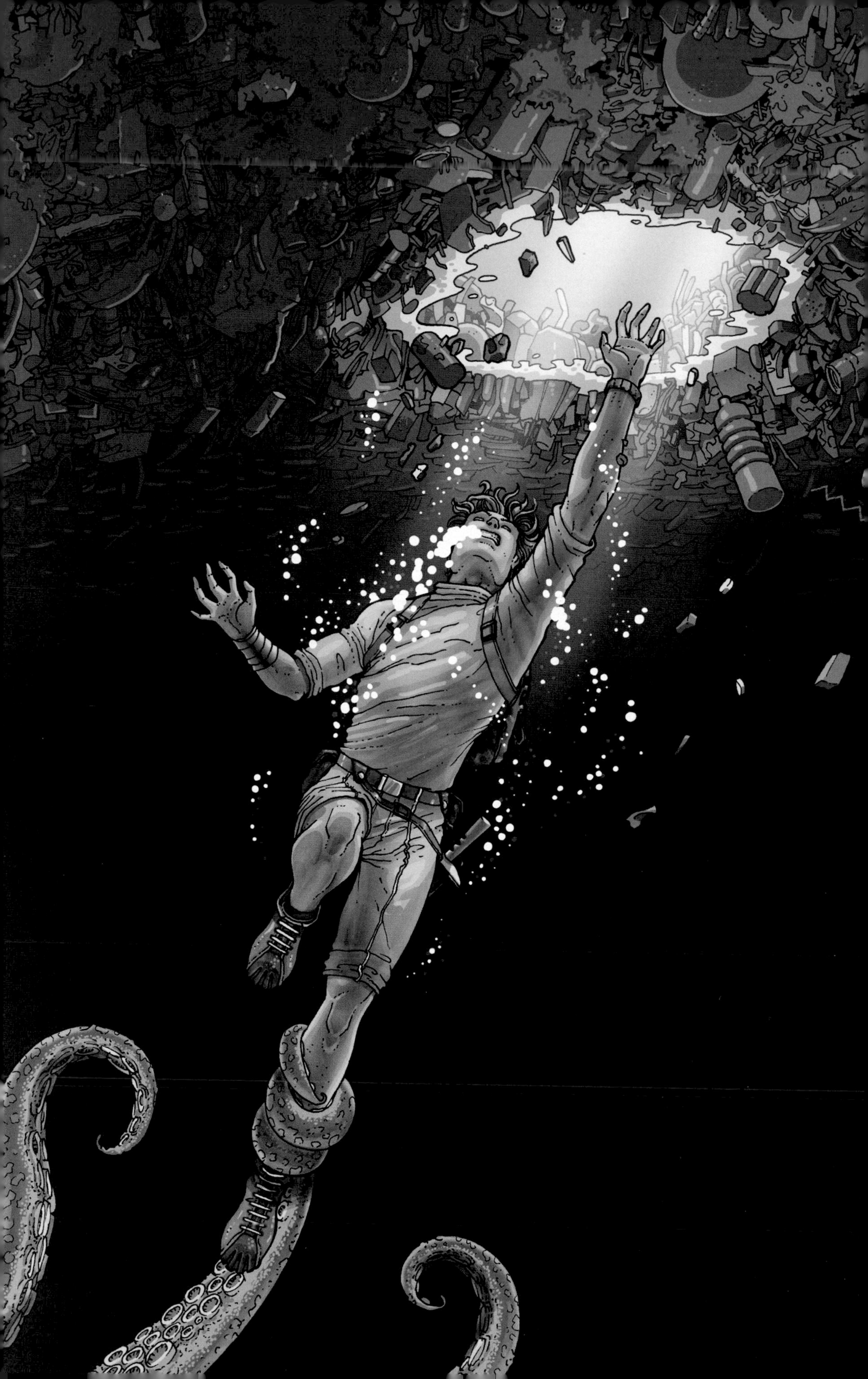

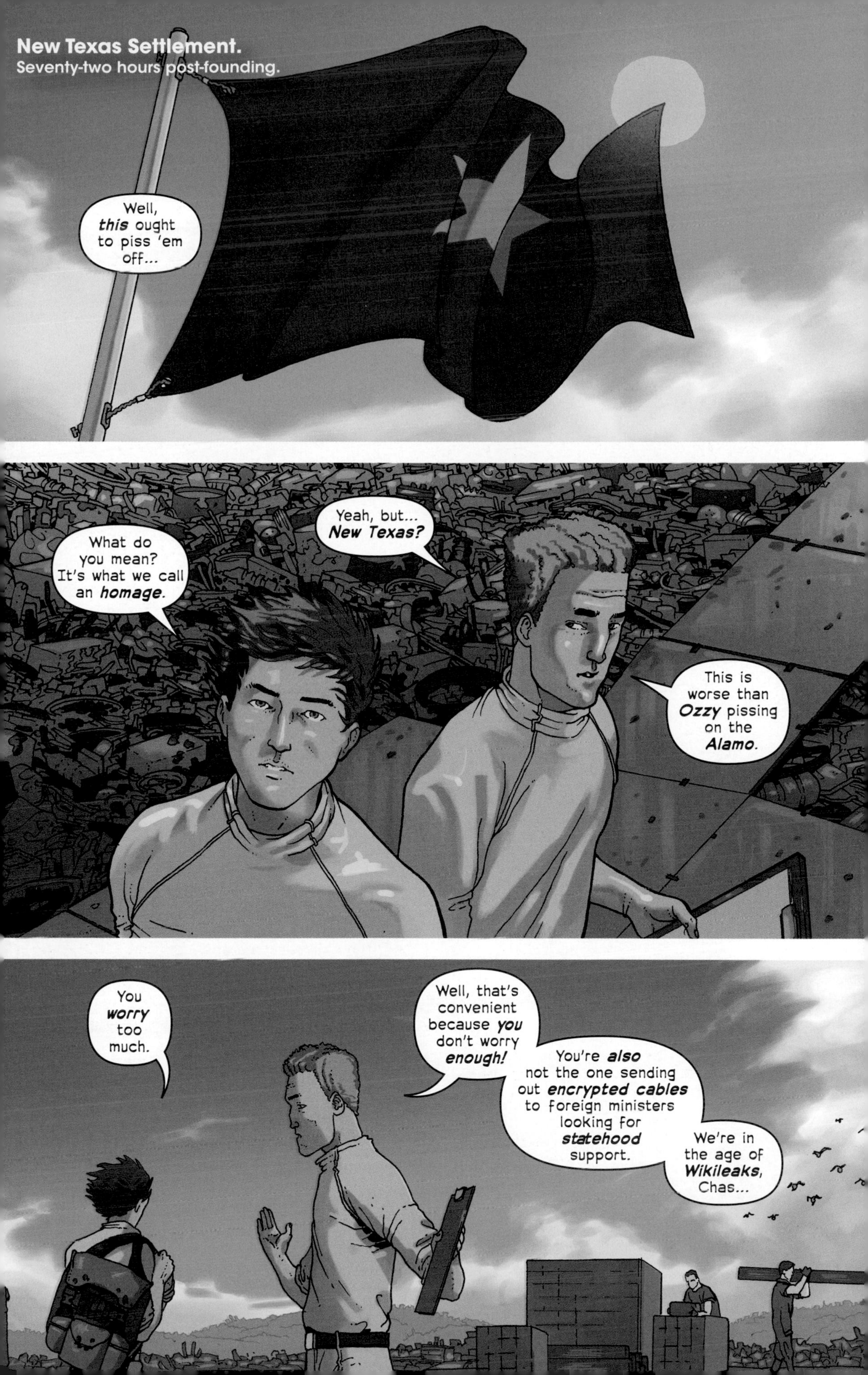
New Texas Settlement.
Seventy-two hours post-founding.
Well, this ought to piss 'em off...
What do you mean? It's what we call an homage.
Yeah, but... New Texas?
This is worse than Ozzy pissing on the Alamo.
You worry too much.
Well, that's convenient because you don't worry enough!
You're also not the one sending out encrypted cables to foreign ministers looking for statehood support.
We're in the age of Wikileaks, Chas...

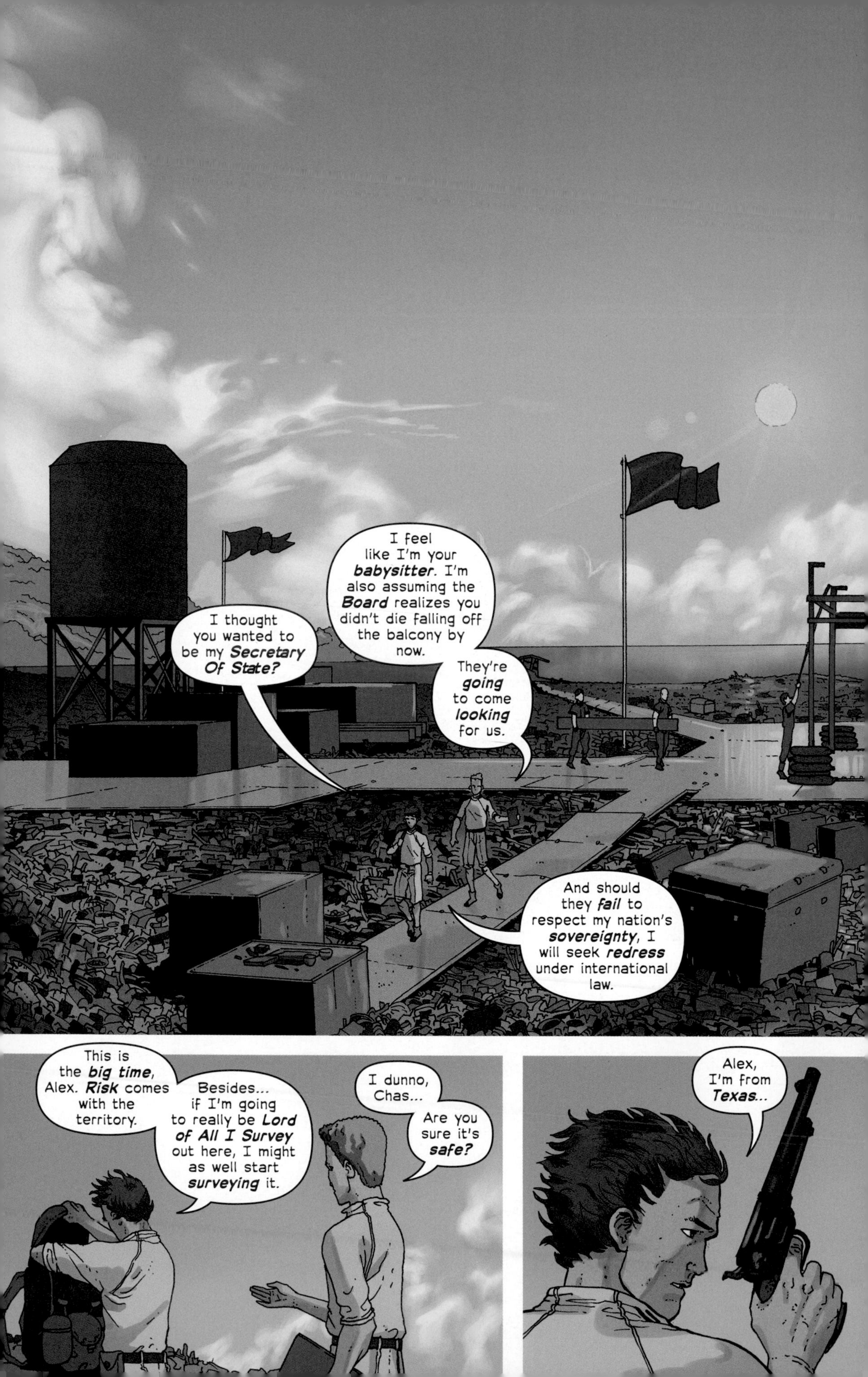
I thought you wanted to be my Secretary Of State?
I feel like I'm your babysitter. I'm also assuming the Board realizes you didn't die falling off the balcony by now.
They're going to come looking for us.
And should they fail to respect my nation's sovereignty, I will seek redress under international law.
This is the big time, Alex. Risk comes with the territory.
Besides... if I'm going to really be Lord of All I Survey out here, I might as well start surveying it.
I dunno, Chas...
Are you sure it's safe?
Alex, I'm from Texas...

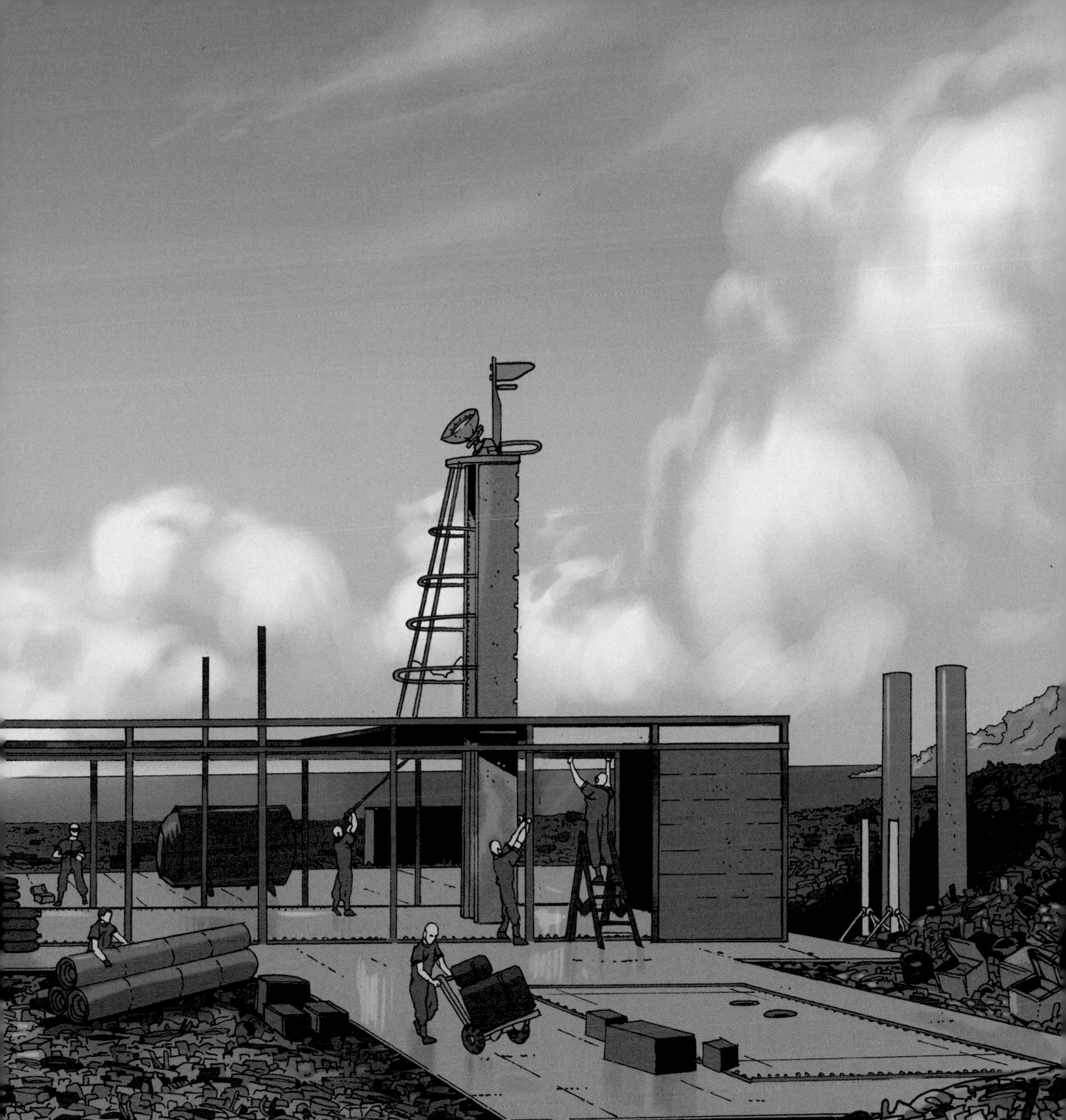

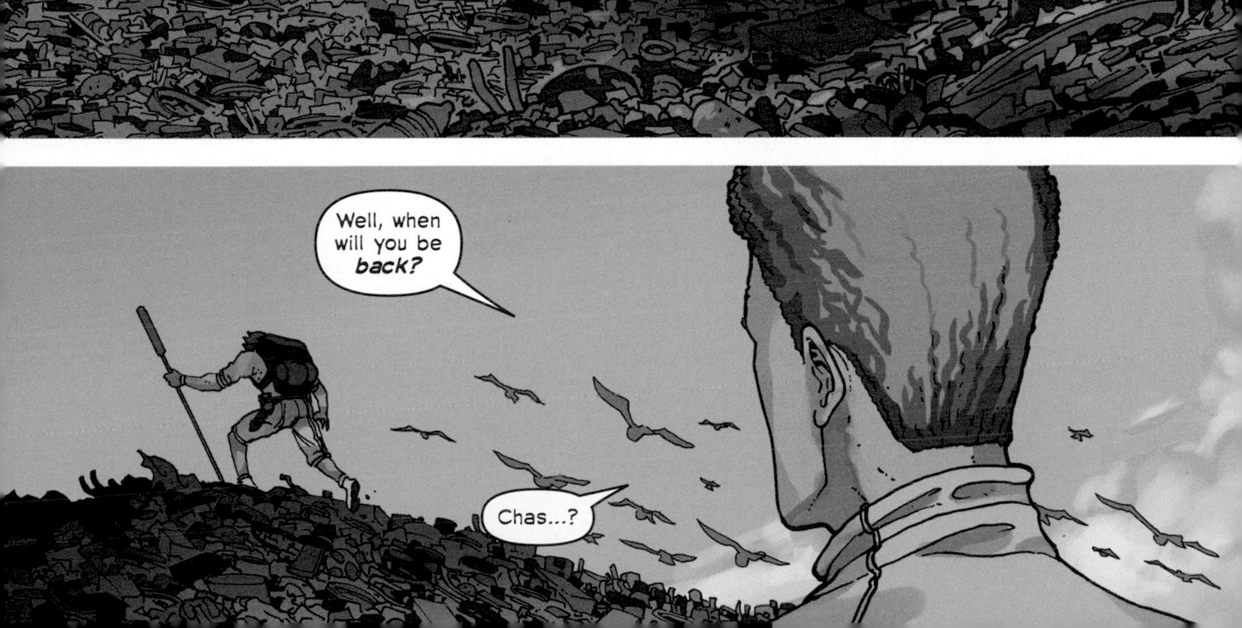
Well, when will you be back?
Chas...?

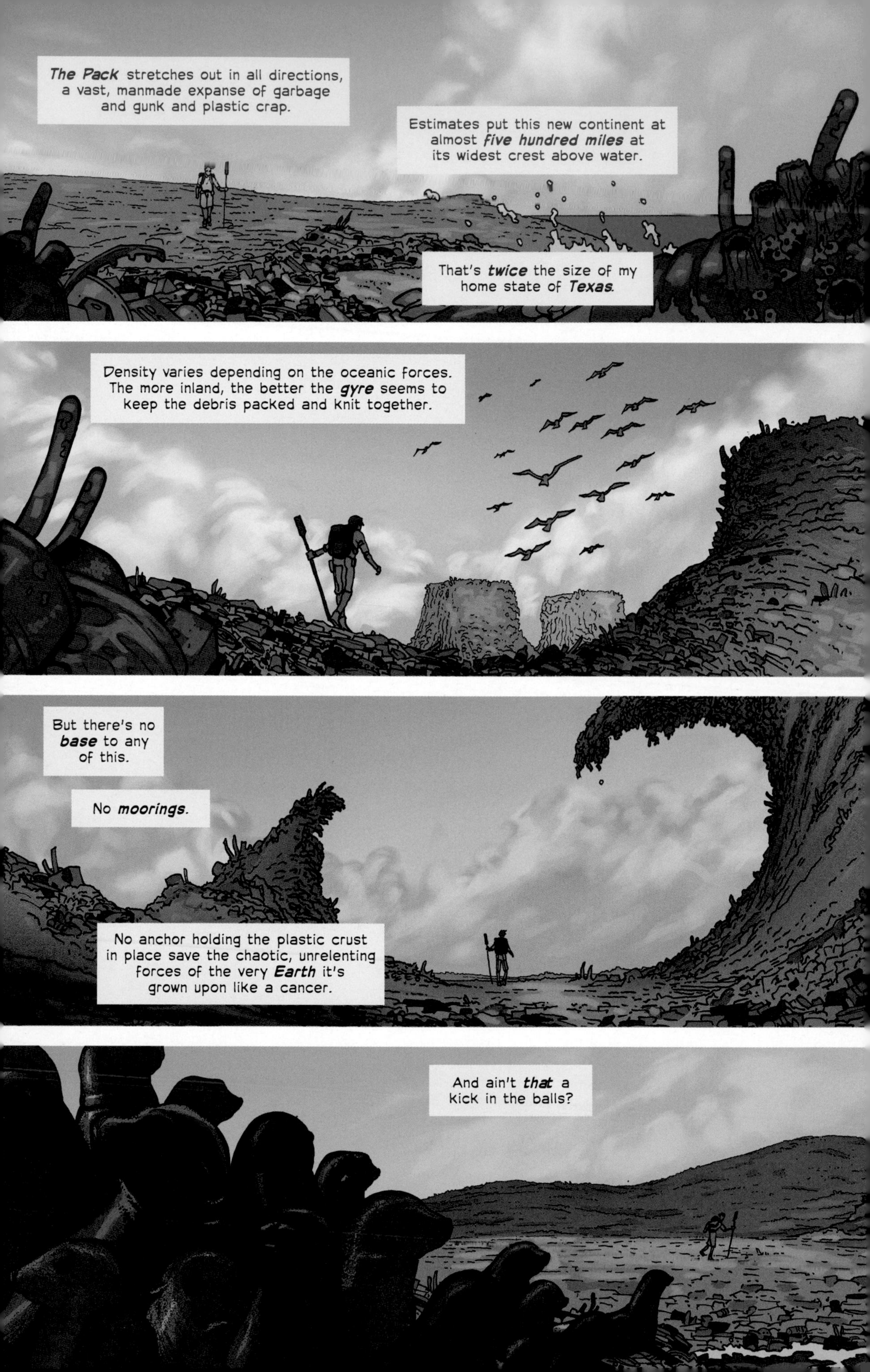
The Pack stretches out in all directions, a vast, manmade expanse of garbage and gunk and plastic crap.
Estimates put this new continent at almost five hundred miles at its widest crest above water.
That's twice the size of my home state of Texas.
Density varies depending on the oceanic forces. The more inland, the better the gyre seems to keep the debris packed and knit together.
But there's no base to any of this.
No moorings.
No anchor holding the plastic crust in place save the chaotic, unrelenting forces of the very Earth it's grown upon like a cancer.
And ain't that a kick in the balls?

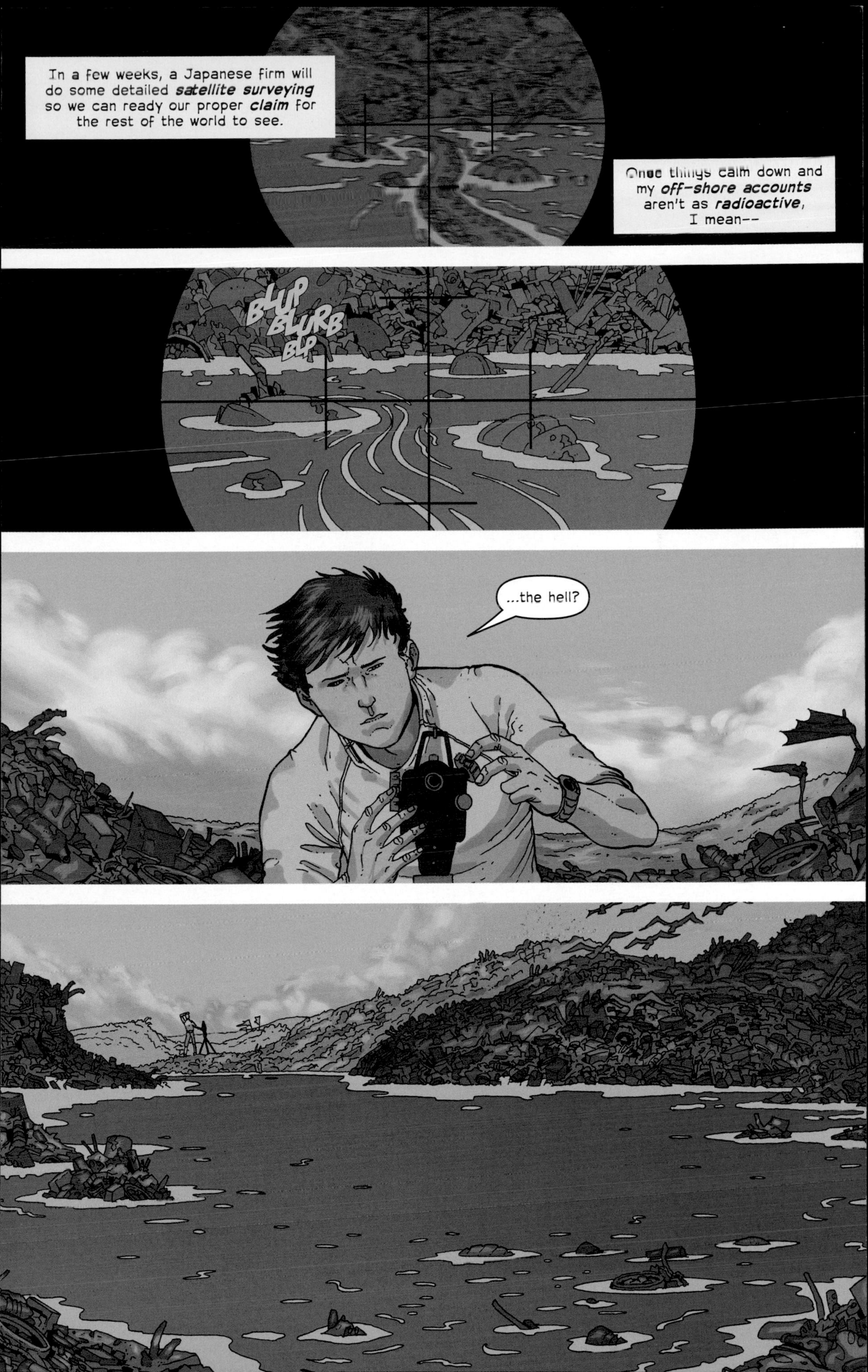
In a few weeks, a Japanese firm will do some detailed *satellite surveying* so we can ready our proper *claim* for the rest of the world to see.
Once things calm down and my *off-shore accounts* aren't as *radioactive*, I mean--
BLUP
BLURB
BLP
...the hell?

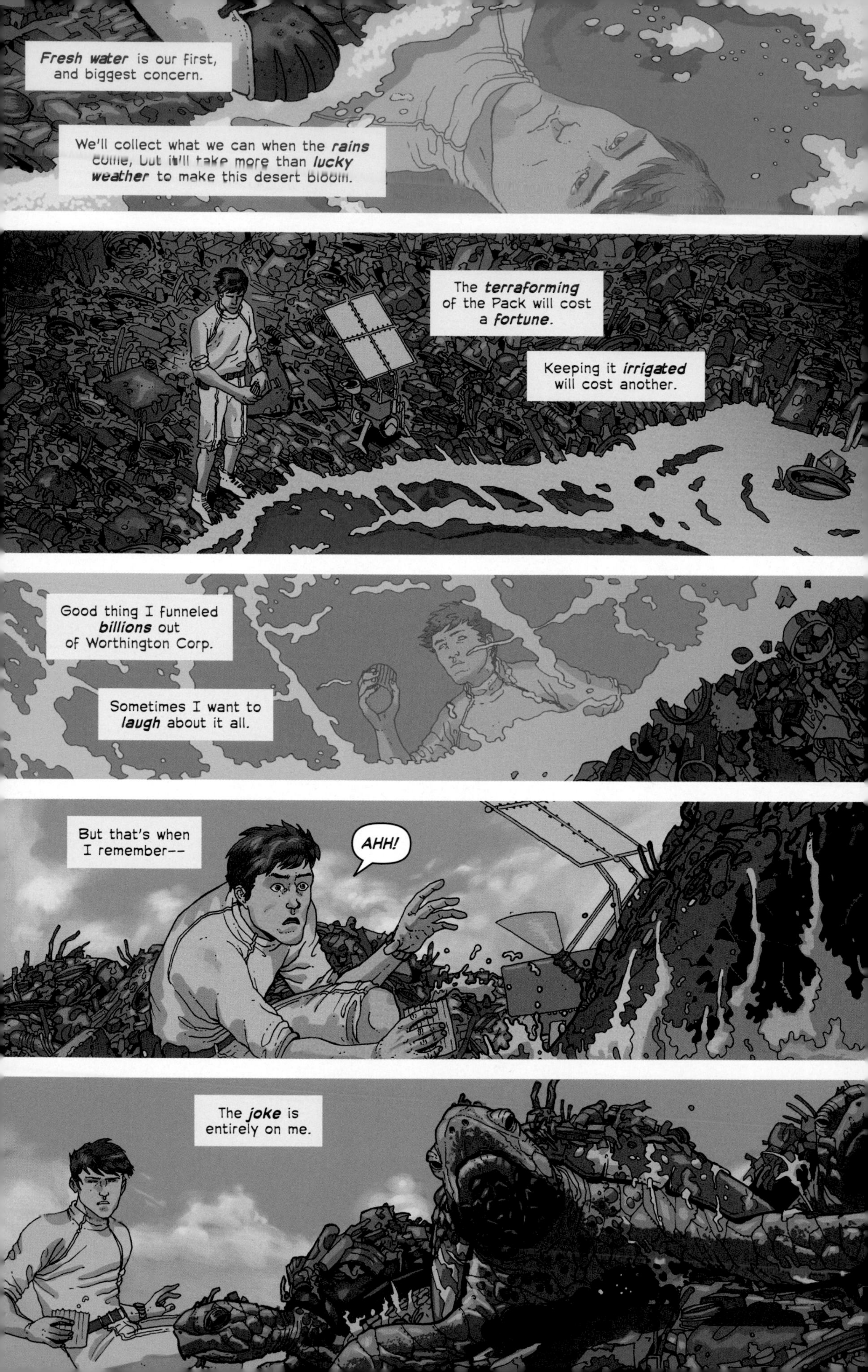
Fresh water is our first, and biggest concern.
We'll collect what we can when the rains come, but it'll take more than lucky weather to make this desert bloom.
The terraforming of the Pack will cost a fortune.
Keeping it irrigated will cost another.
Good thing I funneled billions out of Worthington Corp.
Sometimes I want to laugh about it all.
But that's when I remember--
AHH!
The joke is entirely on me.

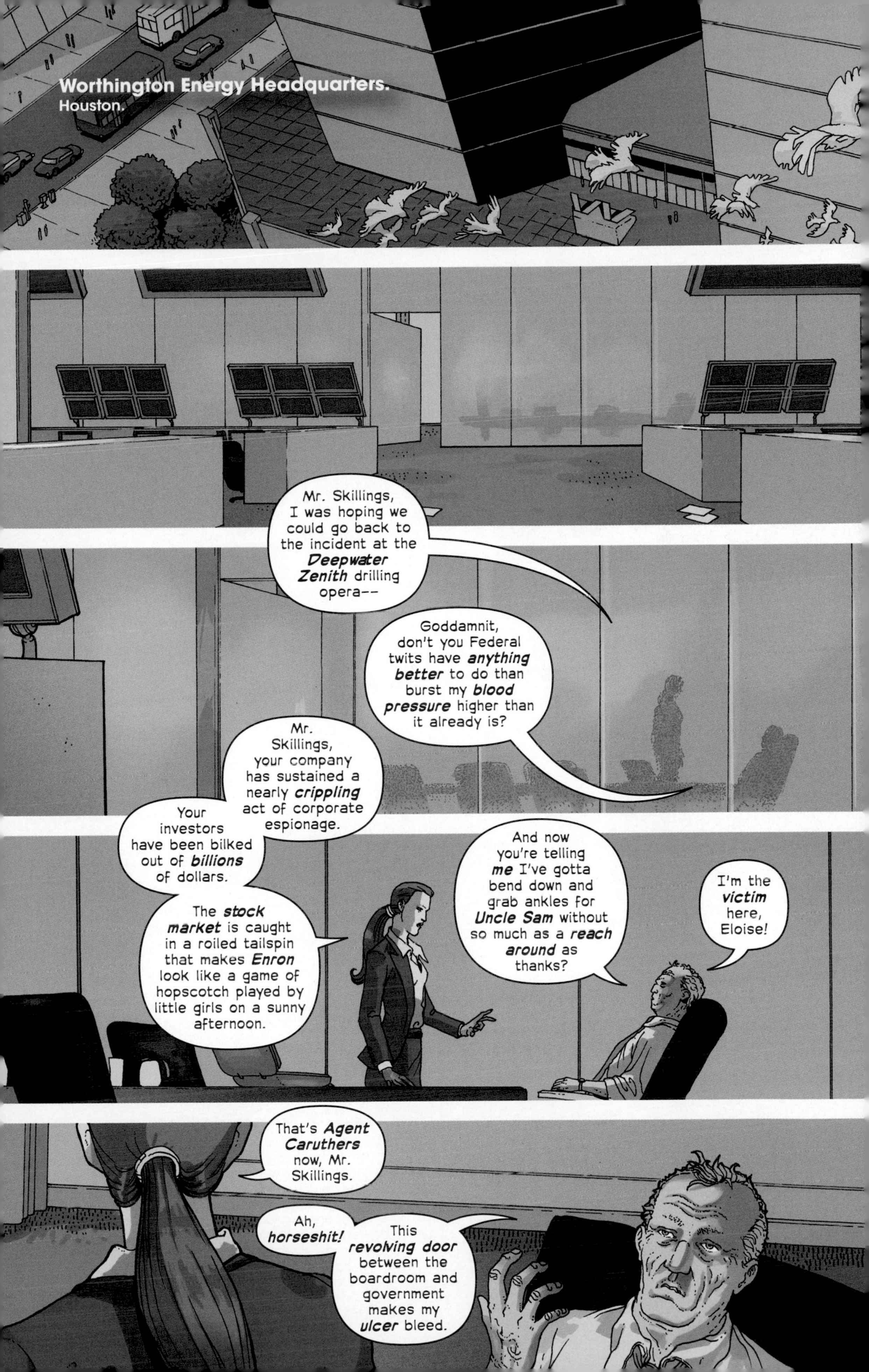
Worthington Energy Headquarters.
Houston.
Mr. Skillings, I was hoping we could go back to the incident at the *Deepwater Zenith* drilling opera--
Goddamnit, don't you Federal twits have *anything better* to do than burst my *blood pressure* higher than it already is?
Mr. Skillings, your company has sustained a nearly *crippling* act of corporate espionage.
Your investors have been bilked out of *billions* of dollars.
The *stock market* is caught in a roiled tailspin that makes *Enron* look like a game of hopscotch played by little girls on a sunny afternoon.
And now you're telling *me* I've gotta bend down and grab ankles for *Uncle Sam* without so much as a *reach around* as thanks?
I'm the *victim* here, Eloise!
That's *Agent Caruthers* now, Mr. Skillings.
Ah, *horseshit!*
This *revolving door* between the boardroom and government makes my *ulcer* bleed.

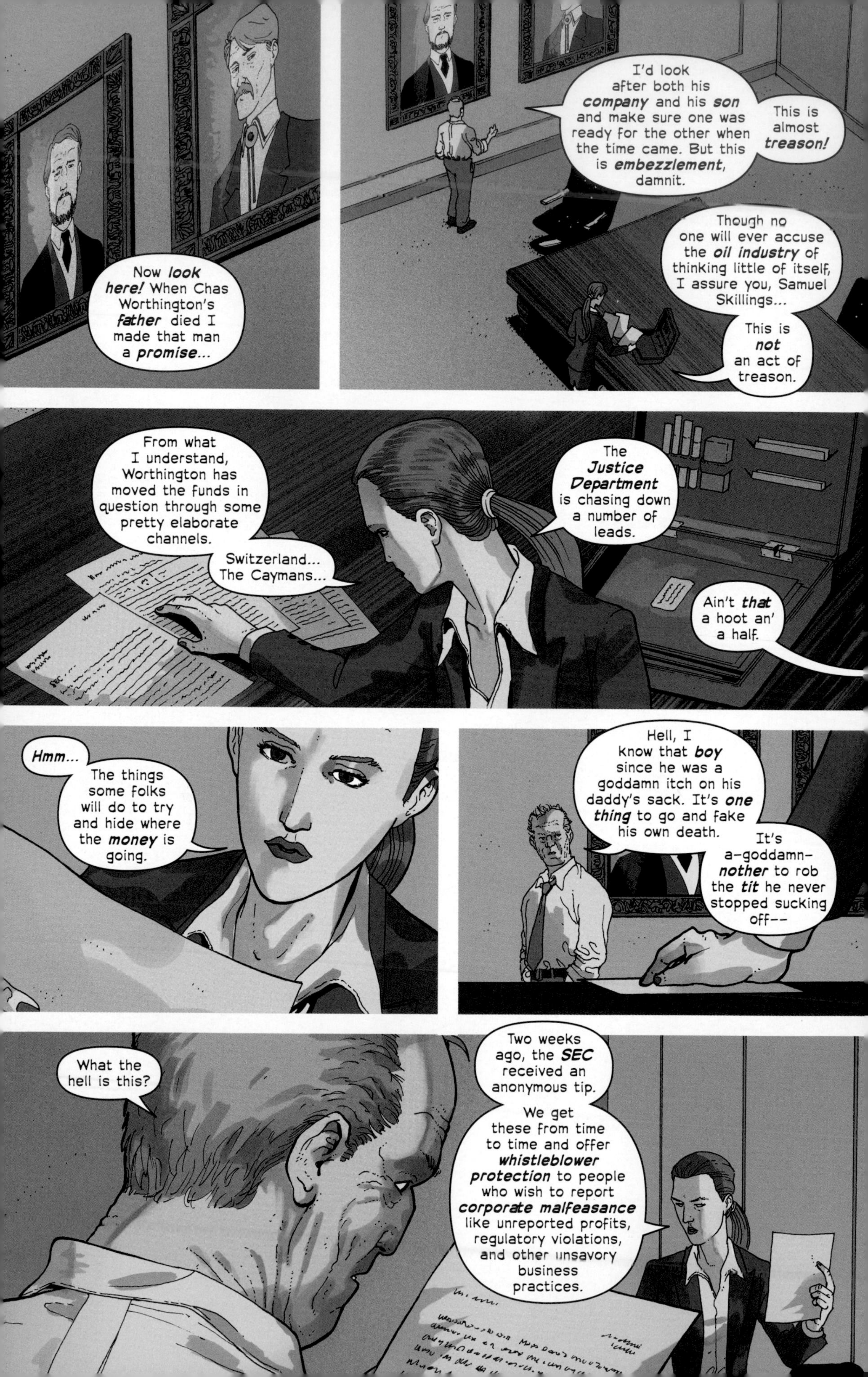
Now look here! When Chas Worthington's father died I made that man a promise...
I'd look after both his company and his son and make sure one was ready for the other when the time came. But this is embezzlement, damnit.
This is almost treason!
Though no one will ever accuse the oil industry of thinking little of itself, I assure you, Samuel Skillings...
This is not an act of treason.
From what I understand, Worthington has moved the funds in question through some pretty elaborate channels.
Switzerland... The Caymans...
The Justice Department is chasing down a number of leads.
Ain't that a hoot an' a half.
Hmm...
The things some folks will do to try and hide where the money is going.
Hell, I know that boy since he was a goddamn itch on his daddy's sack. It's one thing to go and fake his own death.
It's a-goddamn-nother to rob the tit he never stopped sucking off--
What the hell is this?
Two weeks ago, the SEC received an anonymous tip.
We get these from time to time and offer whistleblower protection to people who wish to report corporate malfeasance like unreported profits, regulatory violations, and other unsavory business practices.

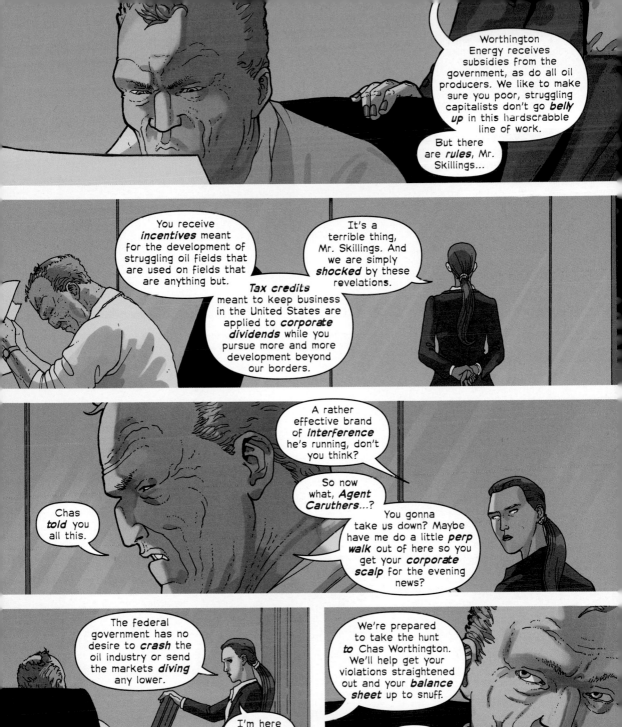

Worthington Energy receives subsidies from the government, as do all oil producers. We like to make sure you poor, struggling capitalists don't go *belly up* in this hardscrabble line of work.

But there are *rules*, Mr. Skillings...

You receive *incentives* meant for the development of struggling oil fields that are used on fields that are anything but. *Tax credits* meant to keep business in the United States are applied to *corporate dividends* while you pursue more and more development beyond our borders.

It's a terrible thing, Mr. Skillings. And we are simply *shocked* by these revelations.

A rather effective brand of *interference* he's running, don't you think?

So now what, *Agent Caruthers*...?

You gonna take us down? Maybe have me do a little *perp walk* out of here so you get your *corporate scalp* for the evening news?

Chas *told* you all this.

The federal government has no desire to *crash* the oil industry or send the markets *diving* any lower.

I'm here to make you an *offer*, Sam.

We're prepared to take the hunt *to* Chas Worthington. We'll help get your violations straightened out and your *balance sheet* up to snuff.

And...?

And in return, you're going to tell us *everything* you can...

...about the *Hydrocarbon Remediation Project*.

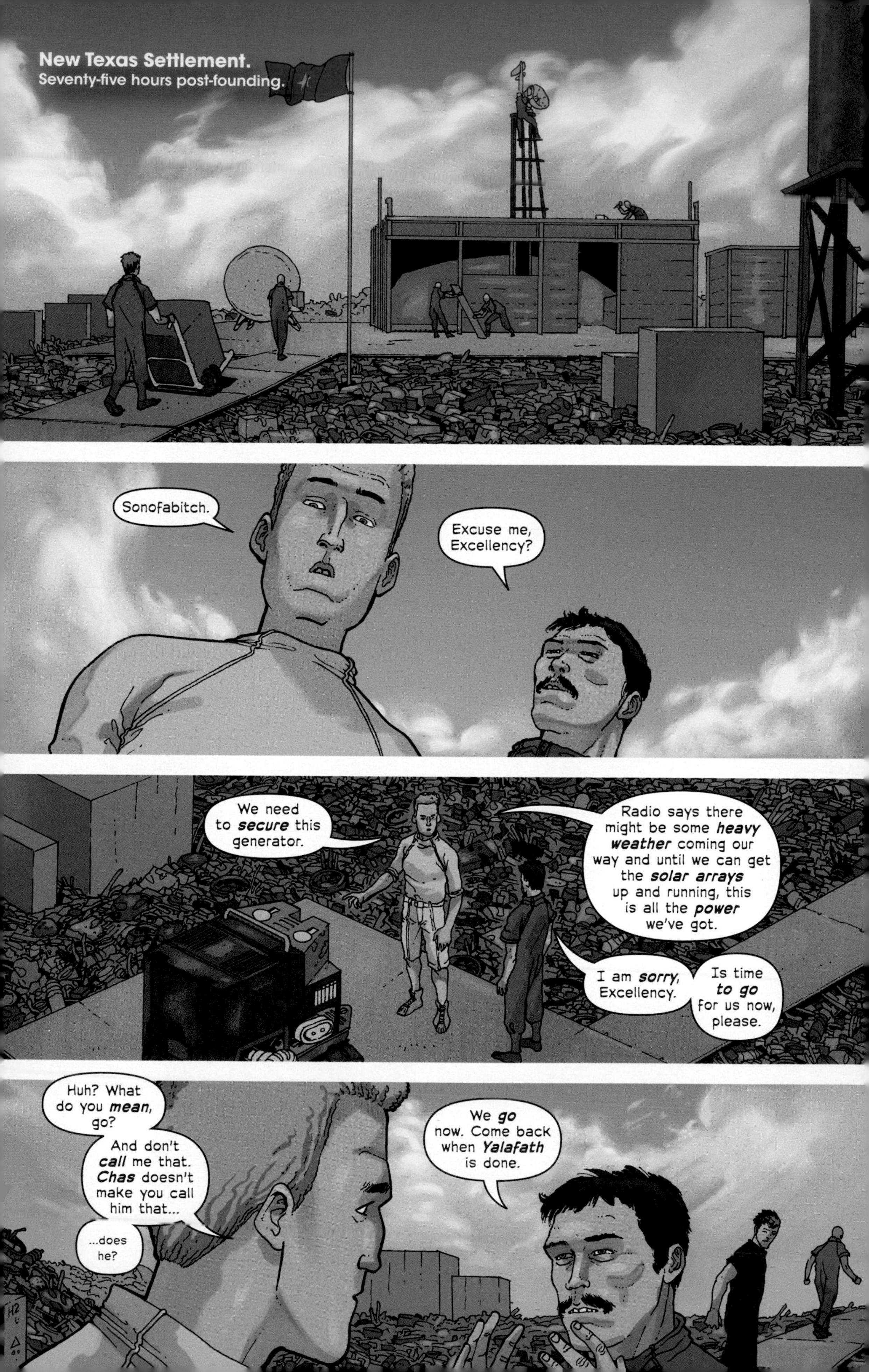
New Texas Settlement.
Seventy-five hours post-founding.
Sonofabitch.
Excuse me, Excellency?
We need to *secure* this generator.
Radio says there might be some *heavy weather* coming our way and until we can get the *solar arrays* up and running, this is all the *power* we've got.
I am *sorry*, Excellency.
Is time *to go* for us now, please.
Huh? What do you *mean*, go?
And don't *call* me that. *Chas* doesn't make you call him that...
...does he?
We *go* now. Come back when *Yalafath* is done.

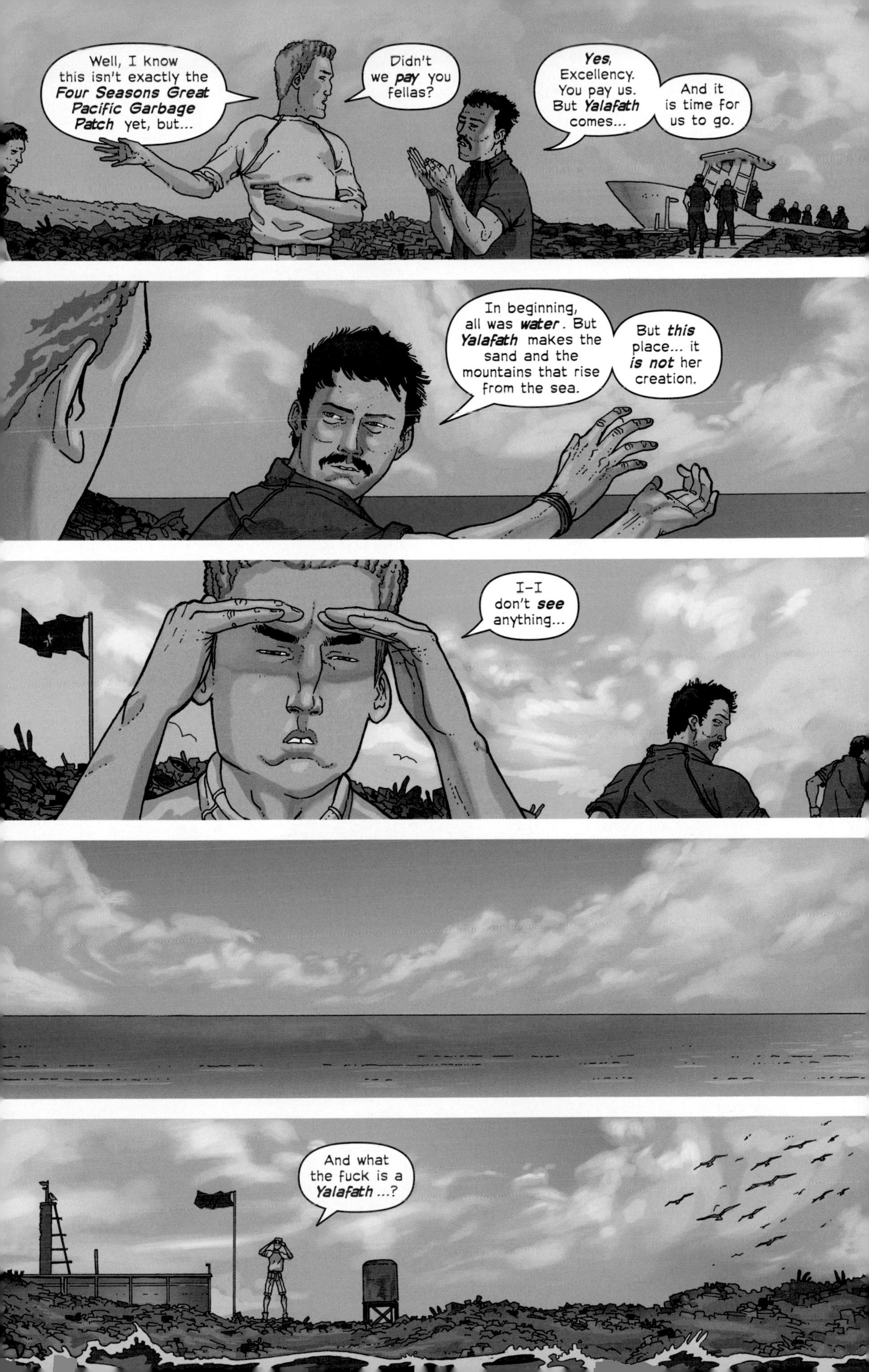
Well, I know this isn't exactly the *Four Seasons Great Pacific Garbage Patch* yet, but...
Didn't we *pay* you fellas?
Yes, Excellency. You pay us. But *Yalafath* comes...
And it is time for us to go.
In beginning, all was *water*. But *Yalafath* makes the sand and the mountains that rise from the sea.
But *this* place... it *is not* her creation.
I-I don't *see* anything...
And what the fuck is a *Yalafath*...?

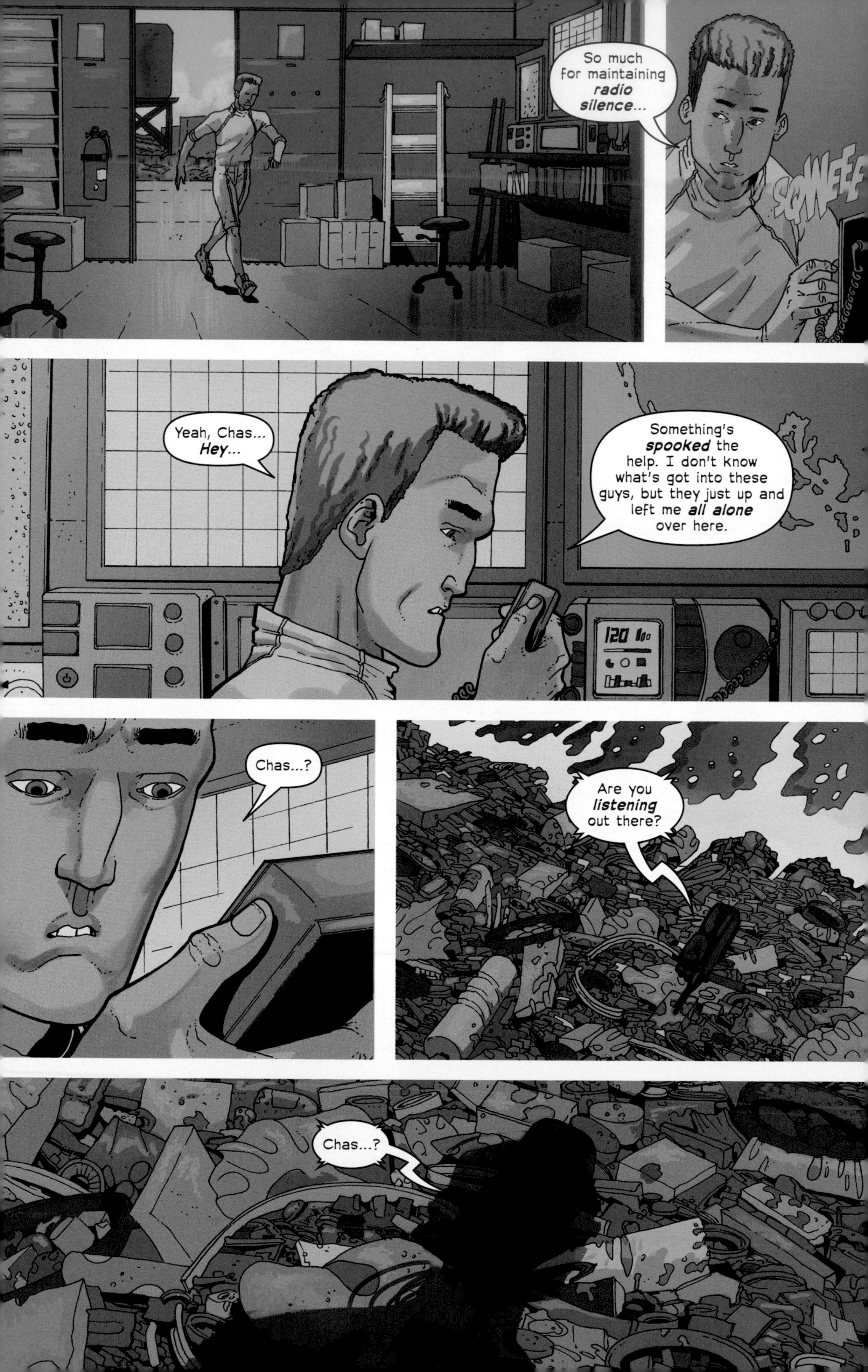
So much for maintaining *radio silence...*
SQWEEE
Yeah, Chas... *Hey...*
Something's *spooked* the help. I don't know what's got into these guys, but they just up and left me *all alone* over here.
Chas...?
Are you *listening* out there?
Chas...?

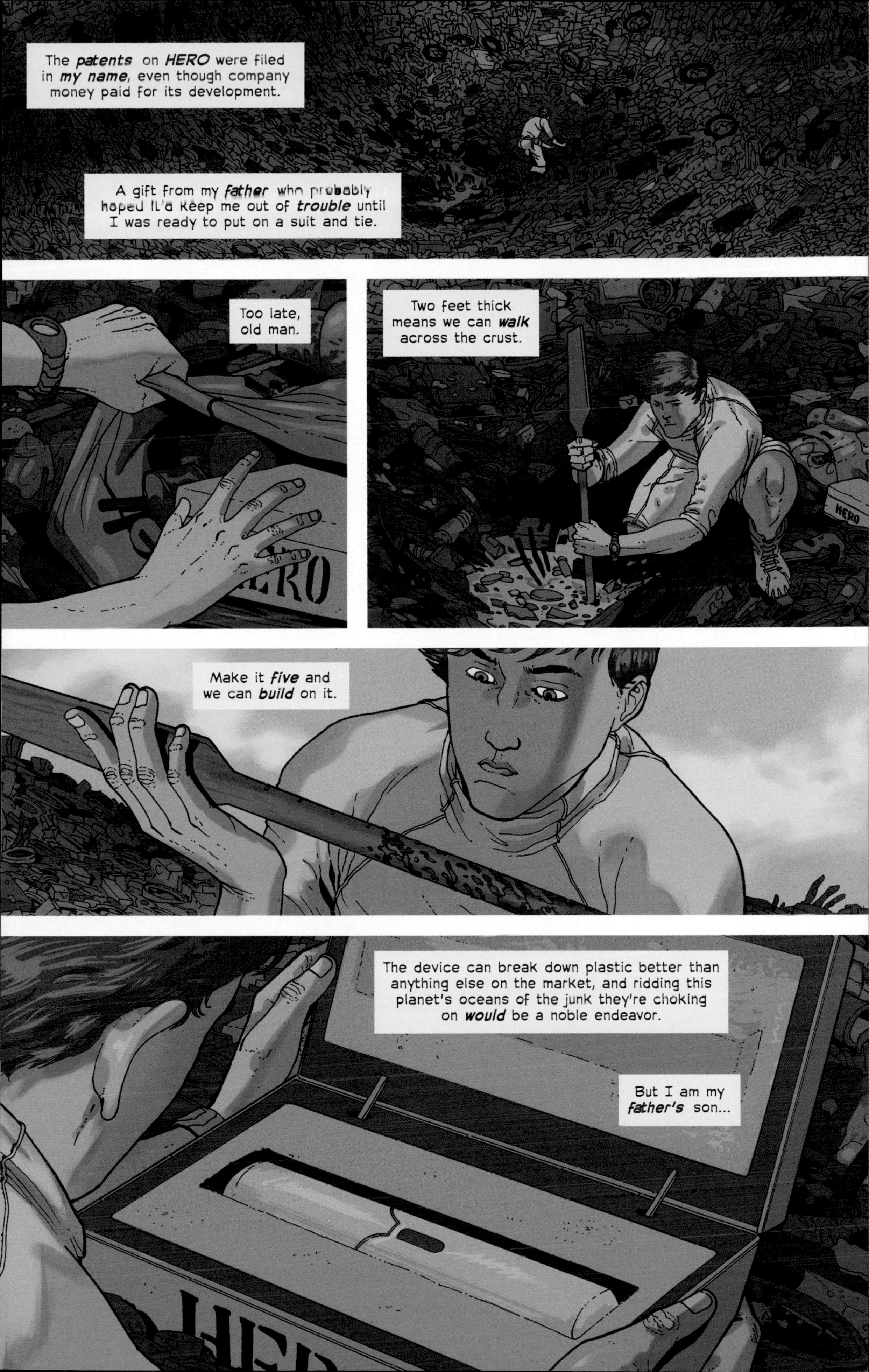

The patents on HERO were filed in my name, even though company money paid for its development.
A gift from my father who probably hoped it'd keep me out of trouble until I was ready to put on a suit and tie.
Too late, old man.
HERO
Two feet thick means we can walk across the crust.
HERO
Make it five and we can build on it.
The device can break down plastic better than anything else on the market, and ridding this planet's oceans of the junk they're choking on would be a noble endeavor.
But I am my father's son...

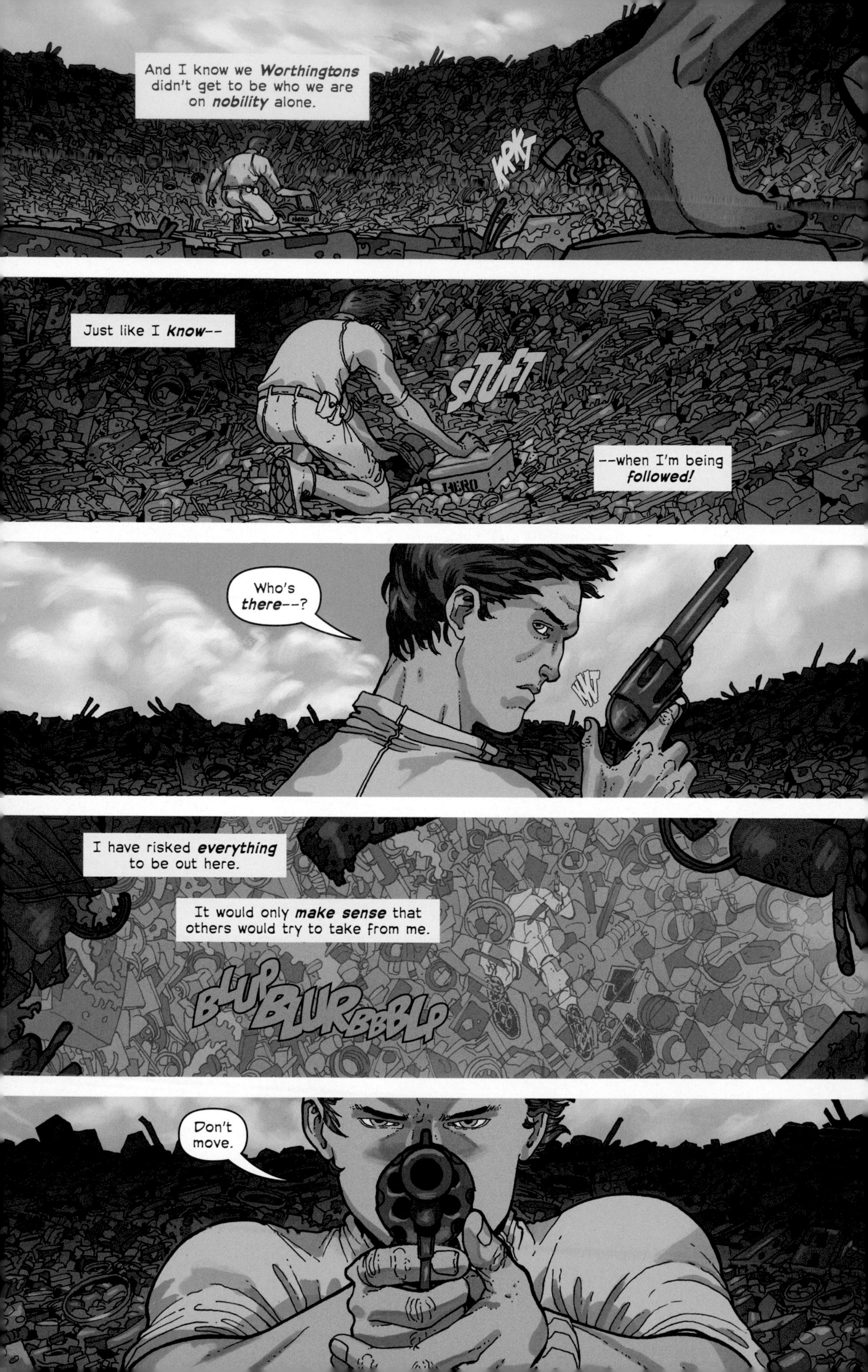

And I know we Worthingtons didn't get to be who we are on nobility alone.
KRKT
Just like I know--
STUFT
--when I'm being followed!
Who's there--?
KNT
I have risked everything to be out here.
It would only make sense that others would try to take from me.
BLUP BLUR BBBLP
Don't move.

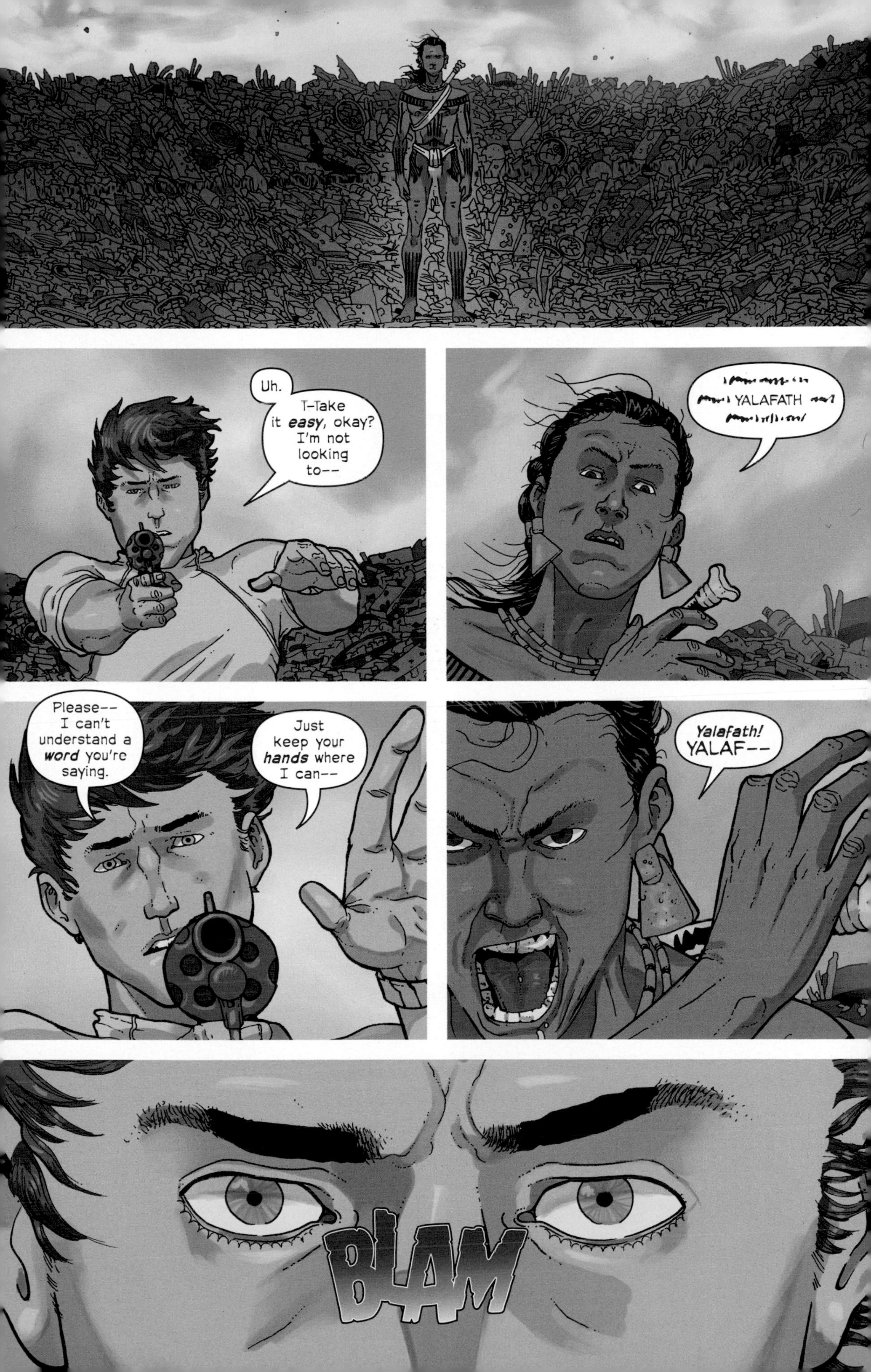
Uh.
T-Take it *easy*, okay? I'm not looking to--
YALAFATH
Please-- I can't understand a *word* you're saying.
Just keep your *hands* where I can--
Yalafath! YALAF--
BLAM

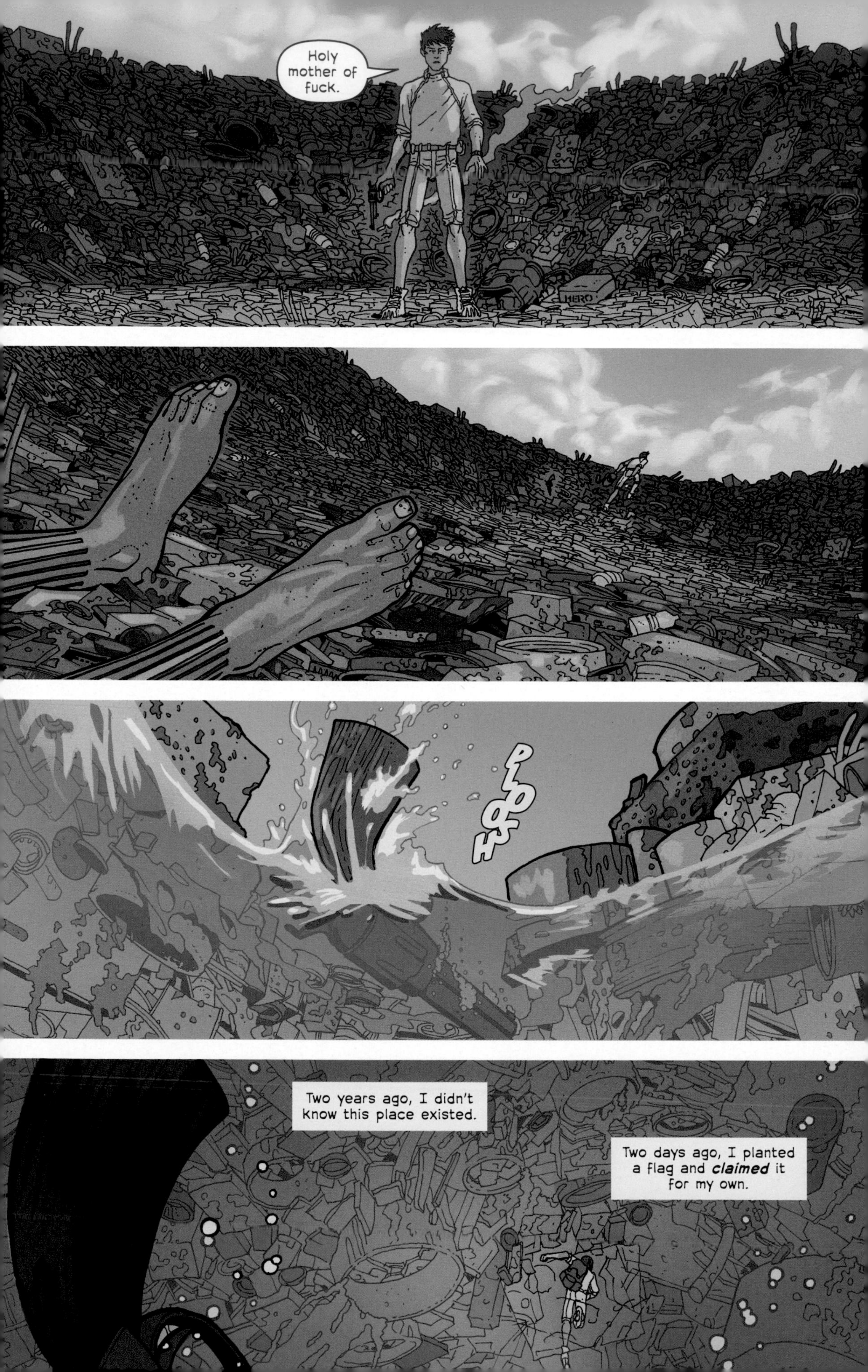
Holy mother of fuck.
HERO
PLOOSH
Two years ago, I didn't know this place existed.
Two days ago, I planted a flag and *claimed* it for my own.

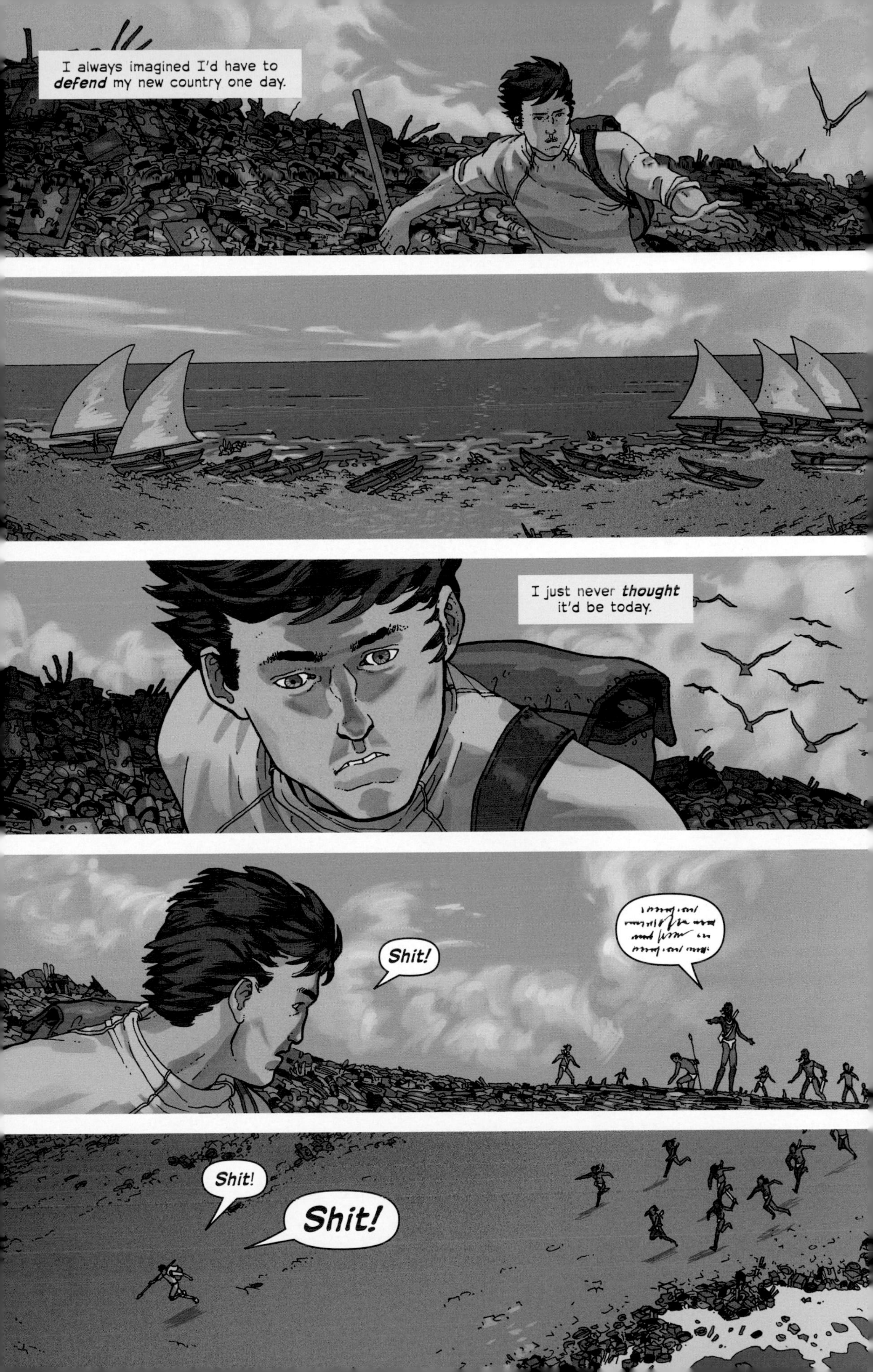
I always imagined I'd have to *defend* my new country one day.
I just never *thought* it'd be today.
Shit!
Shit!
Shit!

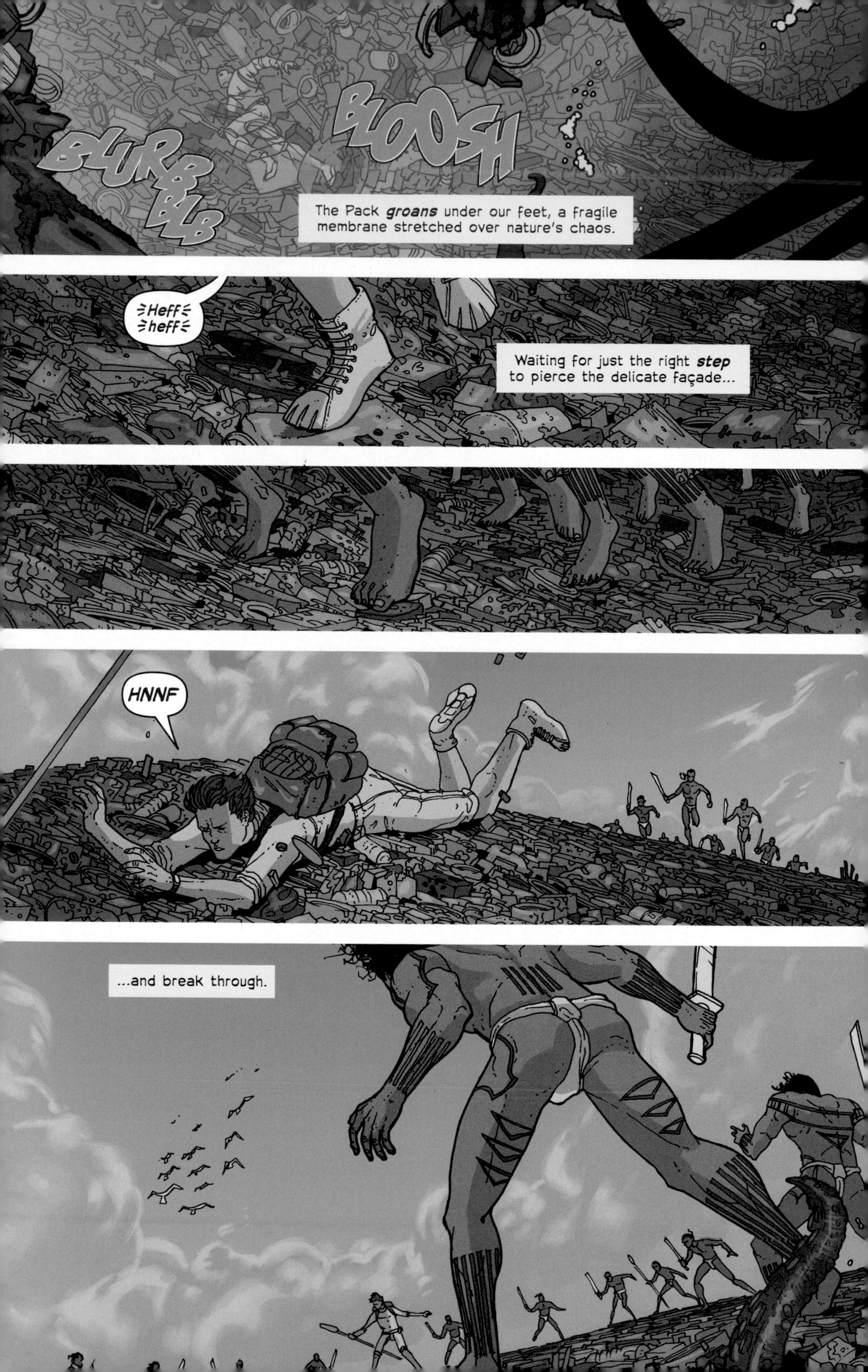
BLURB BLB
BLOOSH
The Pack *groans* under our feet, a fragile membrane stretched over nature's chaos.
Heff heff
Waiting for just the right *step* to pierce the delicate façade...
HNNF
...and break through.

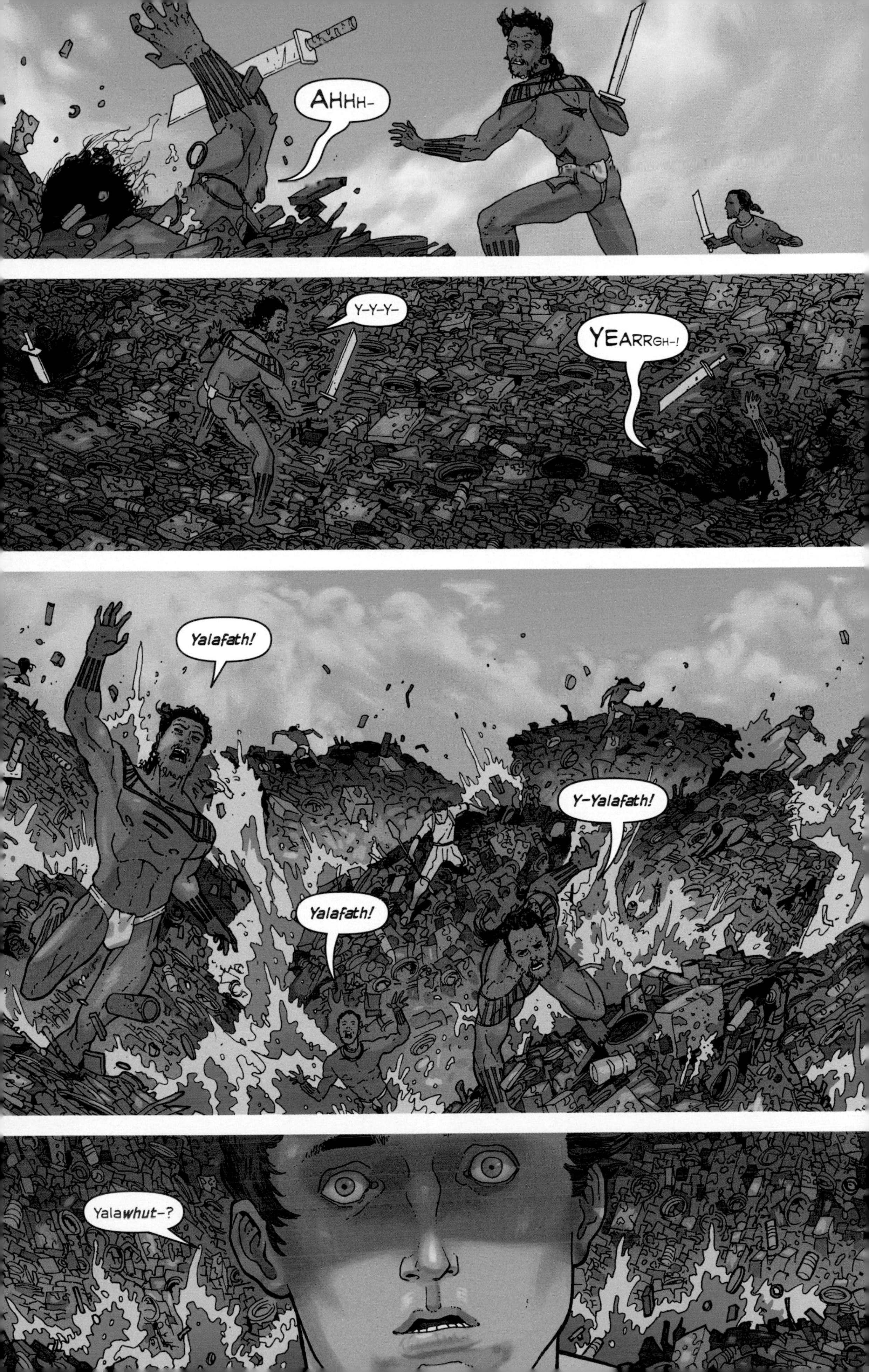
AHHH-
Y-Y-Y-
YEARRGH-!
Yalafath!
Y-Yalafath!
Yalafath!
Yalawhut-?

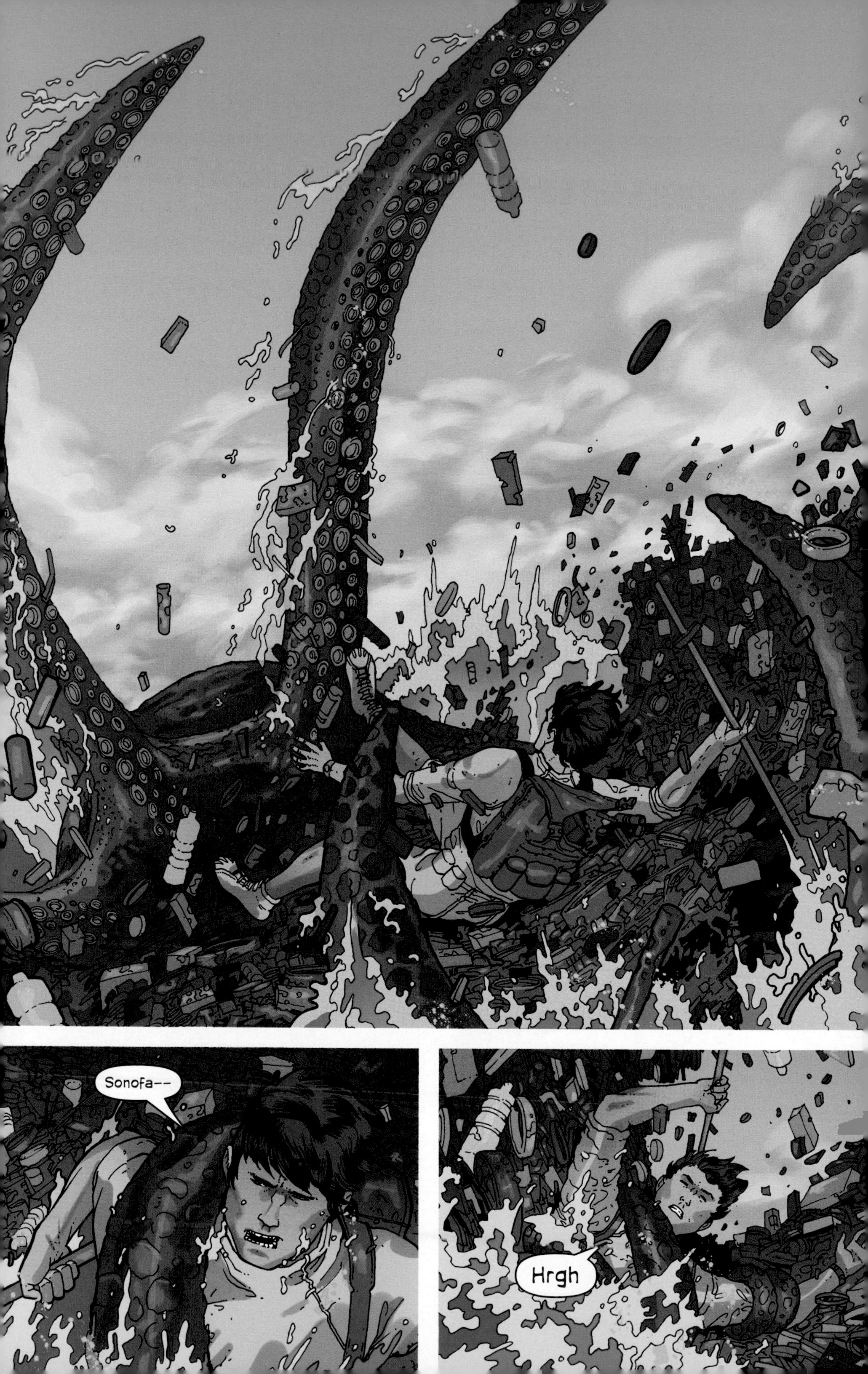
Sonofa--
Hrgh

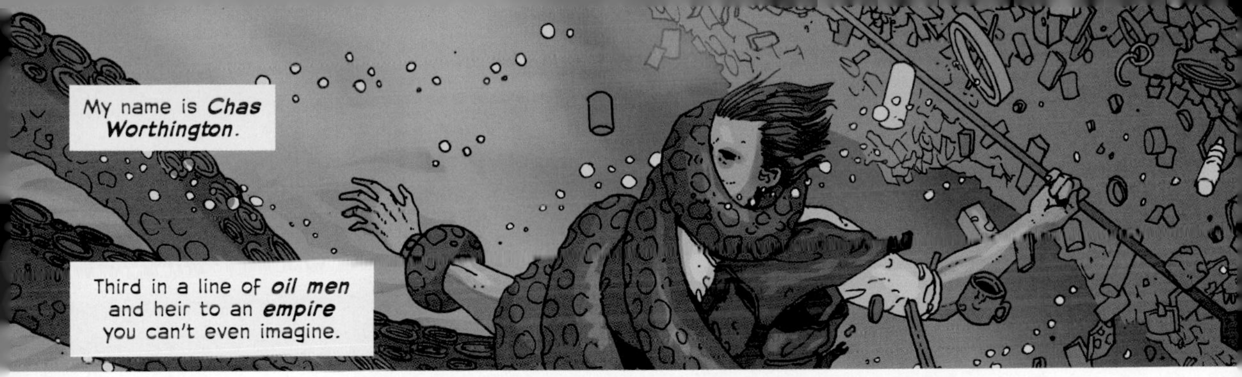
My name is *Chas Worthington*.
Third in a line of ***oil men*** and heir to an ***empire*** you can't even imagine.

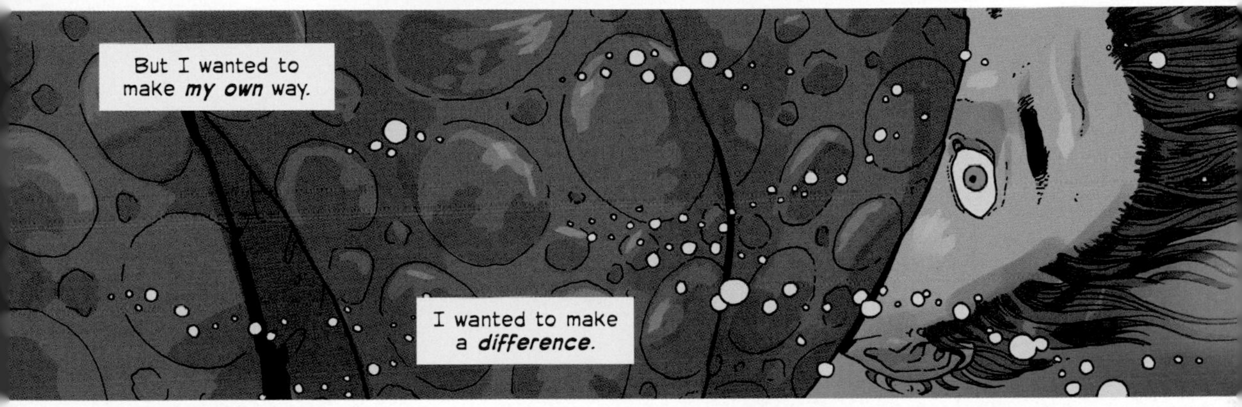
But I wanted to make ***my own*** way.
I wanted to make a ***difference***.

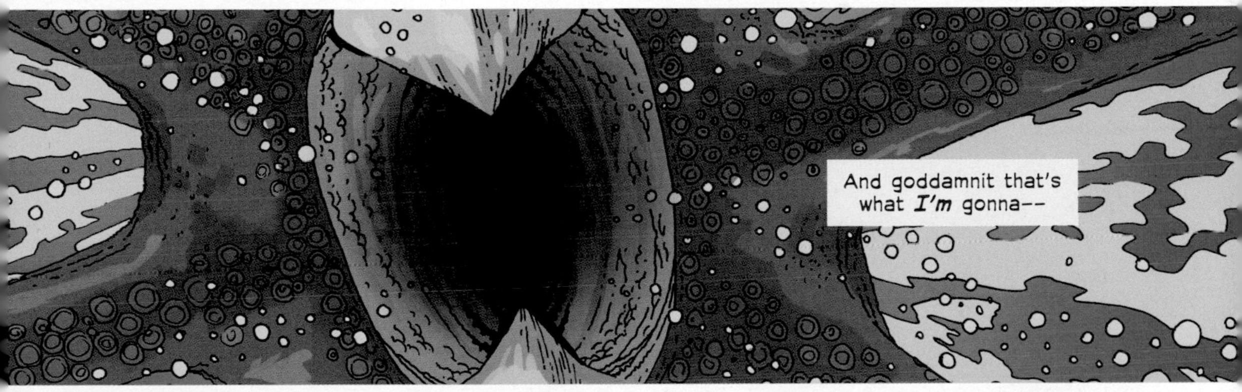
And goddamnit that's what ***I'm*** gonna--

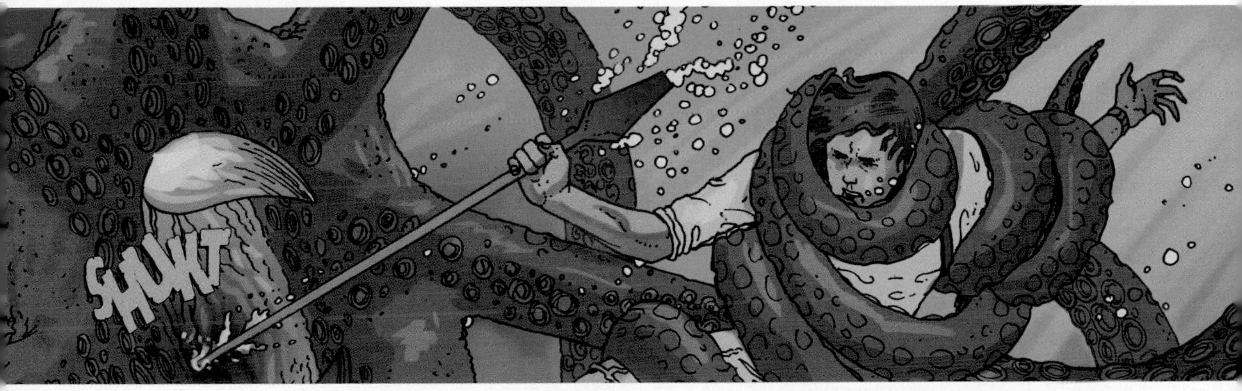
SHUNT

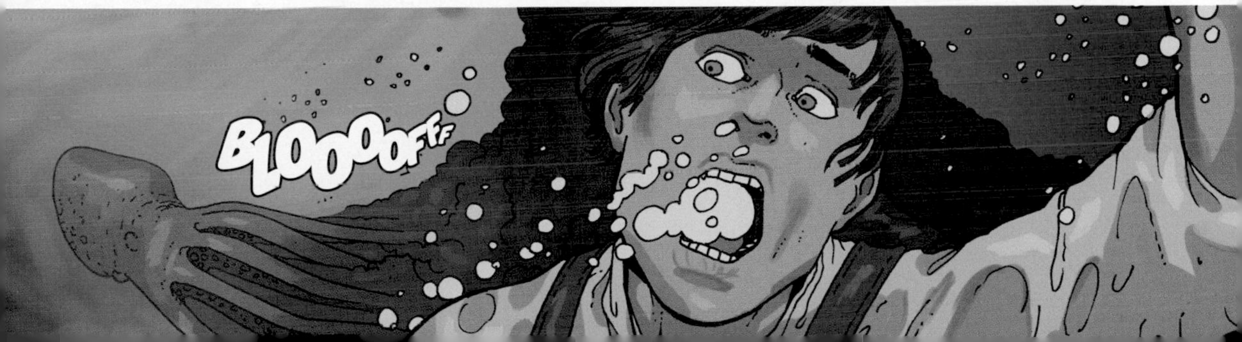
BLOOOOOFFF

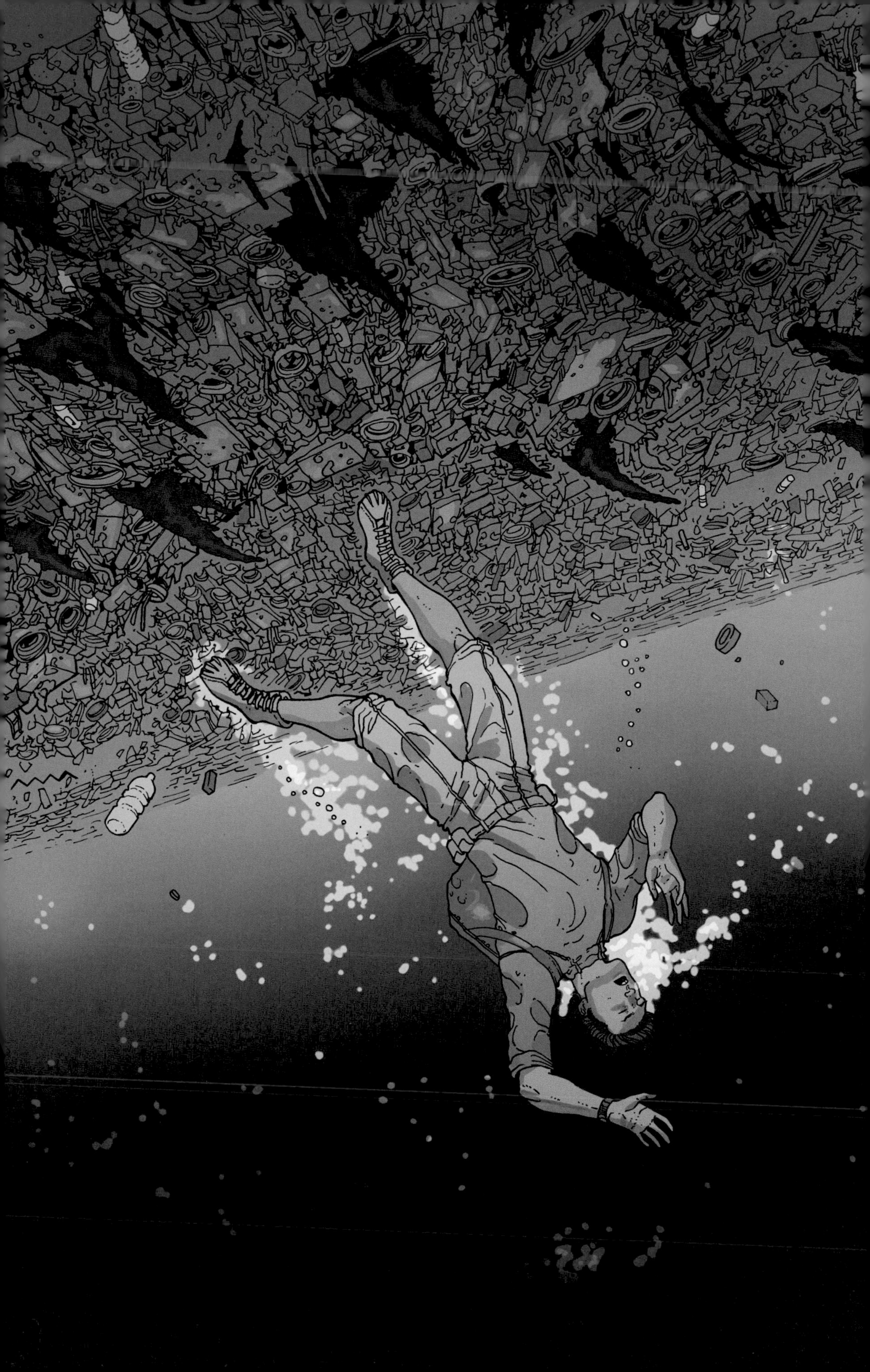

CHAPTER **THREE**

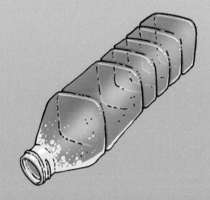

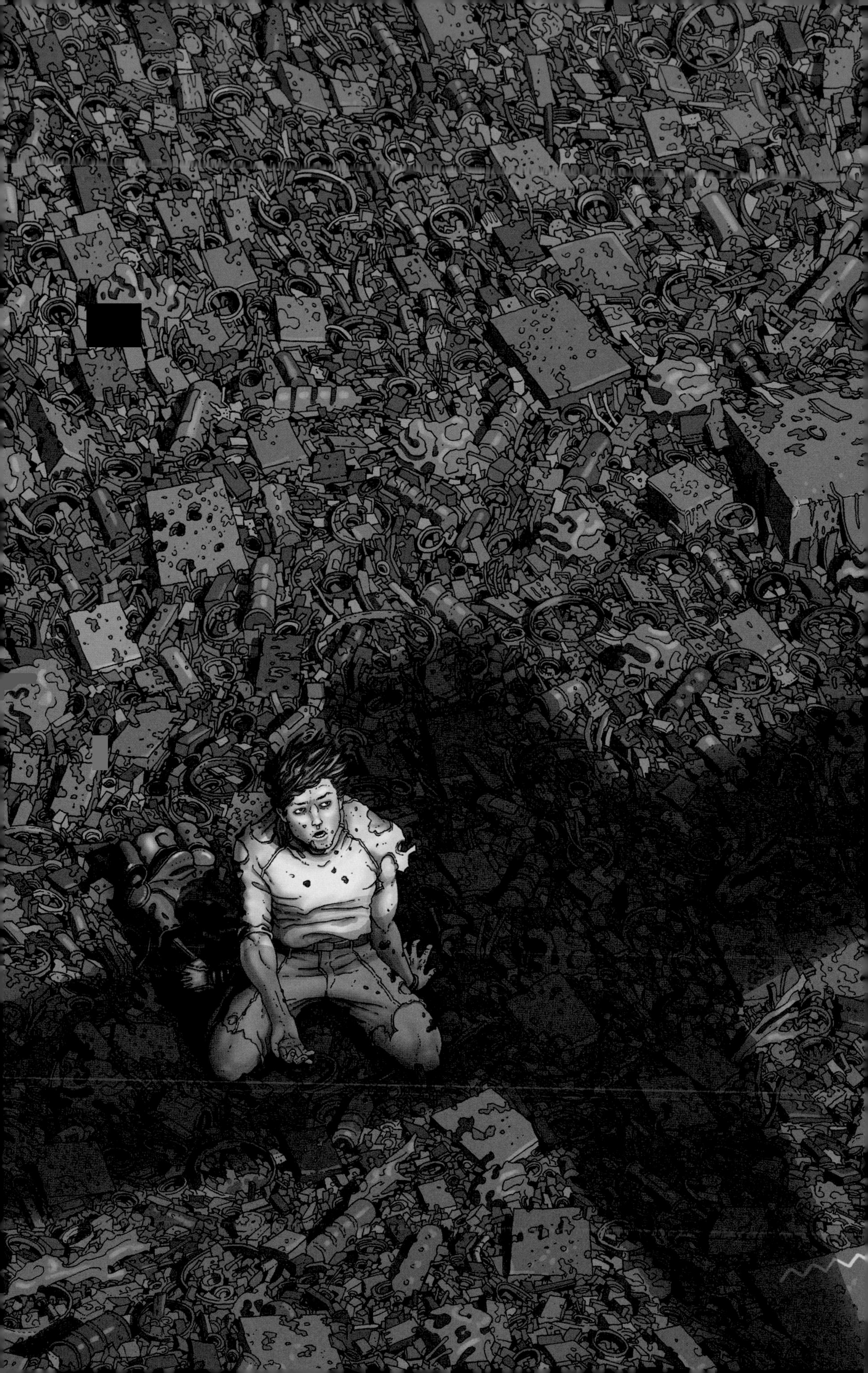

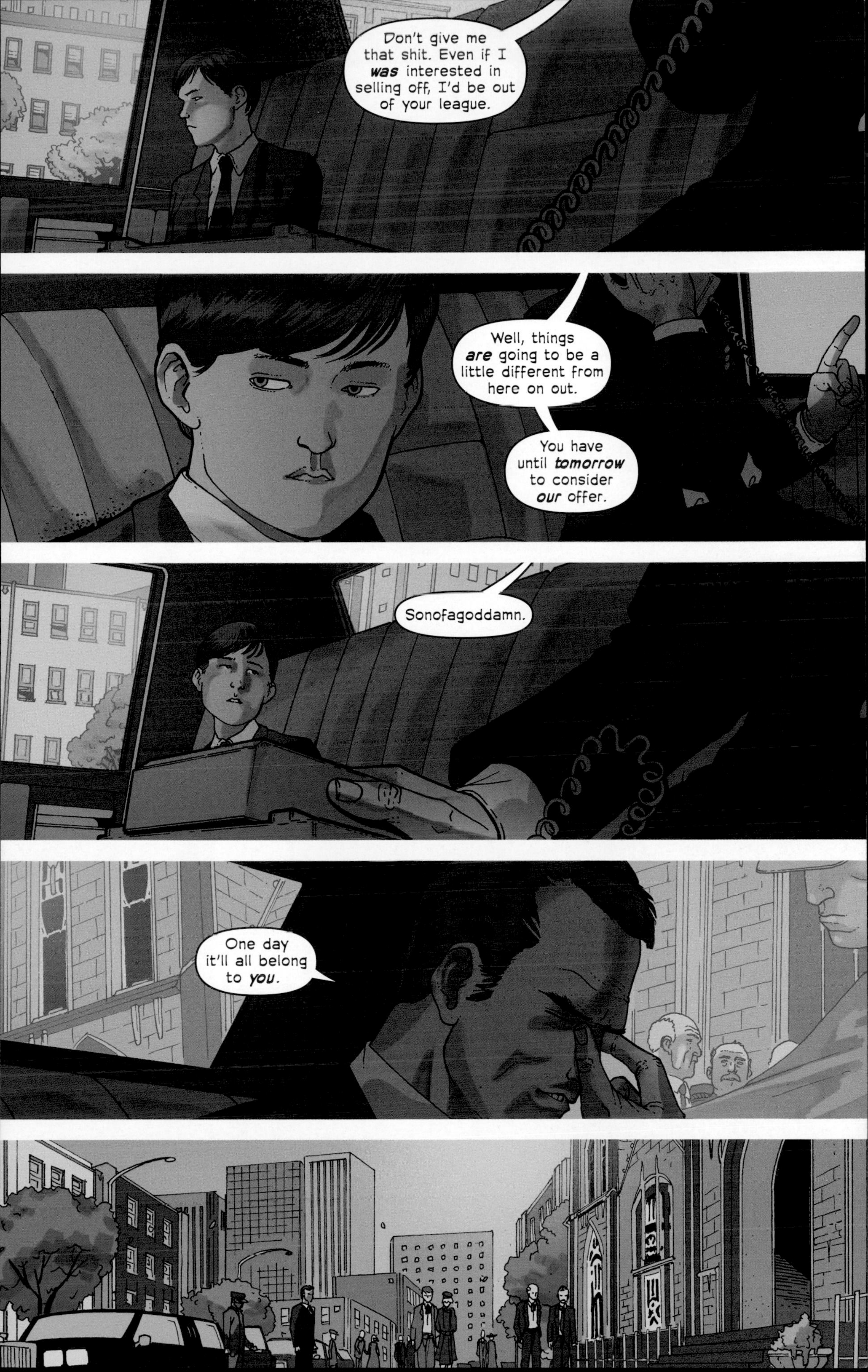
Don't give me that shit. Even if I *was* interested in selling off, I'd be out of your league.
Well, things *are* going to be a little different from here on out.
You have until *tomorrow* to consider *our* offer.
Sonofagoddamn.
One day it'll all belong to *you*.

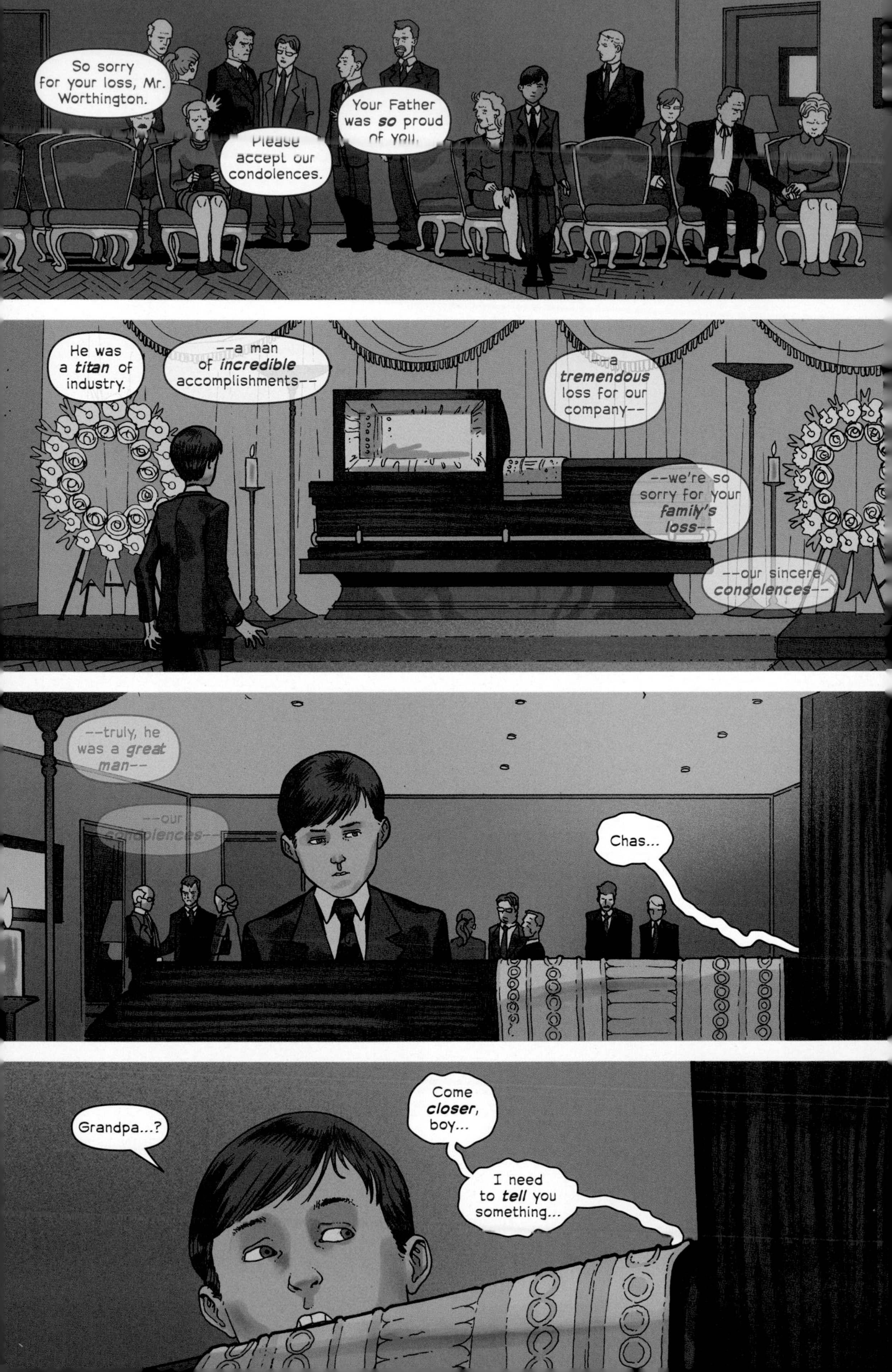
So sorry for your loss, Mr. Worthington.
Please accept our condolences.
Your Father was so proud of you.
He was a titan of industry.
--a man of incredible accomplishments--
--a tremendous loss for our company--
--we're so sorry for your family's loss--
--our sincere condolences--
--truly, he was a great man--
--our condolences--
Chas...
Grandpa...?
Come closer, boy...
I need to tell you something...

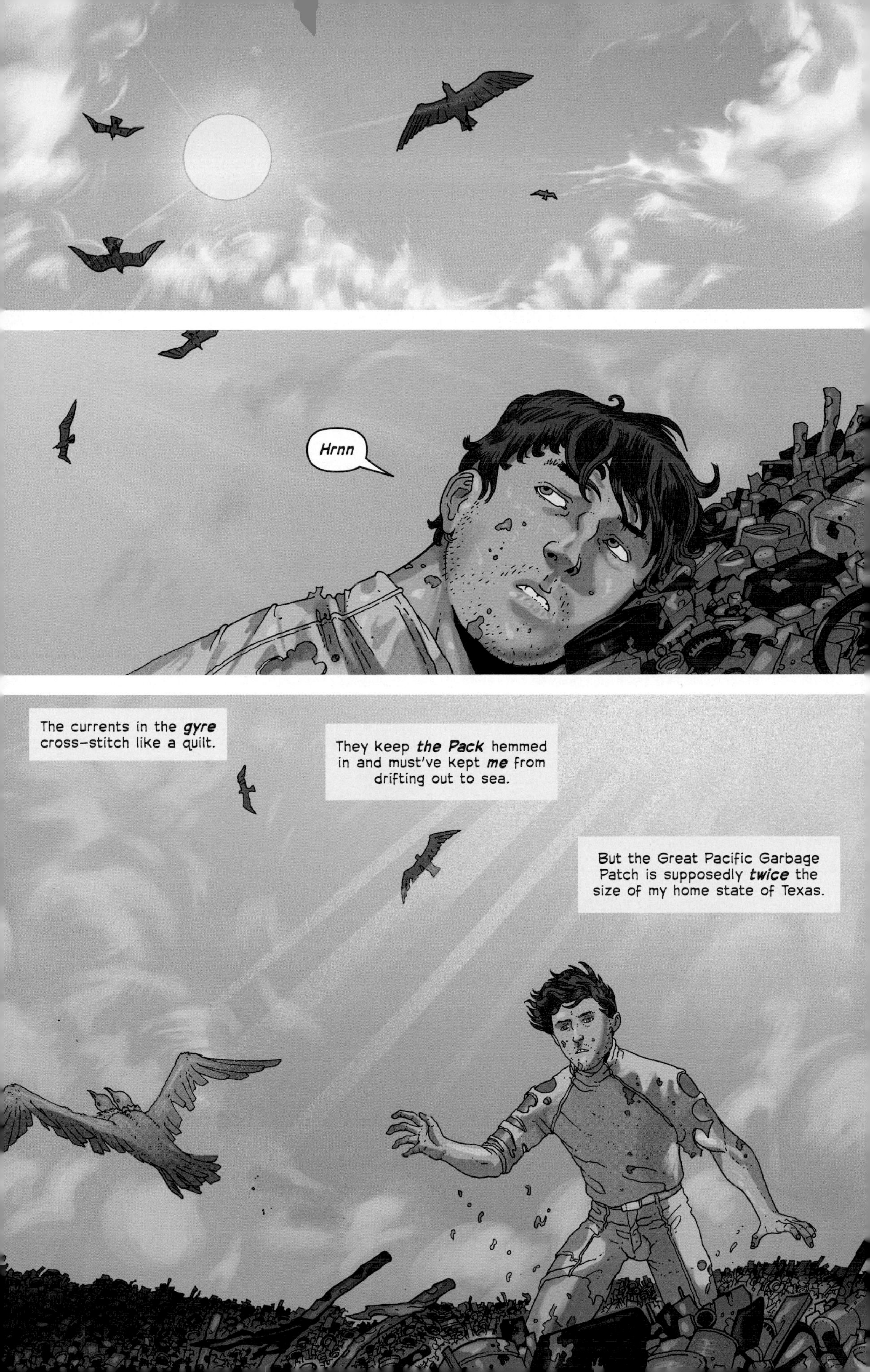
Hrnn
The currents in the gyre cross-stitch like a quilt.
They keep the Pack hemmed in and must've kept me from drifting out to sea.
But the Great Pacific Garbage Patch is supposedly twice the size of my home state of Texas.

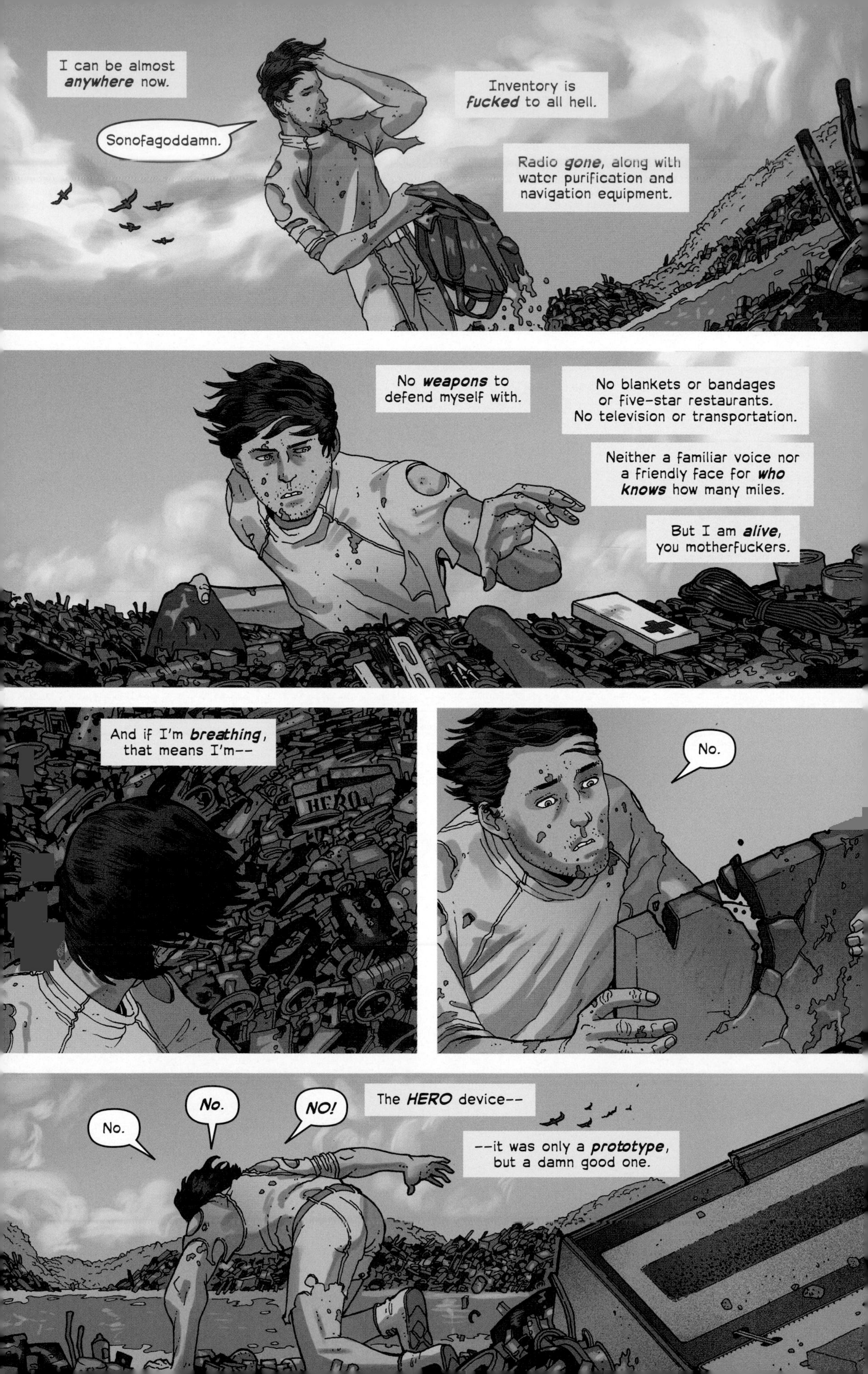
I can be almost *anywhere* now.
Sonofagoddamn.
Inventory is *fucked* to all hell.
Radio *gone*, along with water purification and navigation equipment.
No *weapons* to defend myself with.
No blankets or bandages or five-star restaurants. No television or transportation.
Neither a familiar voice nor a friendly face for *who knows* how many miles.
But I am *alive*, you motherfuckers.
And if I'm *breathing*, that means I'm--
No.
No.
No.
NO!
The *HERO* device--
--it was only a *prototype*, but a damn good one.

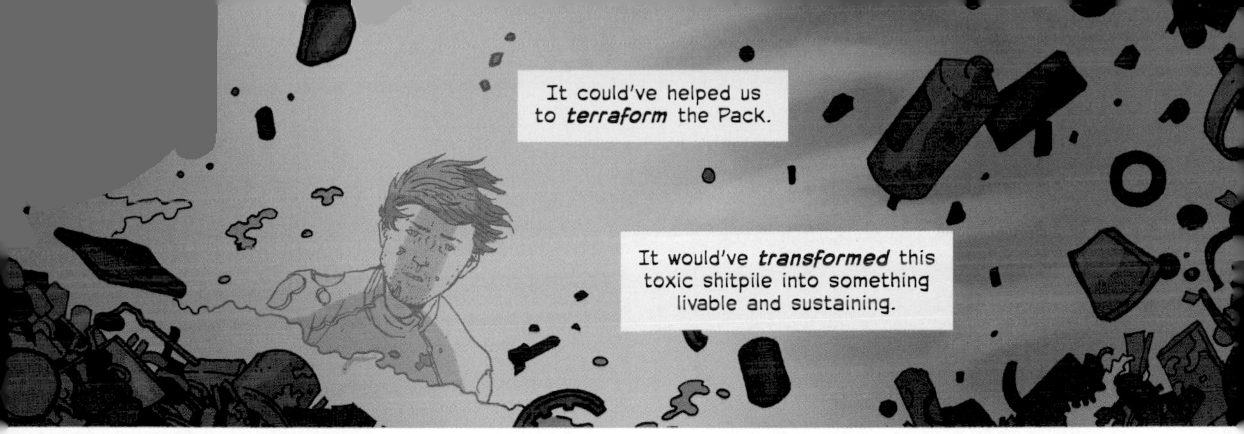
It could've helped us to *terraform* the Pack.
It would've *transformed* this toxic shitpile into something livable and sustaining.

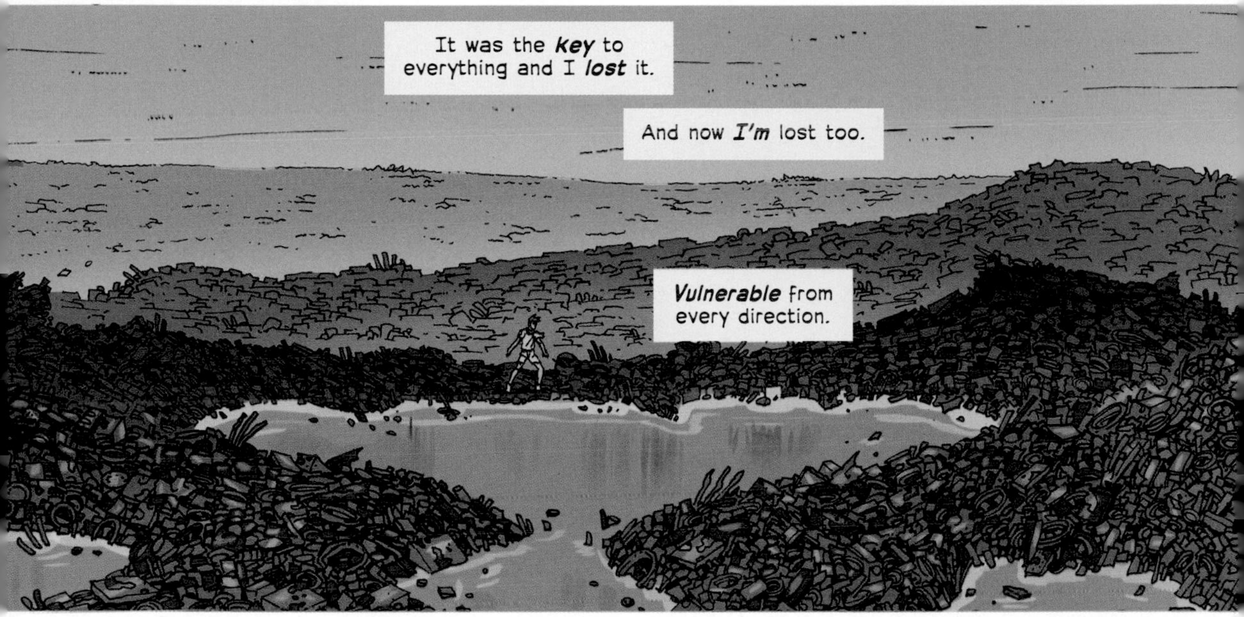
It was the *key* to everything and I *lost* it.
And now *I'm* lost too.
Vulnerable from every direction.

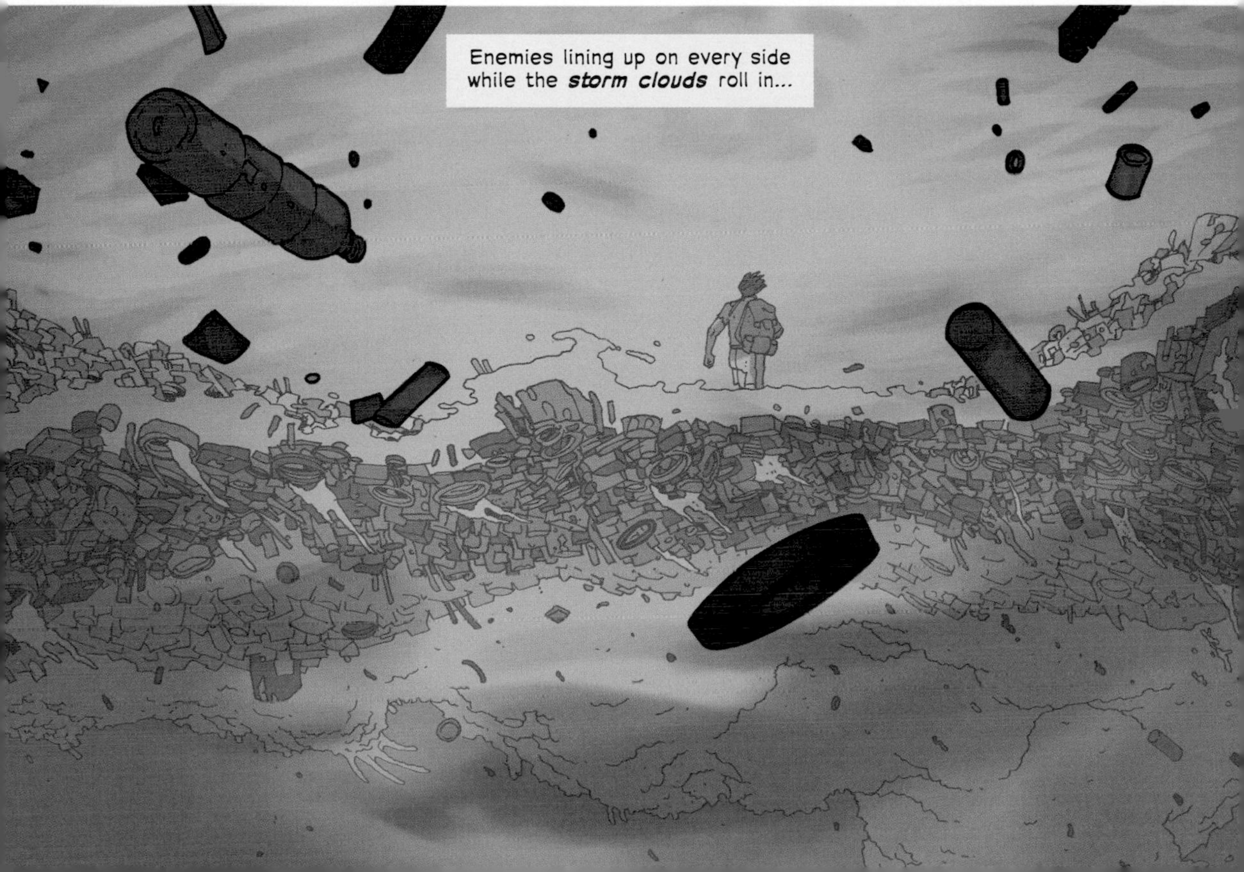
Enemies lining up on every side while the *storm clouds* roll in...

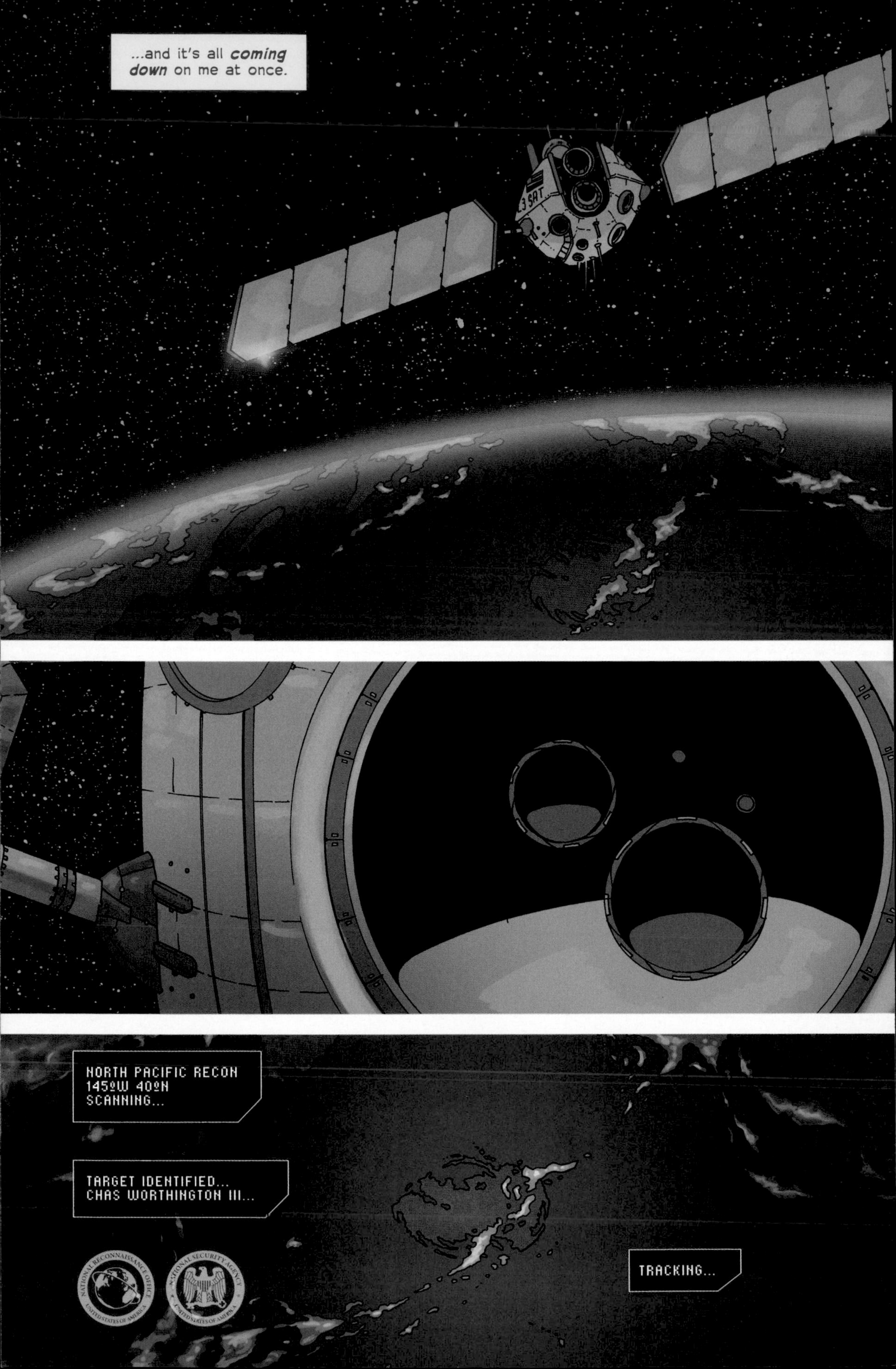
...and it's all *coming down* on me at once.
NORTH PACIFIC RECON
145ºW 40ºN
SCANNING...
TARGET IDENTIFIED...
CHAS WORTHINGTON III...
TRACKING...

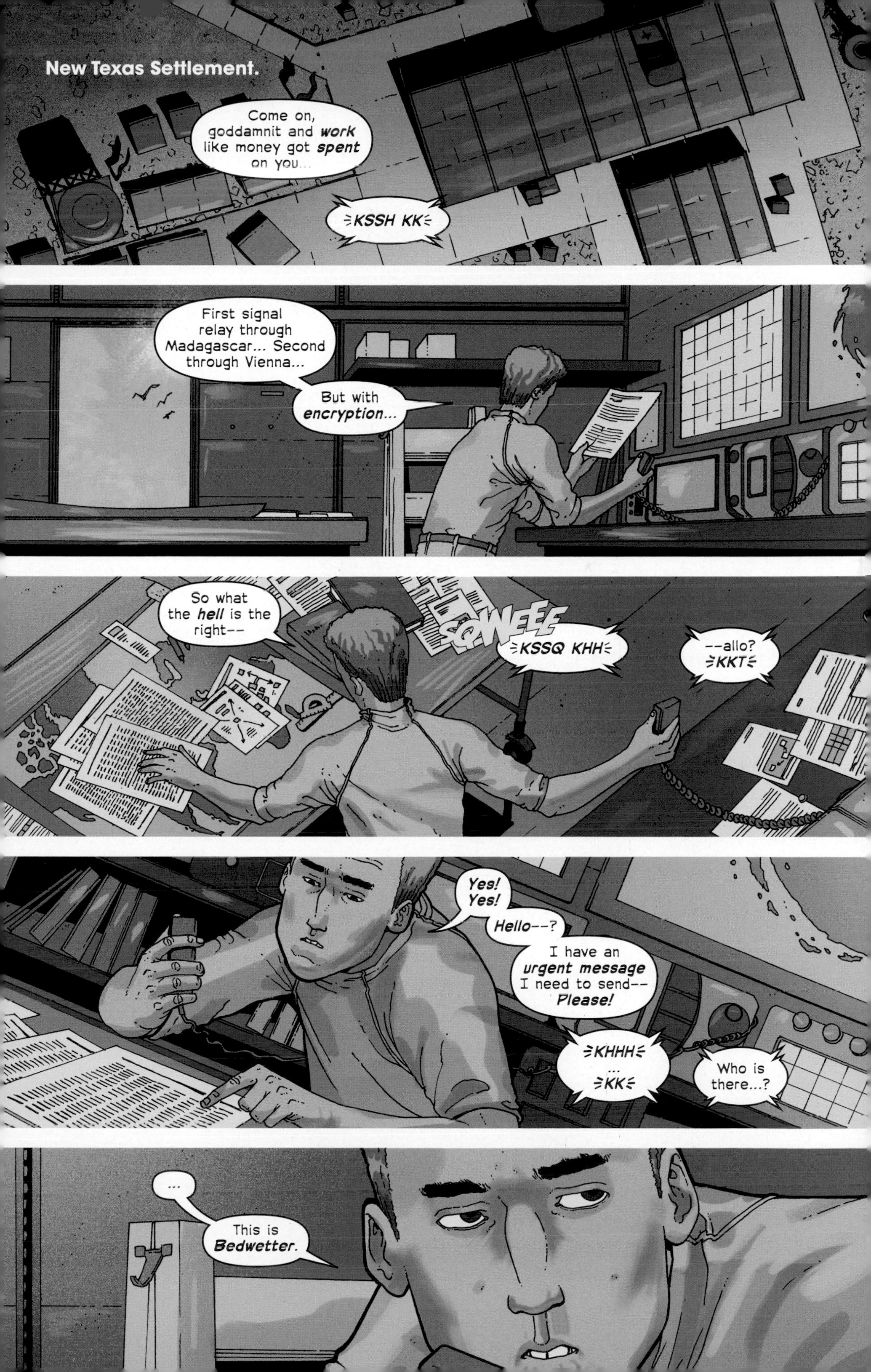

New Texas Settlement.
Come on, goddamnit and work like money got spent on you...
KSSH KK
First signal relay through Madagascar... Second through Vienna...
But with encryption...
So what the hell is the right--
SQWEEE
KSSQ KHH
--allo? KKT
Yes! Yes!
Hello--?
I have an urgent message I need to send-- Please!
KHHH ... KK
Who is there...?
...
This is Bedwetter.

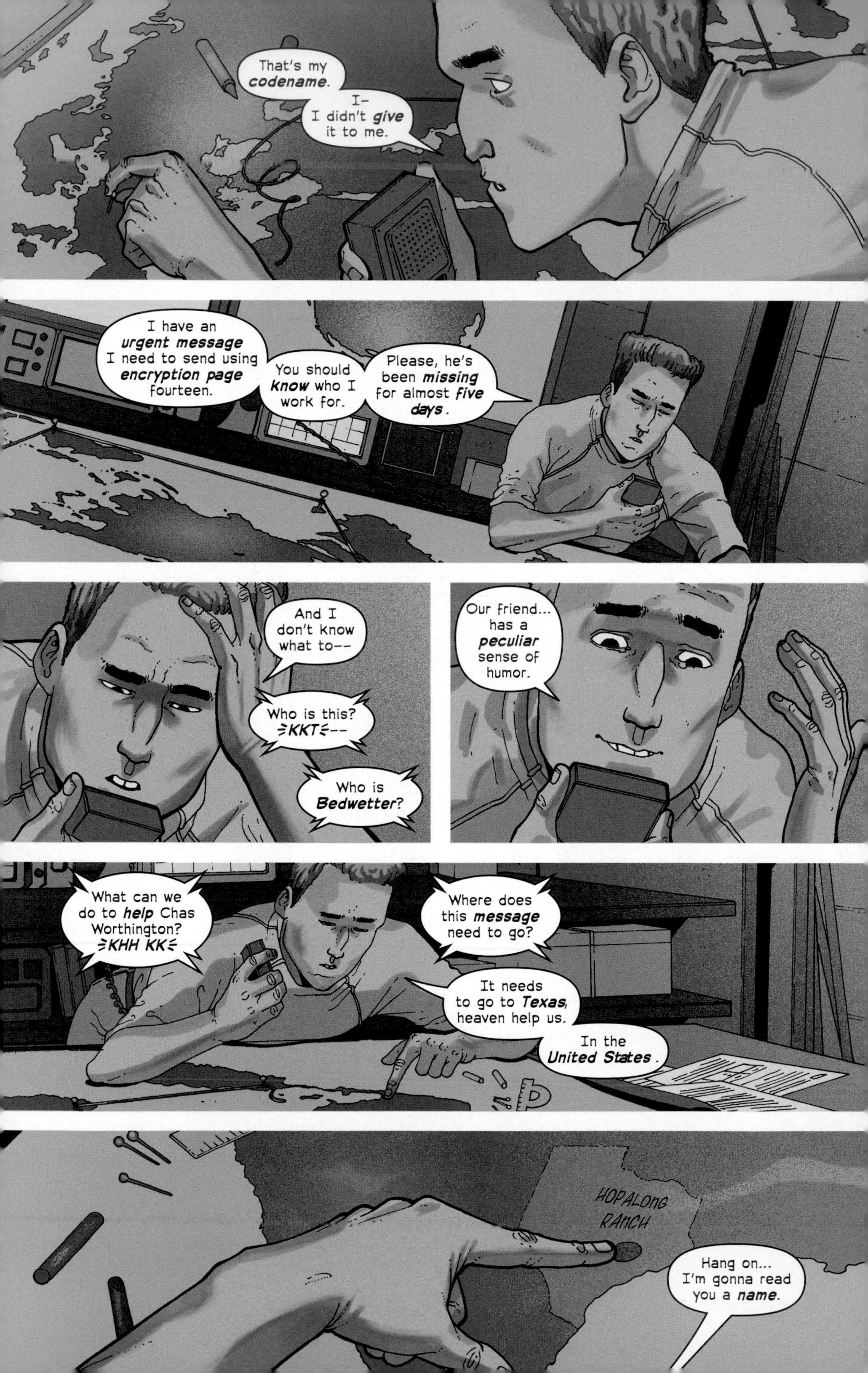
That's my *codename*.
I– I didn't *give* it to me.
I have an *urgent message* I need to send using *encryption page* fourteen.
You should *know* who I work for.
Please, he's been *missing* for almost *five days*.
And I don't know what to--
Who is this? KKT--
Who is *Bedwetter*?
Our friend... has a *peculiar* sense of humor.
What can we do to *help* Chas Worthington? KHH KK
Where does this *message* need to go?
It needs to go to *Texas*, heaven help us.
In the *United States*.
HOPALONG RANCH
Hang on... I'm gonna read you a *name*.

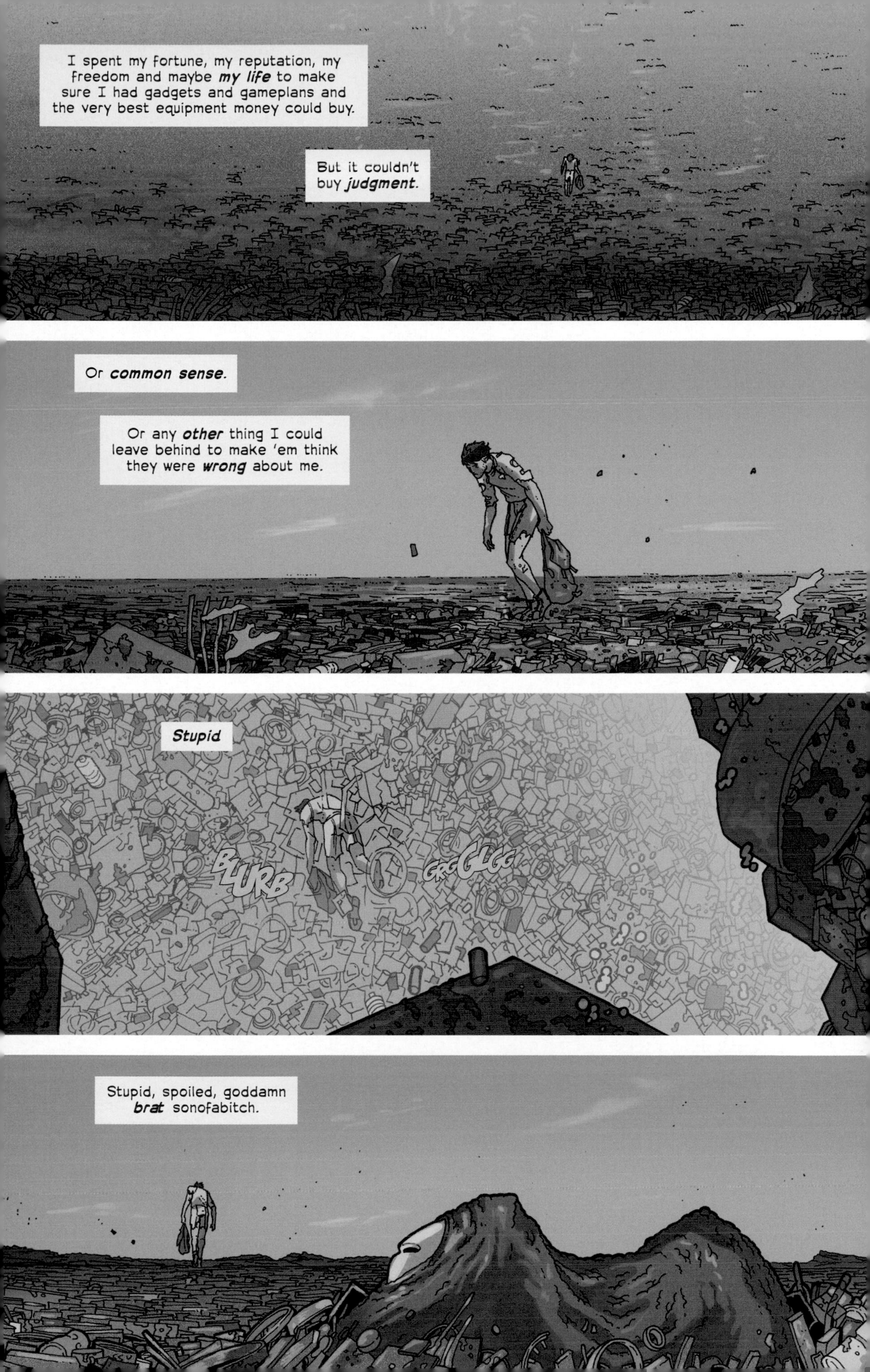
I spent my fortune, my reputation, my freedom and maybe *my life* to make sure I had gadgets and gameplans and the very best equipment money could buy.
But it couldn't buy *judgment*.
Or *common sense*.
Or any *other* thing I could leave behind to make 'em think they were *wrong* about me.
Stupid
BLURB
GRGGLGG
Stupid, spoiled, goddamn *brat* sonofabitch.

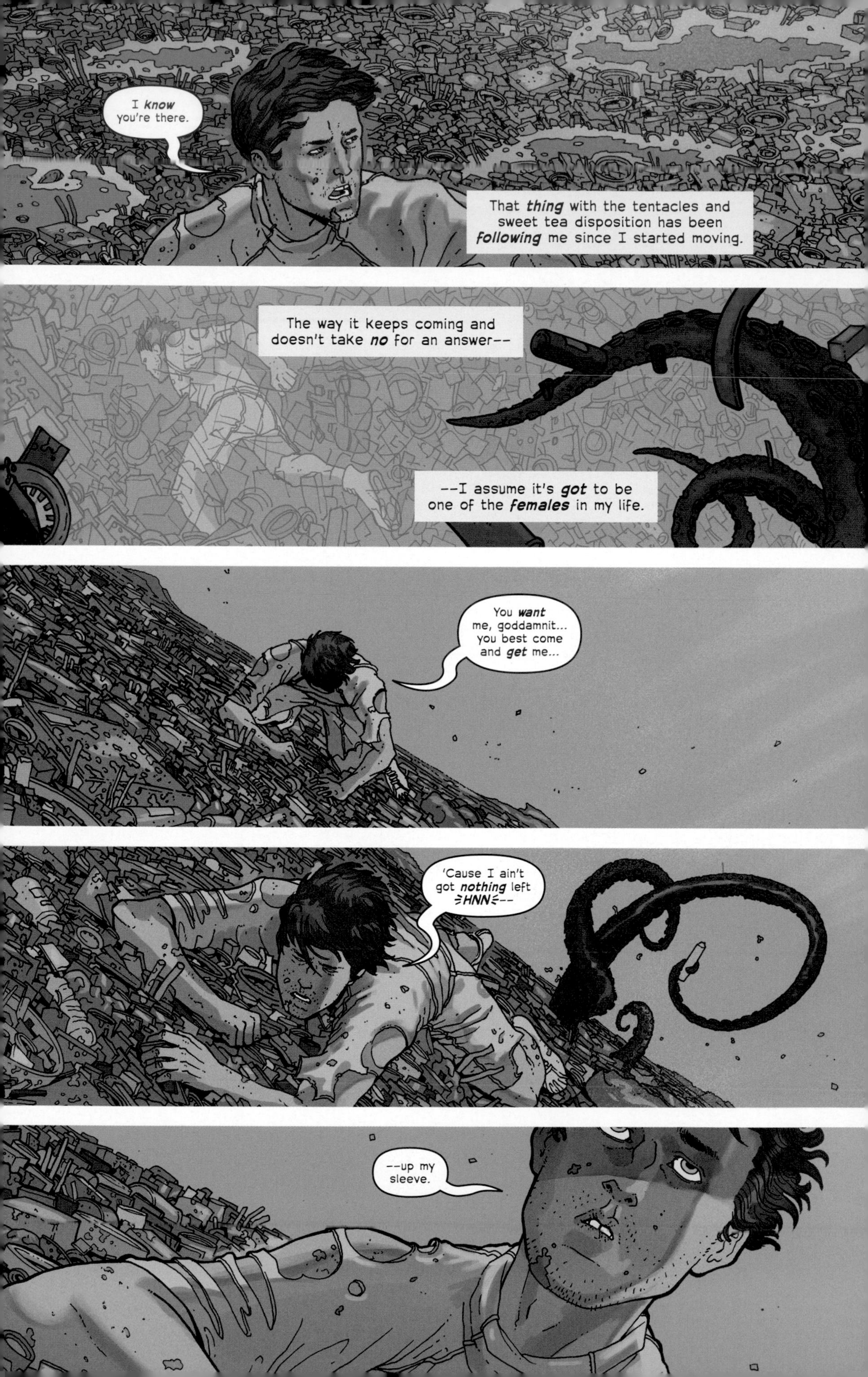
I *know* you're there.
That *thing* with the tentacles and sweet tea disposition has been *following* me since I started moving.
The way it keeps coming and doesn't take *no* for an answer--
--I assume it's *got* to be one of the *females* in my life.
You *want* me, goddamnit... you best come and *get* me...
'Cause I ain't got *nothing* left HNN--
--up my sleeve.

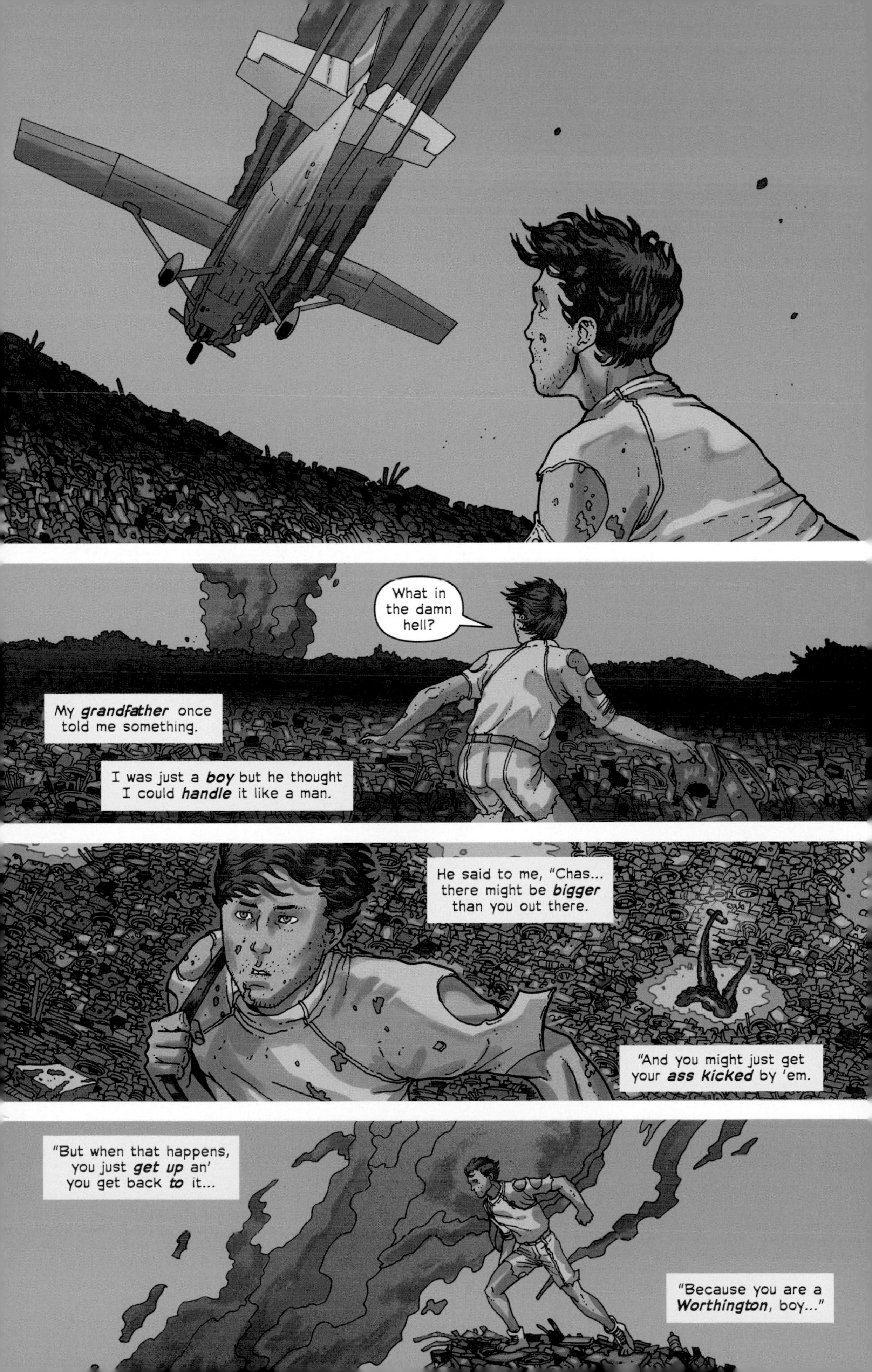

What in the damn hell?
My *grandfather* once told me something.
I was just a *boy* but he thought I could *handle* it like a man.
He said to me, "Chas... there might be *bigger* than you out there.
"And you might just get your *ass kicked* by 'em.
"But when that happens, you just *get up* an' you get back *to* it...
"Because you are a *Worthington*, boy..."

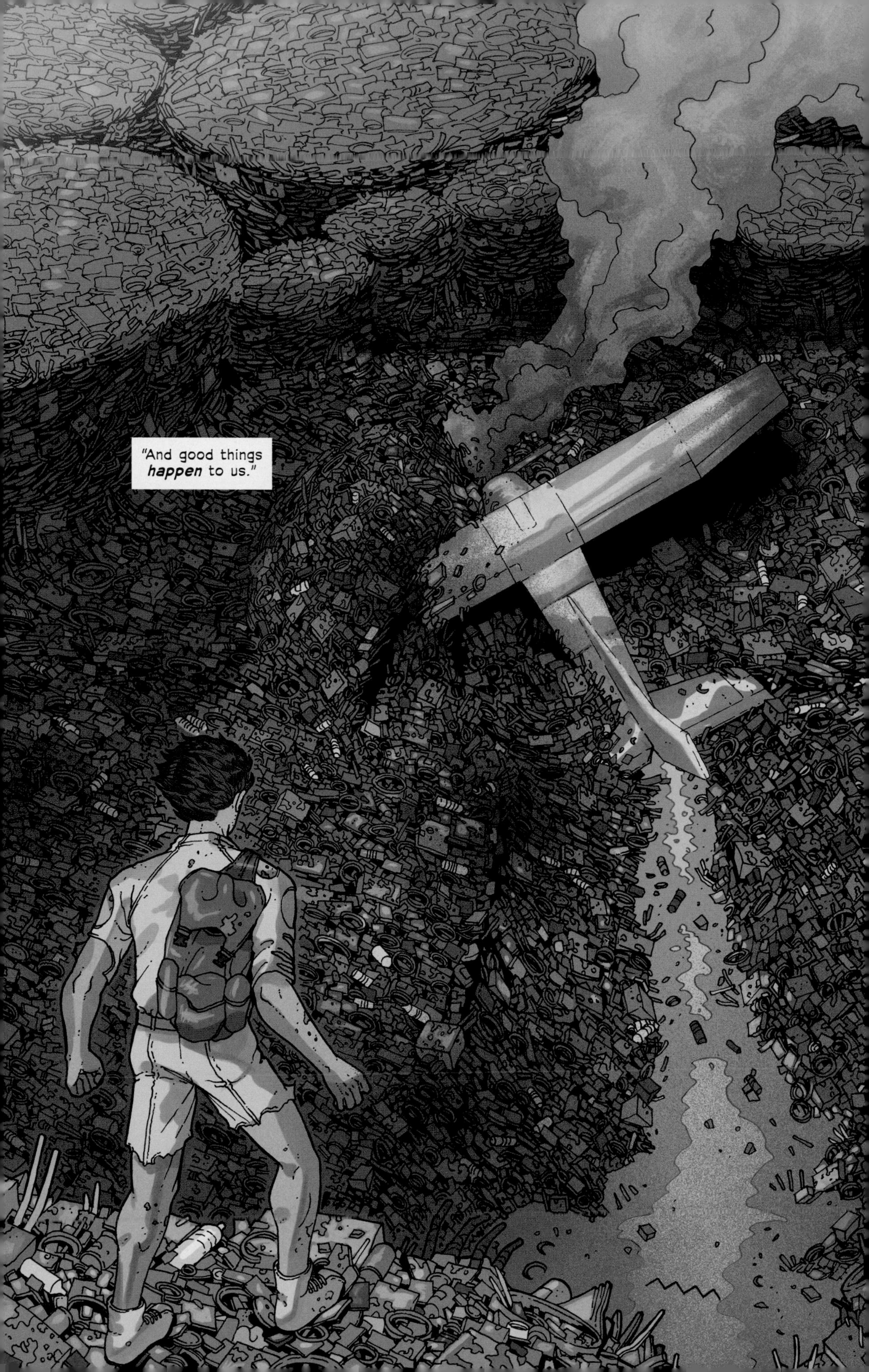
"And good things *happen* to us."

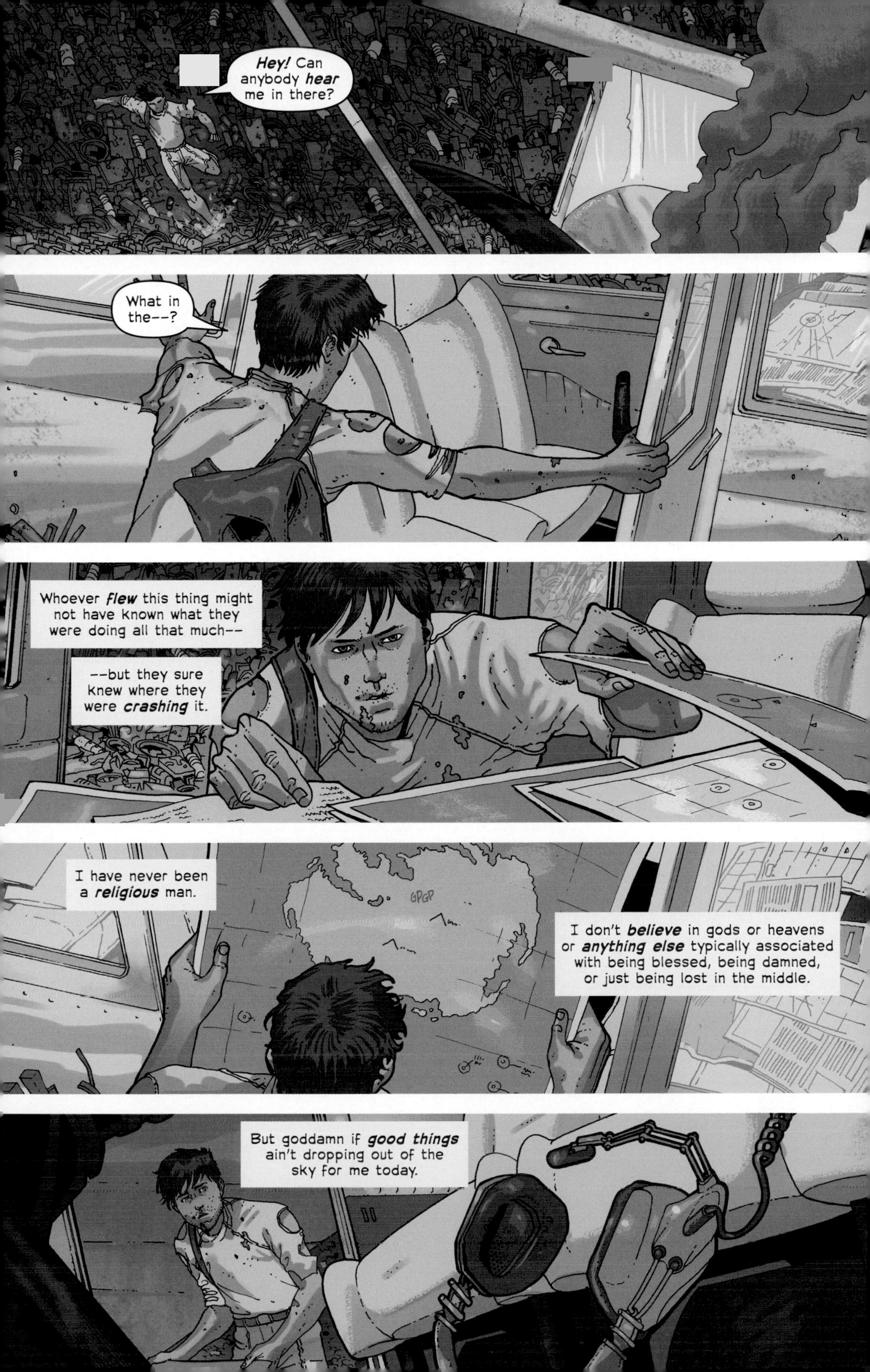
Hey! Can anybody hear me in there?
What in the--?
Whoever flew this thing might not have known what they were doing all that much--
--but they sure knew where they were crashing it.
I have never been a religious man.
GPGP
I don't believe in gods or heavens or anything else typically associated with being blessed, being damned, or just being lost in the middle.
But goddamn if good things ain't dropping out of the sky for me today.

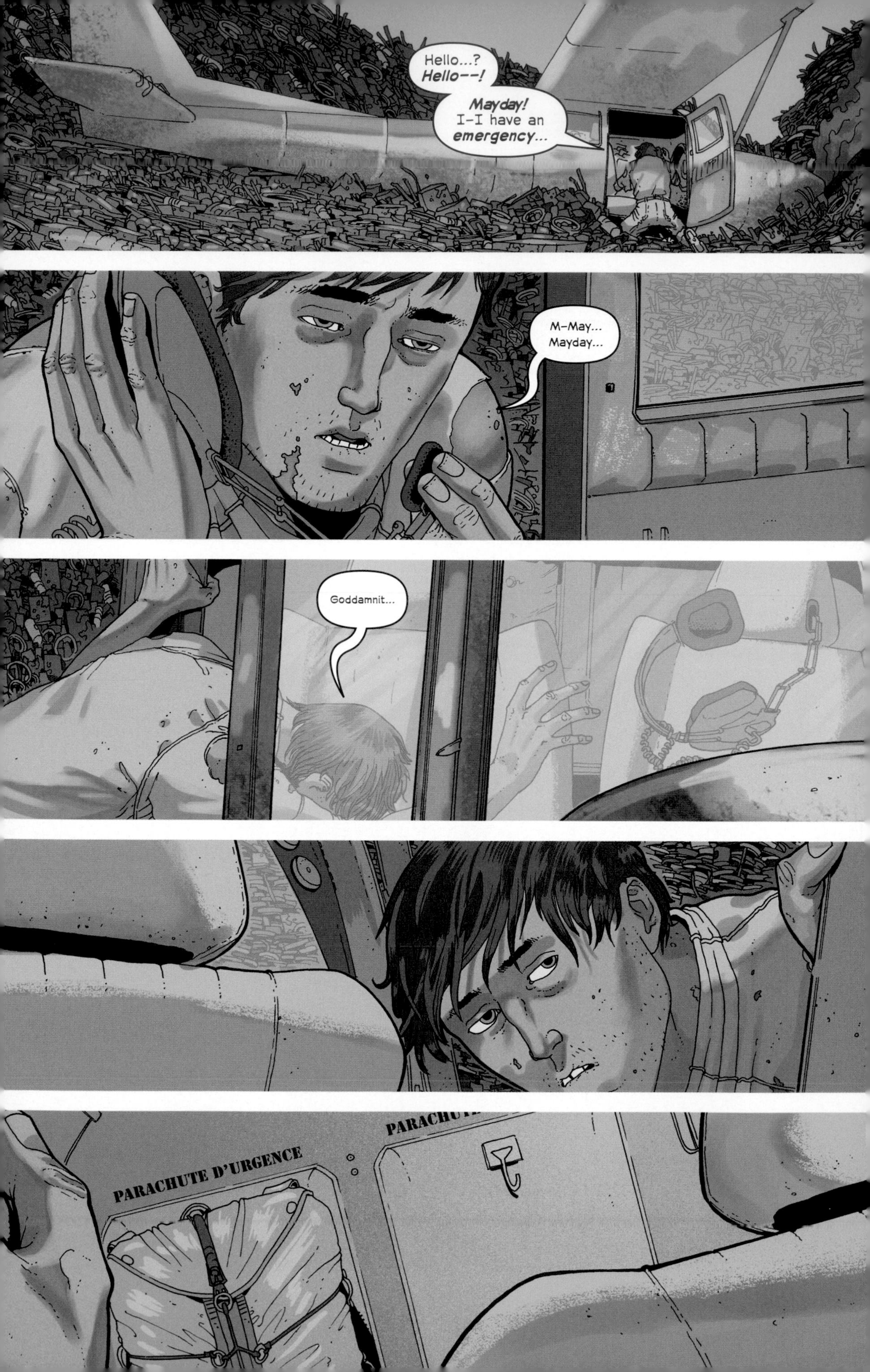
Hello...? Hello--!
Mayday! I-I have an emergency...
M-May... Mayday...
Goddamnit...
PARACHUTE D'URGENCE

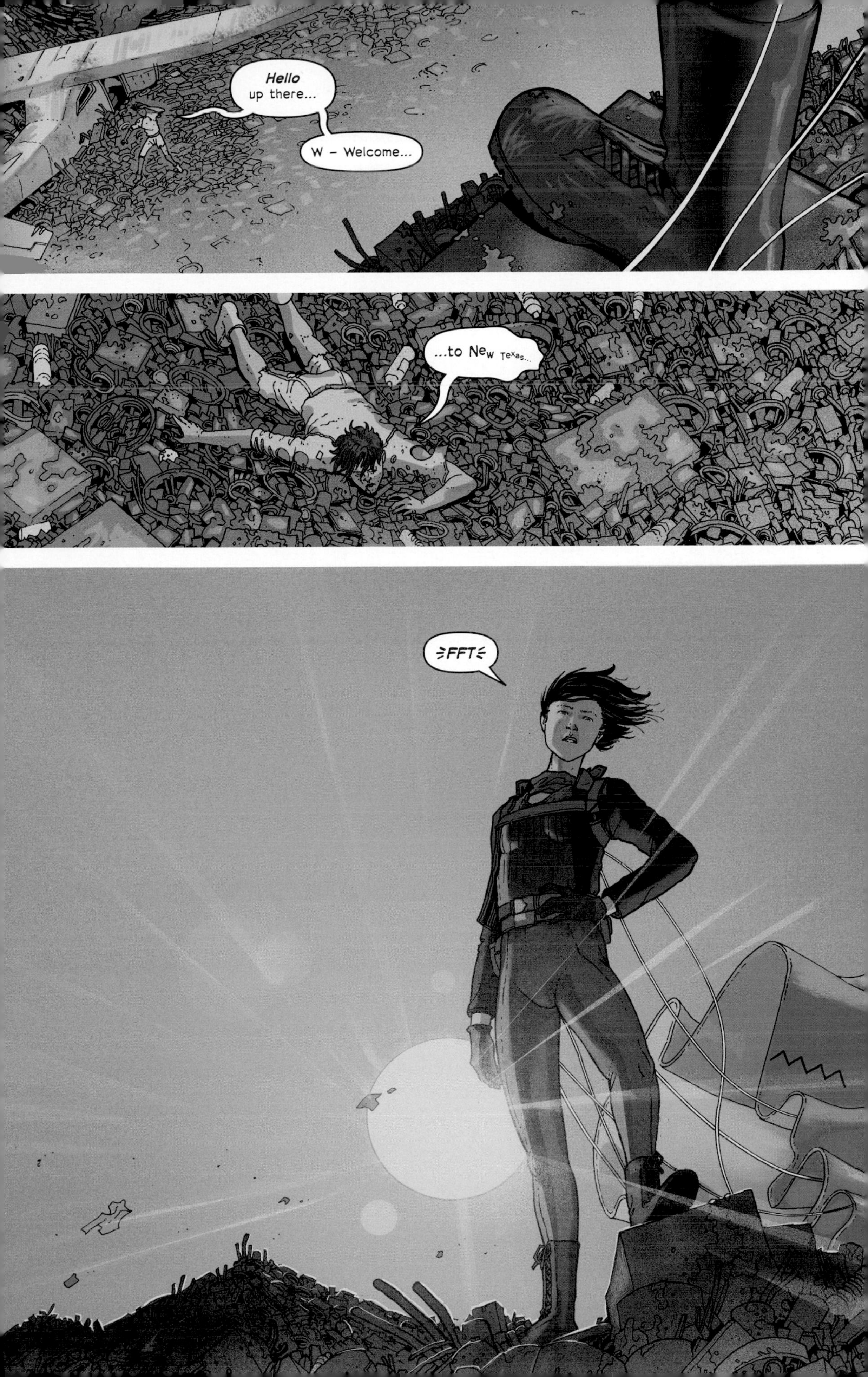
Hello up there...
W - Welcome...
...to New Texas...
FFT

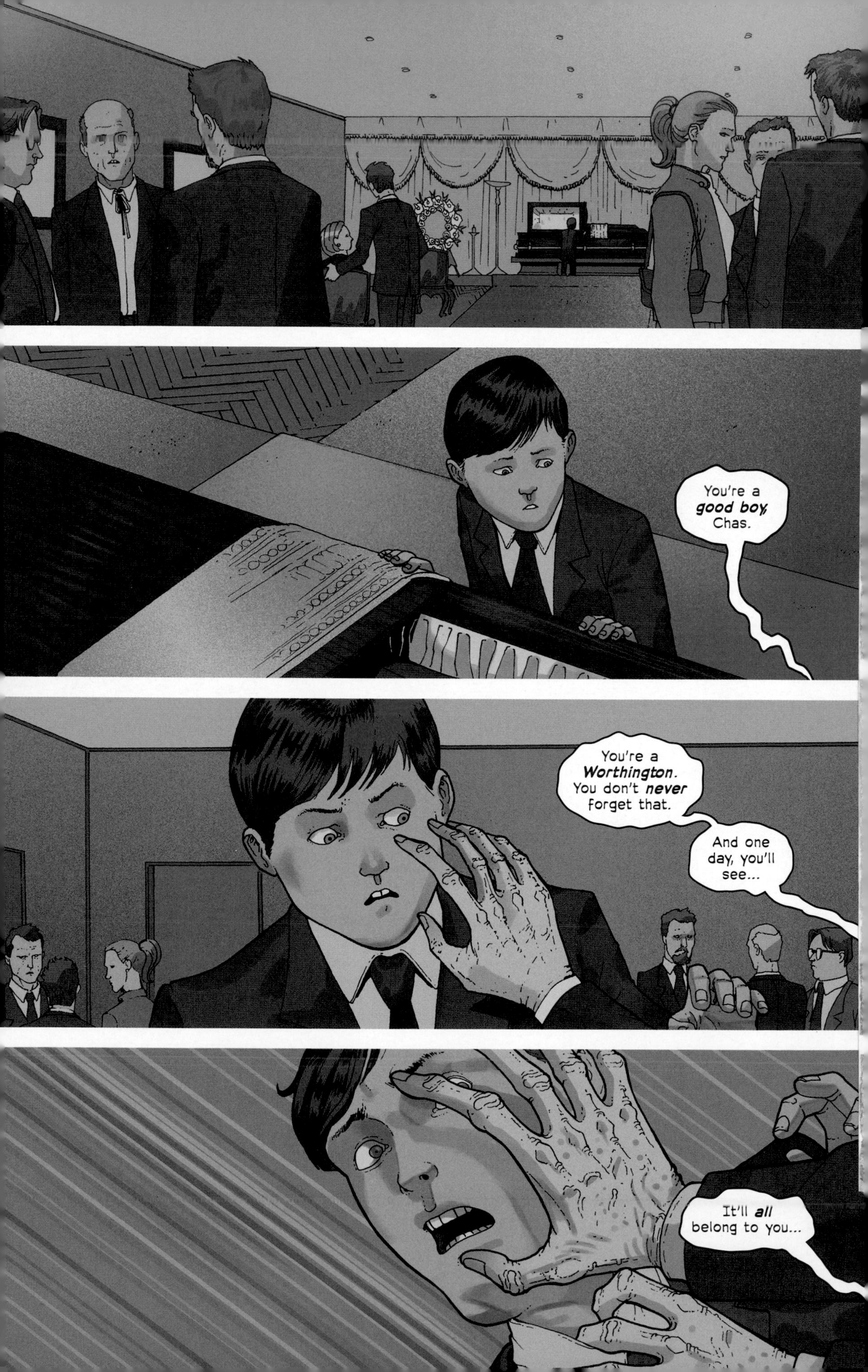
You're a *good boy,* Chas.
You're a *Worthington*. You don't *never* forget that.
And one day, you'll see...
It'll *all* belong to you...

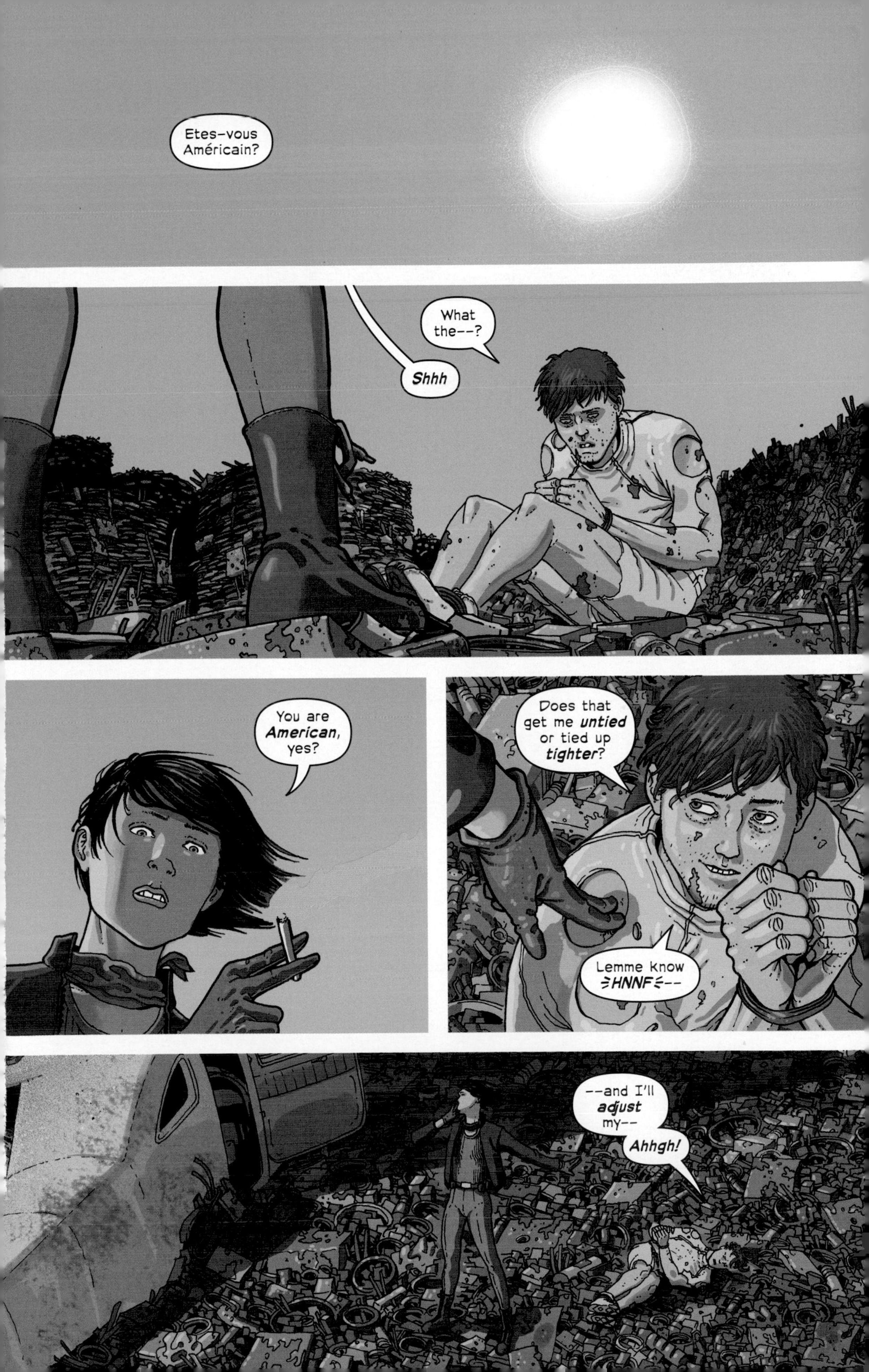
Etes-vous Américain?
What the--?
Shhh
You are *American*, yes?
Does that get me *untied* or tied up *tighter*?
Lemme know *HNNF*--
--and I'll *adjust* my--
Ahhgh!

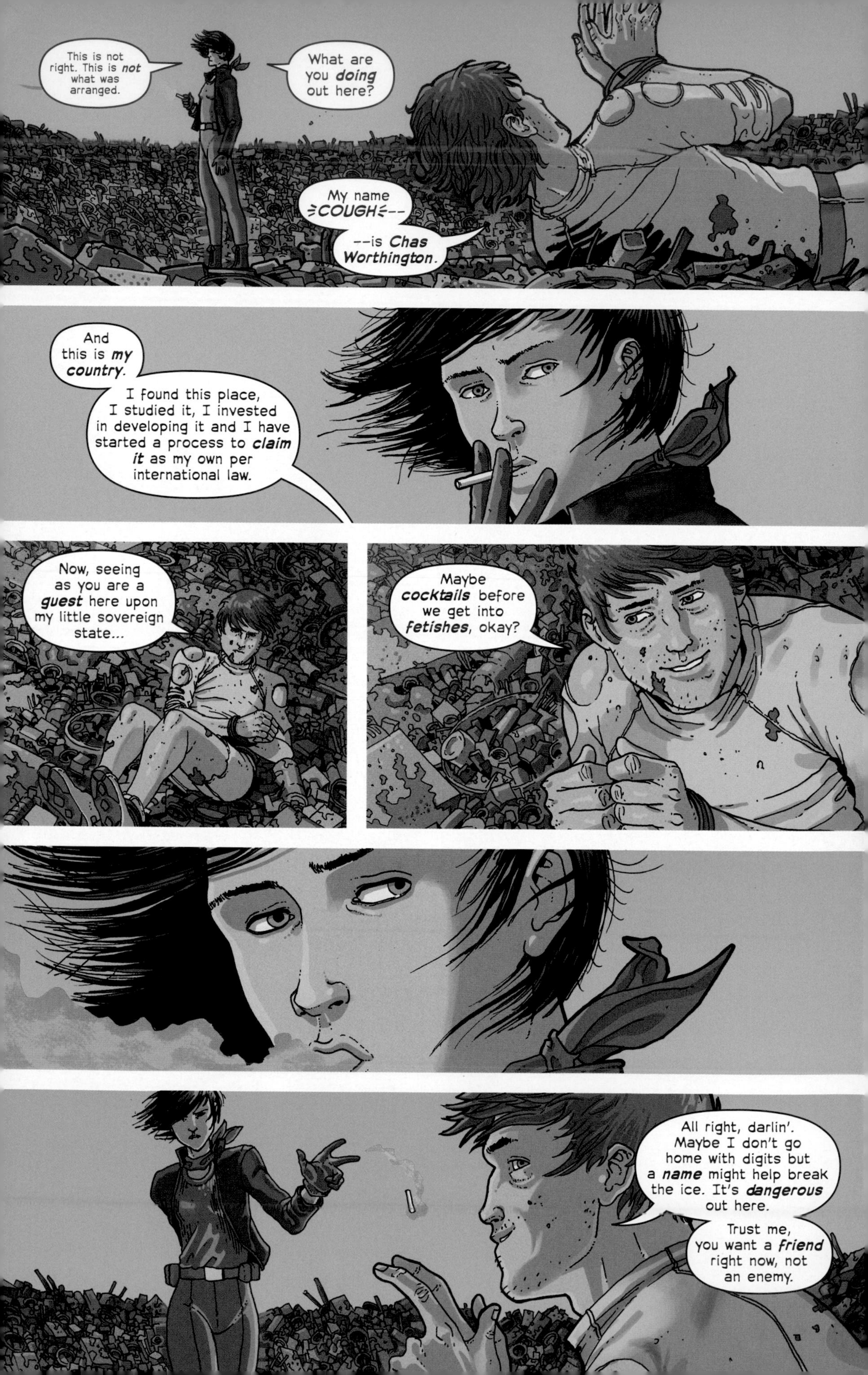

This is not right. This is *not* what was arranged.
What are you *doing* out here?
My name ≶*COUGH*≶--
--is *Chas Worthington*.
And this is *my country*.
I found this place, I studied it, I invested in developing it and I have started a process to *claim it* as my own per international law.
Now, seeing as you are a *guest* here upon my little sovereign state...
Maybe *cocktails* before we get into *fetishes*, okay?
All right, darlin'. Maybe I don't go home with digits but a *name* might help break the ice. It's *dangerous* out here.
Trust me, you want a *friend* right now, not an enemy.

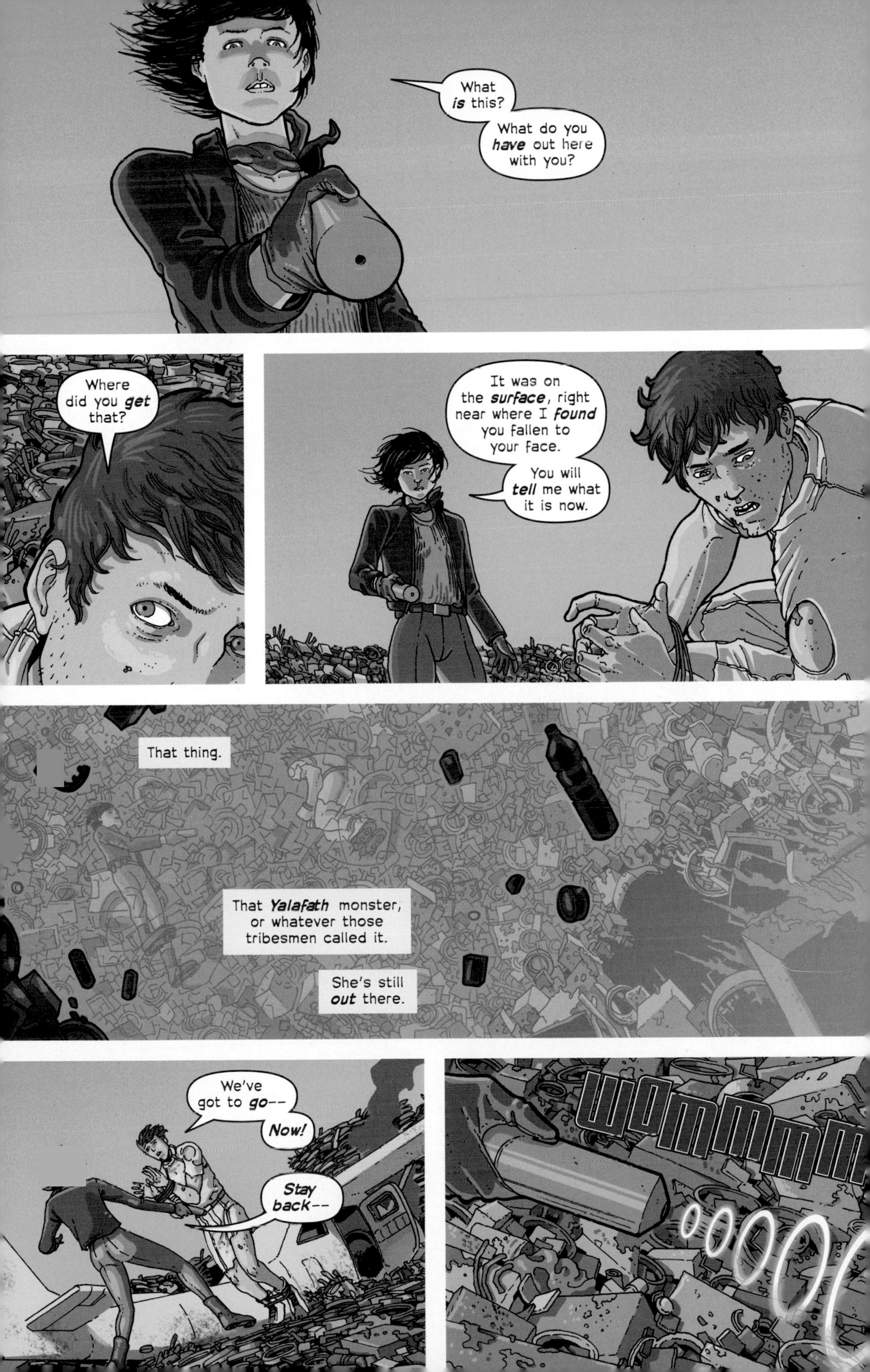

What *is* this?
What do you *have* out here with you?
Where did you *get* that?
It was on the *surface*, right near where I *found* you fallen to your face.
You will *tell* me what it is now.
That thing.
That *Yalafath* monster, or whatever those tribesmen called it.
She's still *out* there.
We've got to *go*--
Now!
Stay back--
WOMMMM

HERO breaks down hydrocarbons into oily compounds.

It then *remediates* that oily sludge into water.

Look out!

KRREEEEAK

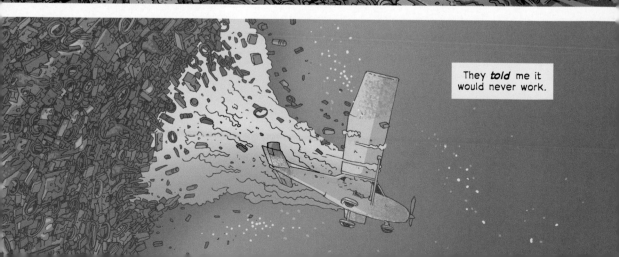

They *told* me it would never work.

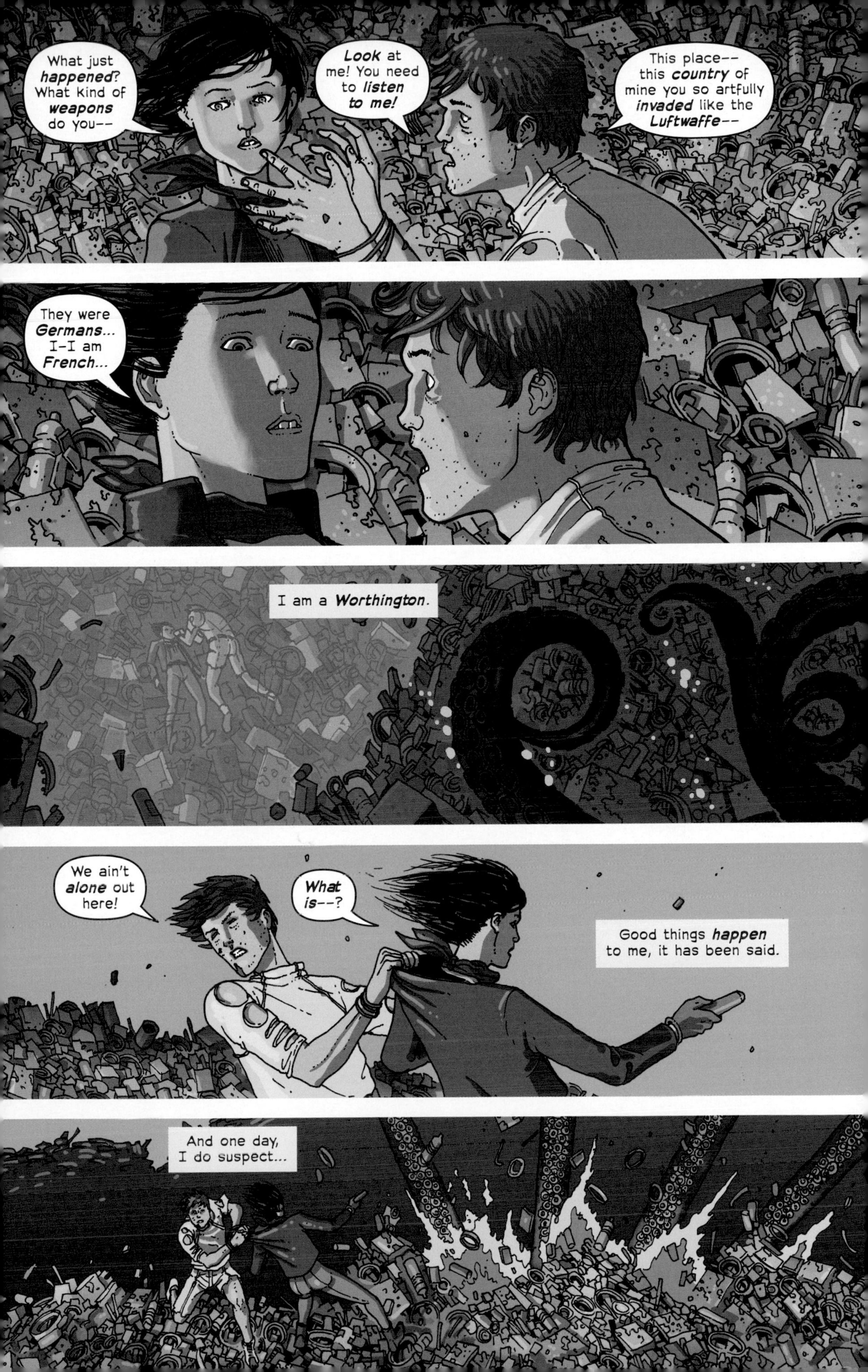
What just *happened*? What kind of *weapons* do you--
Look at me! You need to *listen to me!*
This place-- this *country* of mine you so artfully *invaded* like the *Luftwaffe*--
They were *Germans*... I-I am *French*...
I am a *Worthington*.
We ain't *alone* out here!
What is--?
Good things *happen* to me, it has been said.
And one day, I do suspect...

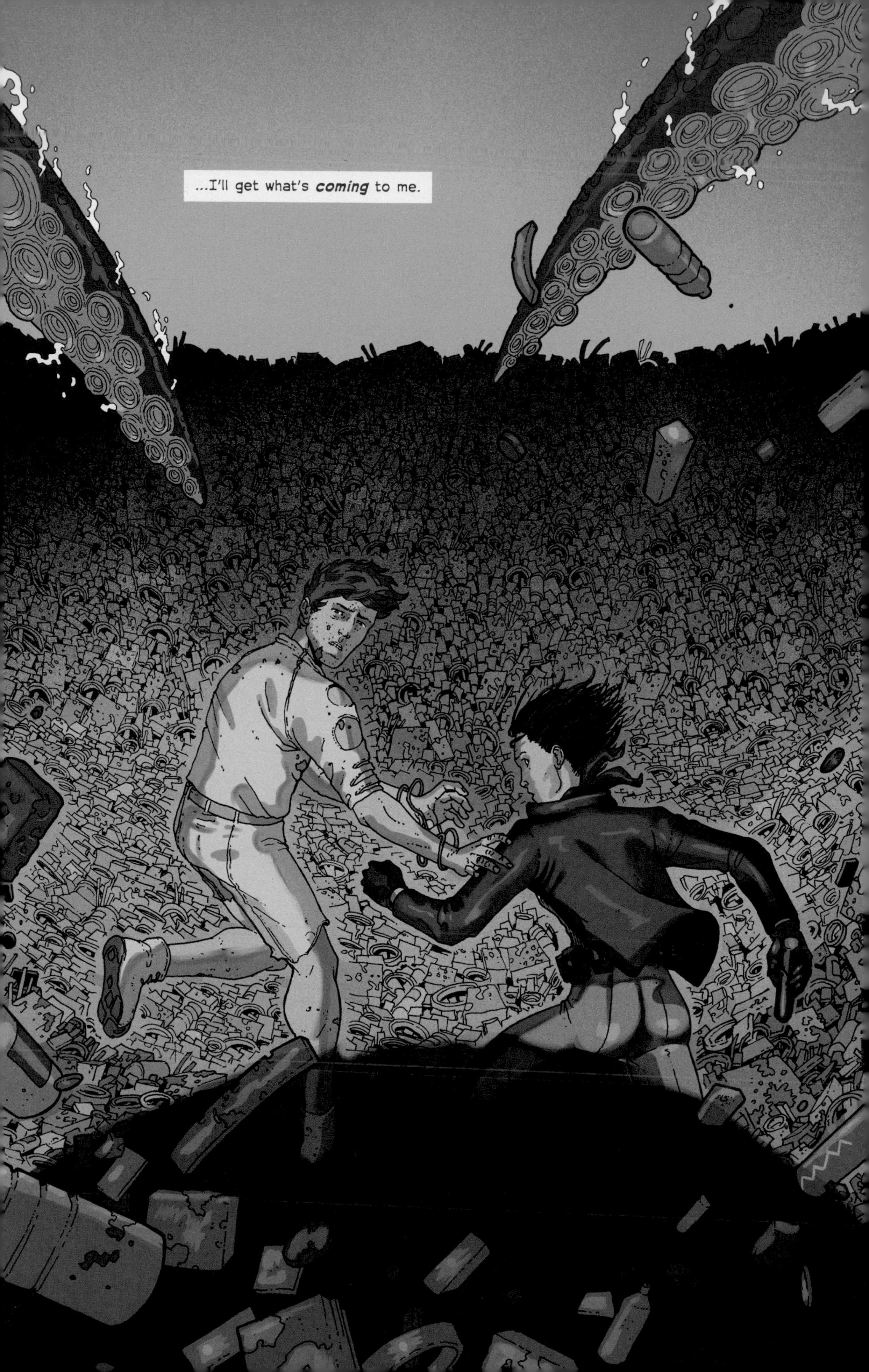
...I'll get what's *coming* to me.

CHAPTER**FOUR**

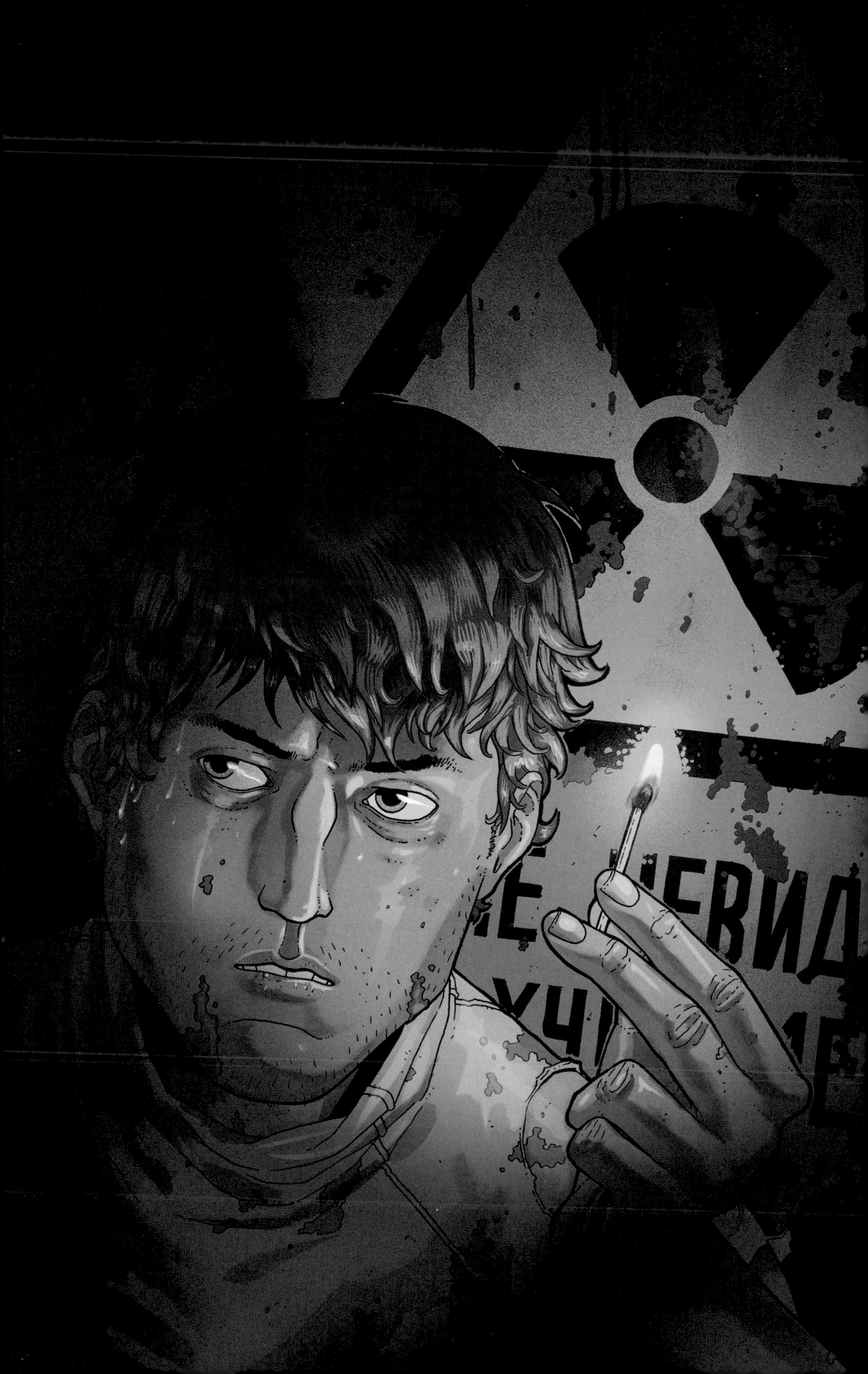

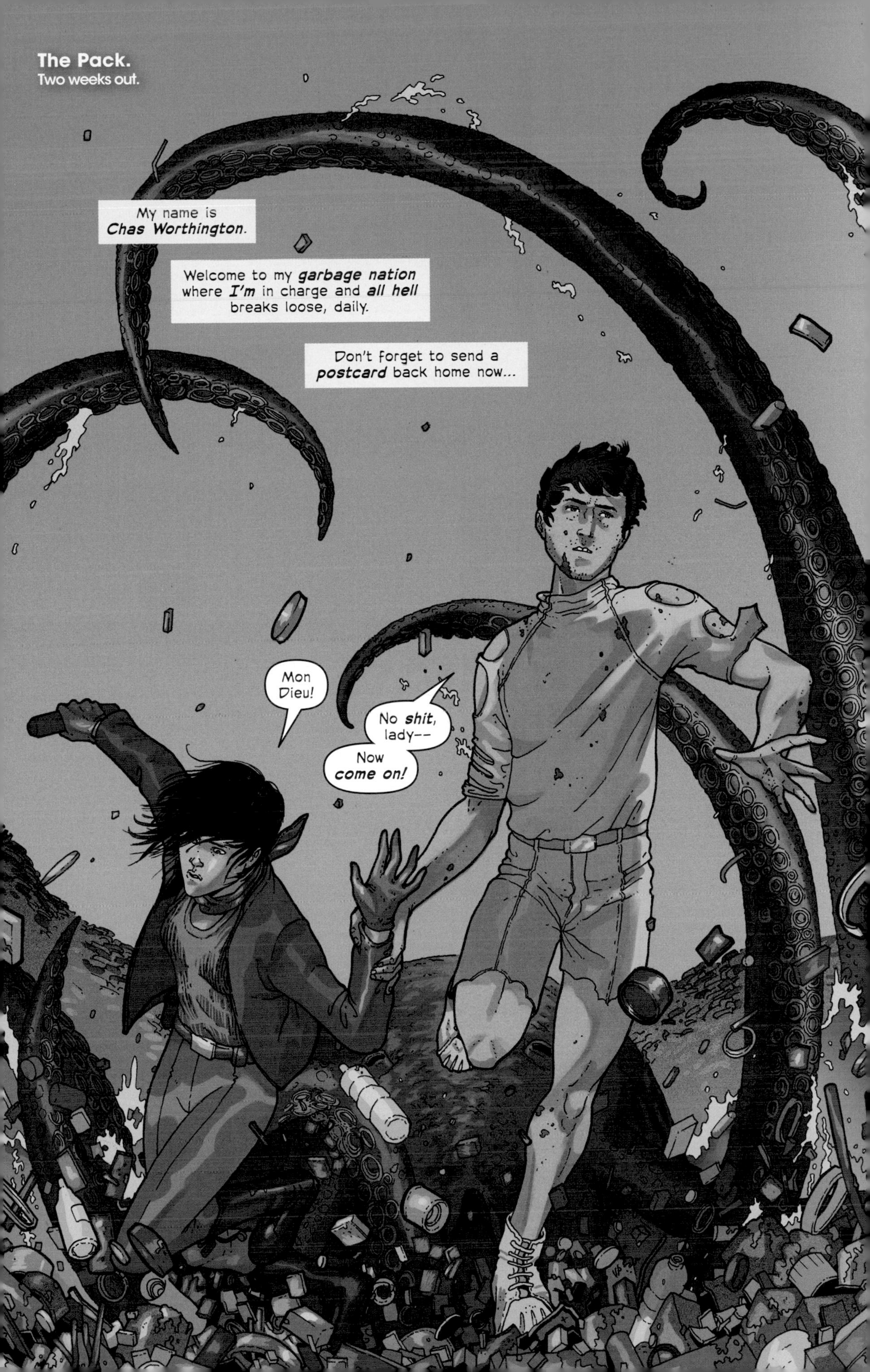
The Pack.
Two weeks out.
My name is *Chas Worthington*.
Welcome to my *garbage nation* where *I'm* in charge and *all hell* breaks loose, daily.
Don't forget to send a *postcard* back home now...
Mon Dieu!
No *shit*, lady--
Now *come on!*

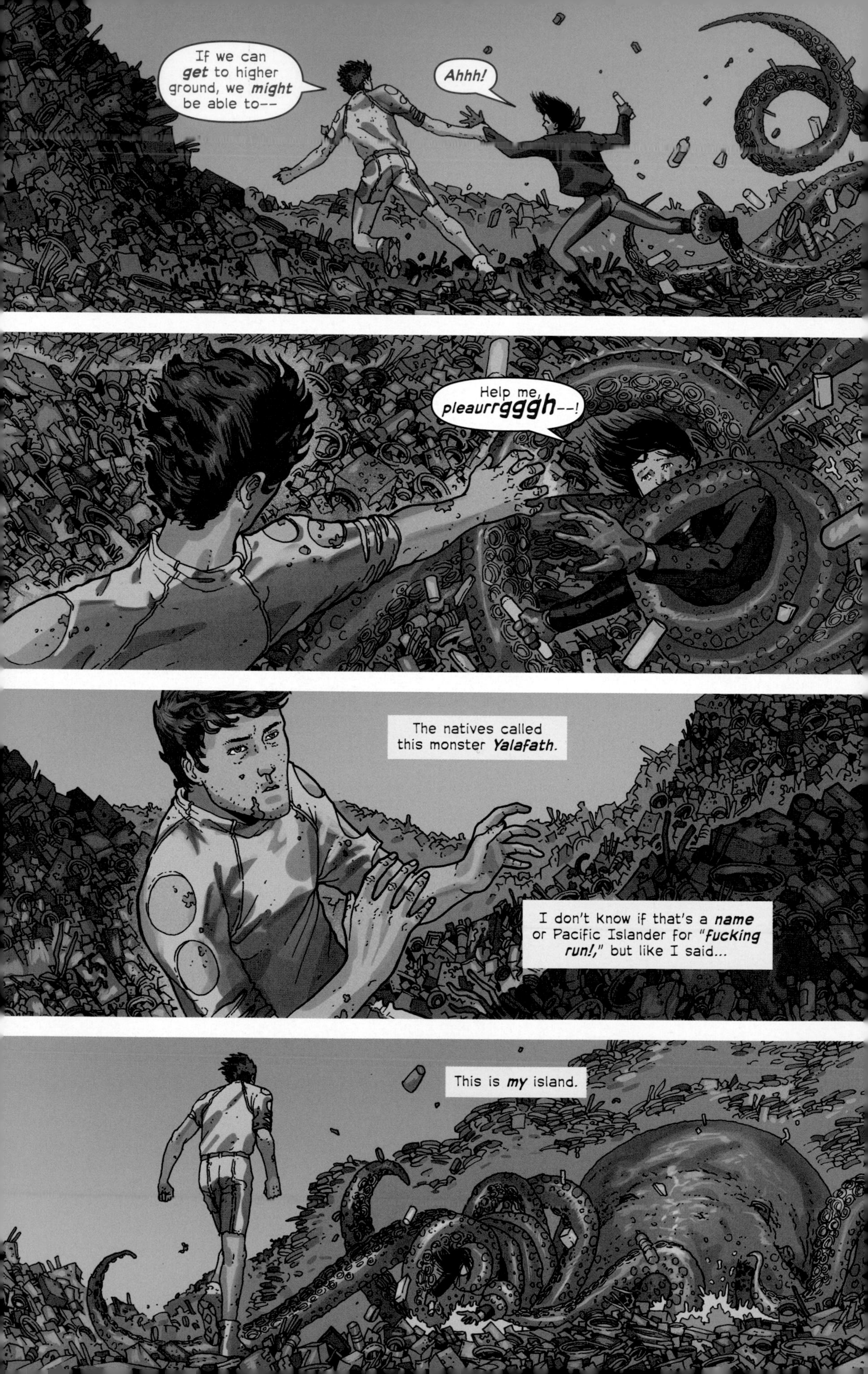

If we can get to higher ground, we might be able to--
Ahhh!
Help me, pleaurrgggh--!
The natives called this monster Yalafath.
I don't know if that's a name or Pacific Islander for "fucking run!," but like I said...
This is my island.

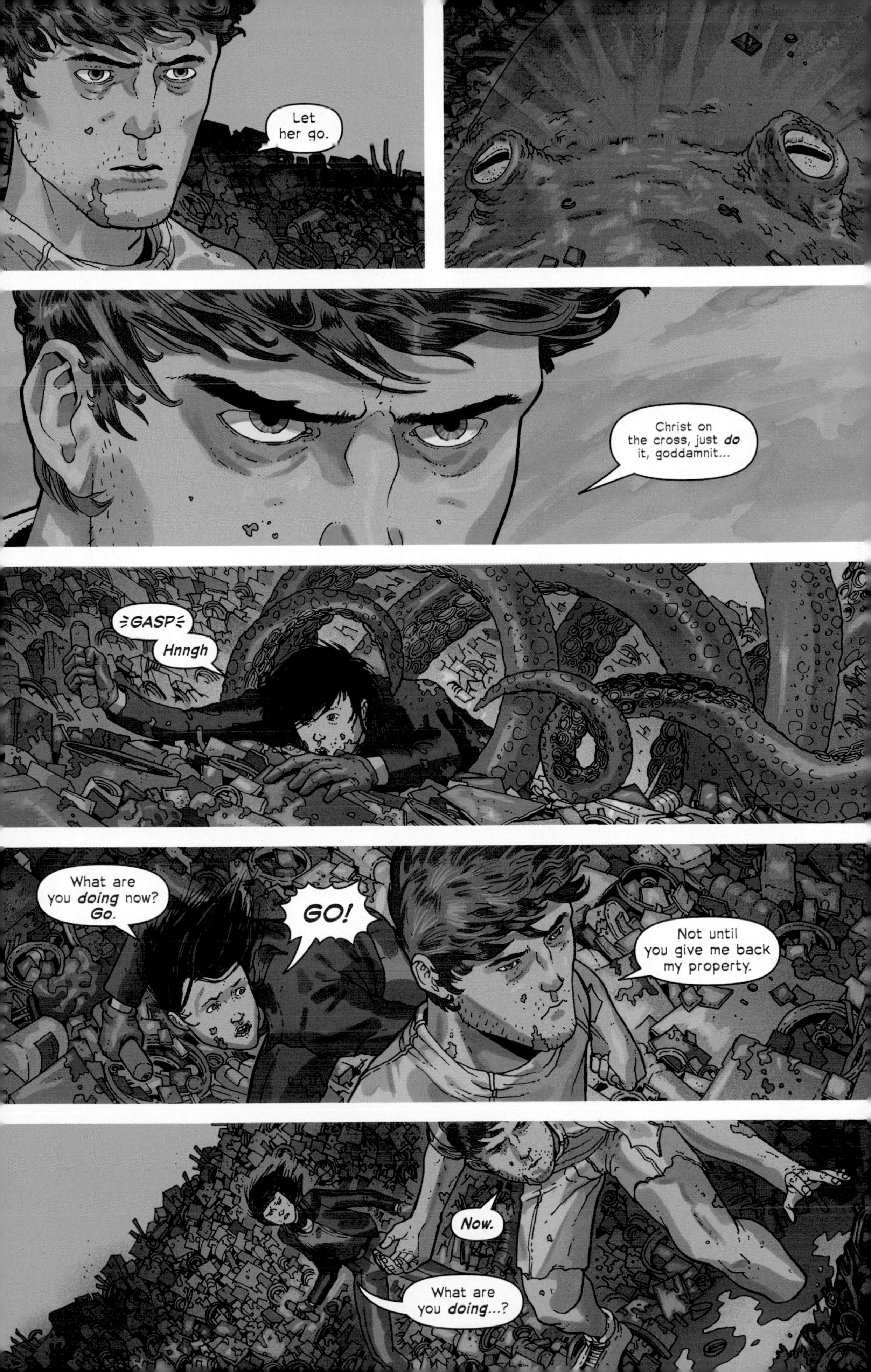
Let her go.
Christ on the cross, just ***do*** it, goddamnit...
GASP
Hnngh
What are you ***doing*** now? ***Go.***
GO!
Not until you give me back my property.
Now.
What are you ***doing...?***

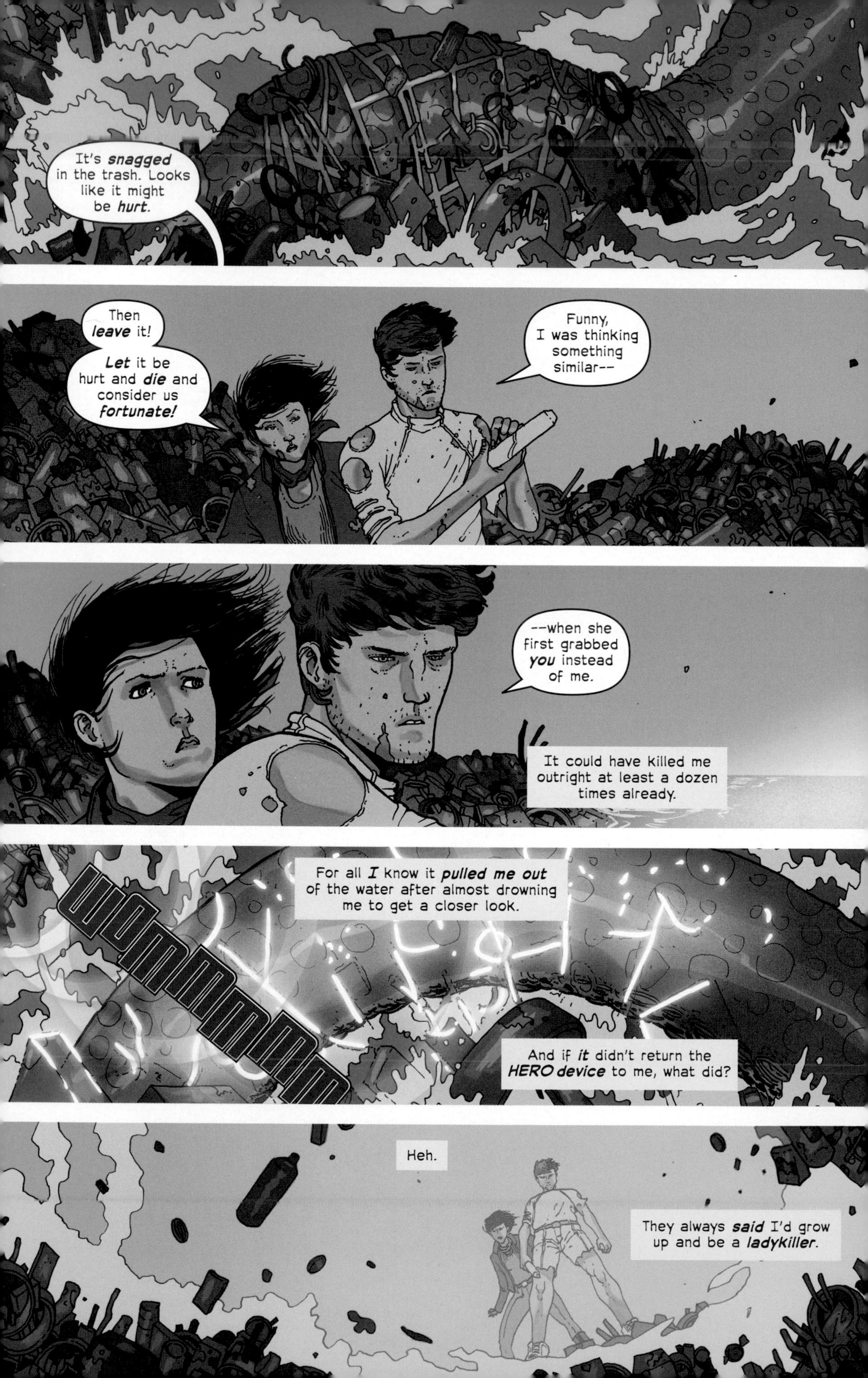
It's ***snagged*** in the trash. Looks like it might be ***hurt***.
Then ***leave*** it!
Let it be hurt and ***die*** and consider us ***fortunate!***
Funny, I was thinking something similar--
--when she first grabbed ***you*** instead of me.
It could have killed me outright at least a dozen times already.
For all ***I*** know it ***pulled me out*** of the water after almost drowning me to get a closer look.
And if ***it*** didn't return the ***HERO device*** to me, what did?
Heh.
They always ***said*** I'd grow up and be a ***ladykiller***.

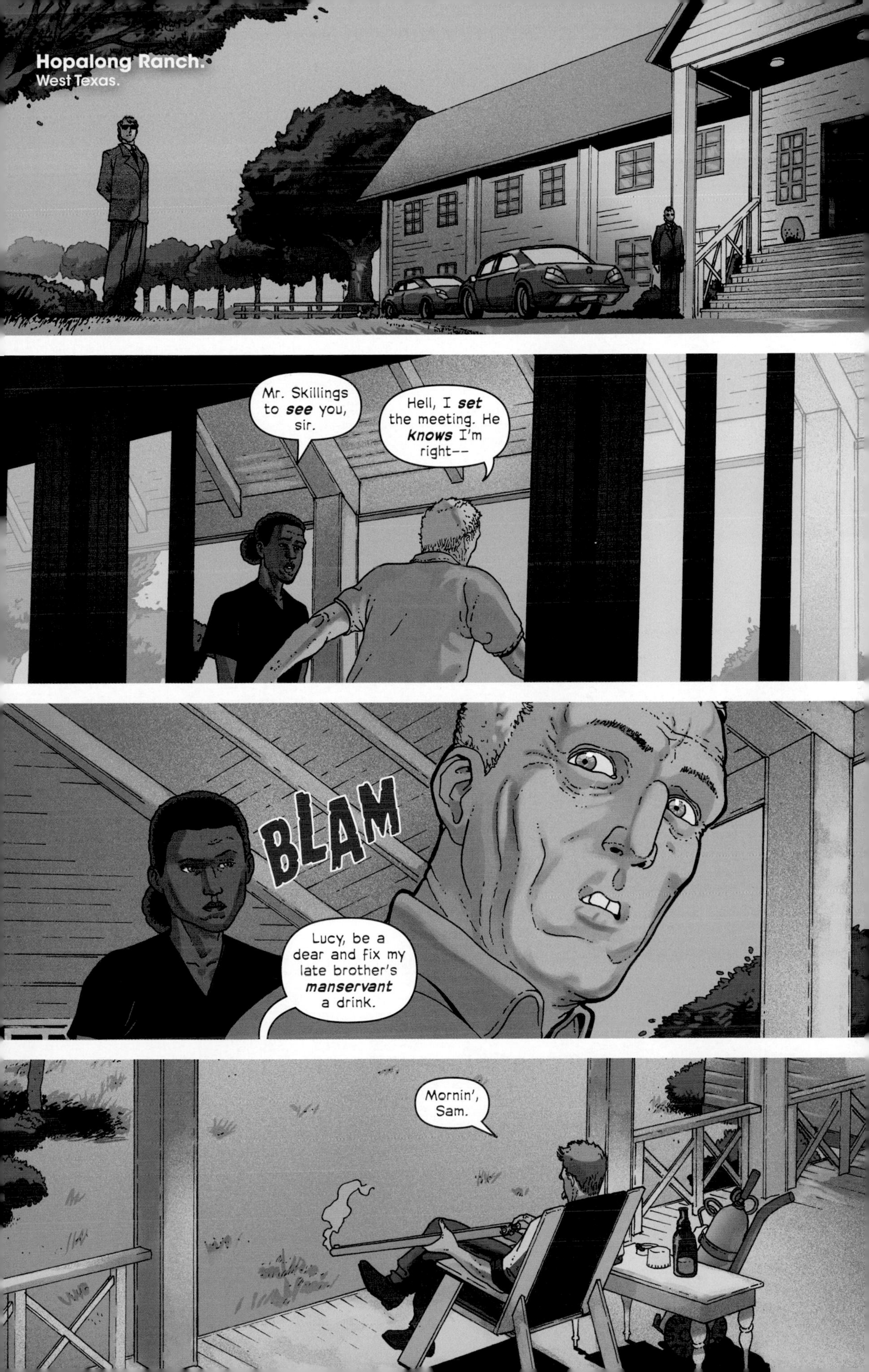
Hopalong Ranch.
West Texas.
Mr. Skillings to **see** you, sir.
Hell, I **set** the meeting. He **knows** I'm right--
BLAM
Lucy, be a dear and fix my late brother's **manservant** a drink.
Mornin', Sam.

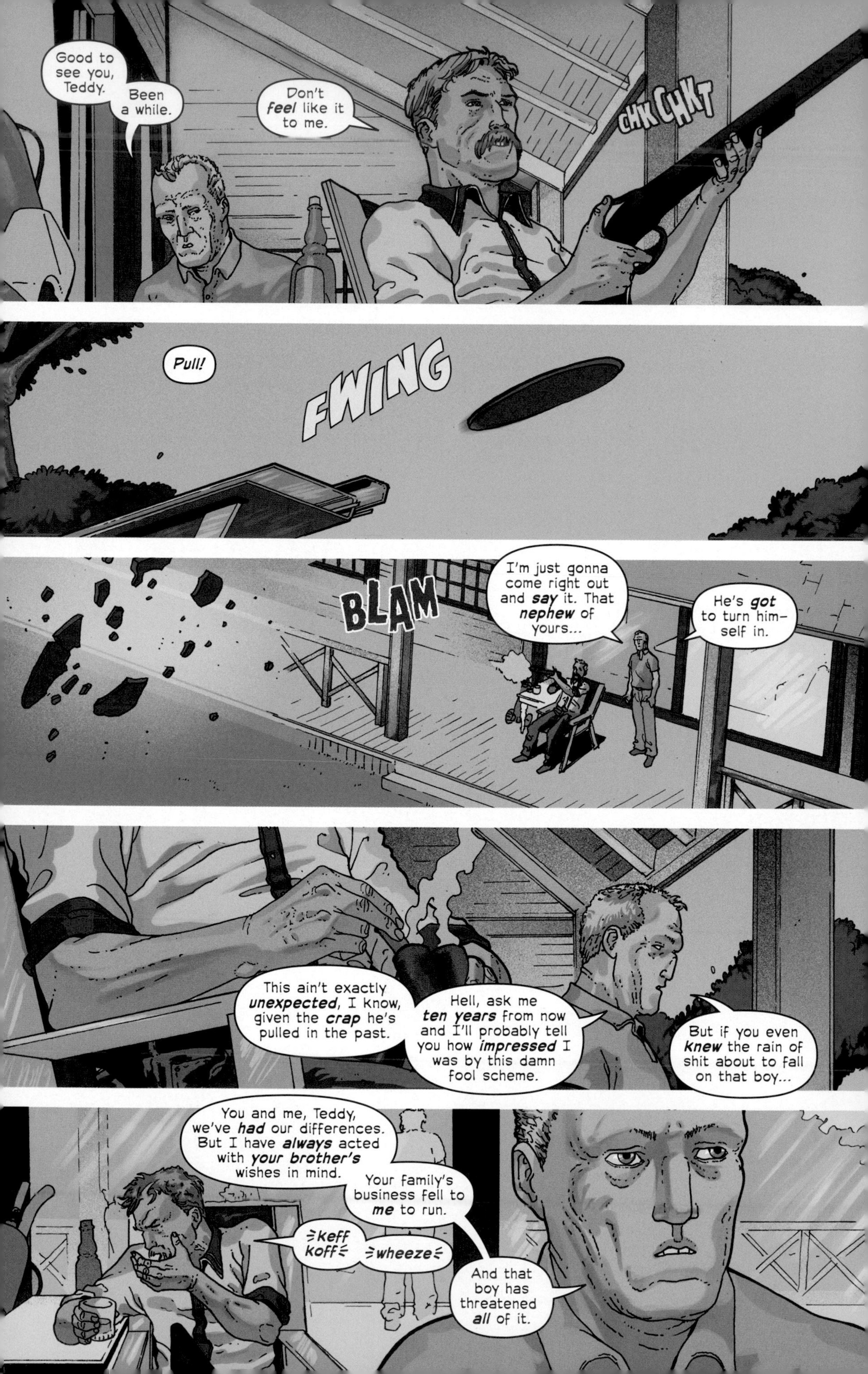
Good to see you, Teddy.
Been a while.
Don't *feel* like it to me.
CHK CHKT
Pull!
FWING
BLAM
I'm just gonna come right out and *say* it. That *nephew* of yours...
He's *got* to turn him-self in.
This ain't exactly *unexpected*, I know, given the *crap* he's pulled in the past.
Hell, ask me *ten years* from now and I'll probably tell you how *impressed* I was by this damn fool scheme.
But if you even *knew* the rain of shit about to fall on that boy...
You and me, Teddy, we've *had* our differences. But I have *always* acted with *your brother's* wishes in mind.
Your family's business fell to *me* to run.
keff koff
wheeze
And that boy has threatened *all* of it.

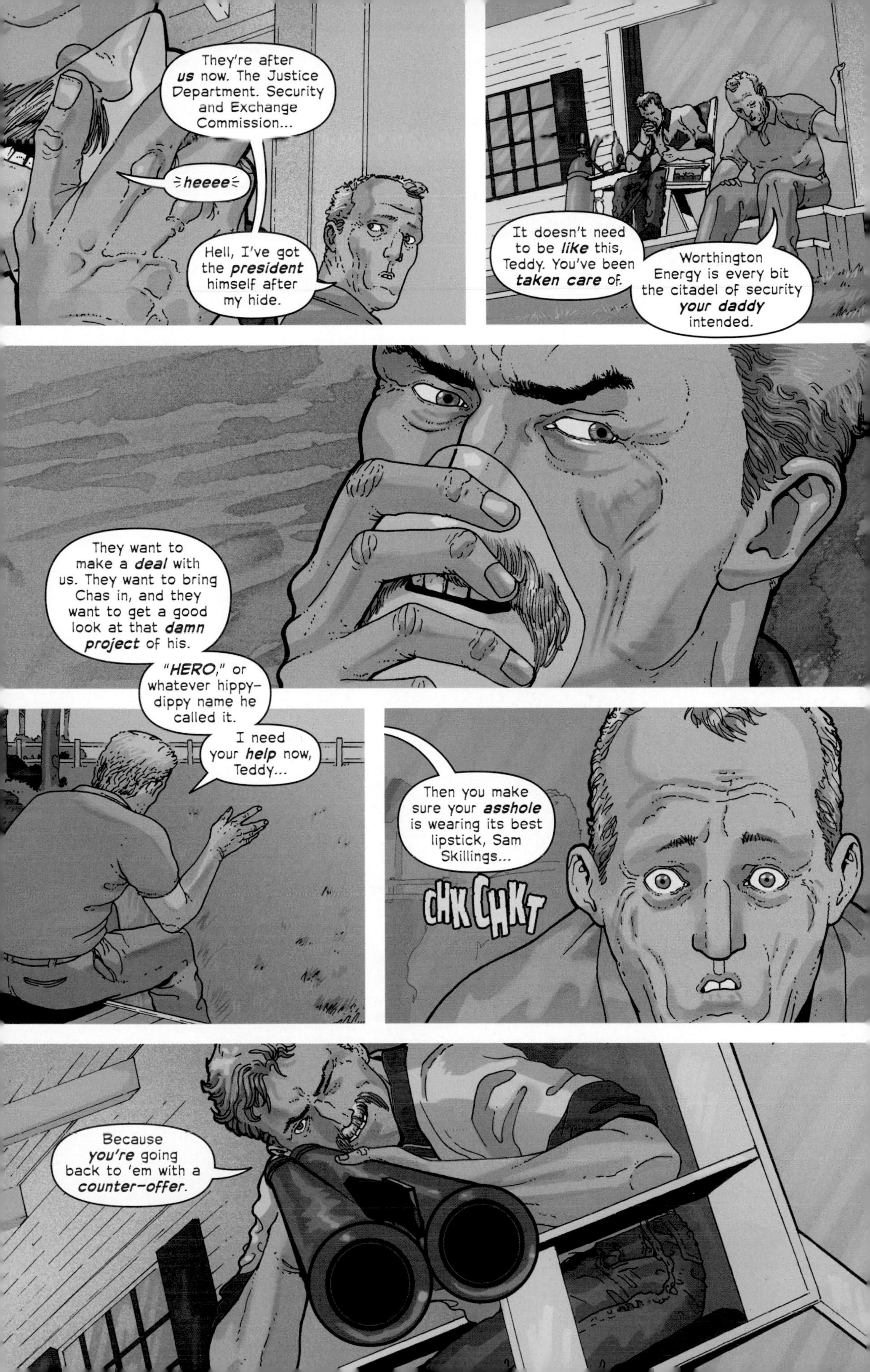
They're after *us* now. The Justice Department. Security and Exchange Commission...
heeee
Hell, I've got the *president* himself after my hide.
It doesn't need to be *like* this, Teddy. You've been *taken care* of.
Worthington Energy is every bit the citadel of security *your daddy* intended.
They want to make a *deal* with us. They want to bring Chas in, and they want to get a good look at that *damn project* of his.
"*HERO*," or whatever hippy-dippy name he called it.
I need your *help* now, Teddy...
Then you make sure your *asshole* is wearing its best lipstick, Sam Skillings...
CHK CHKT
Because *you're* going back to 'em with a *counter-offer*.

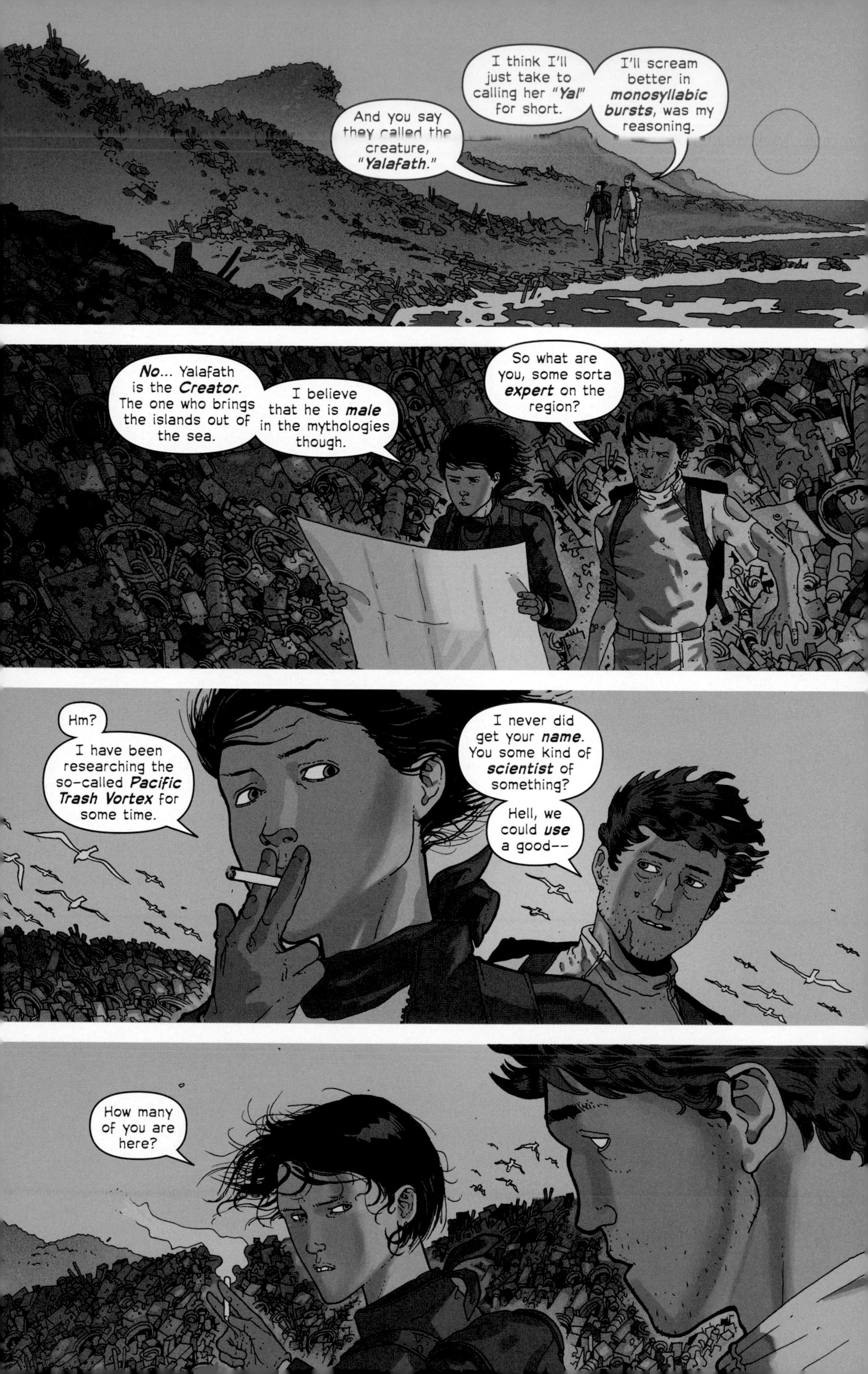
And you say they called the creature, "Yalafath."
I think I'll just take to calling her "Yal" for short.
I'll scream better in monosyllabic bursts, was my reasoning.
No... Yalafath is the Creator. The one who brings the islands out of the sea.
I believe that he is male in the mythologies though.
So what are you, some sorta expert on the region?
Hm?
I have been researching the so-called Pacific Trash Vortex for some time.
I never did get your name. You some kind of scientist of something?
Hell, we could use a good--
How many of you are here?

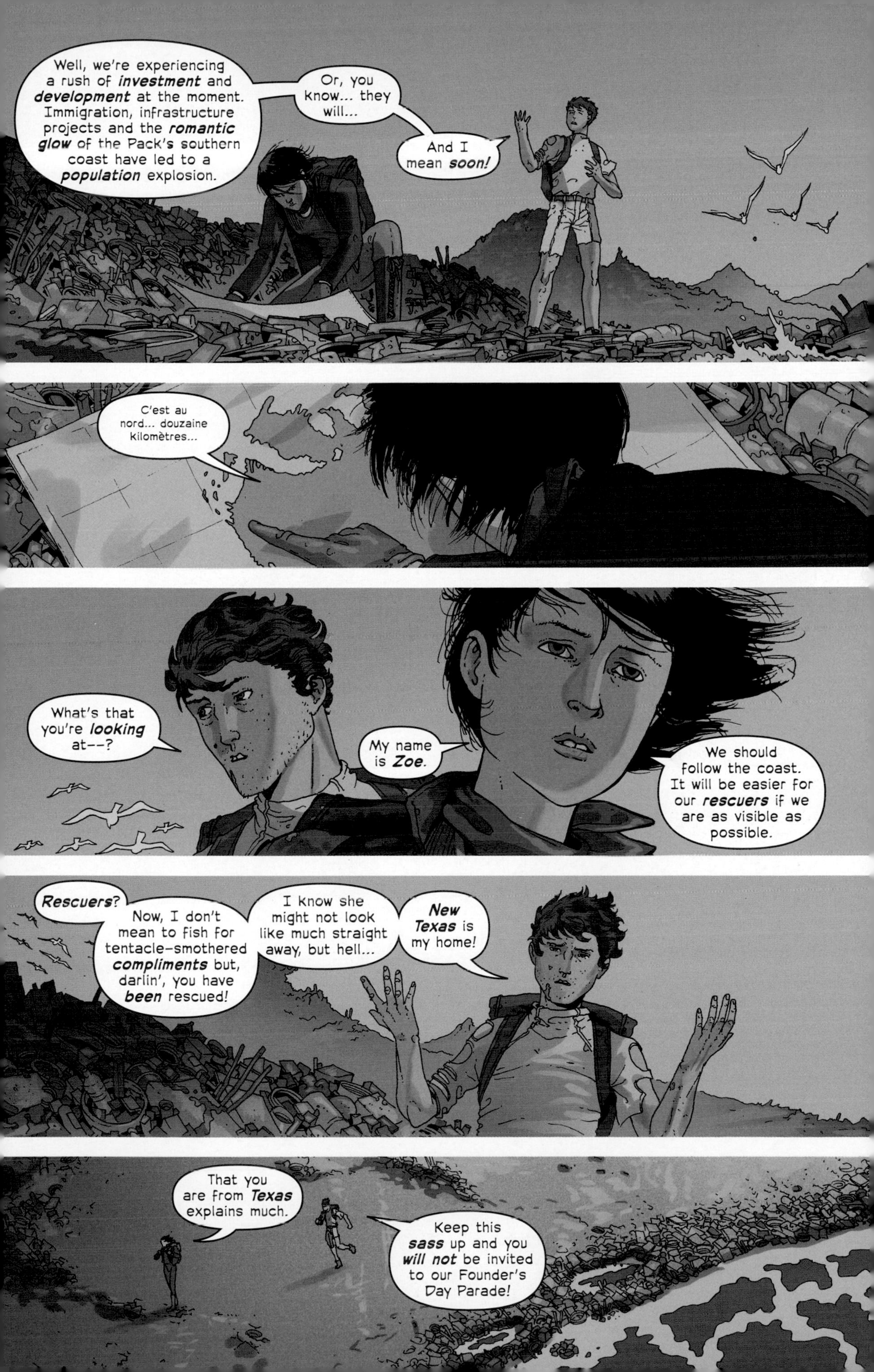

Well, we're experiencing a rush of *investment* and *development* at the moment. Immigration, infrastructure projects and the *romantic glow* of the Pack's southern coast have led to a *population* explosion.
Or, you know... they will...
And I mean *soon!*
C'est au nord... douzaine kilomètres...
What's that you're *looking* at--?
My name is *Zoe*.
We should follow the coast. It will be easier for our *rescuers* if we are as visible as possible.
Rescuers?
Now, I don't mean to fish for tentacle-smothered *compliments* but, darlin', you have *been* rescued!
I know she might not look like much straight away, but hell...
New Texas is my home!
That you are from *Texas* explains much.
Keep this *sass* up and you *will not* be invited to our Founder's Day Parade!

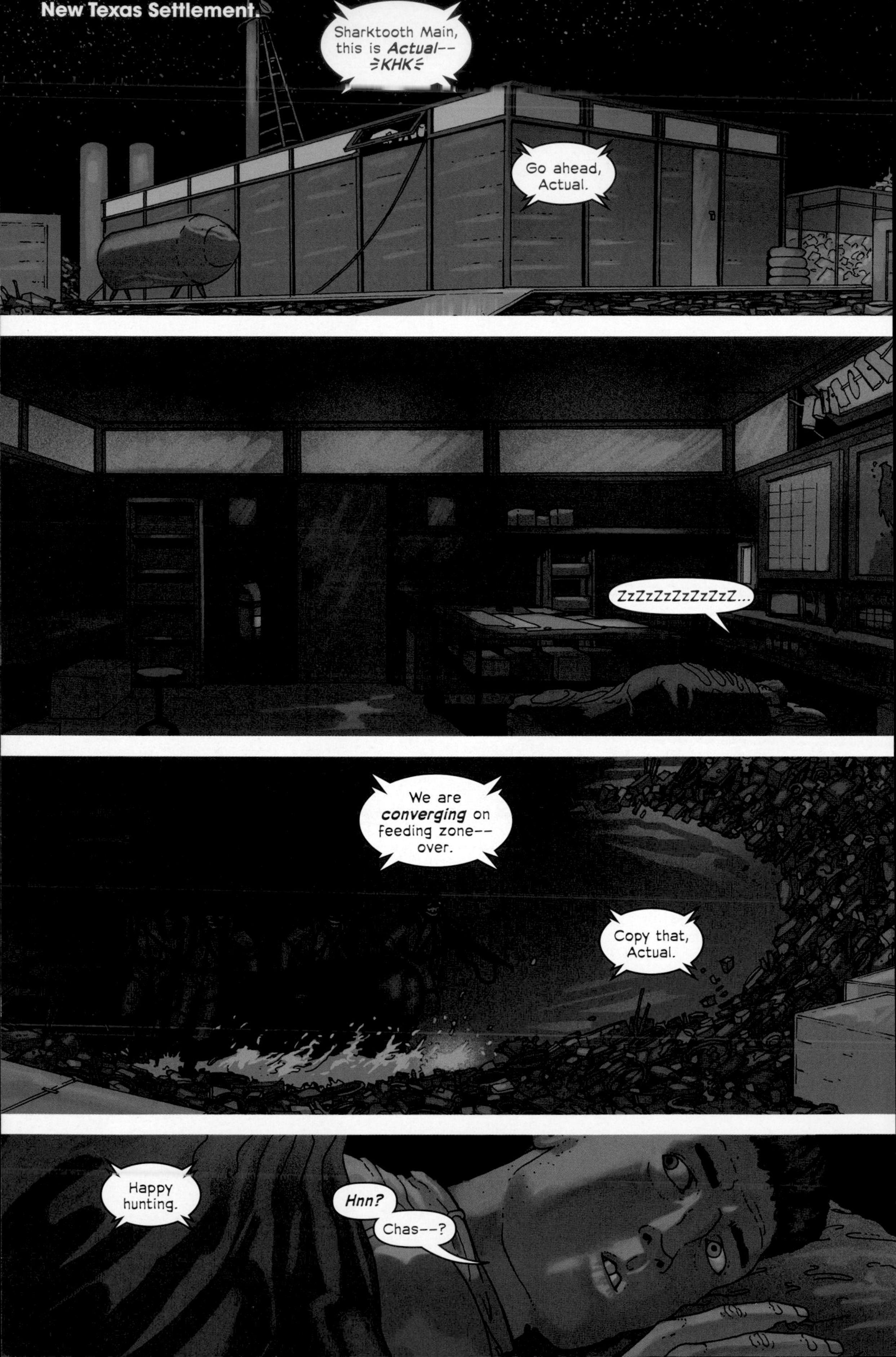
New Texas Settlement.
Sharktooth Main, this is *Actual*-- KHK
Go ahead, Actual.
ZzZzZzZzZzZzZ...
We are *converging* on feeding zone-- over.
Copy that, Actual.
Happy hunting.
Hnn?
Chas--?

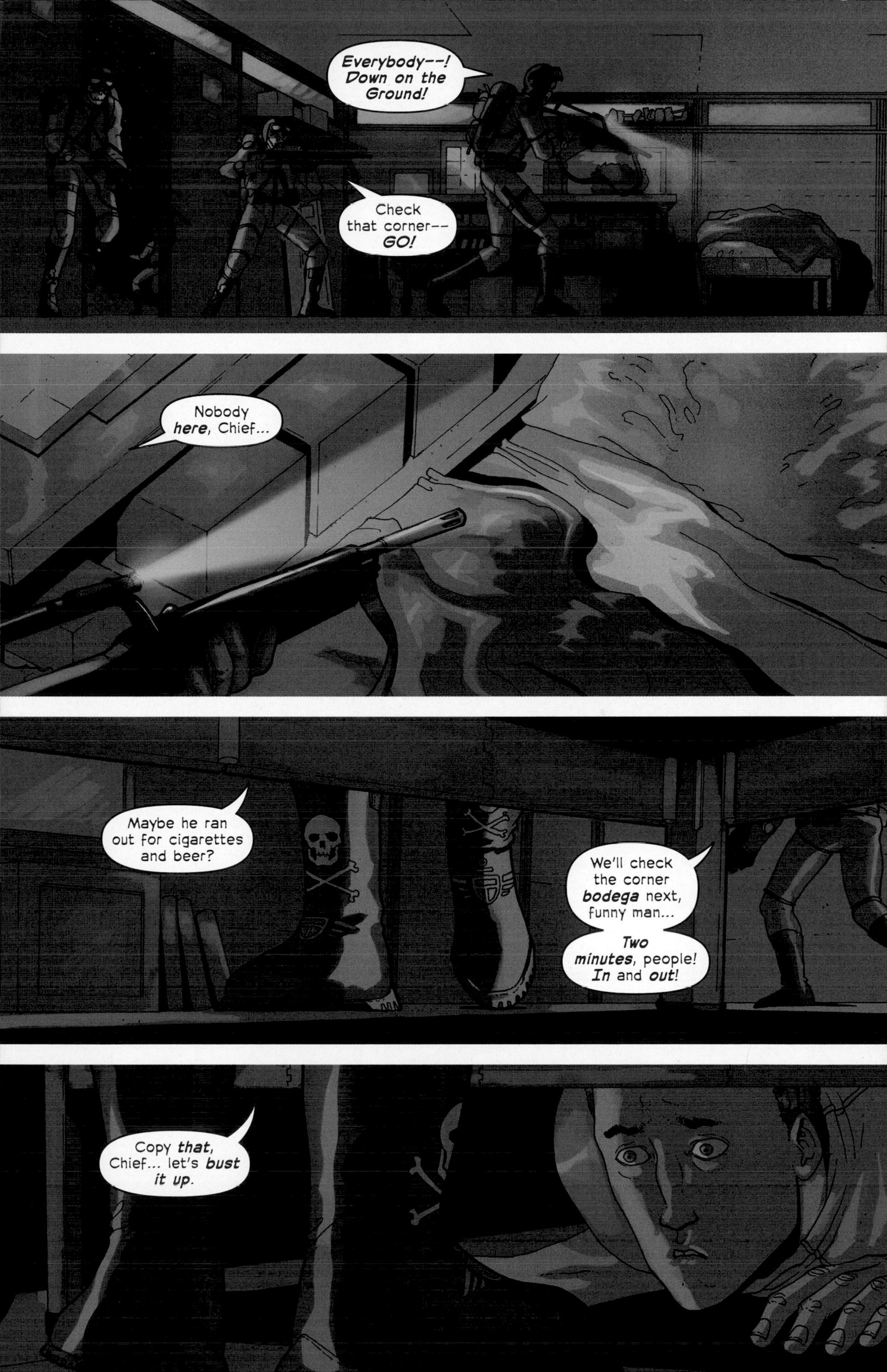
Everybody--! Down on the Ground!
Check that corner-- GO!
Nobody here, Chief...
Maybe he ran out for cigarettes and beer?
We'll check the corner bodega next, funny man...
Two minutes, people! In and out!
Copy that, Chief... let's bust it up.

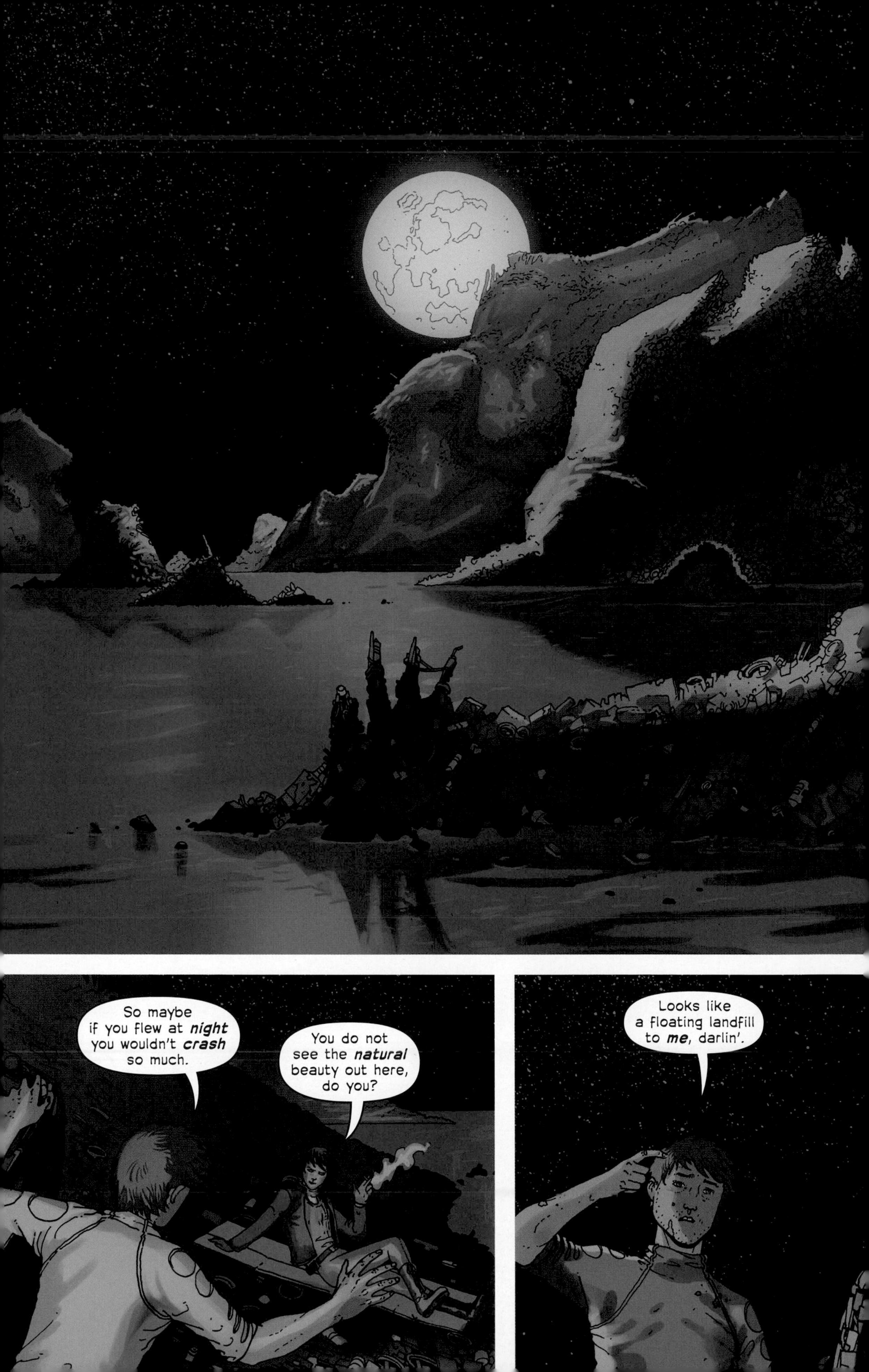
So maybe if you flew at ***night*** you wouldn't ***crash*** so much.
You do not see the ***natural*** beauty out here, do you?
Looks like a floating landfill to ***me***, darlin'.

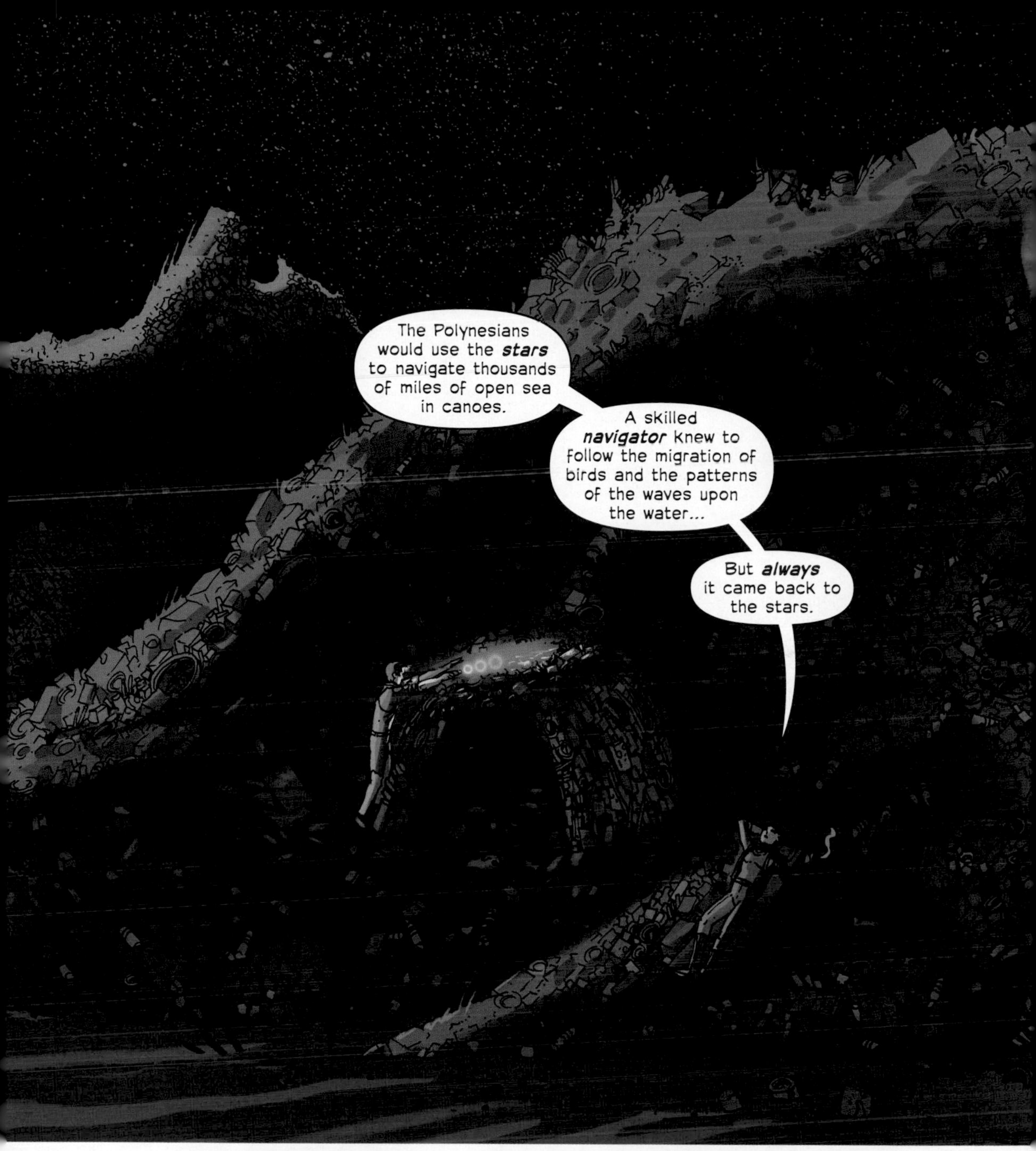
The Polynesians would use the ***stars*** to navigate thousands of miles of open sea in canoes.
A skilled ***navigator*** knew to follow the migration of birds and the patterns of the waves upon the water...
But ***always*** it came back to the stars.

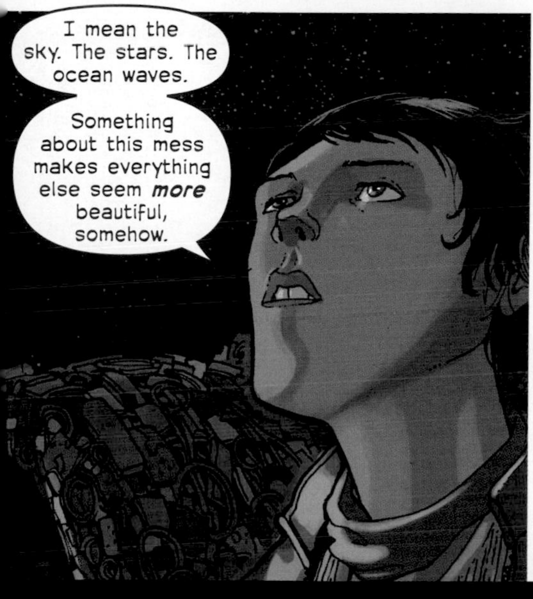
I mean the sky. The stars. The ocean waves.
Something about this mess makes everything else seem ***more*** beautiful, somehow.

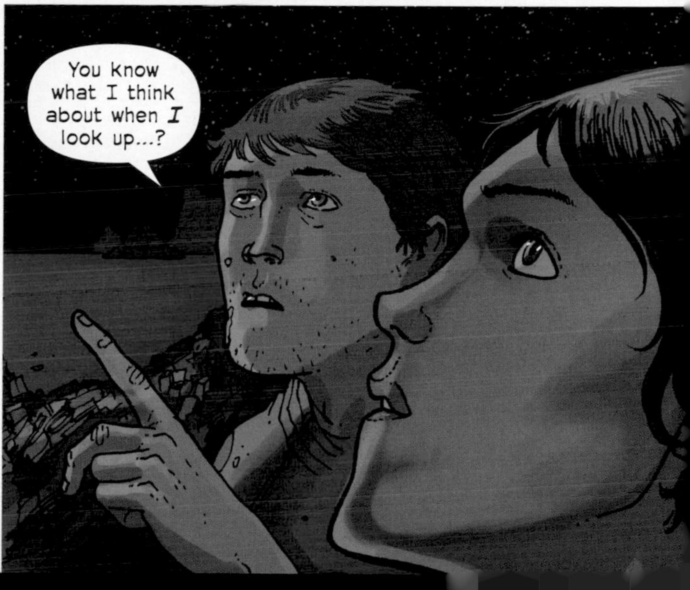
You know what I think about when ***I*** look up...?

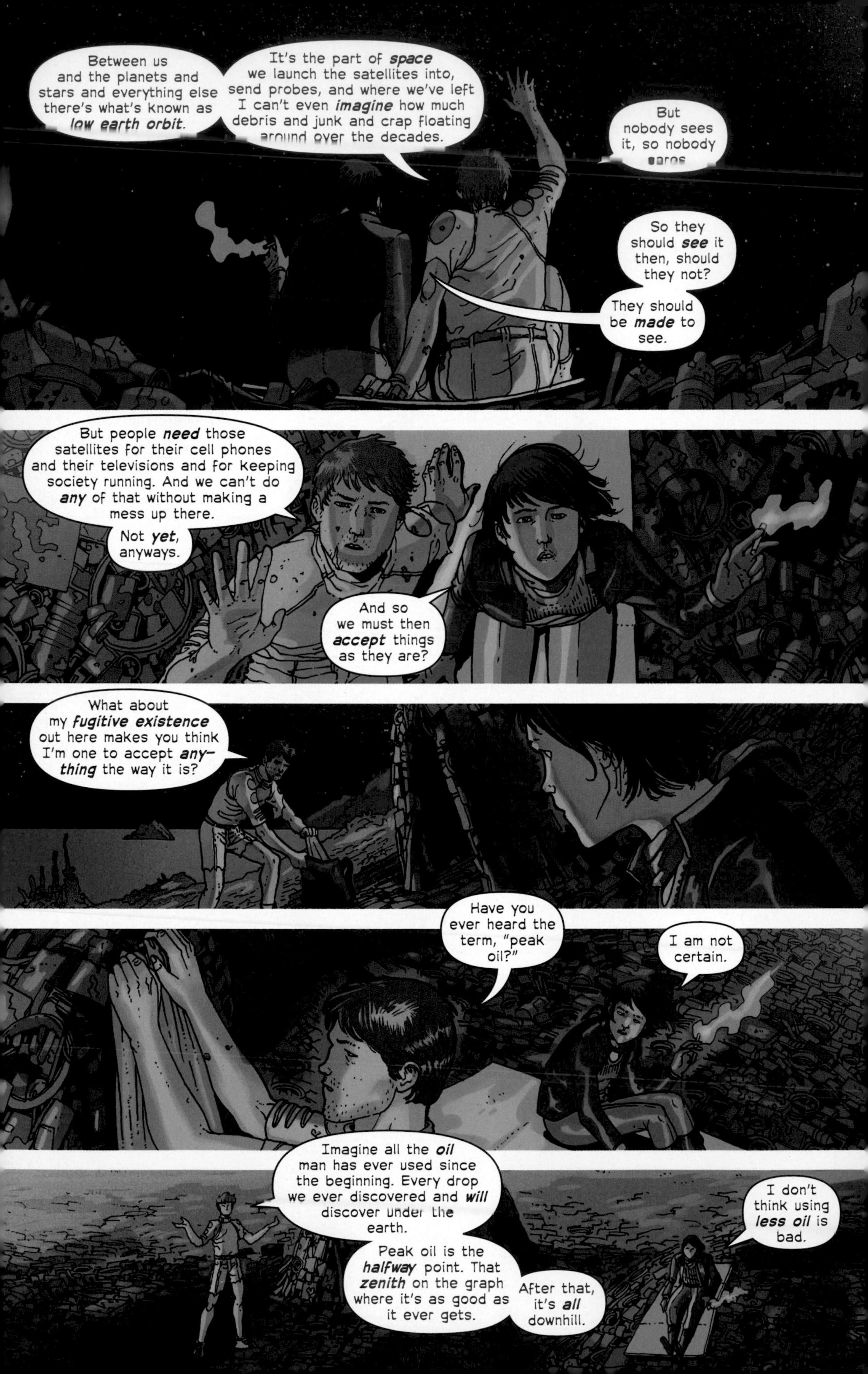
Between us and the planets and stars and everything else there's what's known as *low earth orbit*.
It's the part of *space* we launch the satellites into, send probes, and where we've left I can't even *imagine* how much debris and junk and crap floating around over the decades.
But nobody sees it, so nobody
So they should *see* it then, should they not?
They should be *made* to see.
But people *need* those satellites for their cell phones and their televisions and for keeping society running. And we can't do *any* of that without making a mess up there.
Not *yet*, anyways.
And so we must then *accept* things as they are?
What about my *fugitive existence* out here makes you think I'm one to accept *any-thing* the way it is?
Have you ever heard the term, "peak oil?"
I am not certain.
Imagine all the *oil* man has ever used since the beginning. Every drop we ever discovered and *will* discover under the earth.
Peak oil is the *halfway* point. That *zenith* on the graph where it's as good as it ever gets.
After that, it's *all* downhill.
I don't think using *less oil* is bad.

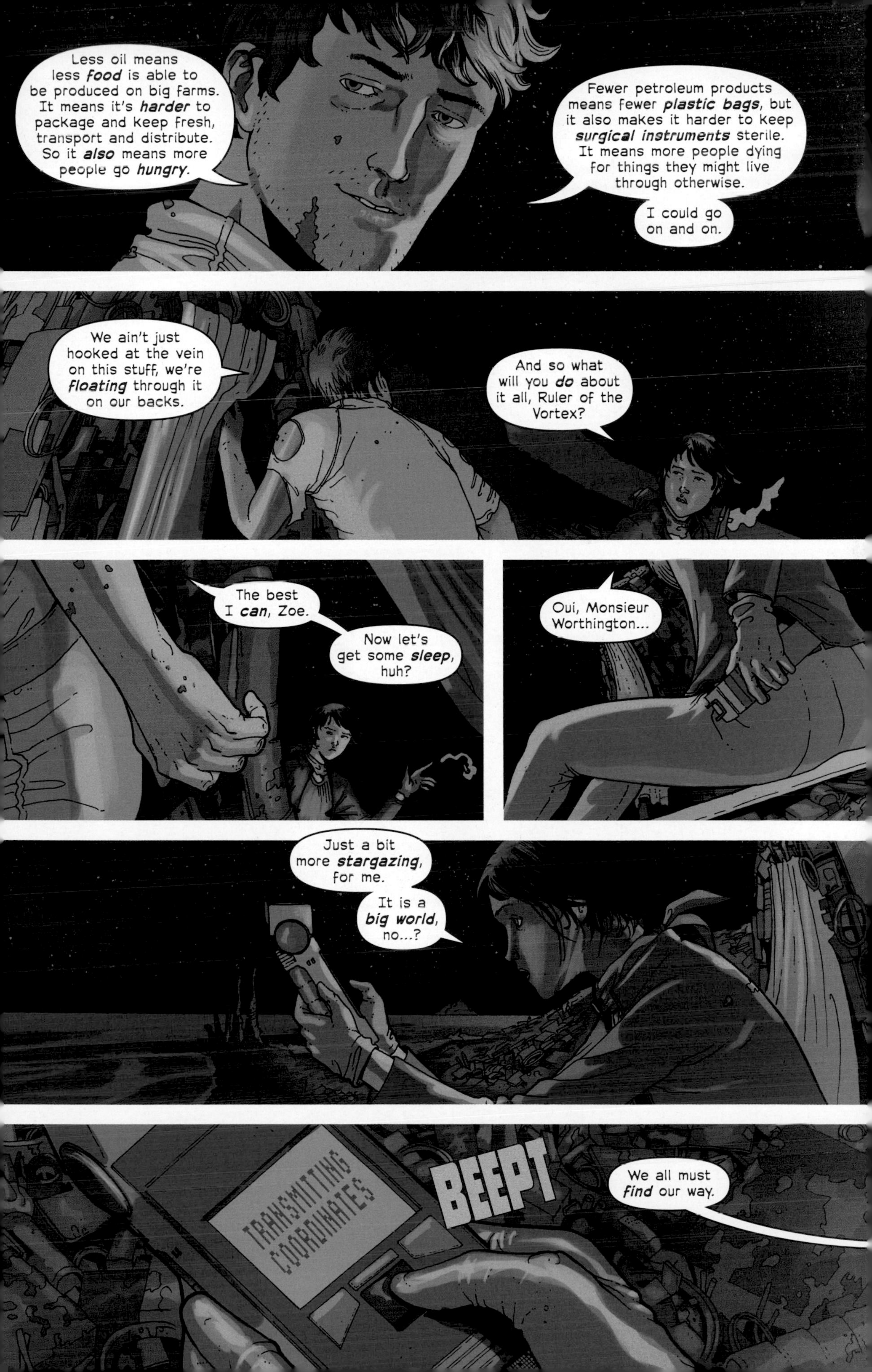
Less oil means less *food* is able to be produced on big farms. It means it's *harder* to package and keep fresh, transport and distribute. So it *also* means more people go *hungry*.
Fewer petroleum products means fewer *plastic bags*, but it also makes it harder to keep *surgical instruments* sterile. It means more people dying for things they might live through otherwise.
I could go on and on.
We ain't just hooked at the vein on this stuff, we're *floating* through it on our backs.
And so what will you *do* about it all, Ruler of the Vortex?
The best I *can*, Zoe.
Now let's get some *sleep*, huh?
Oui, Monsieur Worthington...
Just a bit more *stargazing*, for me.
It is a *big world*, no...?
TRANSMITTING COORDINATES
BEEPT
We all must *find* our way.

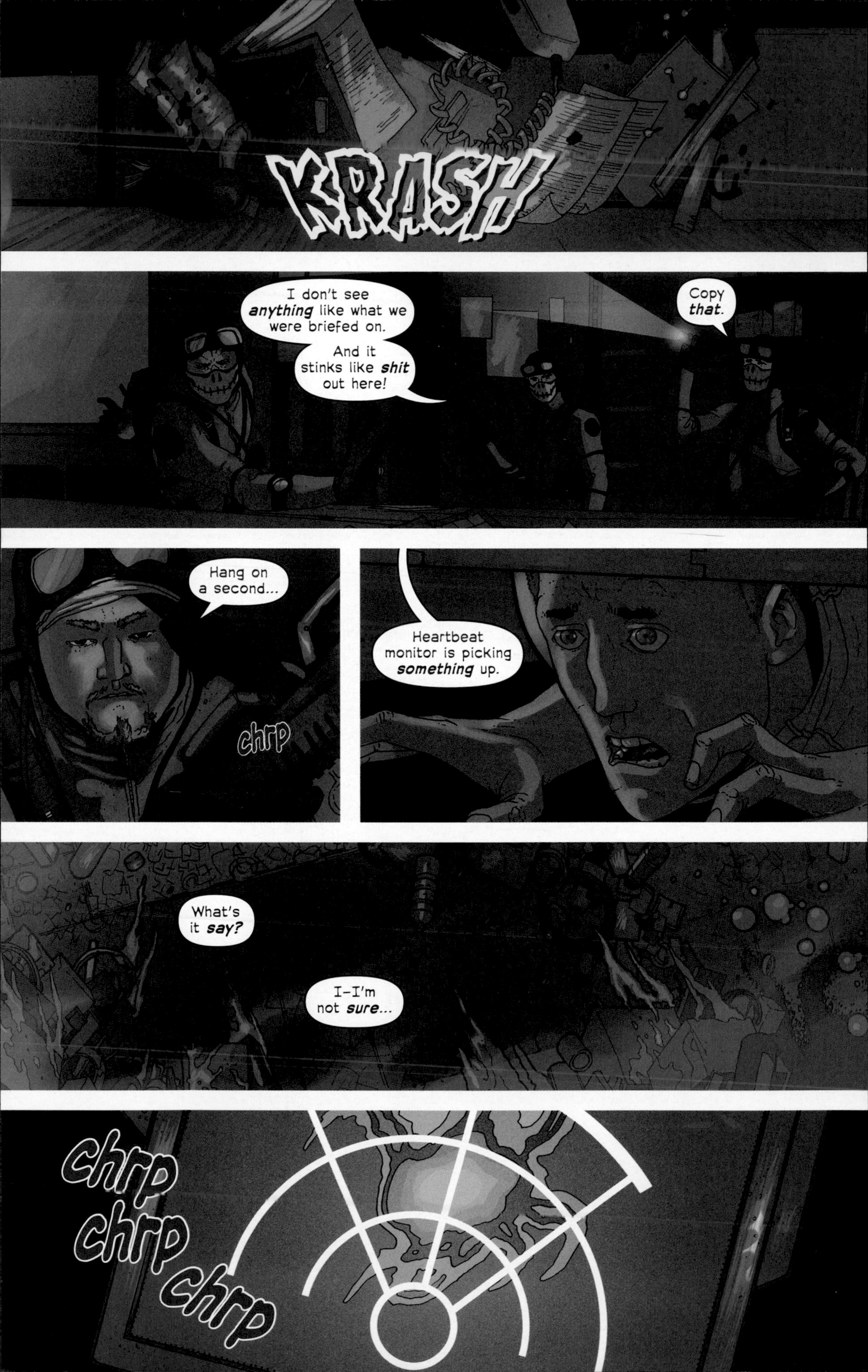
KRASH
I don't see *anything* like what we were briefed on.
And it stinks like *shit* out here!
Copy *that*.
Hang on a second...
chrp
Heartbeat monitor is picking *something* up.
What's it *say?*
I-I'm not *sure*...
chrp
chrp
chrp

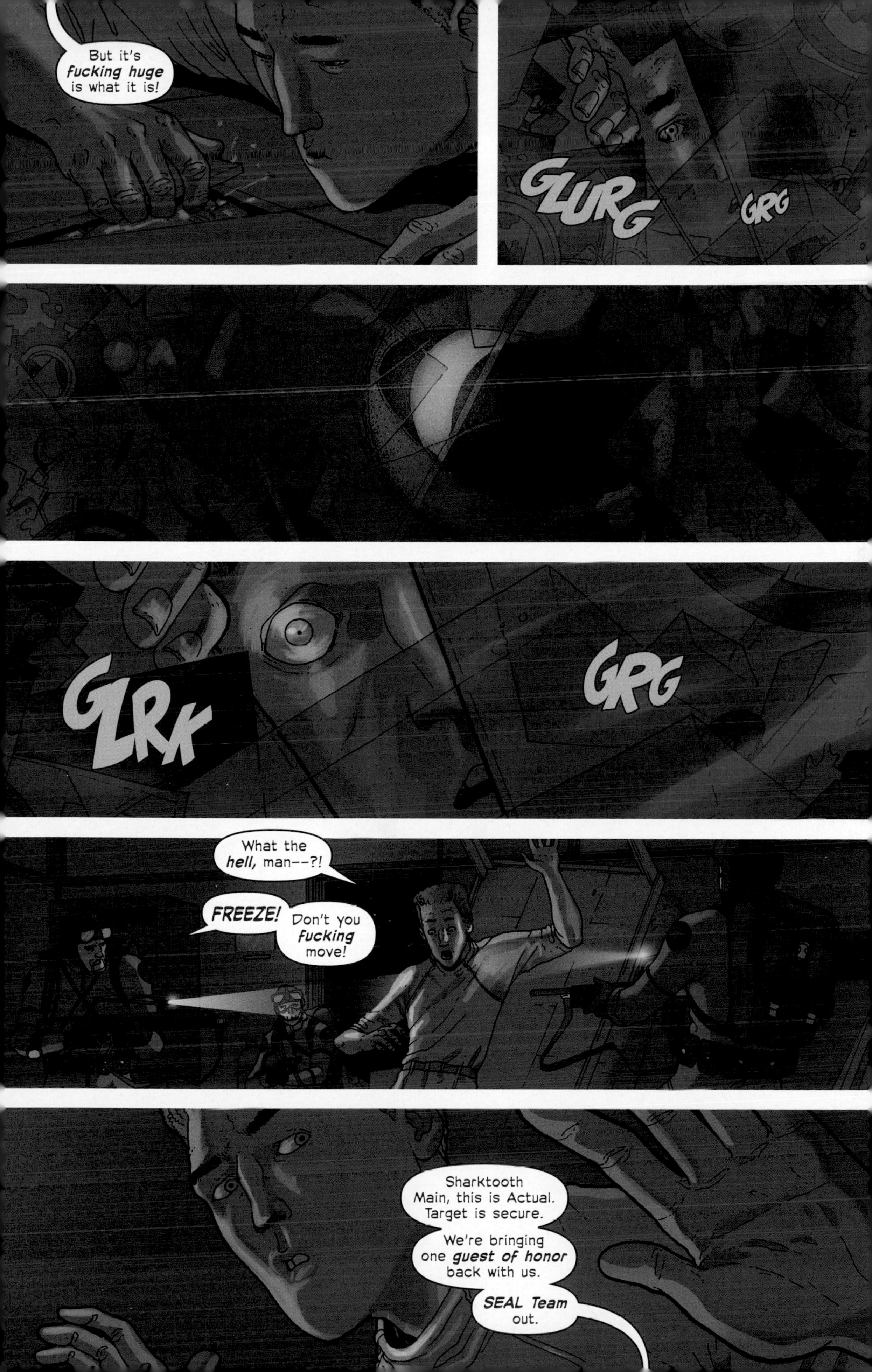
But it's *fucking huge* is what it is!
GLURG
GRG
GLRK
GRG
What the *hell,* man--?!
FREEZE!
Don't you *fucking* move!
Sharktooth Main, this is Actual. Target is secure.
We're bringing one *guest of honor* back with us.
SEAL Team out.

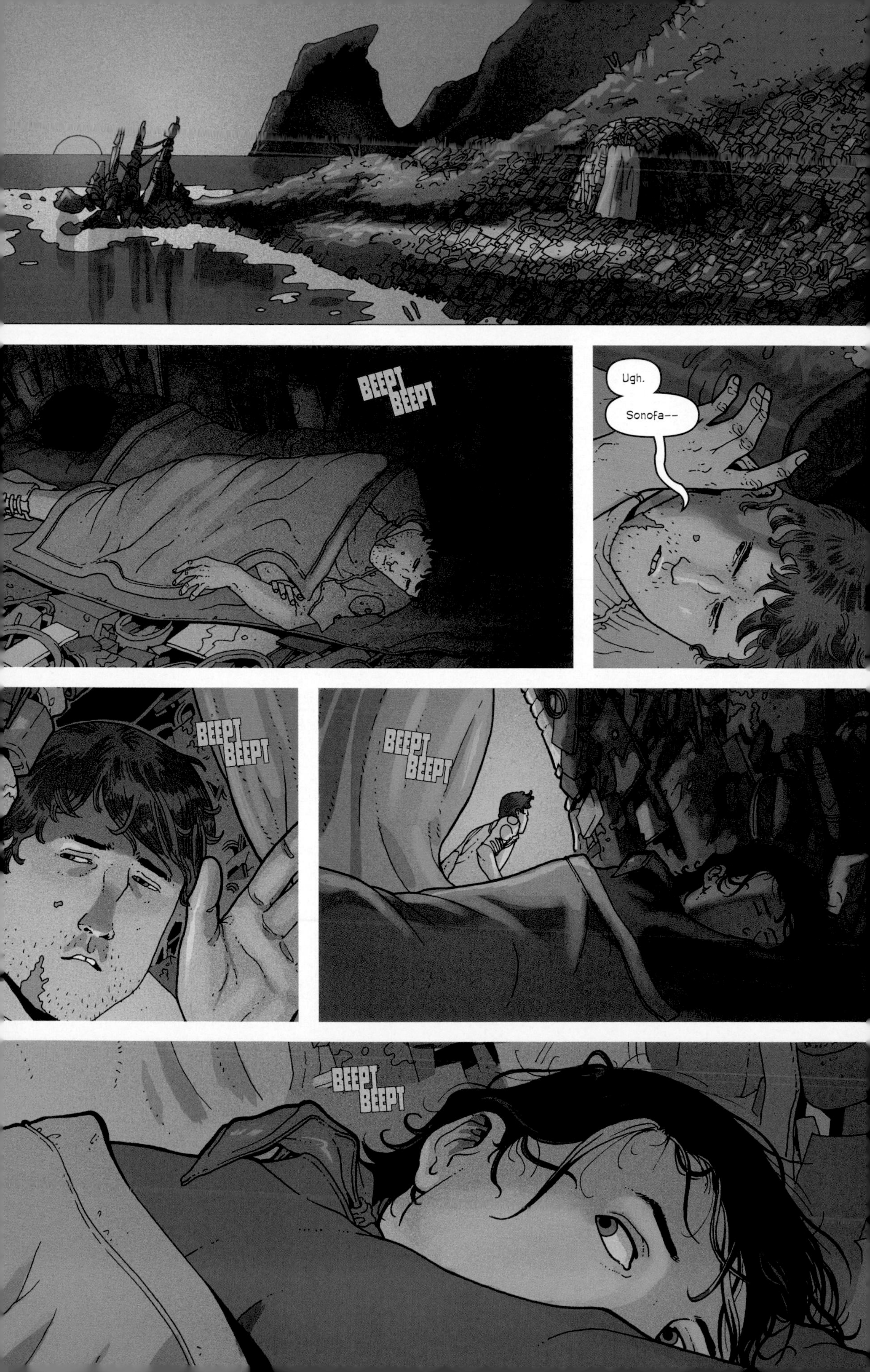
BEEPT BEEPT
Ugh.
Sonofa--
BEEPT BEEPT
BEEPT BEEPT
BEEPT BEEPT

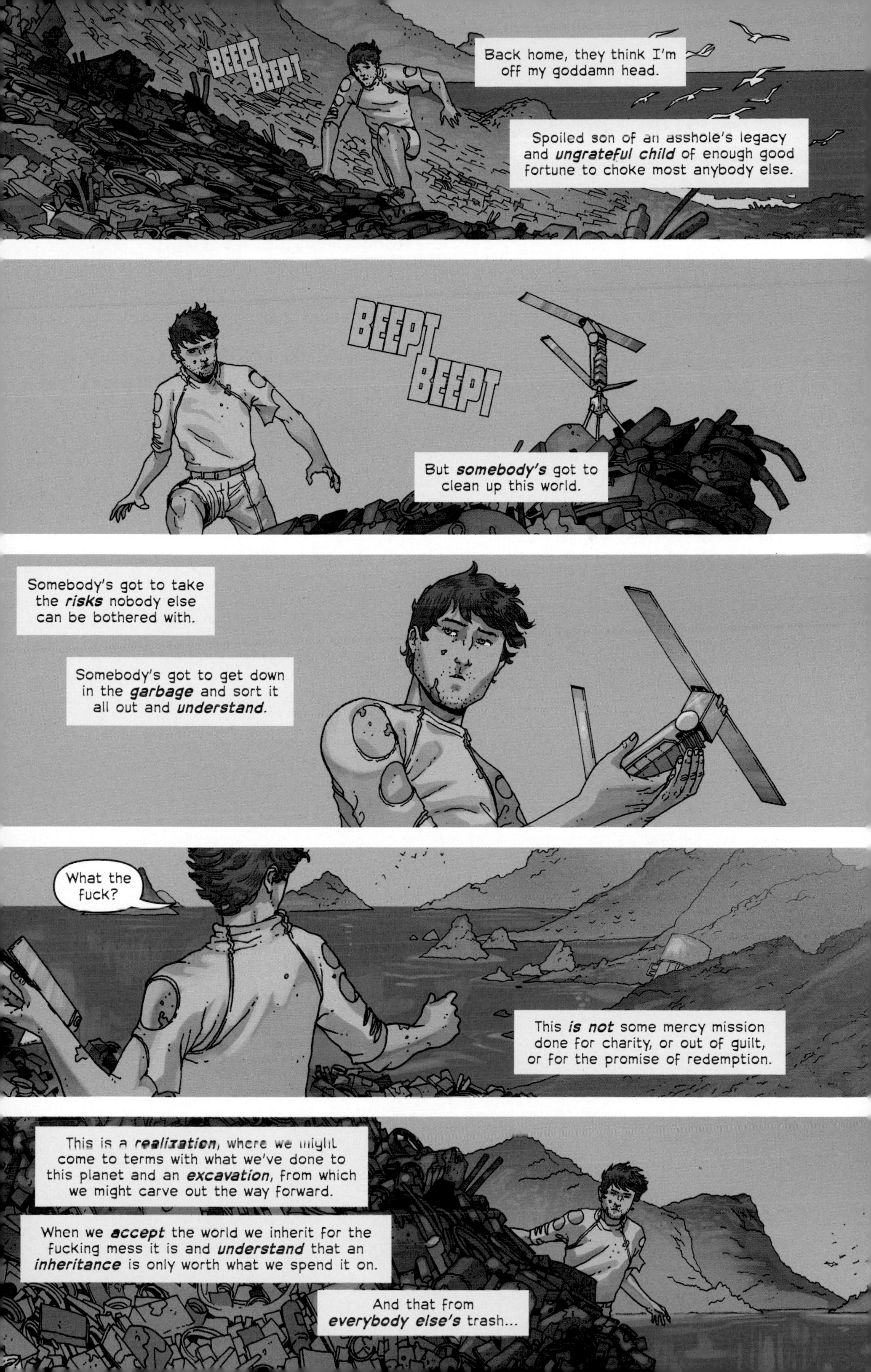
BEEPT BEEPT
Back home, they think I'm off my goddamn head.
Spoiled son of an asshole's legacy and *ungrateful child* of enough good fortune to choke most anybody else.
BEEPT BEEPT
But *somebody's* got to clean up this world.
Somebody's got to take the *risks* nobody else can be bothered with.
Somebody's got to get down in the *garbage* and sort it all out and *understand*.
What the fuck?
This *is not* some mercy mission done for charity, or out of guilt, or for the promise of redemption.
This is a *realization*, where we might come to terms with what we've done to this planet and an *excavation*, from which we might carve out the way forward.
When we *accept* the world we inherit for the fucking mess it is and *understand* that an *inheritance* is only worth what we spend it on.
And that from *everybody else's* trash...

...we might find the *most unexpected* treasure.

The fucking *Russians*...?

CCCP

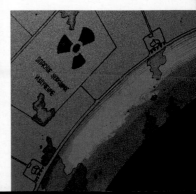

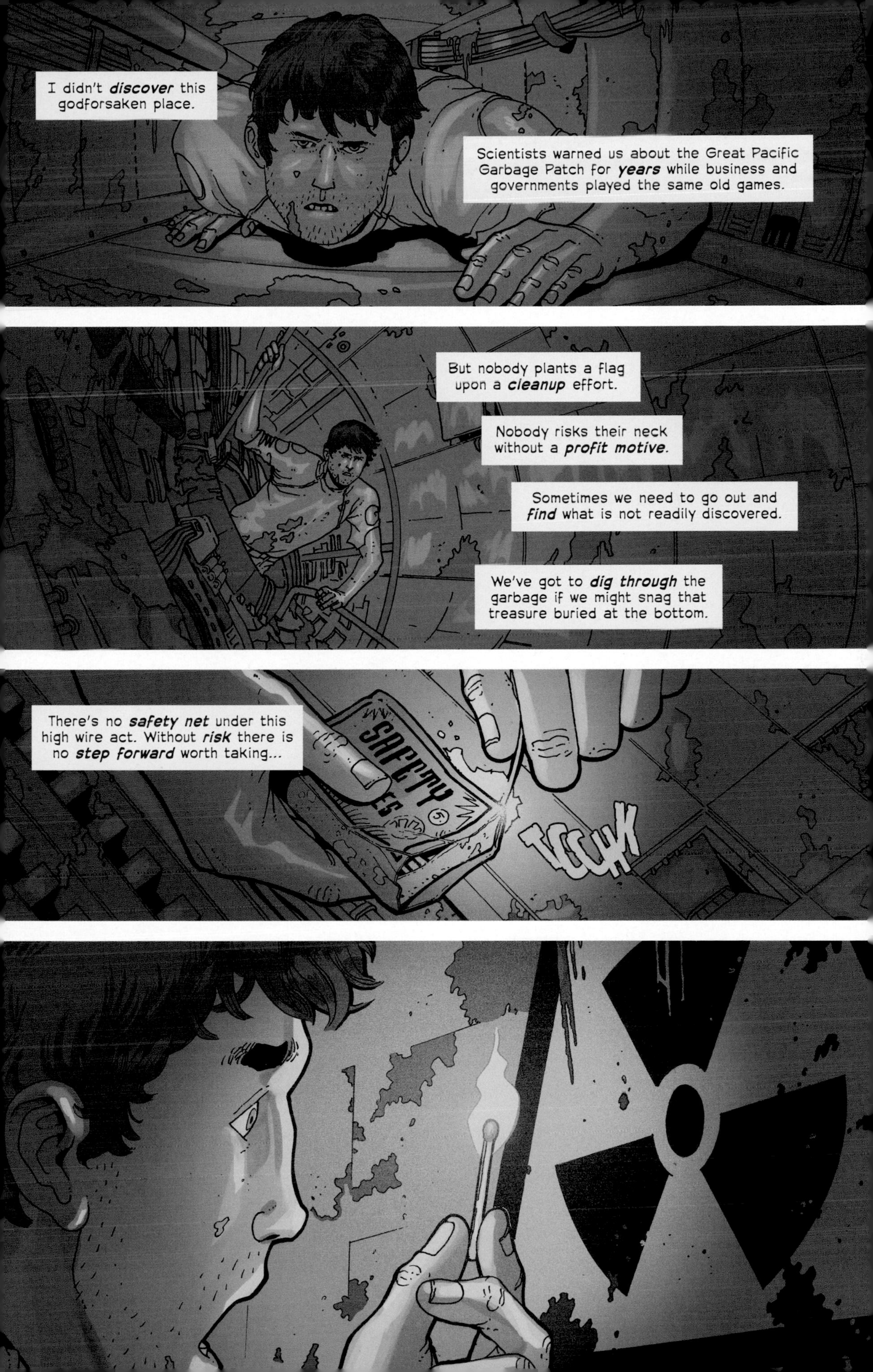
I didn't *discover* this godforsaken place.
Scientists warned us about the Great Pacific Garbage Patch for *years* while business and governments played the same old games.
But nobody plants a flag upon a *cleanup* effort.
Nobody risks their neck without a *profit motive*.
Sometimes we need to go out and *find* what is not readily discovered.
We've got to *dig through* the garbage if we might snag that treasure buried at the bottom.
There's no *safety net* under this high wire act. Without *risk* there is no *step forward* worth taking...
SAFETY
TCCHK

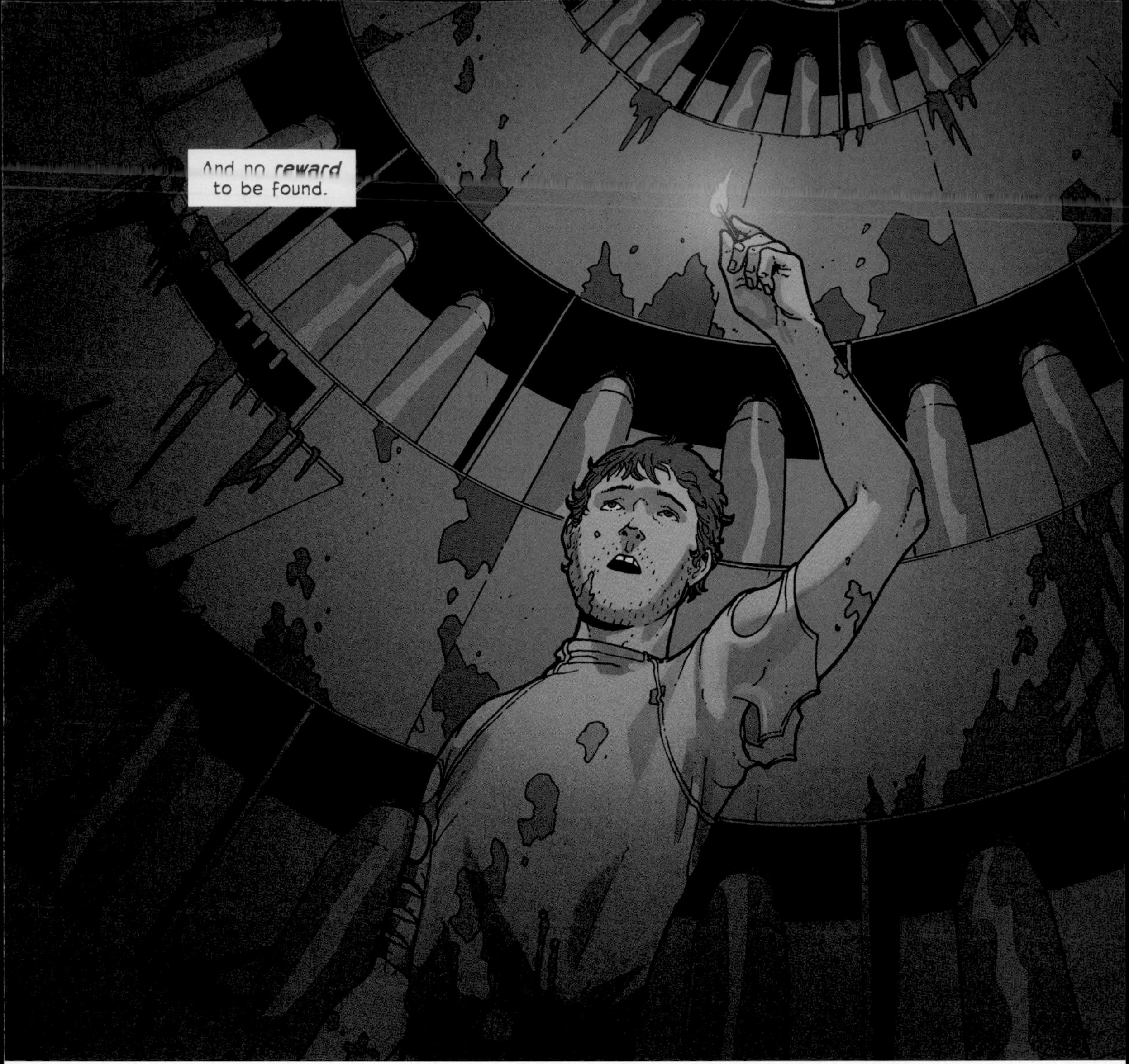
And no reward
to be found.

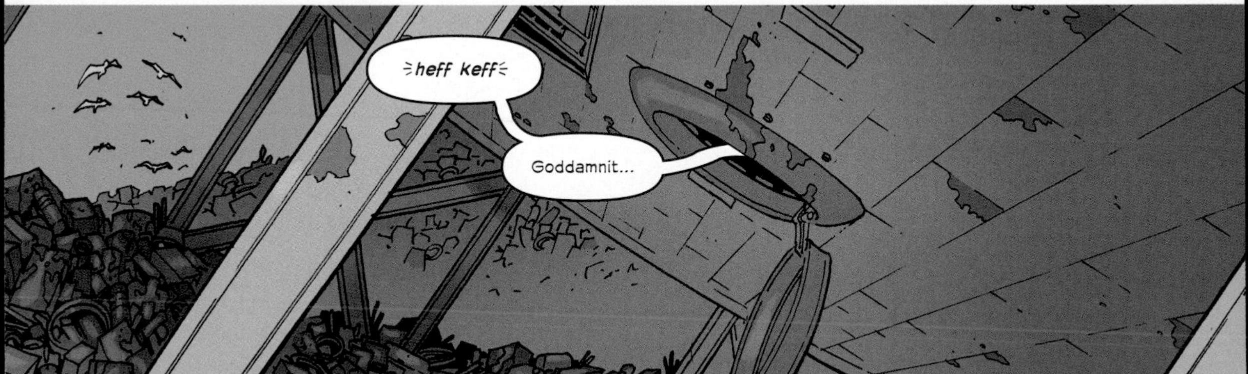
heff keff
Goddamnit...

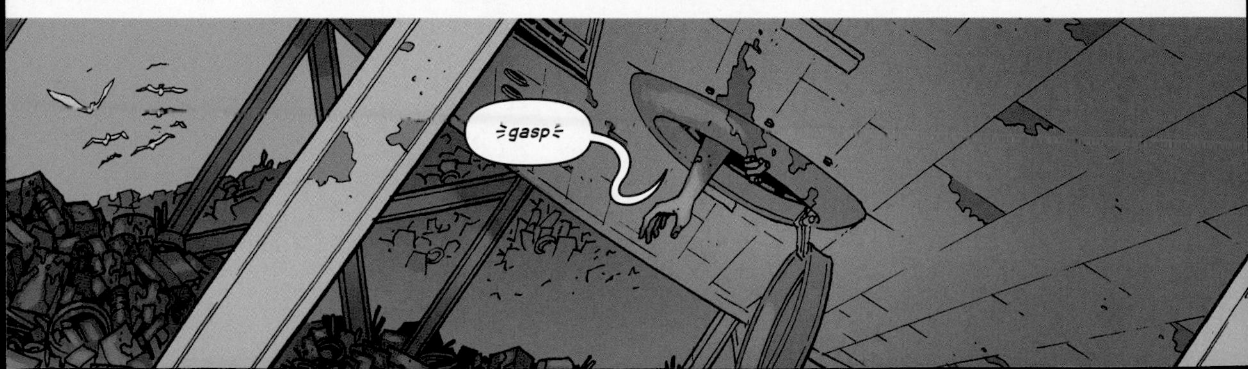
gasp

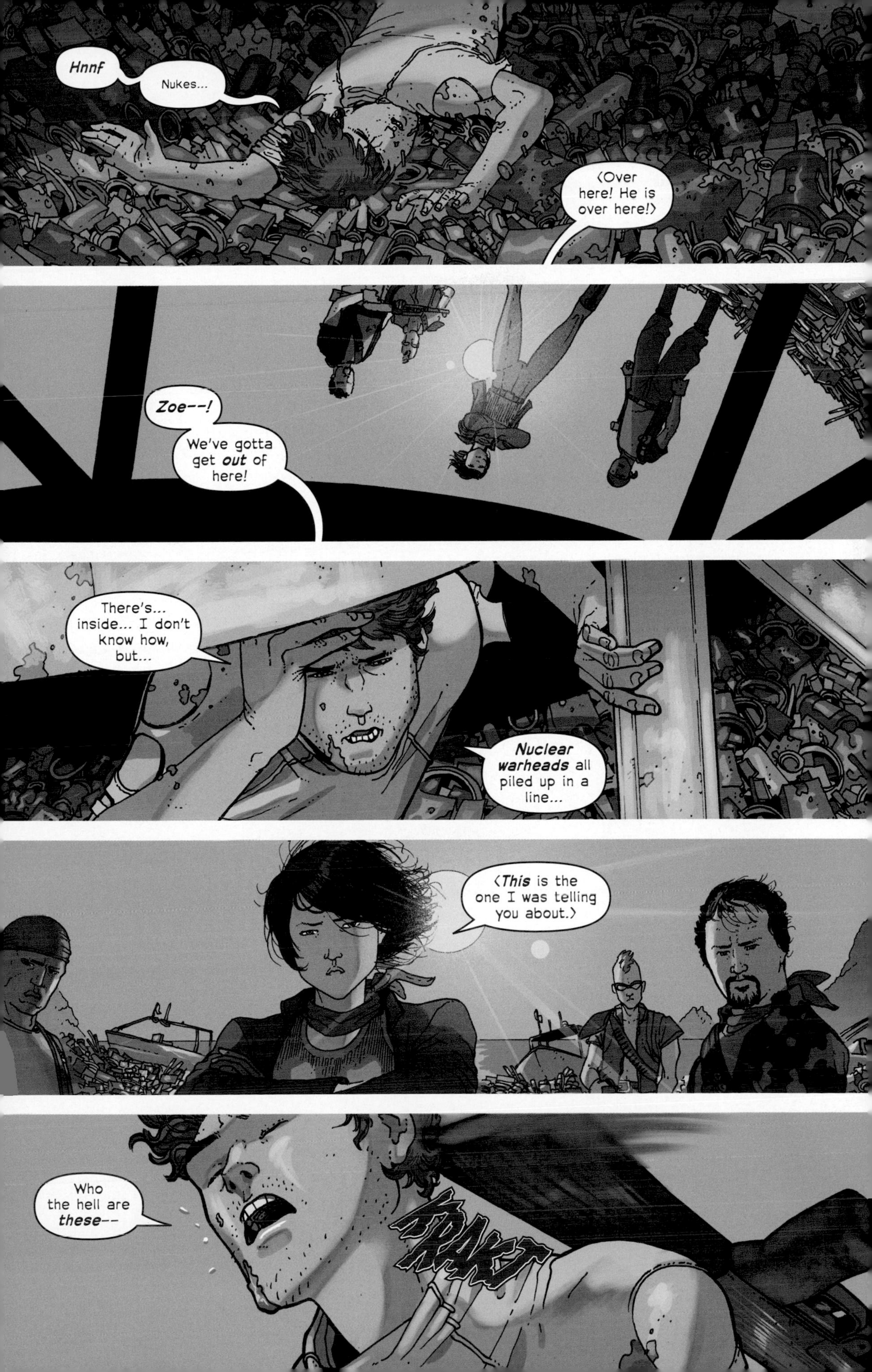
Hnnf
Nukes...
‹Over here! He is over here!›
Zoe--!
We've gotta get out of here!
There's... inside... I don't know how, but...
Nuclear warheads all piled up in a line...
‹This is the one I was telling you about.›
Who the hell are these--
KRAKT

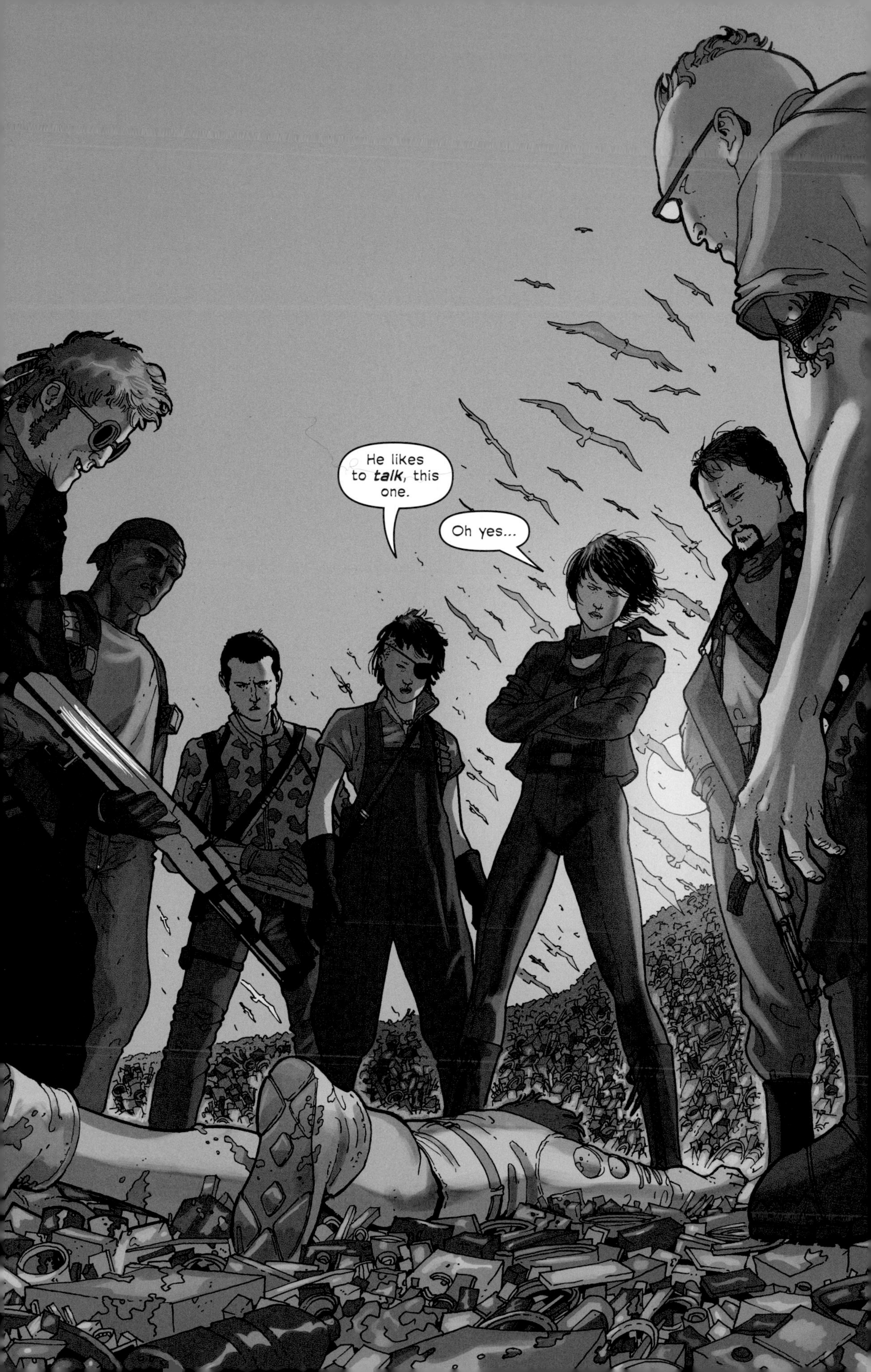
He likes to *talk*, this one.
Oh yes...

CHAPTER**FIVE**

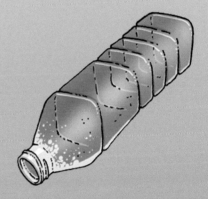

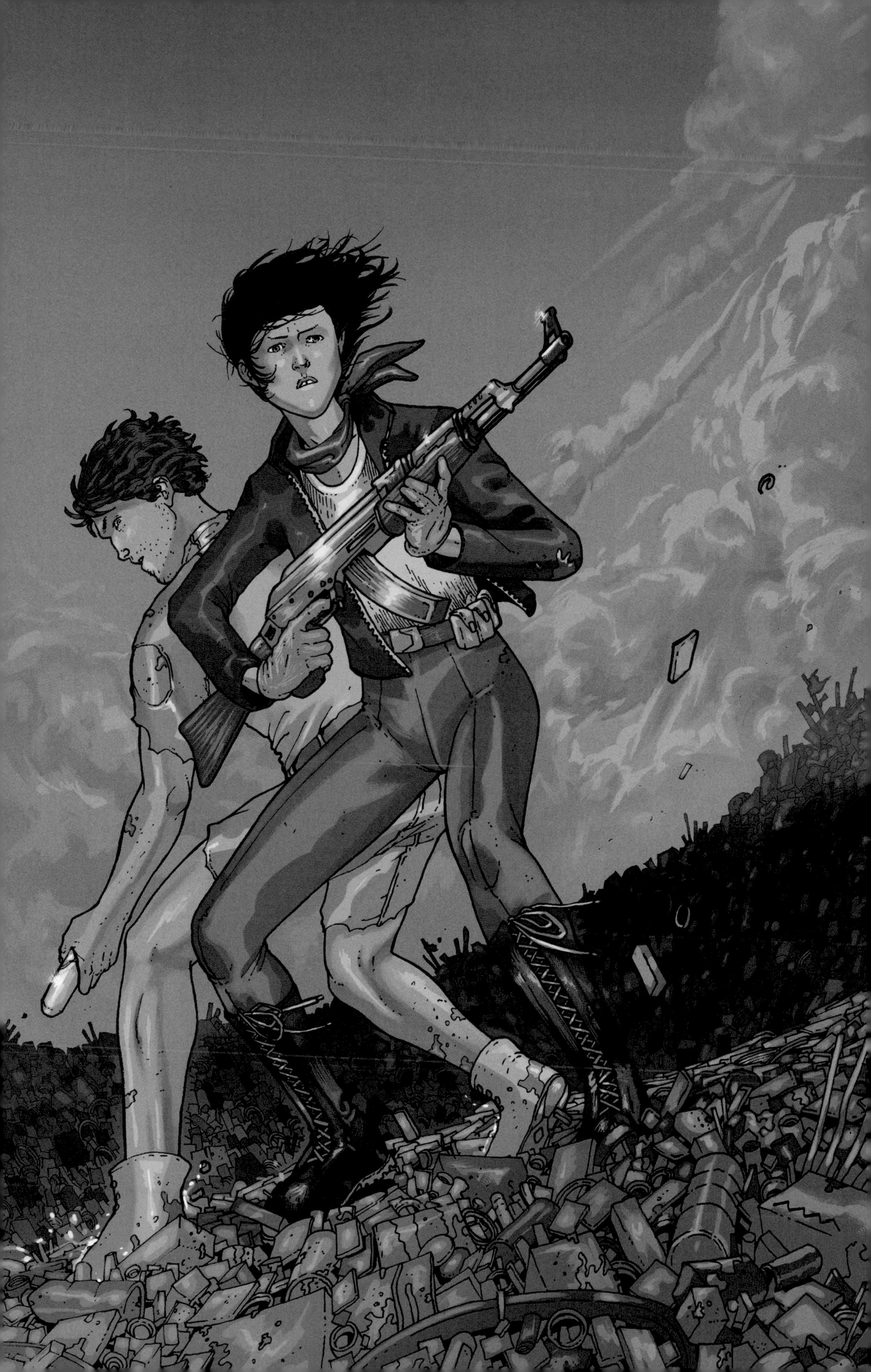

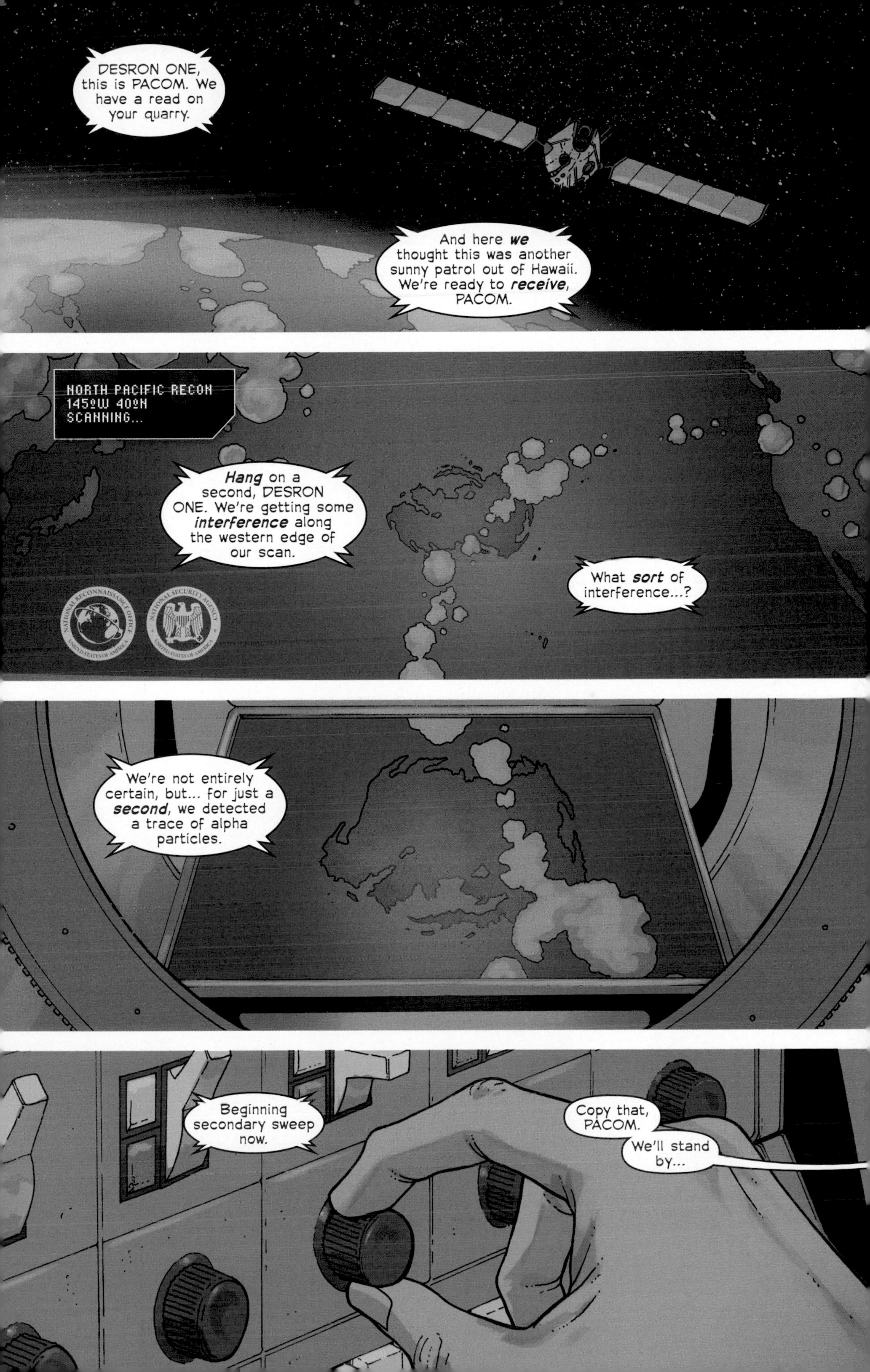
DESRON ONE, this is PACOM. We have a read on your quarry.
And here *we* thought this was another sunny patrol out of Hawaii. We're ready to *receive*, PACOM.
NORTH PACIFIC RECON
145ºW 40ºN
SCANNING...
Hang on a second, DESRON ONE. We're getting some *interference* along the western edge of our scan.
What *sort* of interference...?
We're not entirely certain, but... for just a *second*, we detected a trace of alpha particles.
Beginning secondary sweep now.
Copy that, PACOM.
We'll stand by...

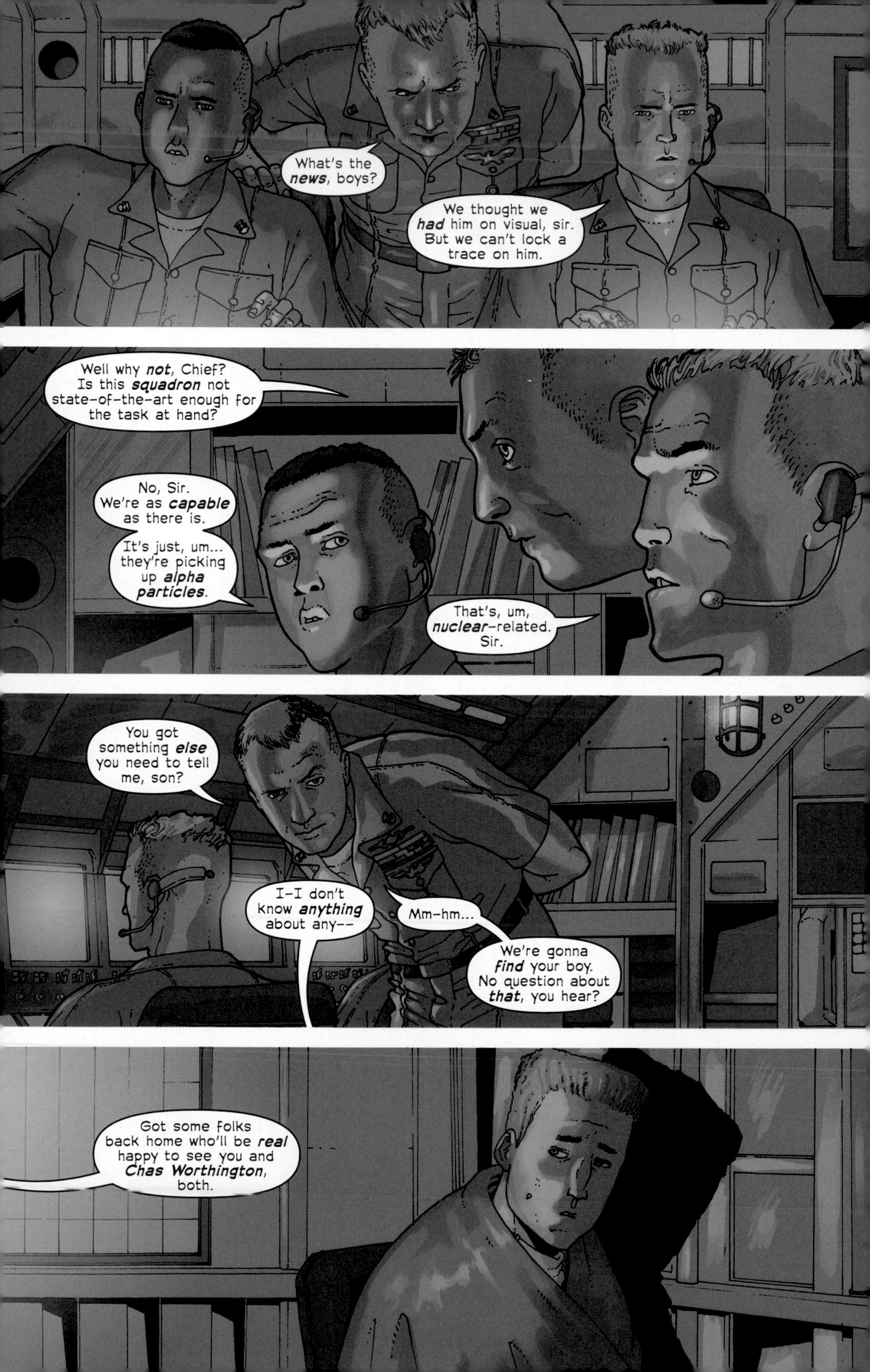
What's the news, boys?
We thought we had him on visual, sir. But we can't lock a trace on him.
Well why not, Chief? Is this squadron not state-of-the-art enough for the task at hand?
No, Sir. We're as capable as there is.
It's just, um... they're picking up alpha particles.
That's, um, nuclear-related. Sir.
You got something else you need to tell me, son?
I-I don't know anything about any--
Mm-hm...
We're gonna find your boy. No question about that, you hear?
Got some folks back home who'll be real happy to see you and Chas Worthington, both.

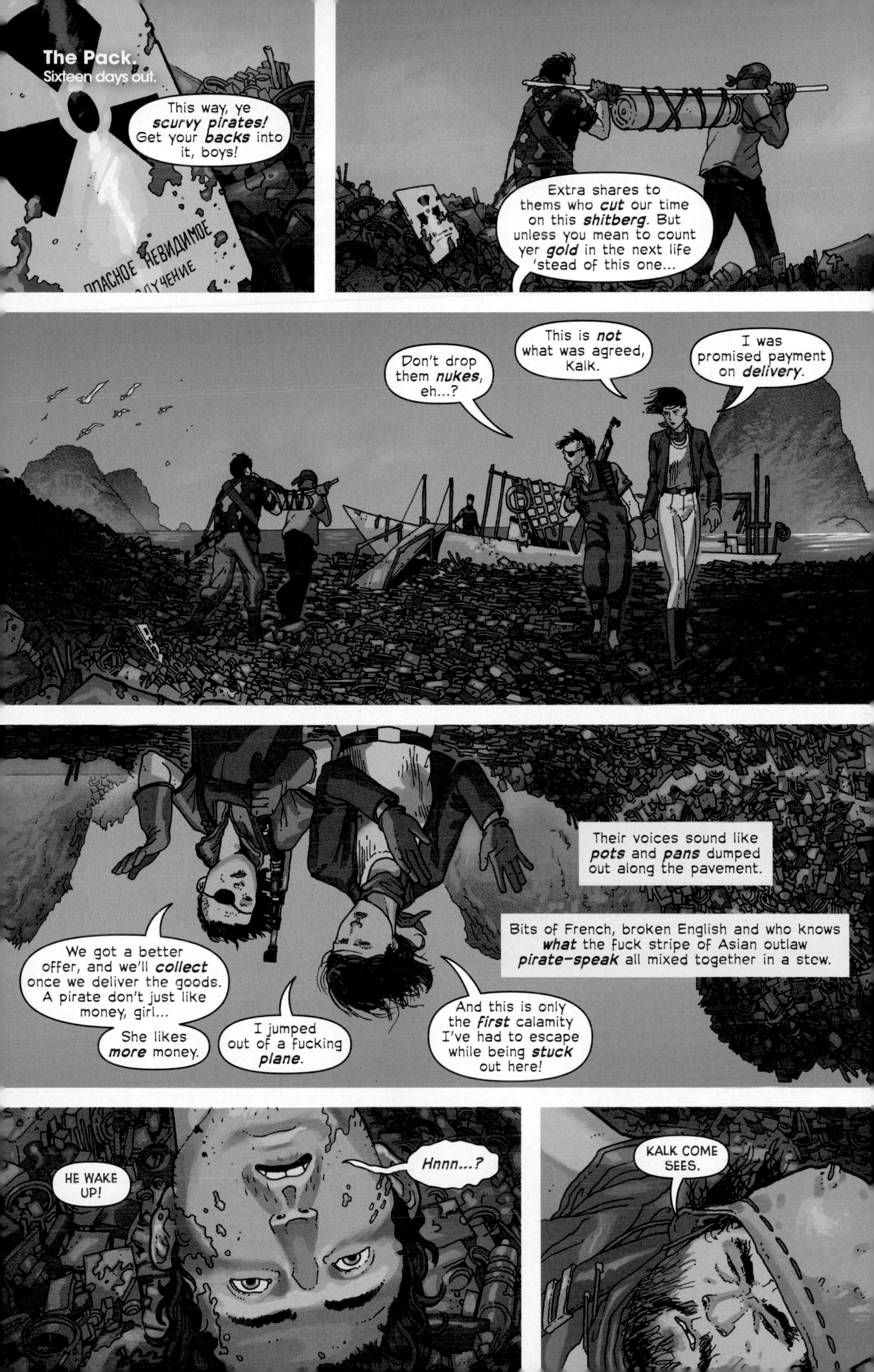
The Pack.
Sixteen days out.
This way, ye scurvy pirates! Get your backs into it, boys!
ОПАСНОЕ НЕВИДИМОЕ ИЗЛУЧЕНИЕ
Extra shares to thems who cut our time on this shitberg. But unless you mean to count yer gold in the next life 'stead of this one...
Don't drop them nukes, eh...?
This is not what was agreed, Kalk.
I was promised payment on delivery.
Their voices sound like pots and pans dumped out along the pavement.
Bits of French, broken English and who knows what the fuck stripe of Asian outlaw pirate-speak all mixed together in a stew.
We got a better offer, and we'll collect once we deliver the goods. A pirate don't just like money, girl...
She likes more money.
I jumped out of a fucking plane.
And this is only the first calamity I've had to escape while being stuck out here!
HE WAKE UP!
Hnnn...?
KALK COME SEES.

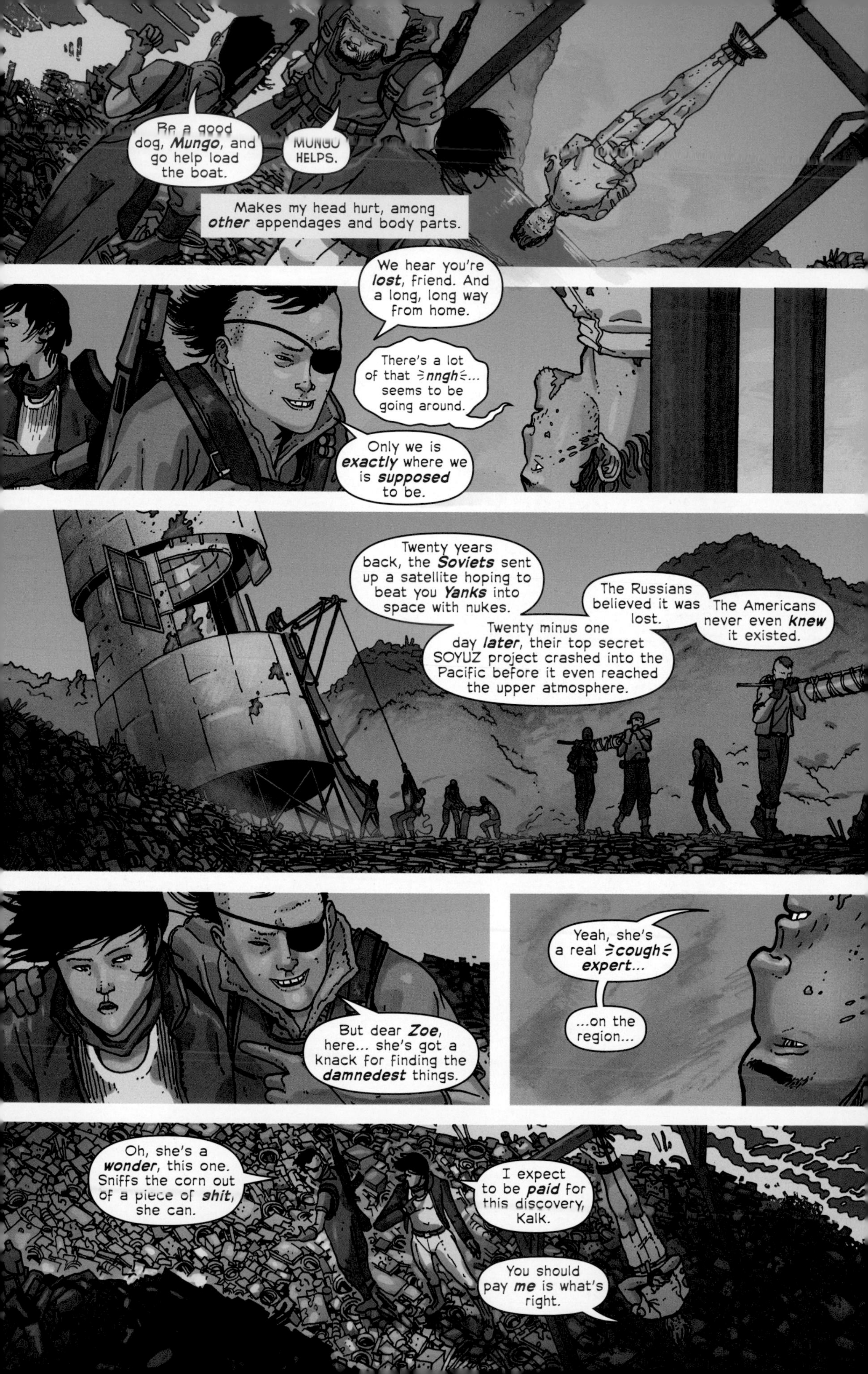

Be a good dog, *Mungo*, and go help load the boat.
MUNGO HELPS.
Makes my head hurt, among *other* appendages and body parts.
We hear you're *lost*, friend. And a long, long way from home.
There's a lot of that *nngh*... seems to be going around.
Only we is *exactly* where we is *supposed* to be.
Twenty years back, the *Soviets* sent up a satellite hoping to beat you *Yanks* into space with nukes.
Twenty minus one day *later*, their top secret SOYUZ project crashed into the Pacific before it even reached the upper atmosphere.
The Russians believed it was lost.
The Americans never even *knew* it existed.
But dear *Zoe*, here... she's got a knack for finding the *damnedest* things.
Yeah, she's a real *cough* *expert*...
...on the region...
Oh, she's a *wonder*, this one. Sniffs the corn out of a piece of *shit*, she can.
I expect to be *paid* for this discovery, Kalk.
You should pay *me* is what's right.

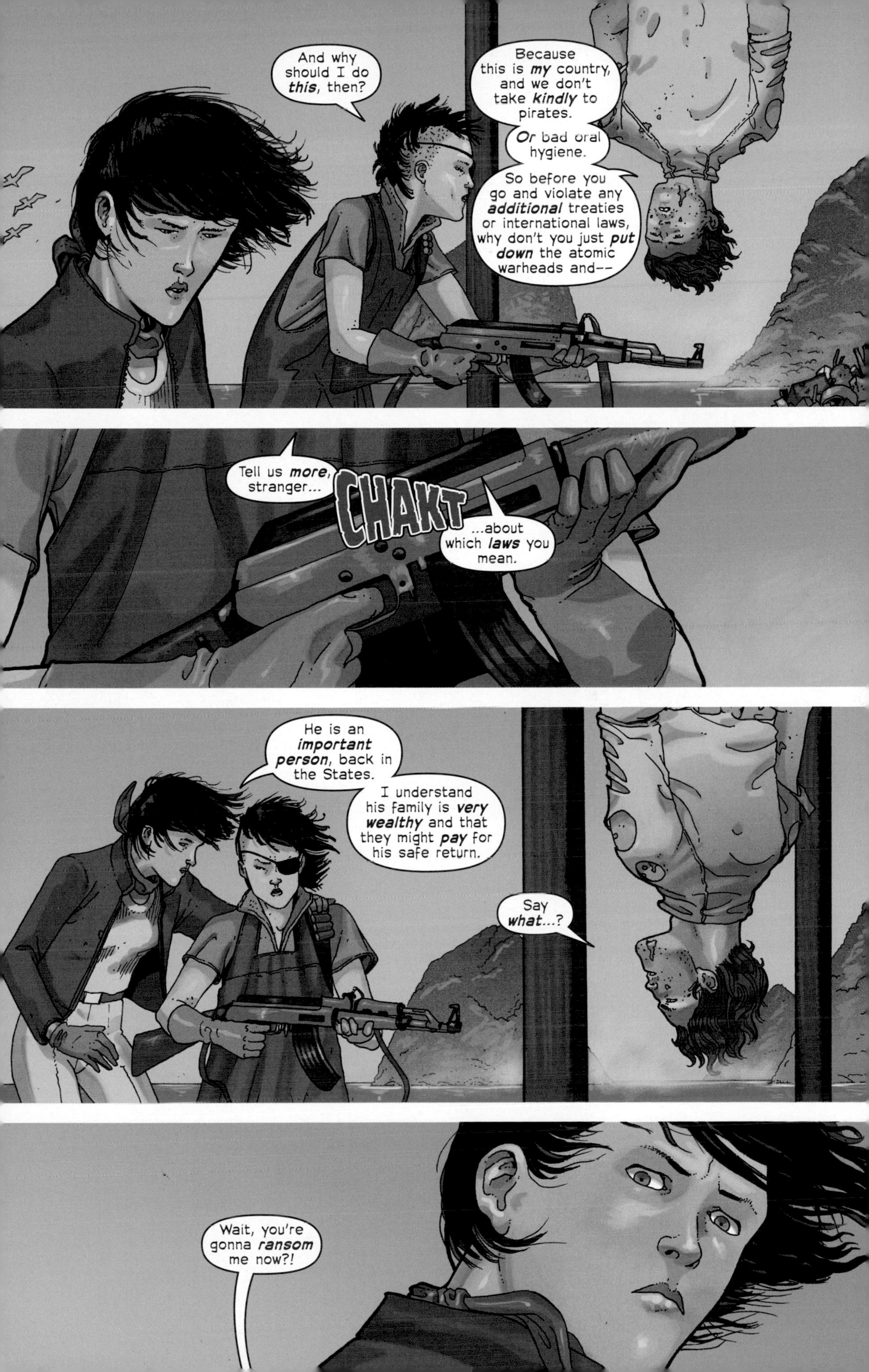
And why should I do this, then?
Because this is my country, and we don't take kindly to pirates.
Or bad oral hygiene.
So before you go and violate any additional treaties or international laws, why don't you just put down the atomic warheads and--
Tell us more, stranger...
CHAKT
...about which laws you mean.
He is an important person, back in the States.
I understand his family is very wealthy and that they might pay for his safe return.
Say what...?
Wait, you're gonna ransom me now?!

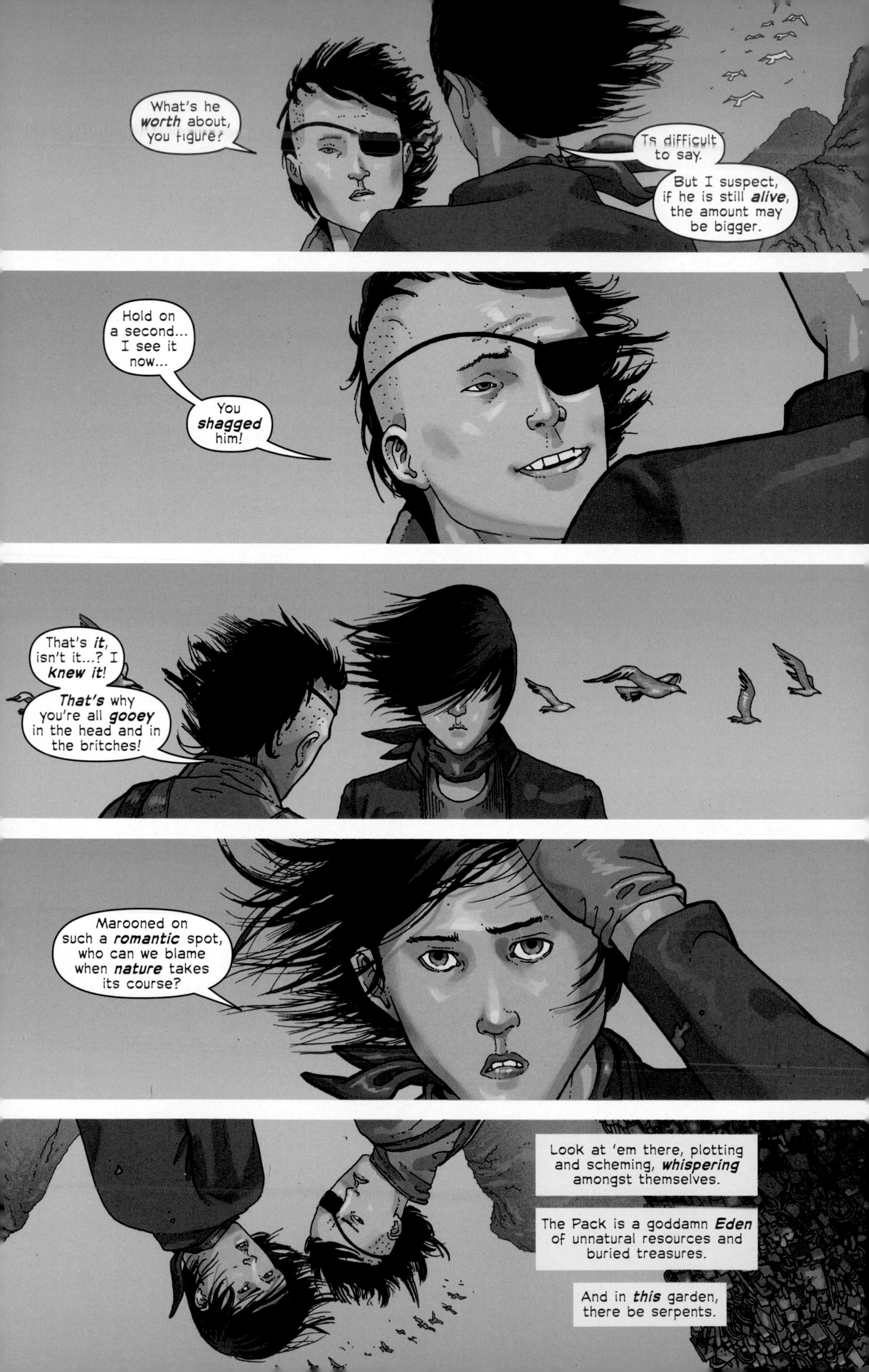

What's he *worth* about, you figure?
'Tis difficult to say.
But I suspect, if he is still *alive*, the amount may be bigger.
Hold on a second... I see it now...
You *shagged* him!
That's *it*, isn't it...? I *knew it*!
That's why you're all *gooey* in the head and in the britches!
Marooned on such a *romantic* spot, who can we blame when *nature* takes its course?
Look at 'em there, plotting and scheming, *whispering* amongst themselves.
The Pack is a goddamn *Eden* of unnatural resources and buried treasures.
And in *this* garden, there be serpents.

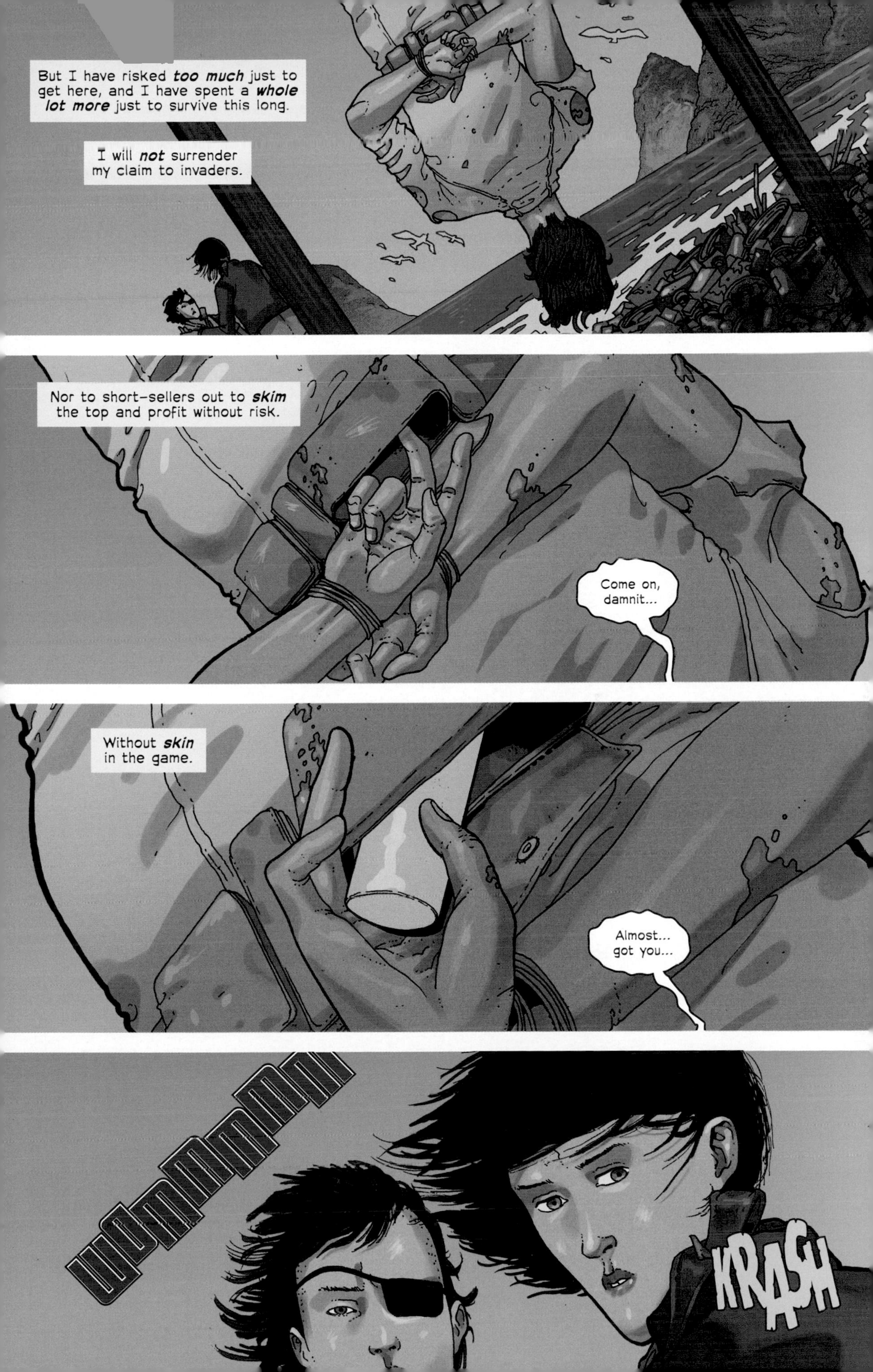
But I have risked too much just to get here, and I have spent a whole lot more just to survive this long.
I will not surrender my claim to invaders.
Nor to short-sellers out to skim the top and profit without risk.
Come on, damnit...
Without skin in the game.
Almost... got you...
WOMMMM
KRASH

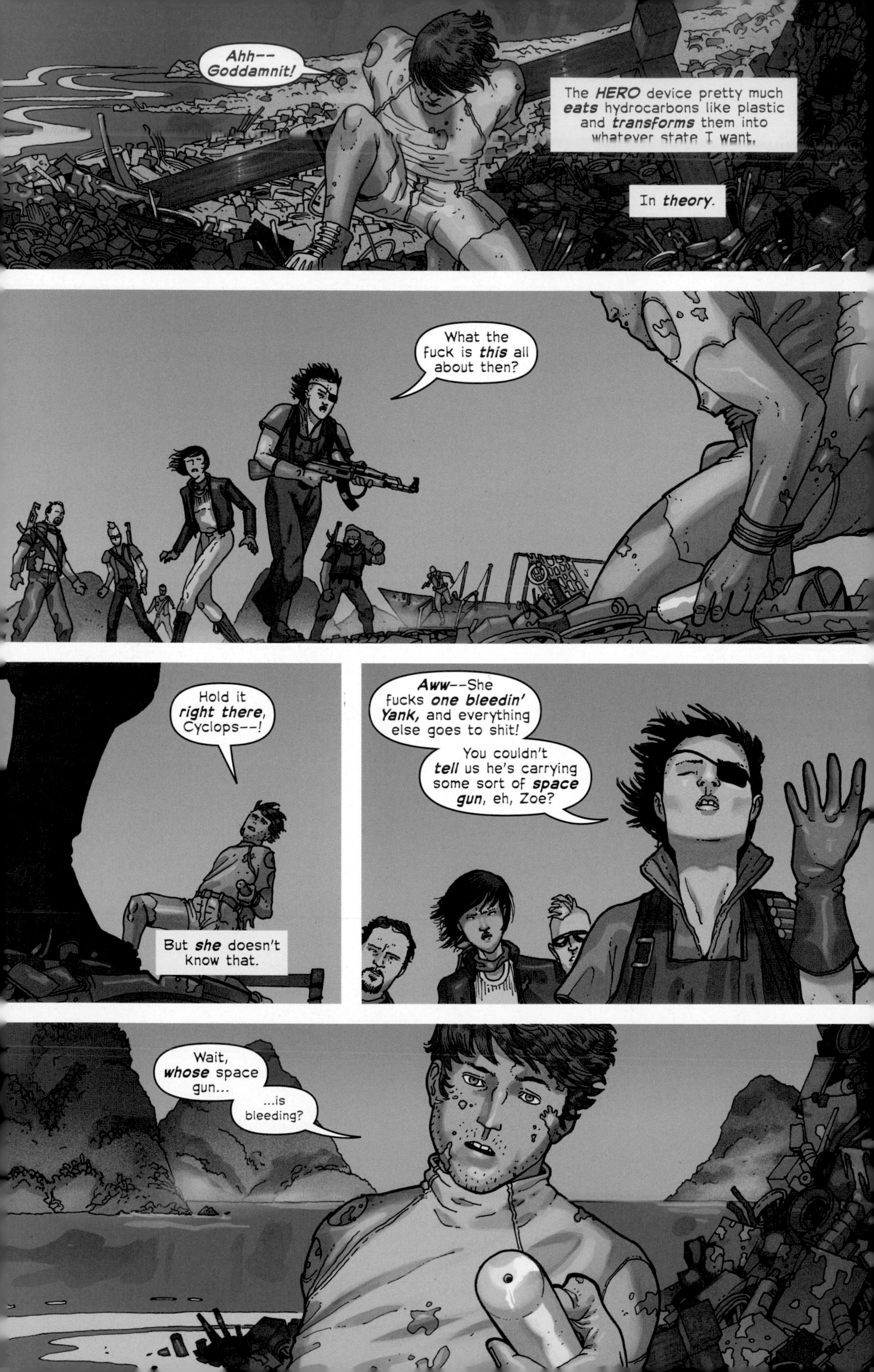
Ahh-- Goddamnit!
The HERO device pretty much eats hydrocarbons like plastic and transforms them into whatever state I want.
In theory.
What the fuck is this all about then?
Hold it right there, Cyclops--!
But she doesn't know that.
Aww--She fucks one bleedin' Yank, and everything else goes to shit!
You couldn't tell us he's carrying some sort of space gun, eh, Zoe?
Wait, whose space gun...
...is bleeding?

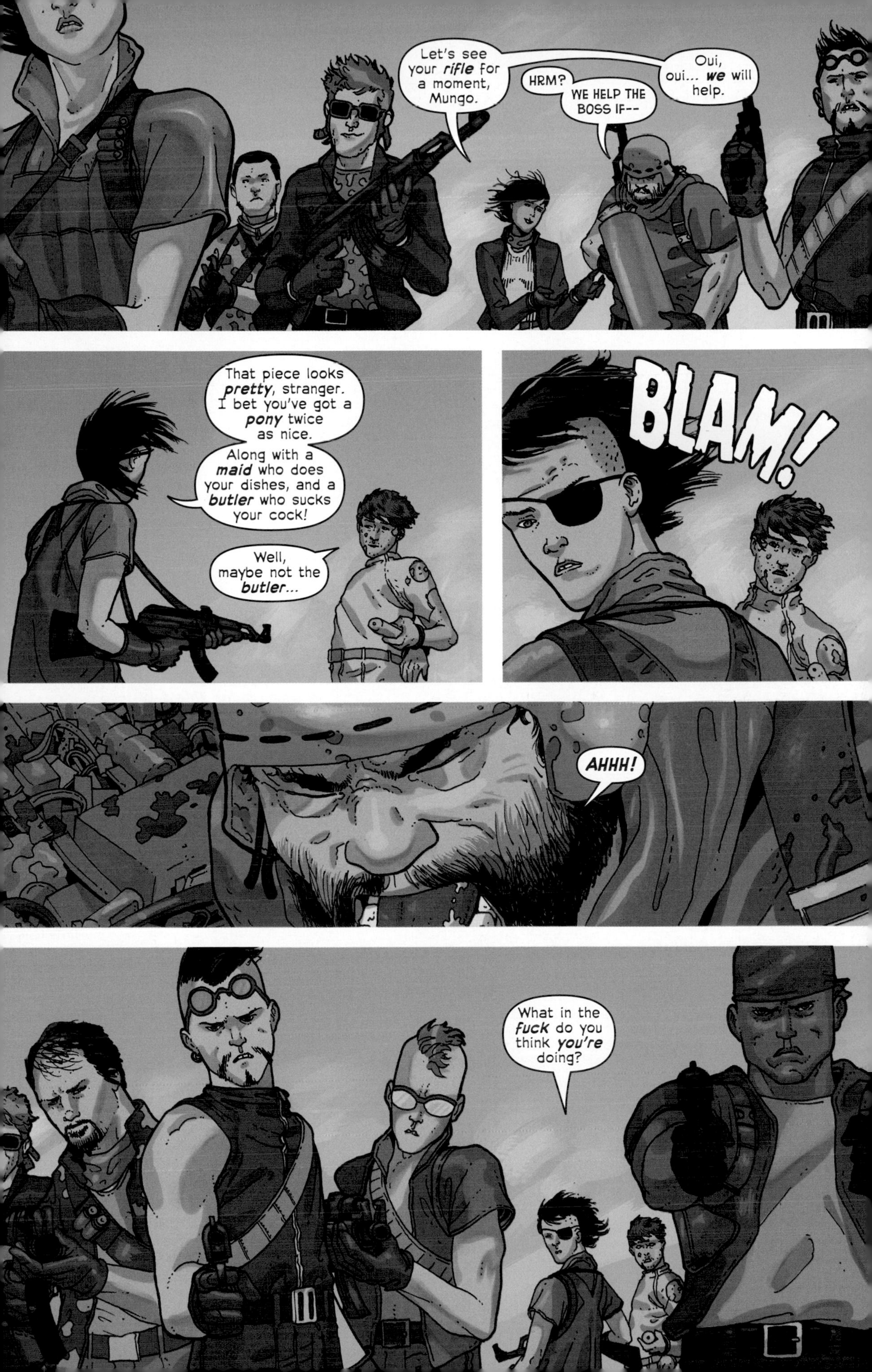
Let's see your *rifle* for a moment, Mungo.
HRM?
WE HELP THE BOSS IF--
Oui, oui... *we* will help.
That piece looks *pretty*, stranger. I bet you've got a *pony* twice as nice.
Along with a *maid* who does your dishes, and a *butler* who sucks your cock!
Well, maybe not the *butler*...
BLAM!
AHHH!
What in the *fuck* do you think *you're* doing?

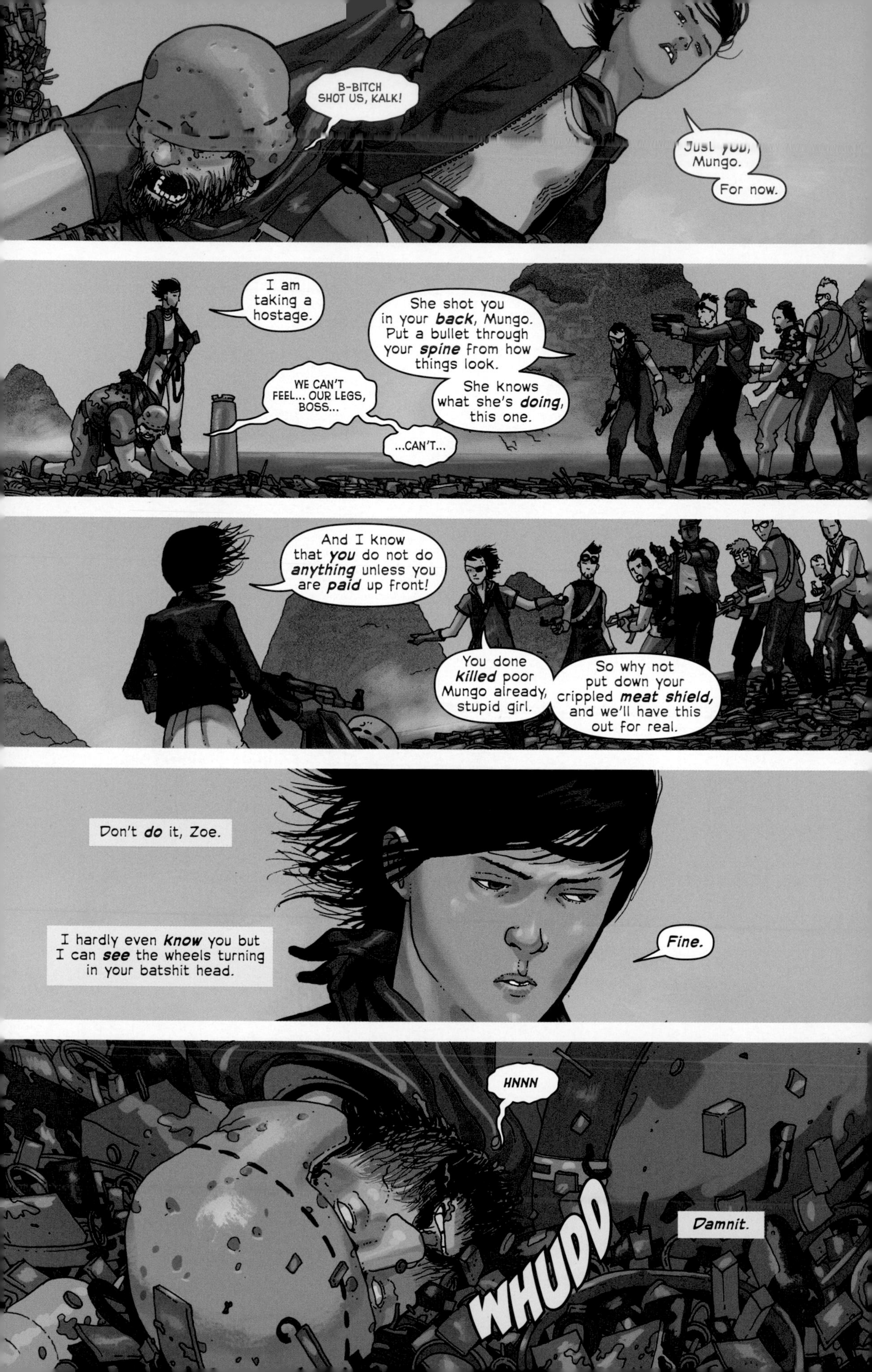
B-BITCH SHOT US, KALK!
Just YOU, Mungo.
For now.
I am taking a hostage.
She shot you in your back, Mungo. Put a bullet through your spine from how things look.
She knows what she's doing, this one.
WE CAN'T FEEL... OUR LEGS, BOSS...
...CAN'T...
And I know that you do not do anything unless you are paid up front!
You done killed poor Mungo already, stupid girl.
So why not put down your crippled meat shield, and we'll have this out for real.
Don't do it, Zoe.
I hardly even know you but I can see the wheels turning in your batshit head.
Fine.
HNNN
WHUDD
Damnit.

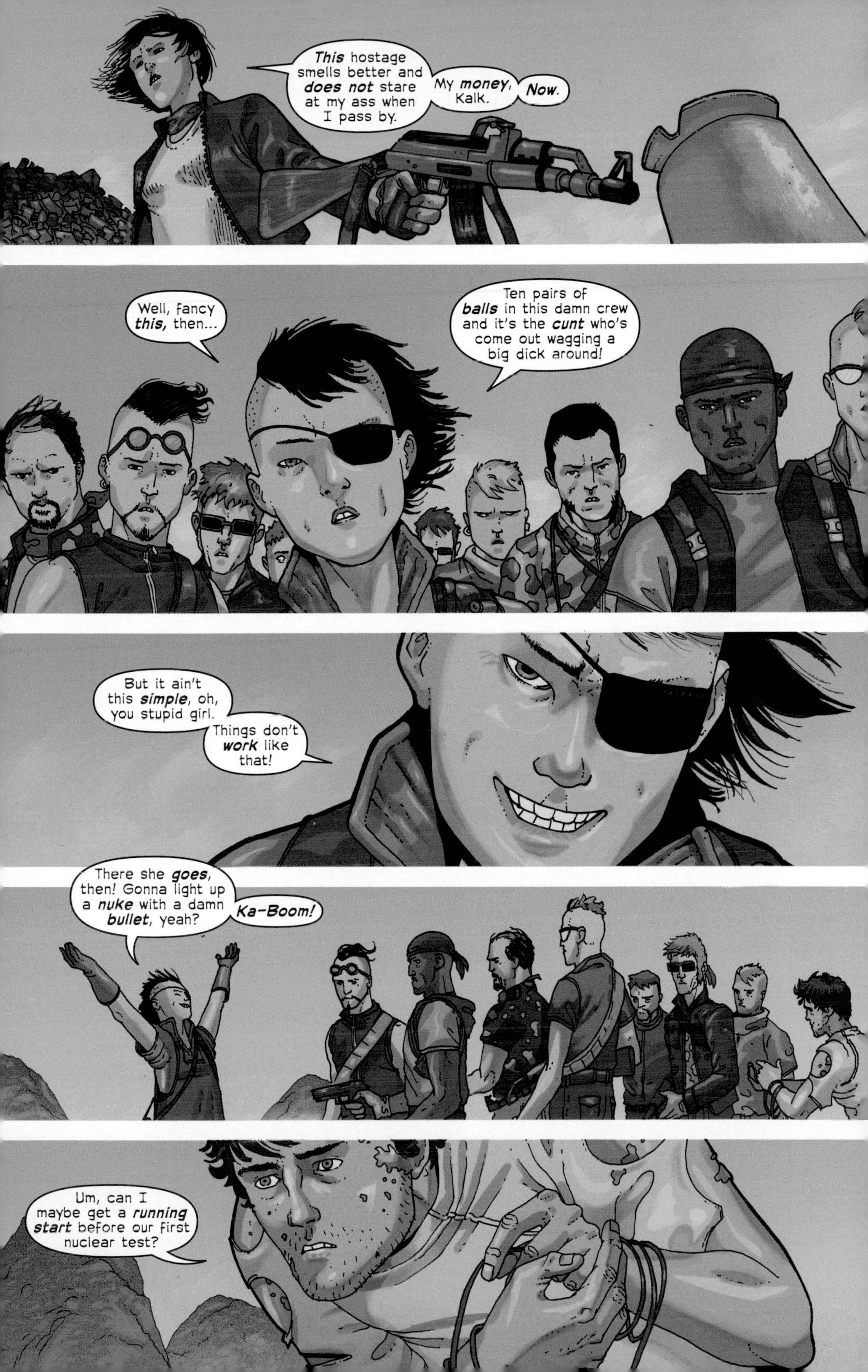
This hostage smells better and does not stare at my ass when I pass by.
My money, Kalk.
Now.
Well, fancy this, then...
Ten pairs of balls in this damn crew and it's the cunt who's come out wagging a big dick around!
But it ain't this simple, oh, you stupid girl.
Things don't work like that!
There she goes, then! Gonna light up a nuke with a damn bullet, yeah?
Ka-Boom!
Um, can I maybe get a running start before our first nuclear test?

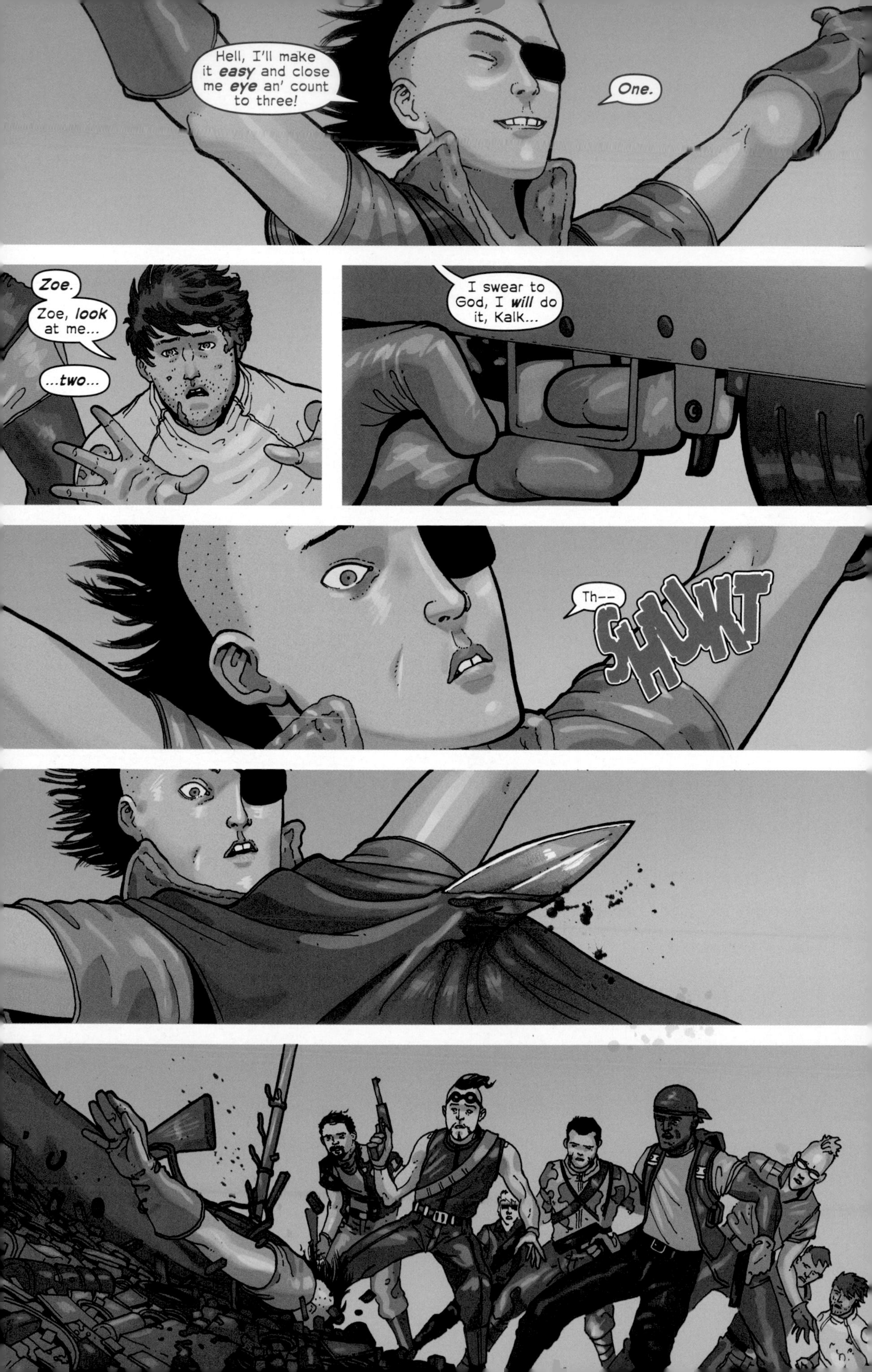

Hell, I'll make it *easy* and close me *eye* an' count to three!
One.
Zoe.
Zoe, *look* at me...
...two...
I swear to God, I *will* do it, Kalk...
Th--
SHUKT

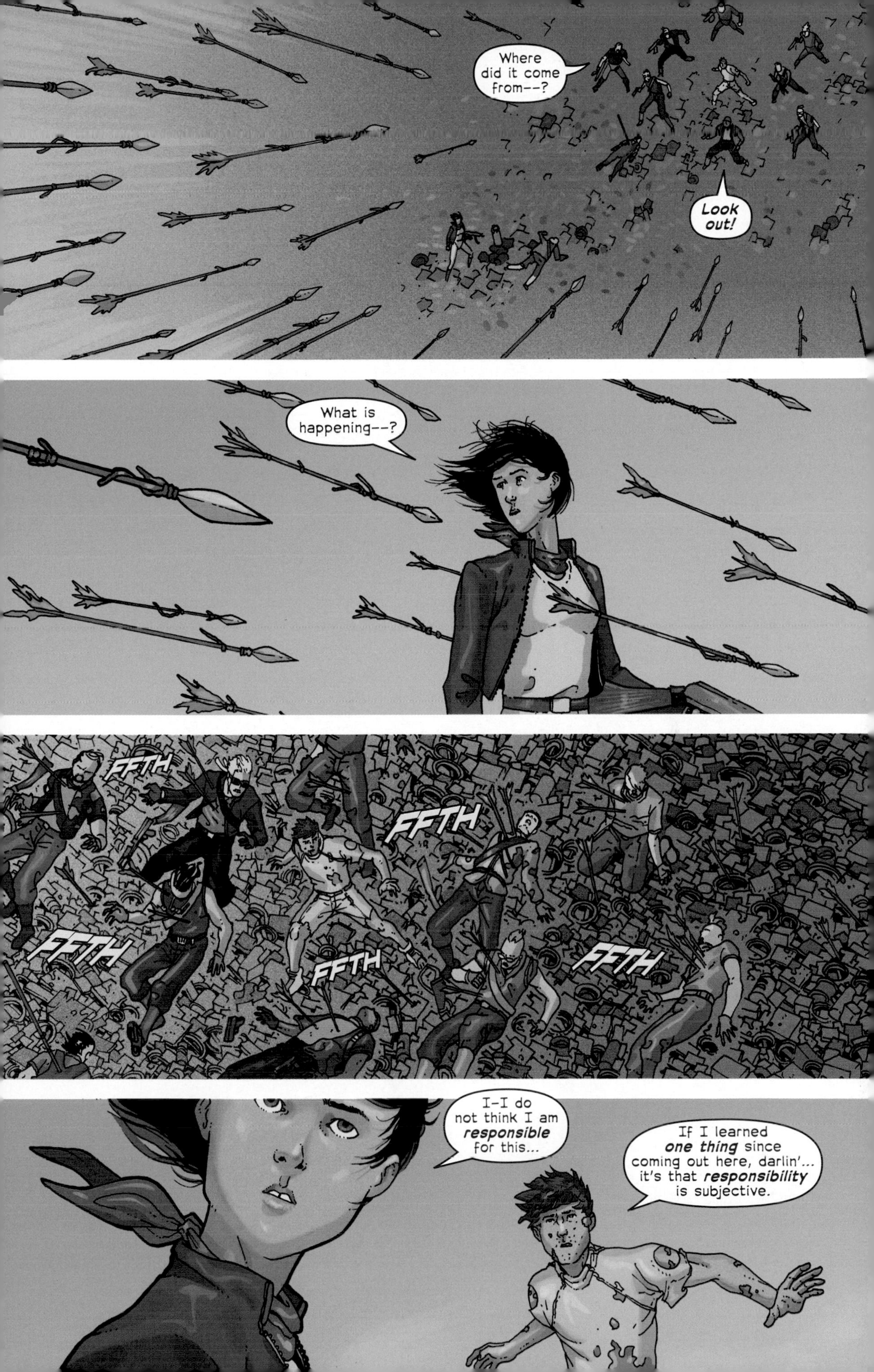
Where did it come from--?
Look out!
What is happening--?
FFTH
FFTH
FFTH
FFTH
FFTH
I-I do not think I am *responsible* for this...
If I learned *one thing* since coming out here, darlin'... it's that *responsibility* is subjective.

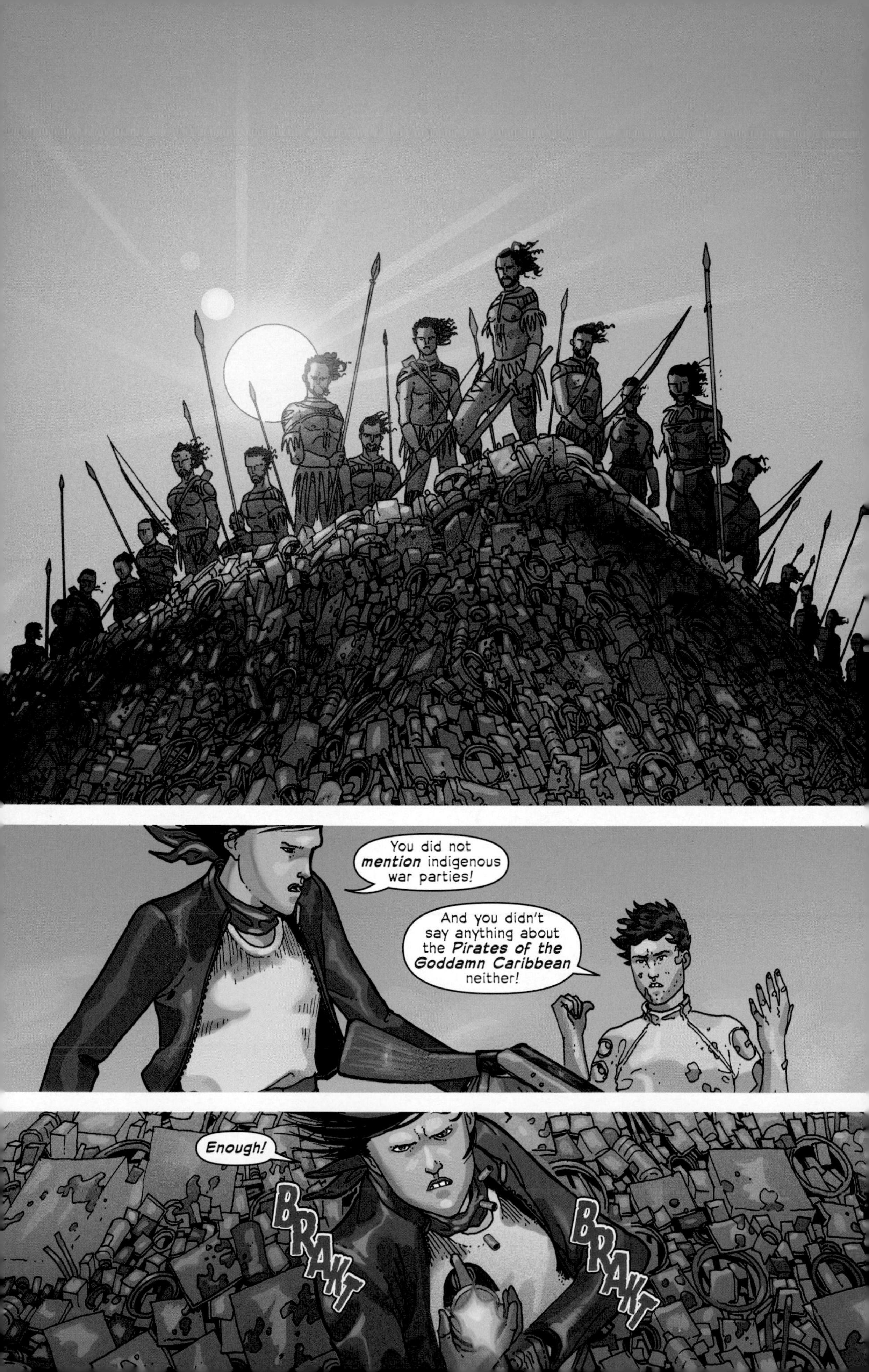

You did not *mention* indigenous war parties!
And you didn't say anything about the *Pirates of the Goddamn Caribbean* neither!
Enough!
BRAKT
BRAKT

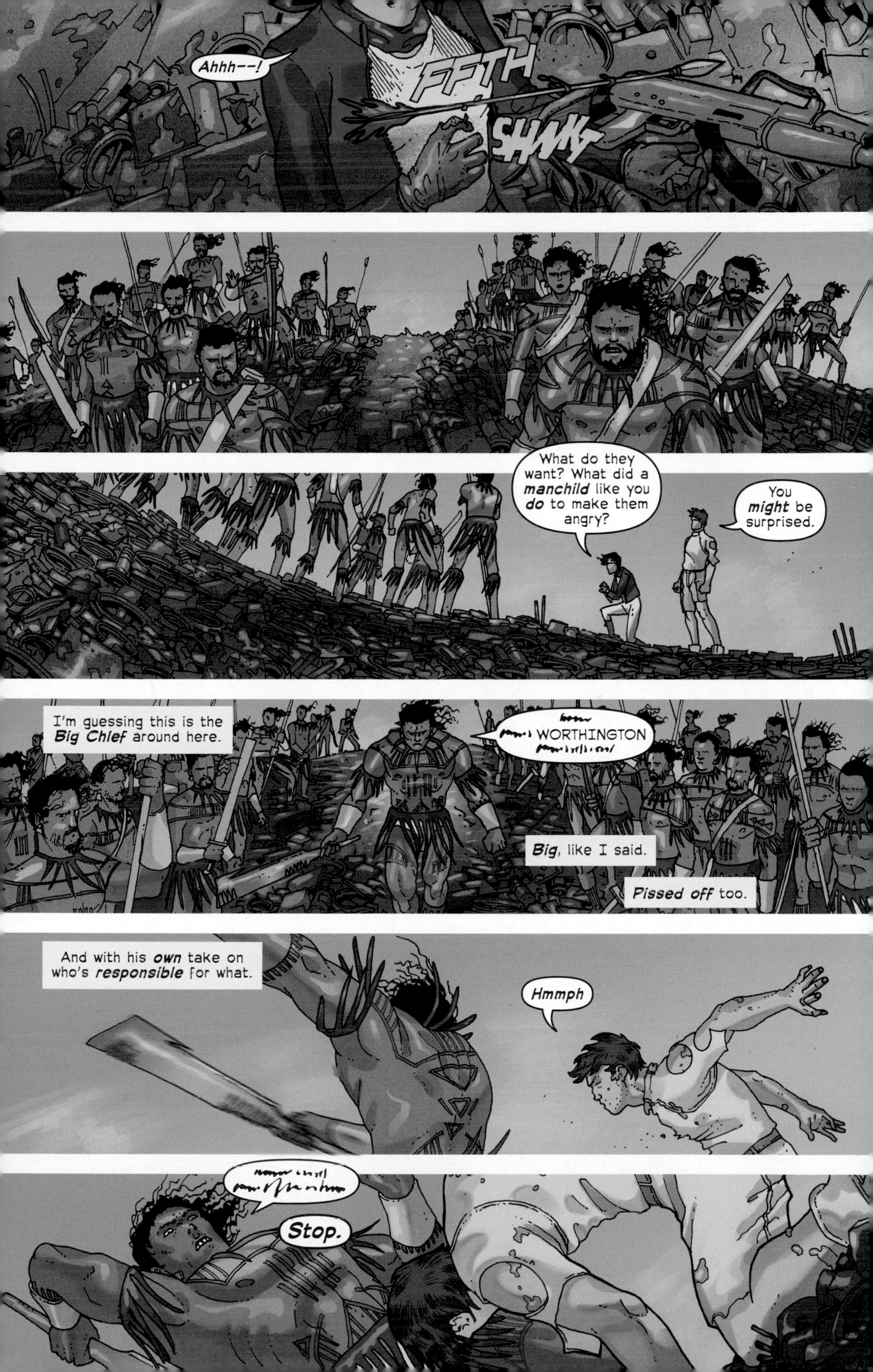
Ahhh--!
FFTH
SHAK
What do they want? What did a manchild like you do to make them angry?
You might be surprised.
I'm guessing this is the Big Chief around here.
WORTHINGTON
Big, like I said.
Pissed off too.
And with his own take on who's responsible for what.
Hmmph
Stop.

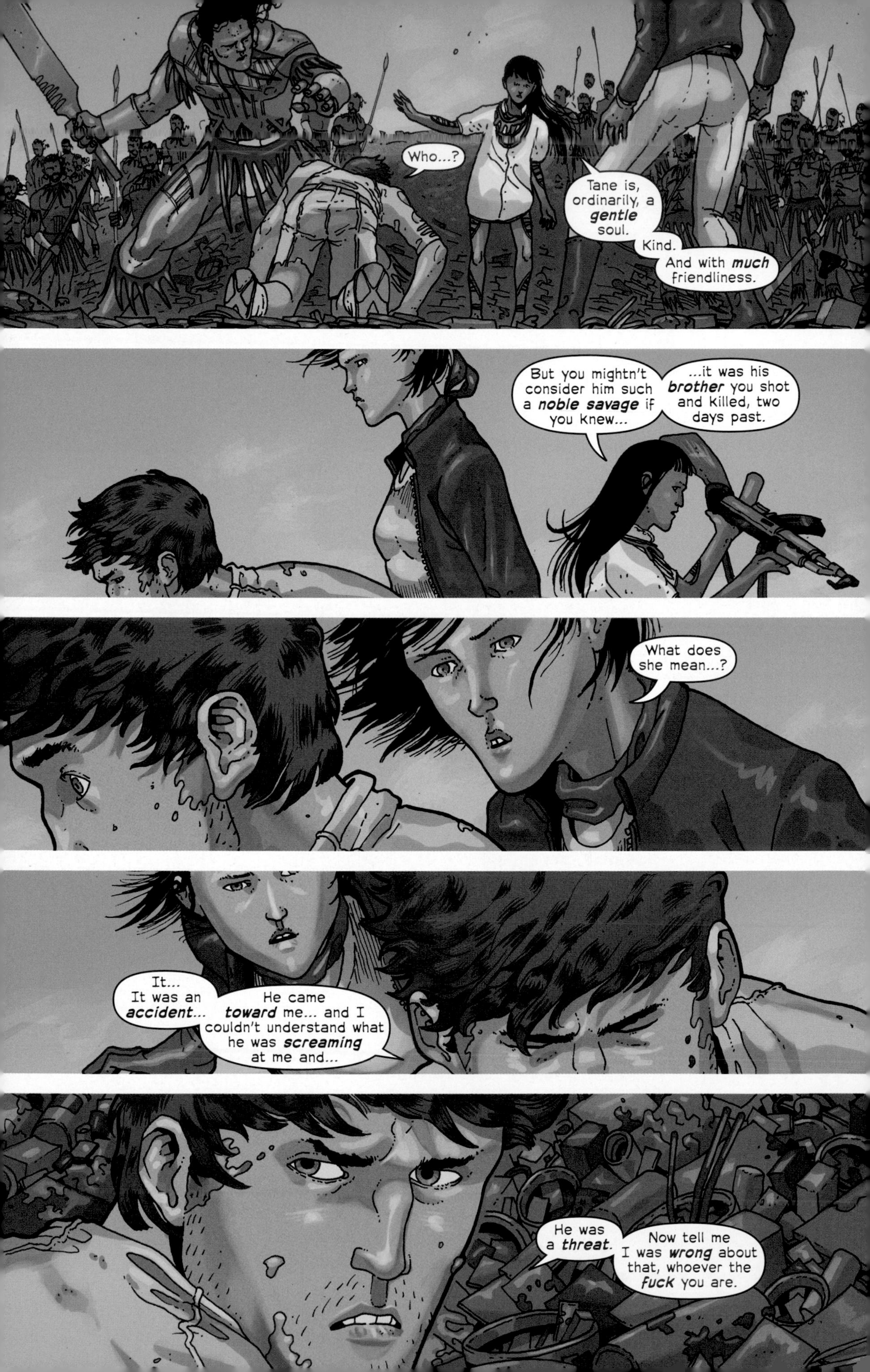

Who...?
Tane is, ordinarily, a *gentle* soul.
Kind.
And with *much* friendliness.
But you mightn't consider him such a *noble savage* if you knew...
...it was his *brother* you shot and killed, two days past.
What does she mean...?
It... It was an *accident*...
He came *toward* me... and I couldn't understand what he was *screaming* at me and...
He was a *threat*.
Now tell me I was *wrong* about that, whoever the *fuck* you are.

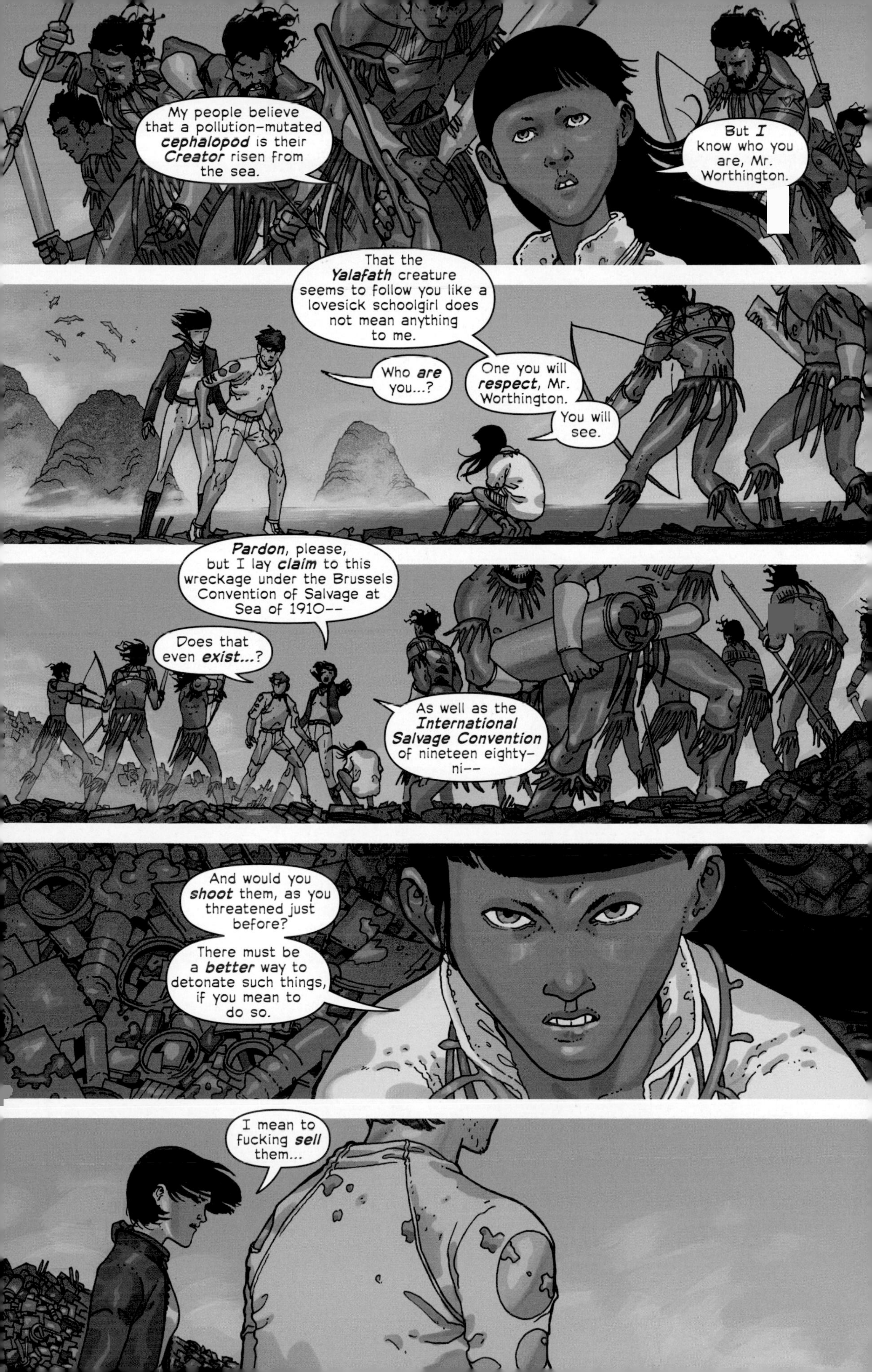
My people believe that a pollution-mutated *cephalopod* is their *Creator* risen from the sea.
But *I* know who you are, Mr. Worthington.
That the *Yalafath* creature seems to follow you like a lovesick schoolgirl does not mean anything to me.
Who *are* you...?
One you will *respect*, Mr. Worthington.
You will see.
Pardon, please, but I lay *claim* to this wreckage under the Brussels Convention of Salvage at Sea of 1910--
Does that even *exist...*?
As well as the *International Salvage Convention* of nineteen eighty-ni--
And would you *shoot* them, as you threatened just before?
There must be a *better* way to detonate such things, if you mean to do so.
I mean to fucking *sell* them...

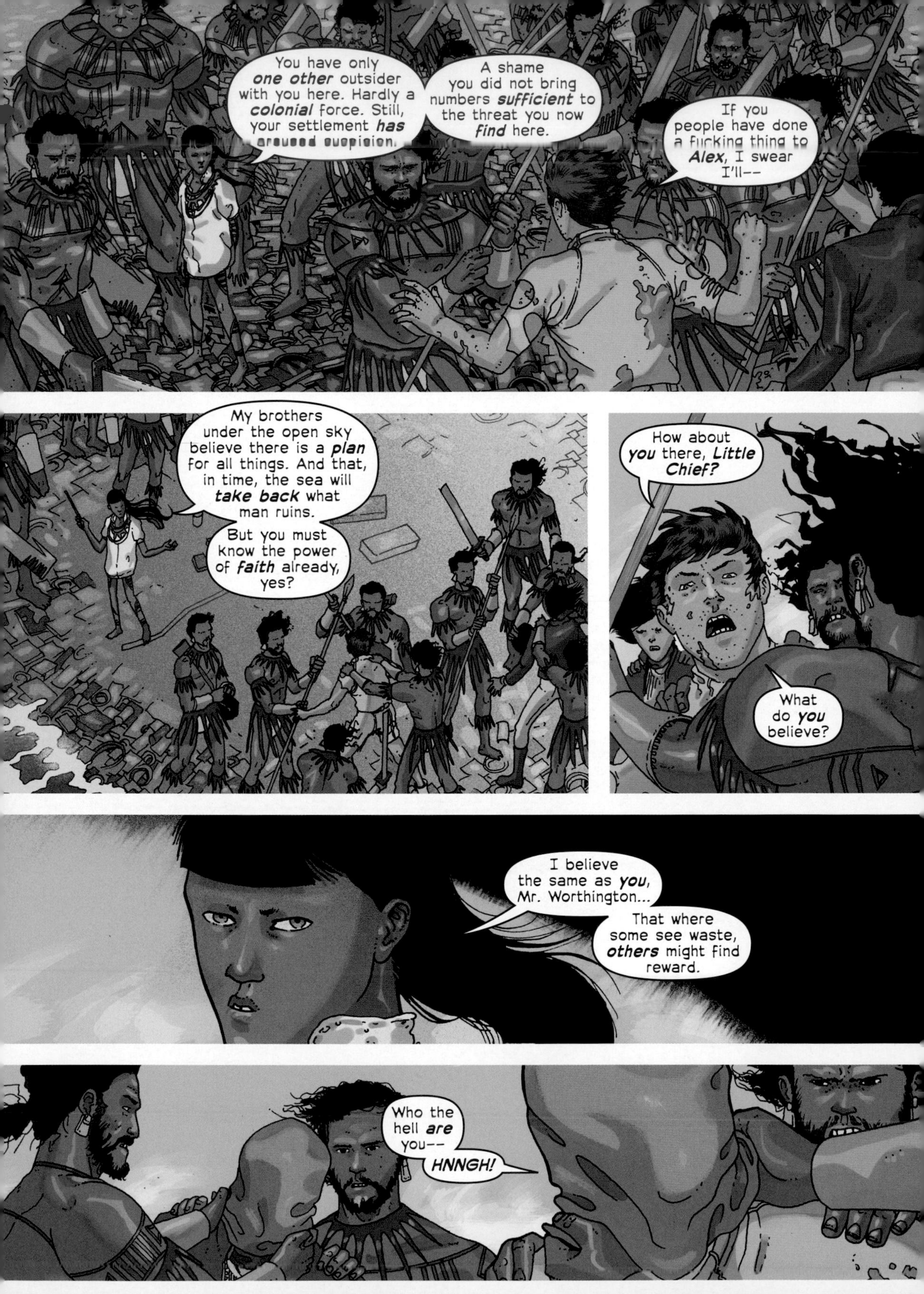
You have only one other outsider with you here. Hardly a colonial force. Still, your settlement has aroused suspicion.
A shame you did not bring numbers sufficient to the threat you now find here.
If you people have done a fucking thing to Alex, I swear I'll--
My brothers under the open sky believe there is a plan for all things. And that, in time, the sea will take back what man ruins.
But you must know the power of faith already, yes?
How about you there, Little Chief?
What do you believe?
I believe the same as you, Mr. Worthington...
That where some see waste, others might find reward.
Who the hell are you--
HNNGH!

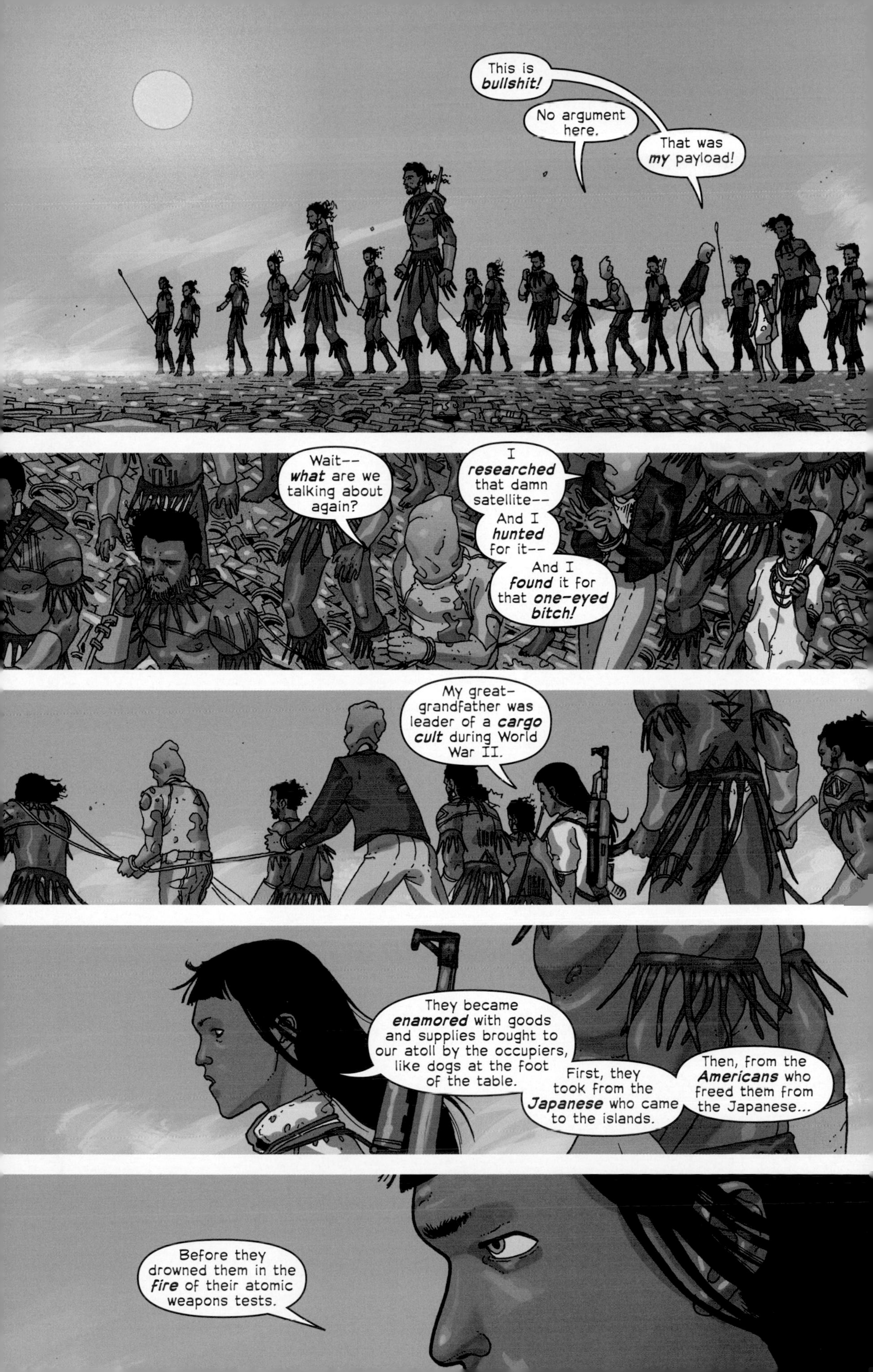
This is bullshit!
No argument here.
That was my payload!
Wait-- what are we talking about again?
I researched that damn satellite--
And I hunted for it--
And I found it for that one-eyed bitch!
My great-grandfather was leader of a cargo cult during World War II.
They became enamored with goods and supplies brought to our atoll by the occupiers, like dogs at the foot of the table.
First, they took from the Japanese who came to the islands.
Then, from the Americans who freed them from the Japanese...
Before they drowned them in the fire of their atomic weapons tests.

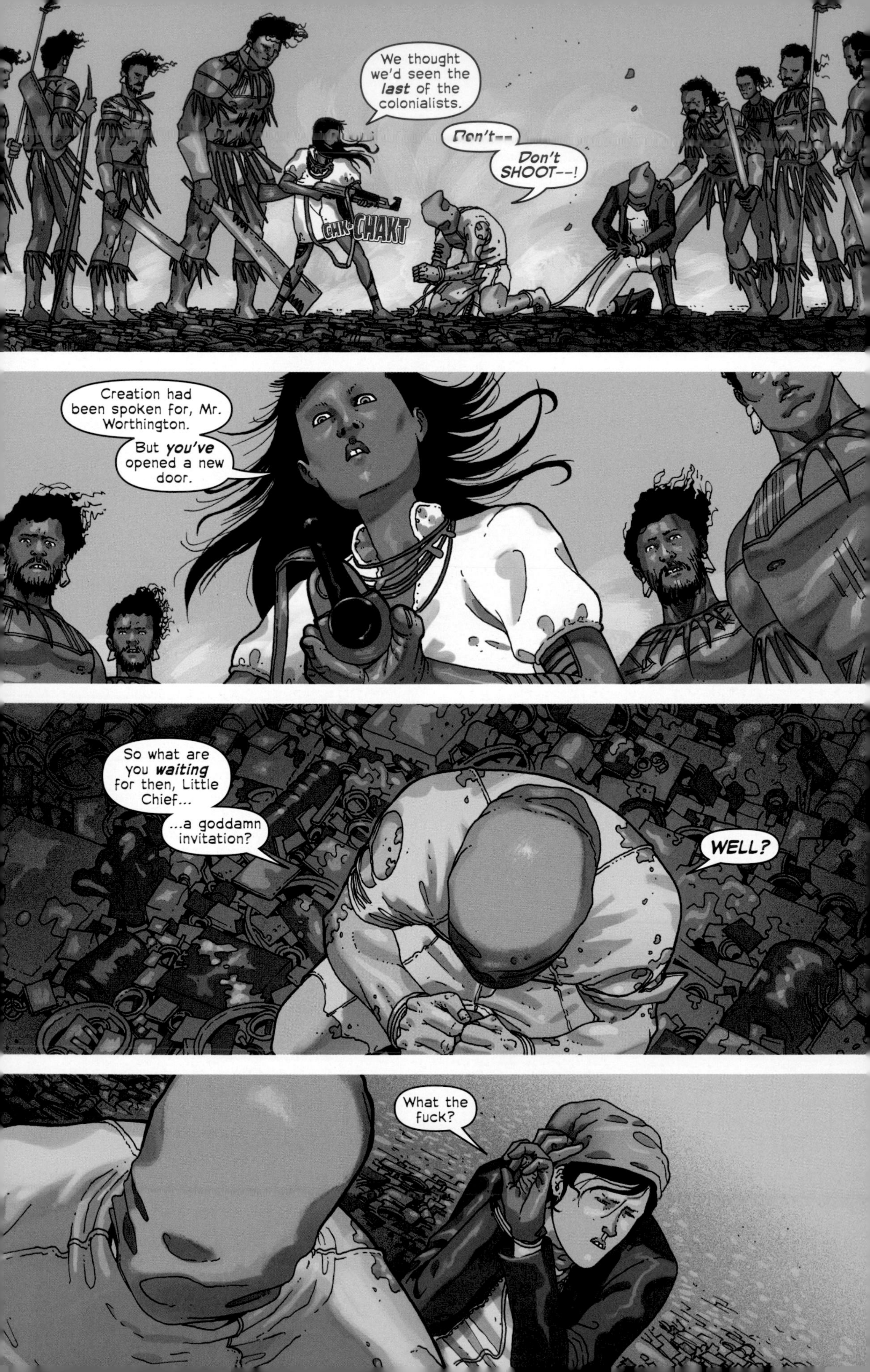
We thought we'd seen the *last* of the colonialists.
Don't--
Don't SHOOT--!
CHK-CHAKT
Creation had been spoken for, Mr. Worthington.
But *you've* opened a new door.
So what are you *waiting* for then, Little Chief...
...a goddamn invitation?
WELL?
What the fuck?

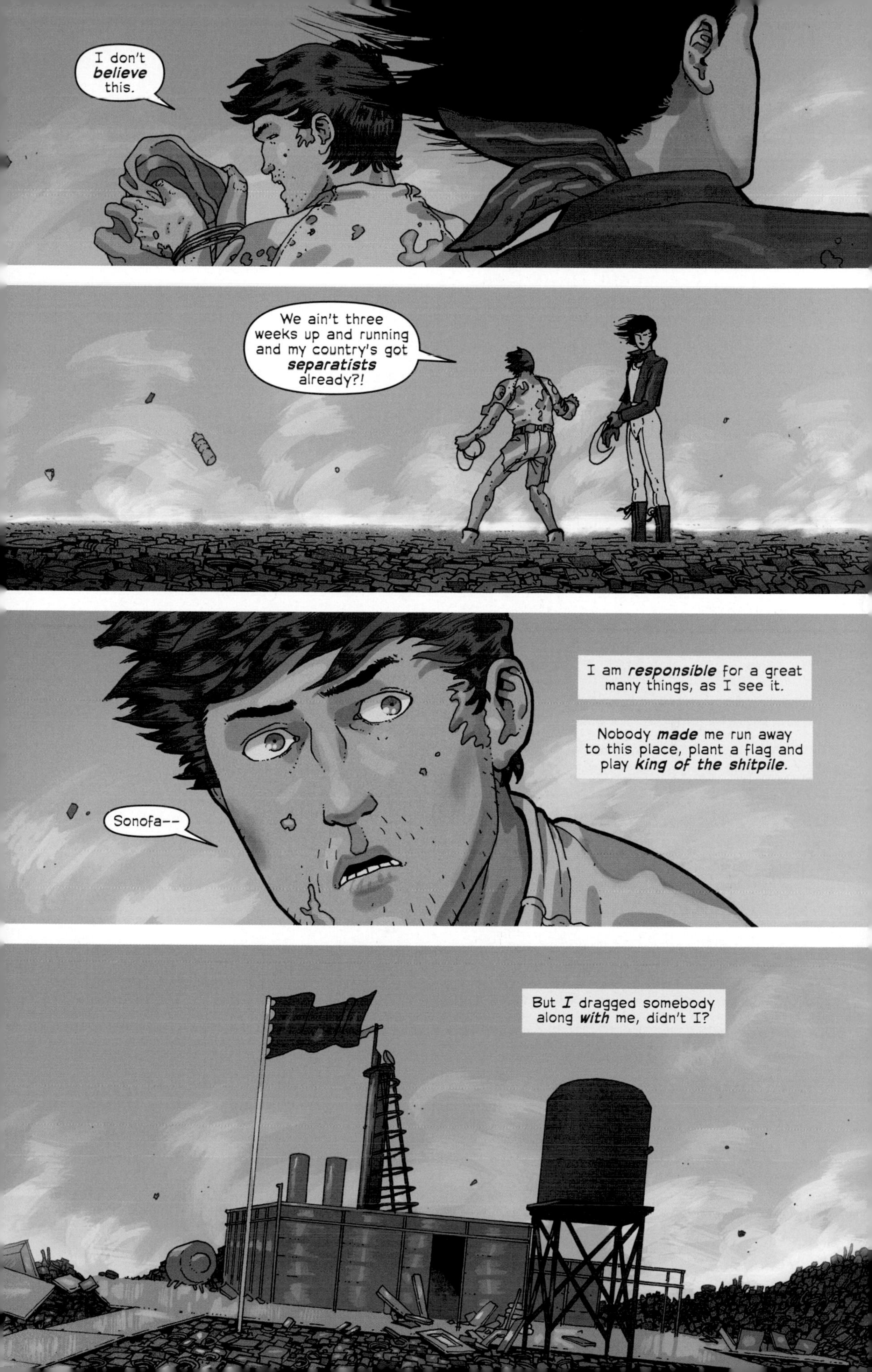
I don't *believe* this.
We ain't three weeks up and running and my country's got *separatists* already?!
I am *responsible* for a great many things, as I see it.
Nobody *made* me run away to this place, plant a flag and play *king of the shitpile*.
Sonofa--
But *I* dragged somebody along *with* me, didn't I?

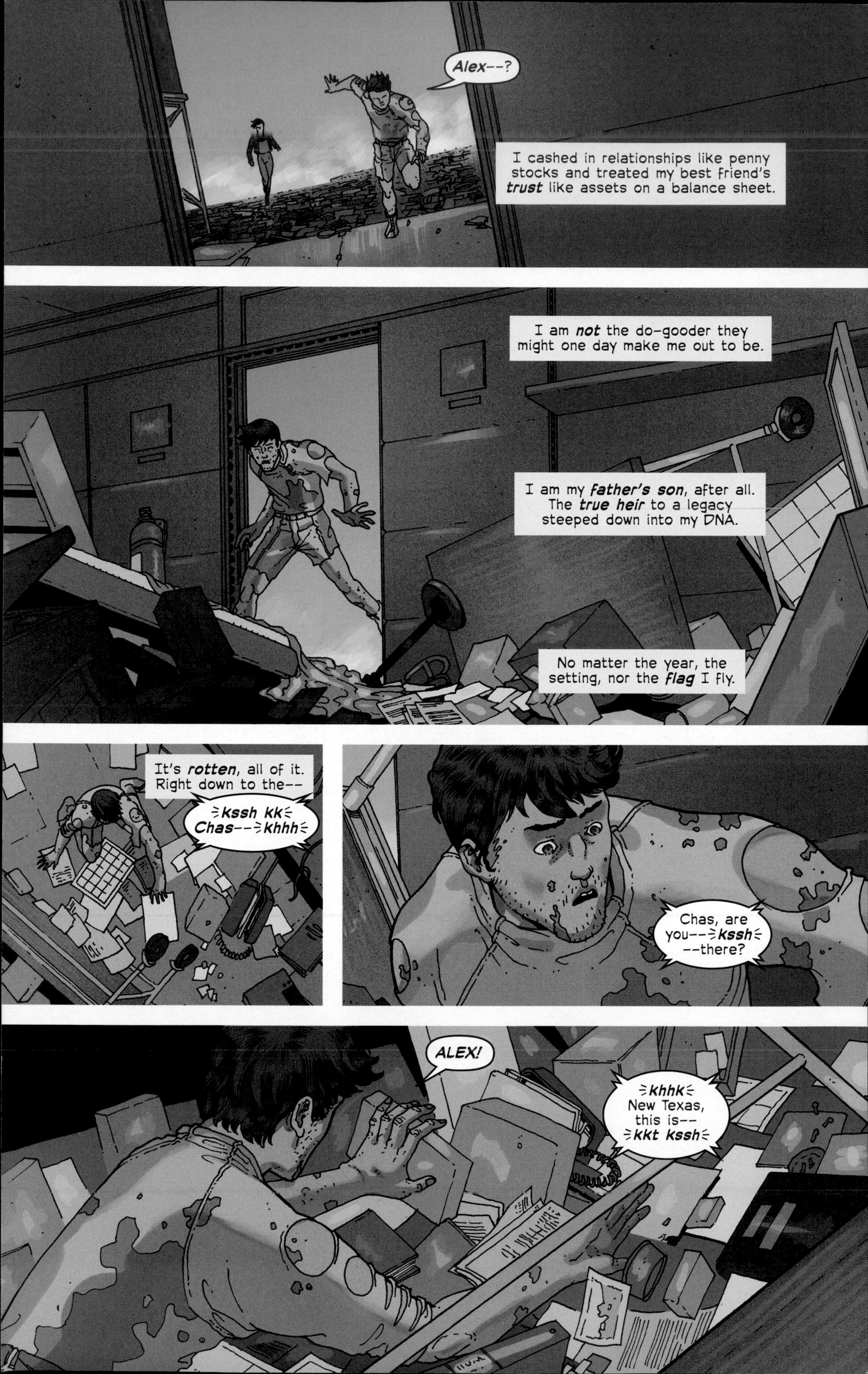
Alex--?
I cashed in relationships like penny stocks and treated my best friend's *trust* like assets on a balance sheet.
I am *not* the do-gooder they might one day make me out to be.
I am my *father's son*, after all. The *true heir* to a legacy steeped down into my DNA.
No matter the year, the setting, nor the *flag* I fly.
It's *rotten*, all of it. Right down to the--
kssh kk Chas-- *khhh*
Chas, are you-- *kssh* --there?
ALEX!
khhk New Texas, this is-- *kkt kssh*

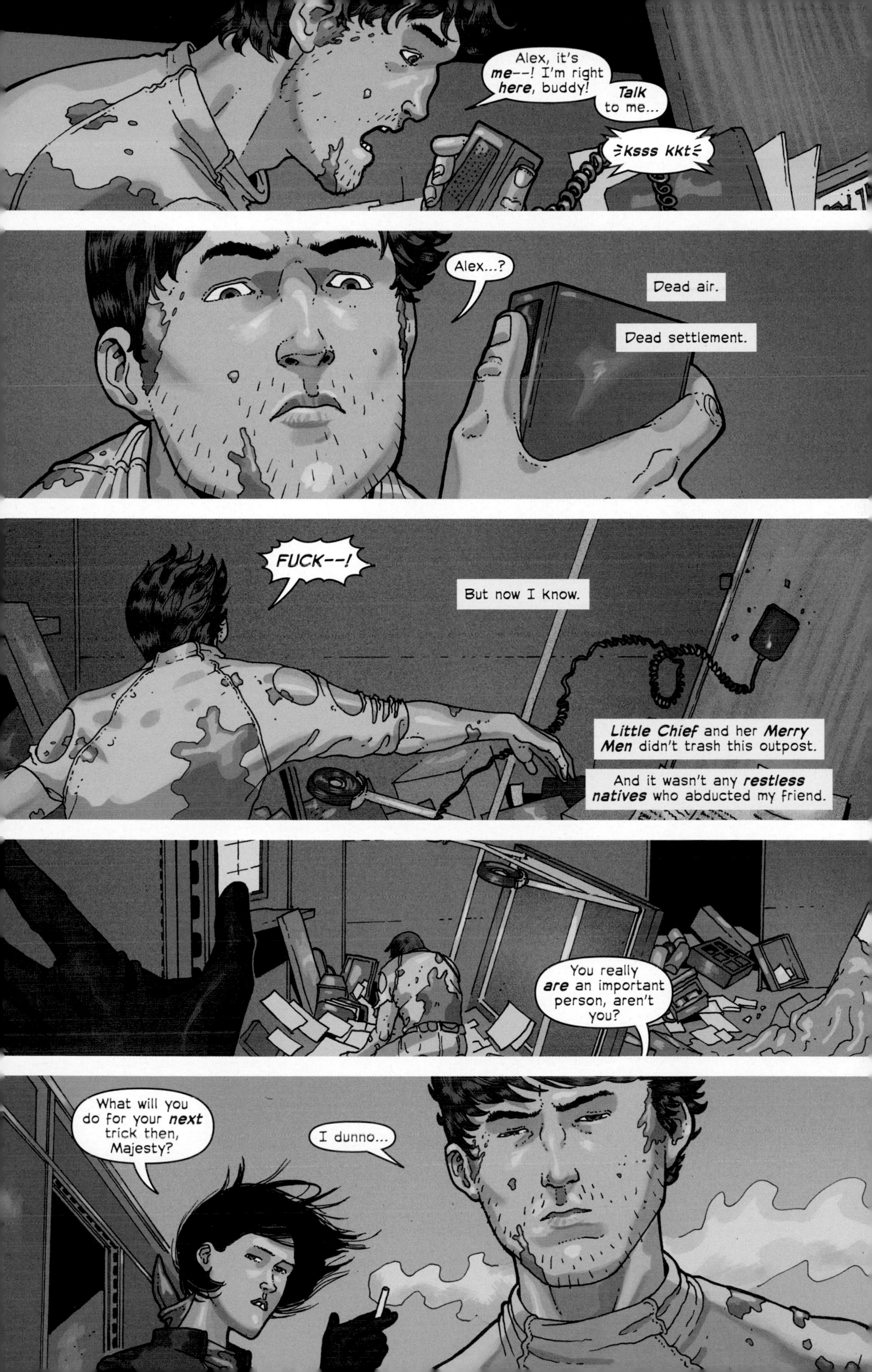
Alex, it's me--! I'm right here, buddy!
Talk to me...
ksss kkt
Alex...?
Dead air.
Dead settlement.
FUCK--!
But now I know.
Little Chief and her Merry Men didn't trash this outpost.
And it wasn't any restless natives who abducted my friend.
You really are an important person, aren't you?
What will you do for your next trick then, Majesty?
I dunno...

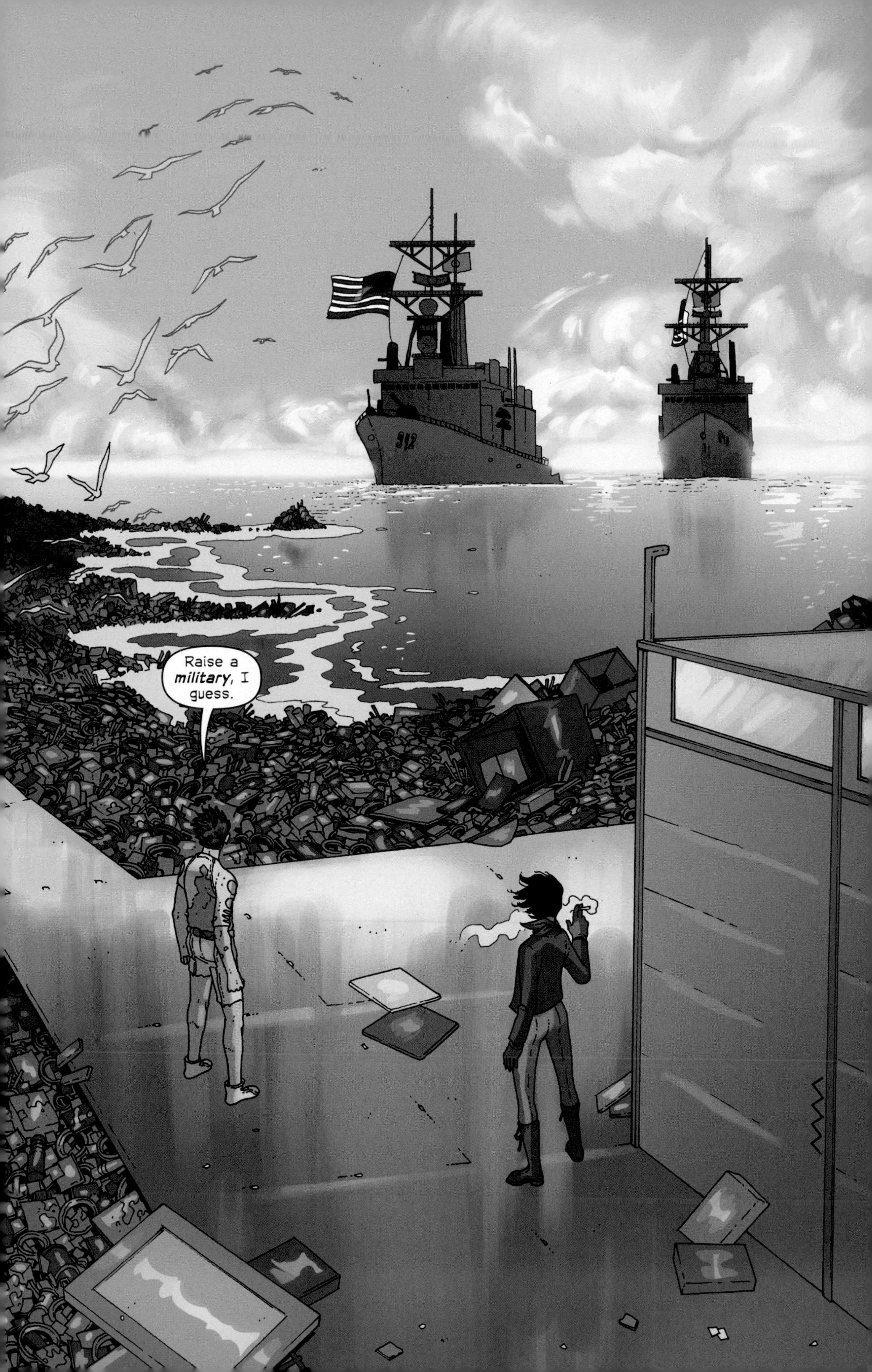
Raise a military, I guess.

CHAPTER**SIX**

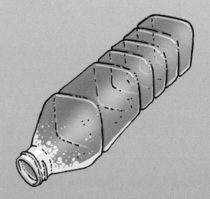

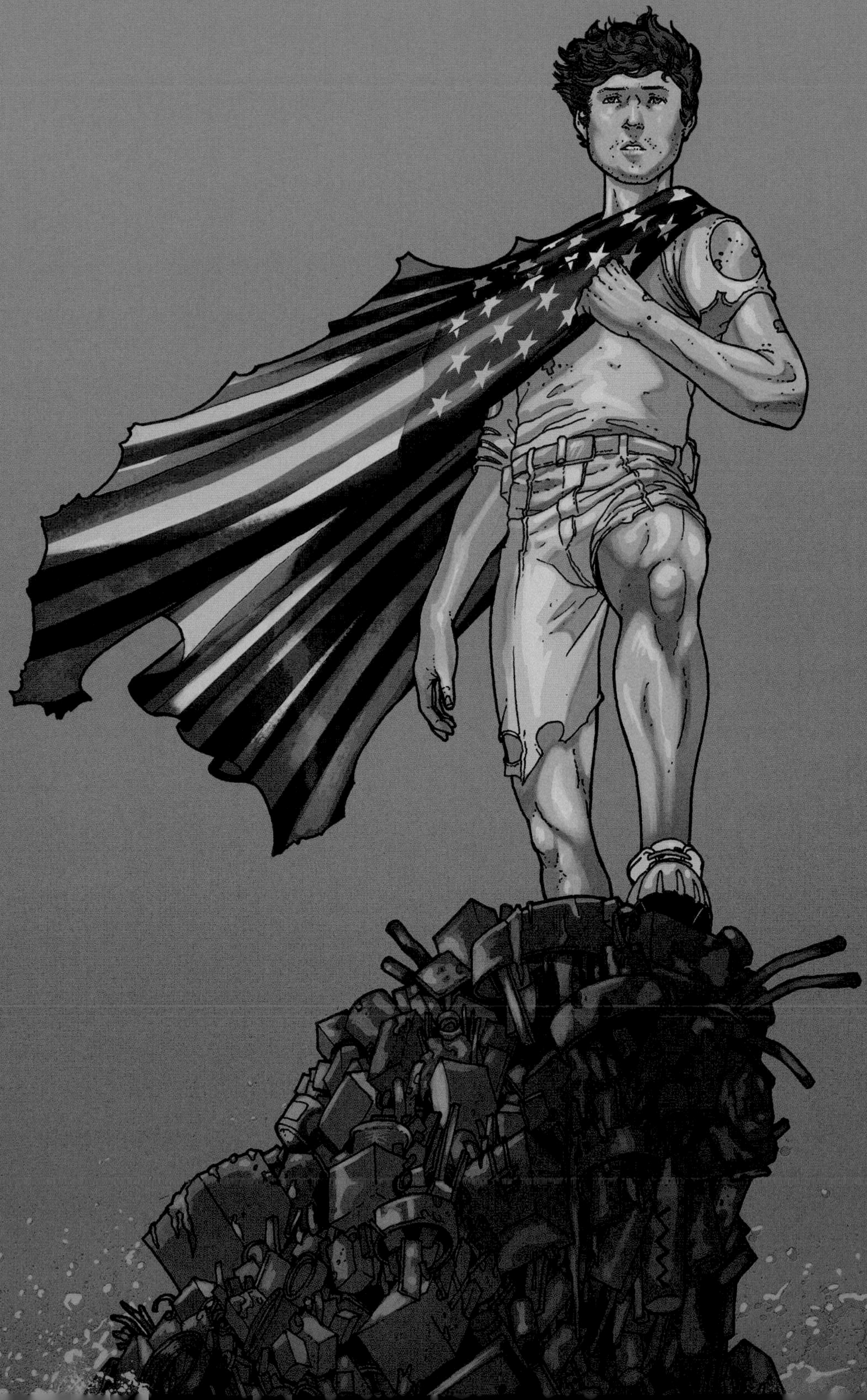

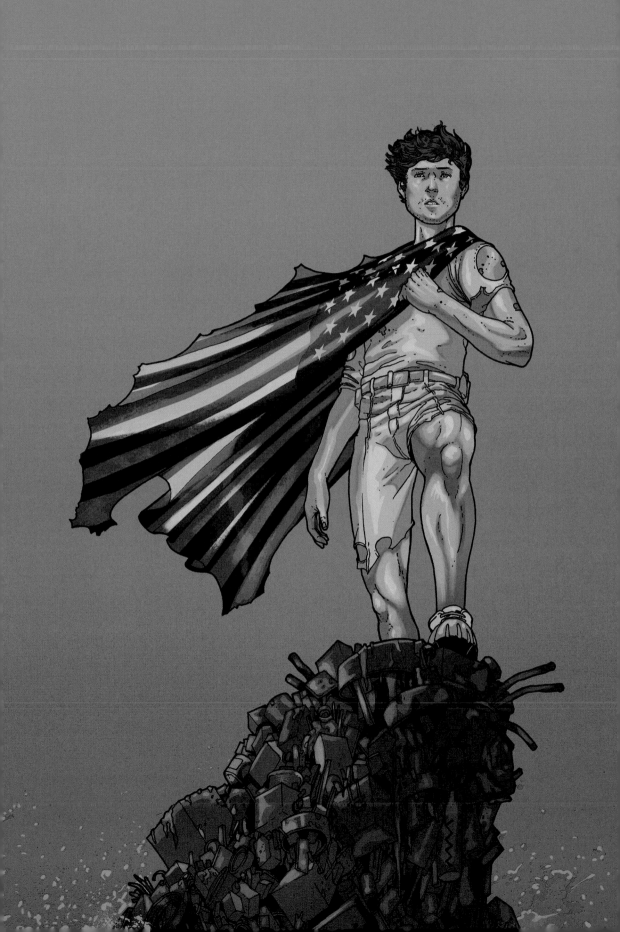

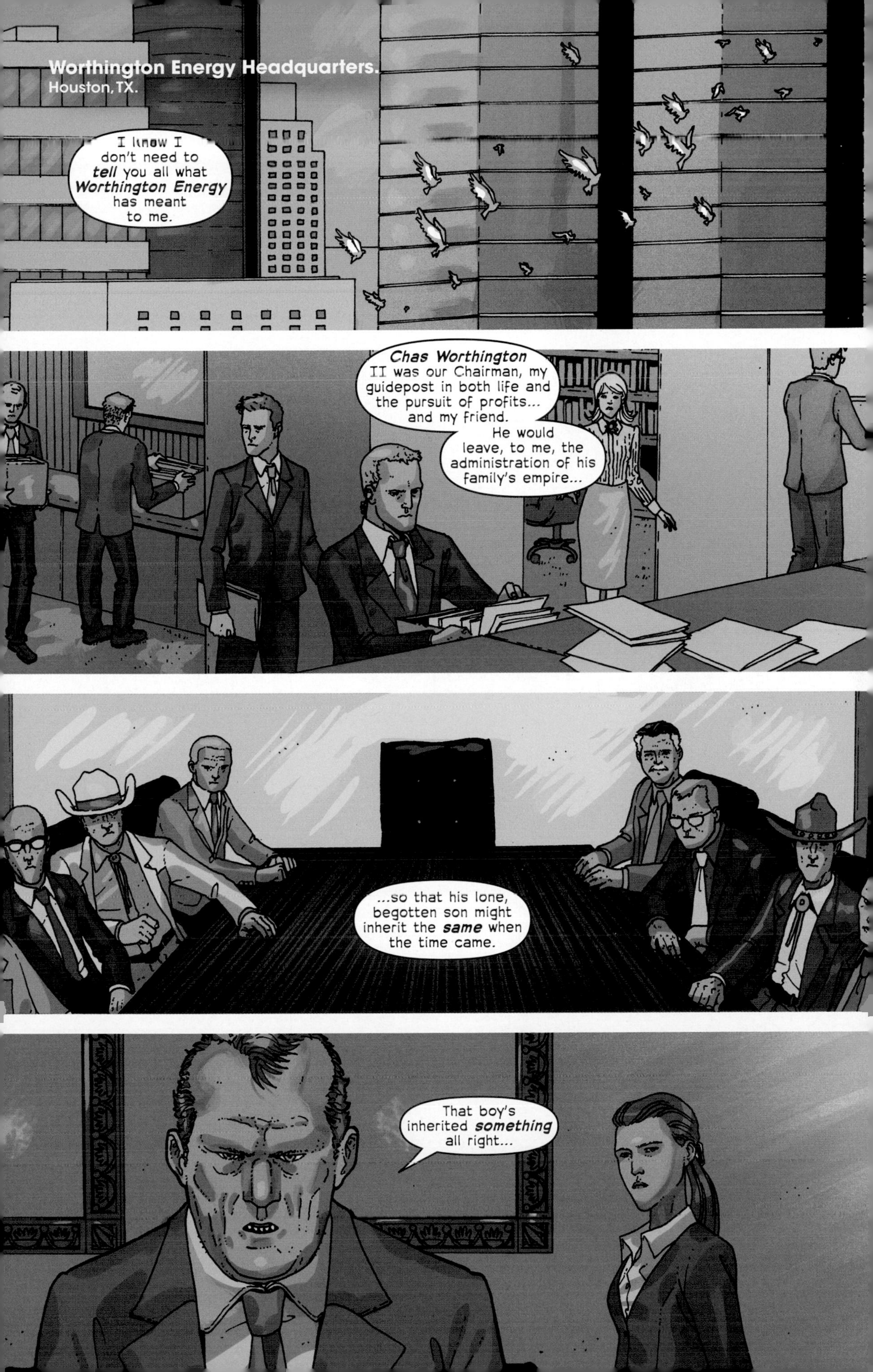

Worthington Energy Headquarters.
Houston, TX.
I know I don't need to *tell* you all what *Worthington Energy* has meant to me.
Chas Worthington II was our Chairman, my guidepost in both life and the pursuit of profits... and my friend.
He would leave, to me, the administration of his family's empire...
...so that his lone, begotten son might inherit the *same* when the time came.
That boy's inherited *something* all right...

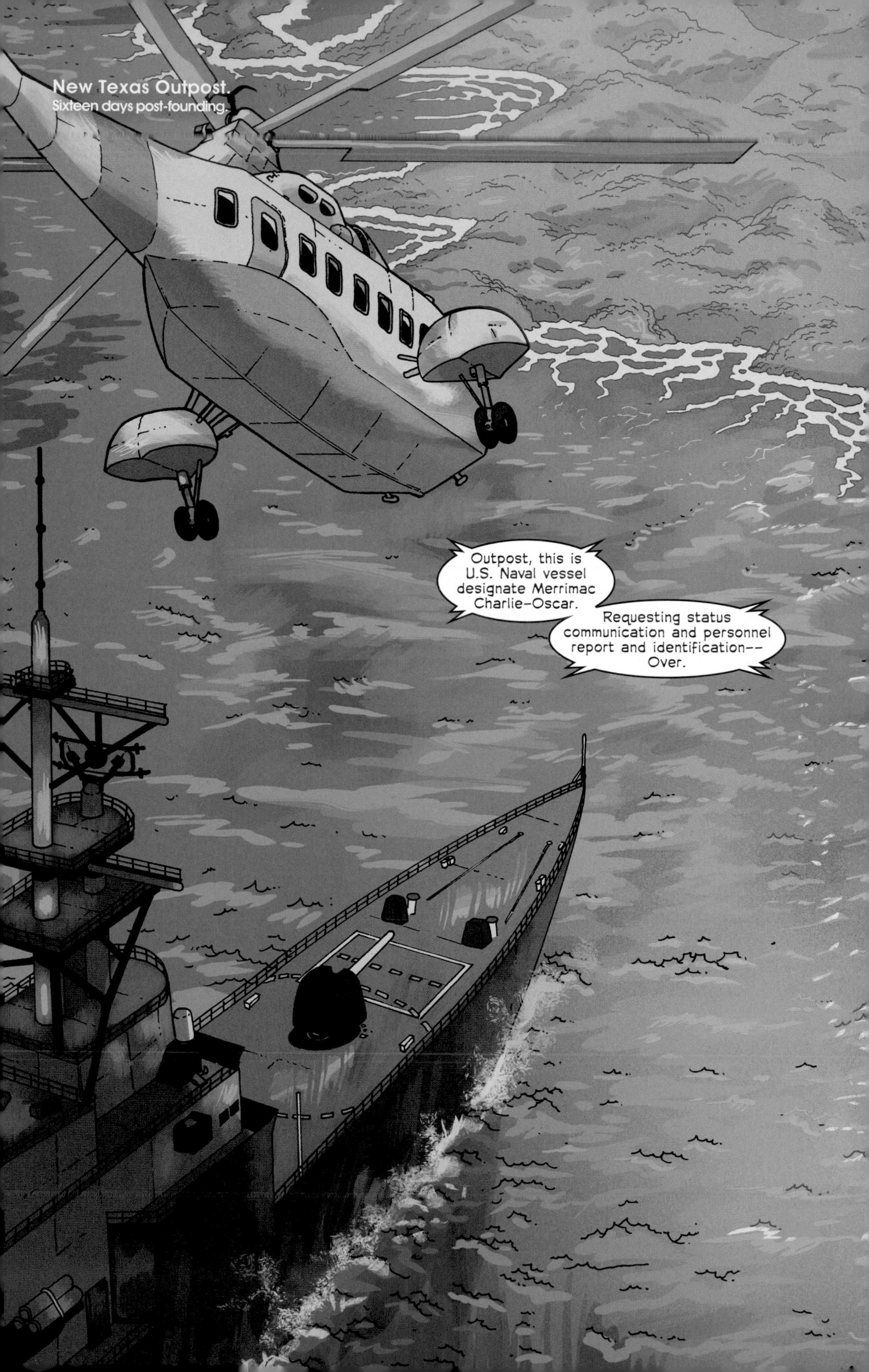
New Texas Outpost.
Sixteen days post-founding.
Outpost, this is U.S. Naval vessel designate Merrimac Charlie-Oscar.
Requesting status communication and personnel report and identification-- Over.

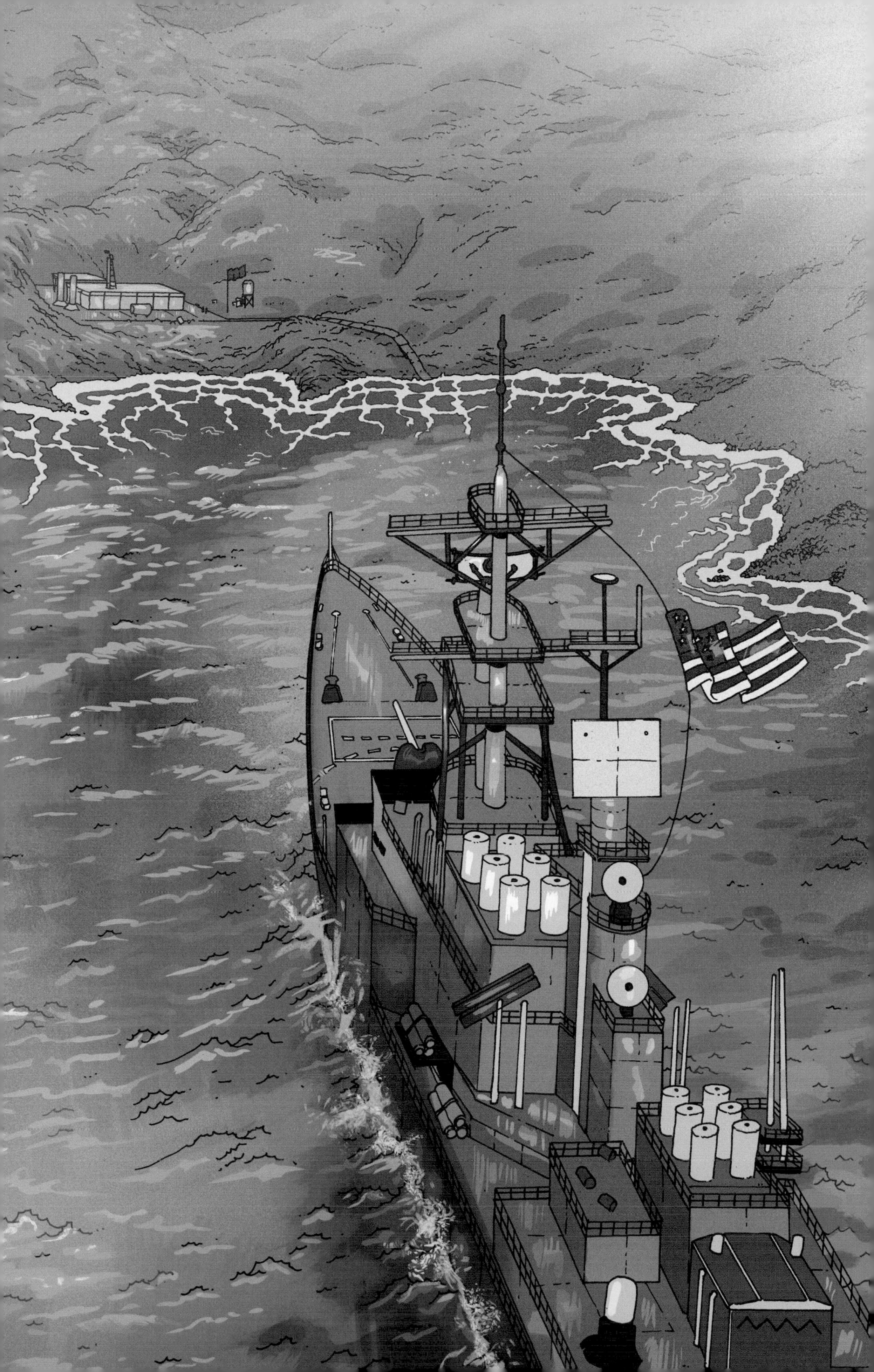

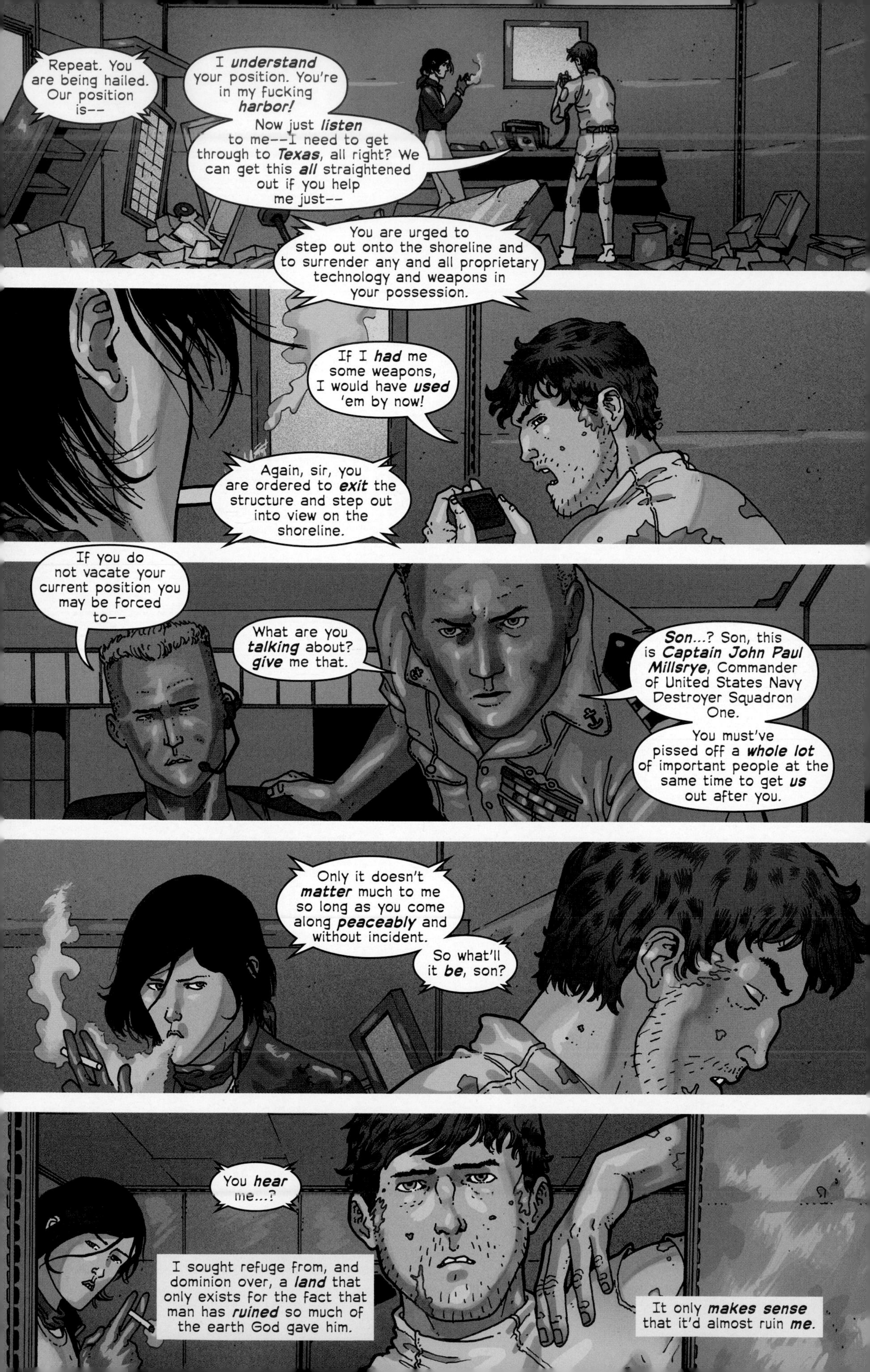
Repeat. You are being hailed. Our position is--
I understand your position. You're in my fucking harbor!
Now just listen to me--I need to get through to Texas, all right? We can get this all straightened out if you help me just--
You are urged to step out onto the shoreline and to surrender any and all proprietary technology and weapons in your possession.
If I had me some weapons, I would have used 'em by now!
Again, sir, you are ordered to exit the structure and step out into view on the shoreline.
If you do not vacate your current position you may be forced to--
What are you talking about? give me that.
Son...? Son, this is Captain John Paul Millsrye, Commander of United States Navy Destroyer Squadron One.
You must've pissed off a whole lot of important people at the same time to get us out after you.
Only it doesn't matter much to me so long as you come along peaceably and without incident.
So what'll it be, son?
You hear me...?
I sought refuge from, and dominion over, a land that only exists for the fact that man has ruined so much of the earth God gave him.
It only makes sense that it'd almost ruin me.

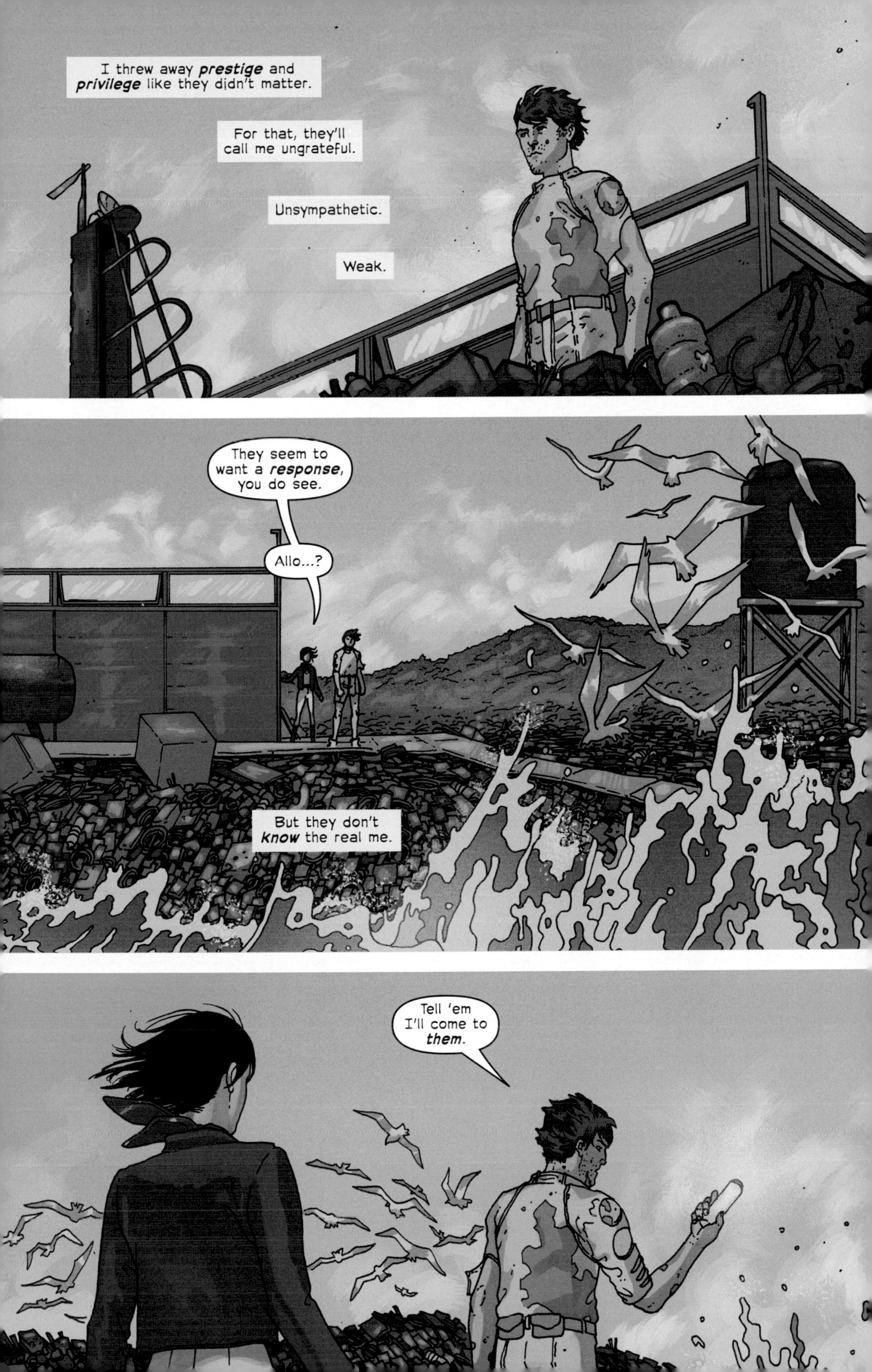

I threw away *prestige* and *privilege* like they didn't matter.
For that, they'll call me ungrateful.
Unsympathetic.
Weak.
They seem to want a *response*, you do see.
Allo...?
But they don't *know* the real me.
Tell 'em I'll come to *them*.

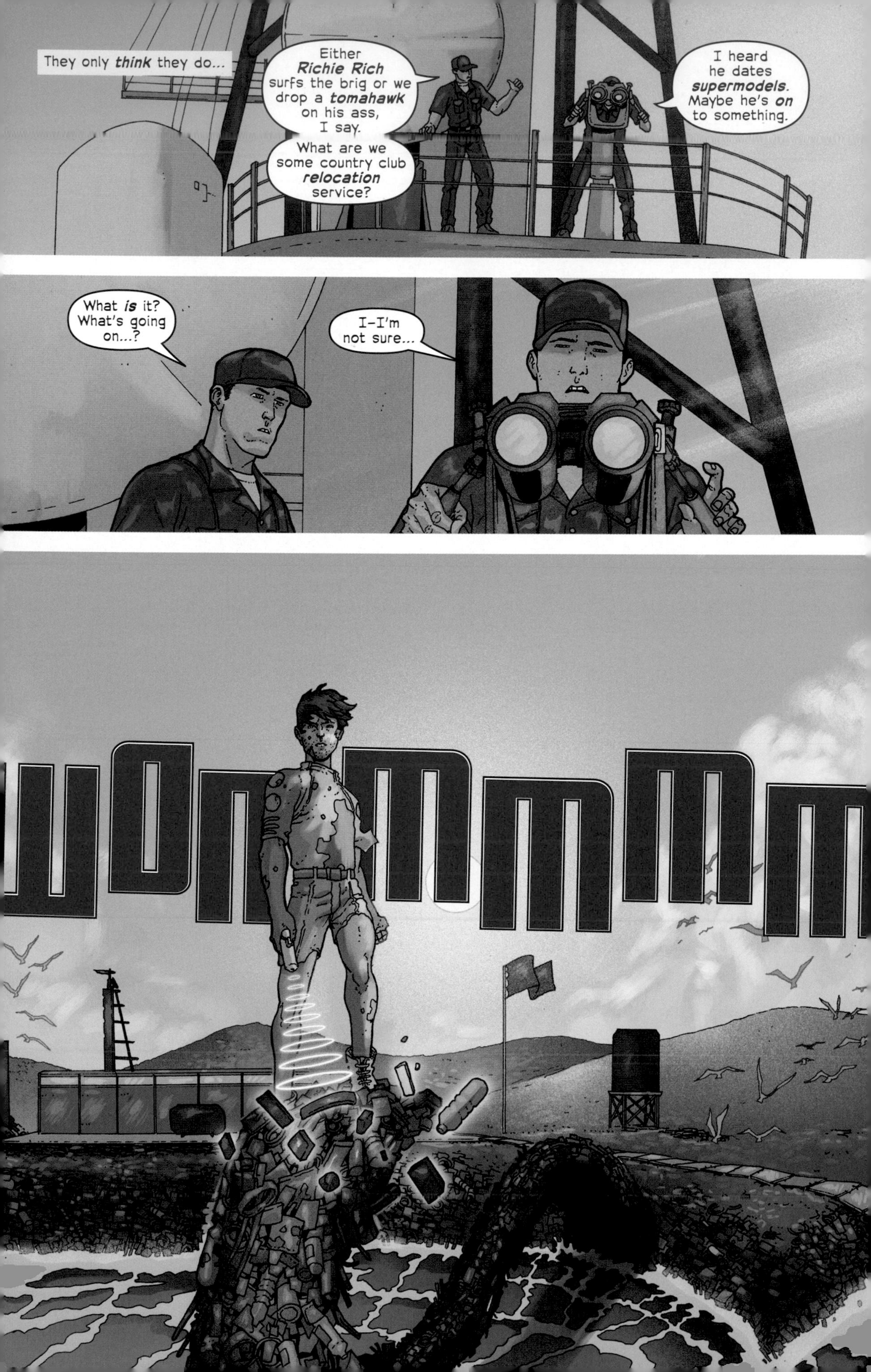
They only *think* they do...
Either *Richie Rich* surfs the brig or we drop a *tomahawk* on his ass, I say.
What are we some country club *relocation* service?
I heard he dates *supermodels*. Maybe he's *on* to something.
What *is* it? What's going on...?
I-I'm not sure...
WOMMMMM

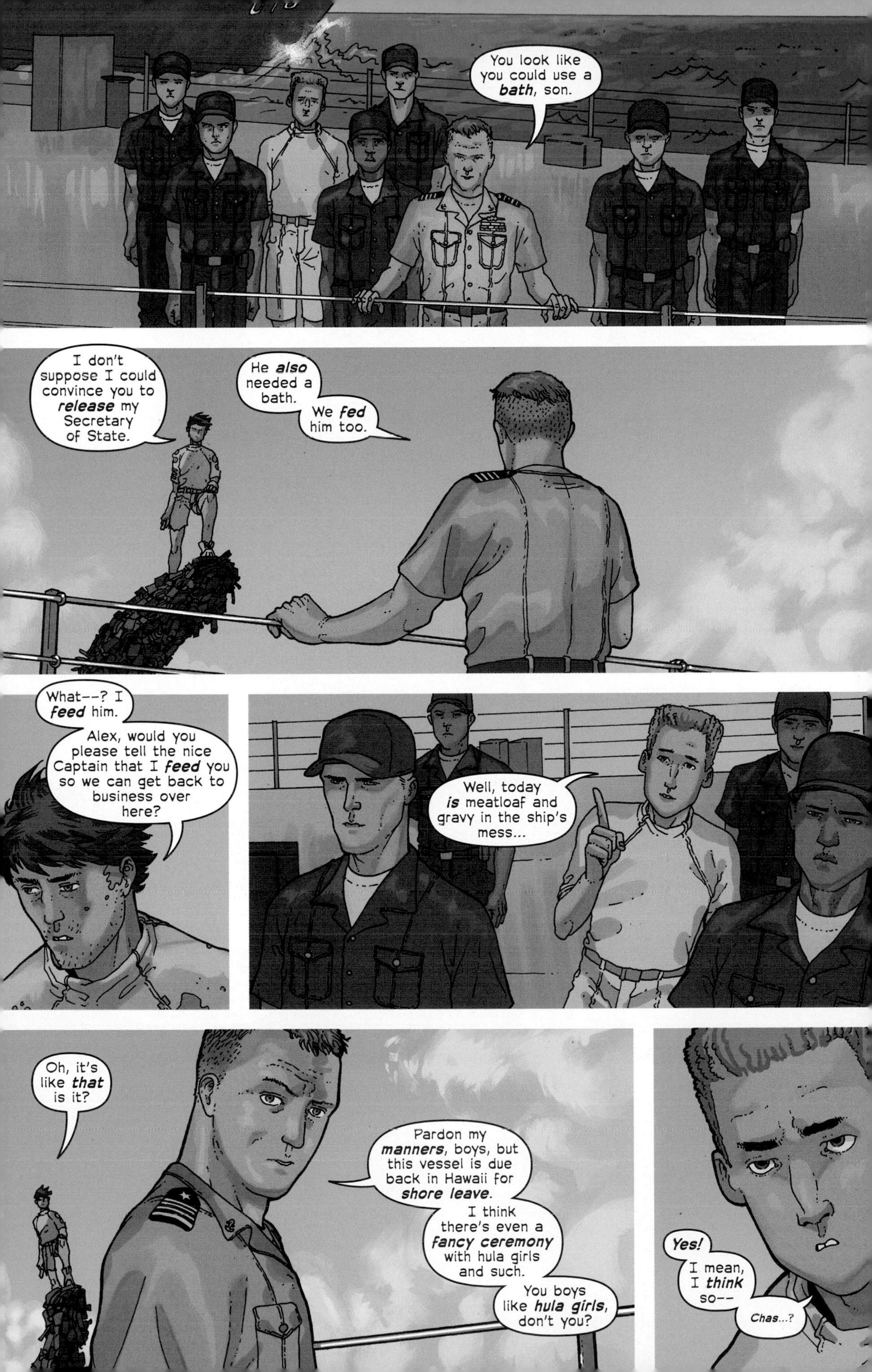

You look like you could use a *bath*, son.
I don't suppose I could convince you to *release* my Secretary of State.
He *also* needed a bath.
We *fed* him too.
What--? I *feed* him.
Alex, would you please tell the nice Captain that I *feed* you so we can get back to business over here?
Well, today *is* meatloaf and gravy in the ship's mess...
Oh, it's like *that* is it?
Pardon my *manners*, boys, but this vessel is due back in Hawaii for *shore leave*.
I think there's even a *fancy ceremony* with hula girls and such.
You boys like *hula girls*, don't you?
Yes!
I mean, I *think* so--
Chas...?

Drop your weapon!

Do it Now!

You people have *no idea* what you're dealing with, right now.

Now, now... there's no need for *hostilities*.

I'm sure *young Master Worthington* only means to *surrender* that piece of stolen proprietary technology so that we all might *push off* for home.

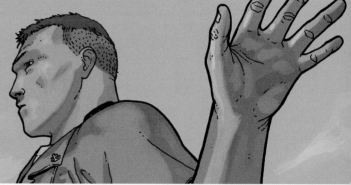

Alex, you remember that *swimming hole* used to fill up whenever we finally got some summer rain? You'd never hold your *nose* right.

You'd almost *drown* yourself with a demented kinda *panic snuffle* when we'd jump in.

Um, *why...?*

We have sailed a ways to *find* you, Chas Worthington, and if you'd prefer to avoid giving me one *damn good* reason to storm that garbage beach you've pissed a claim on...

...we'll welcome you *aboard* and be on our way.

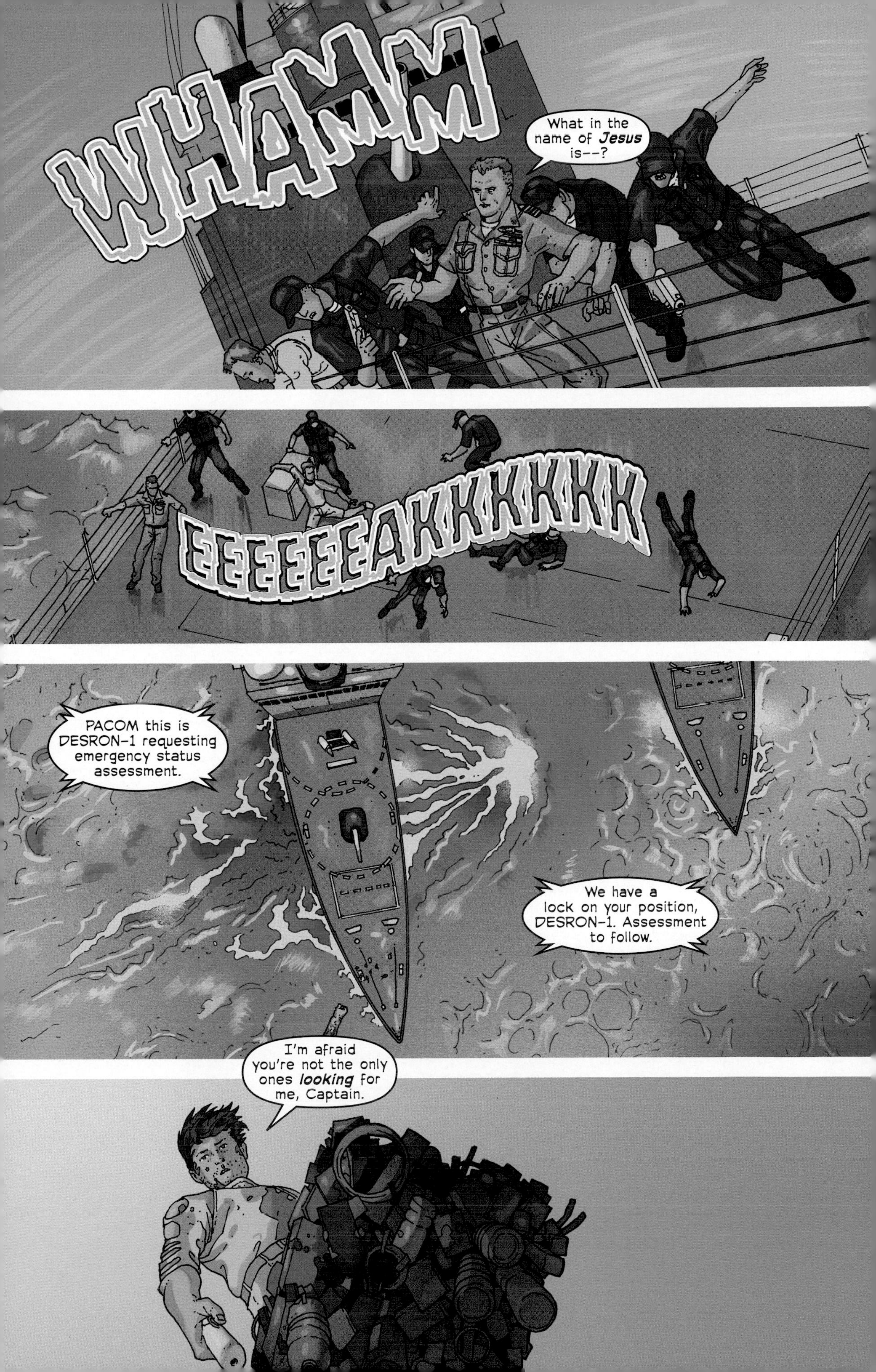
WHAMM
What in the name of *Jesus* is--?
EEEEEEAKKKKKKKK
PACOM this is DESRON-1 requesting emergency status assessment.
We have a lock on your position, DESRON-1. Assessment to follow.
I'm afraid you're not the only ones *looking* for me, Captain.

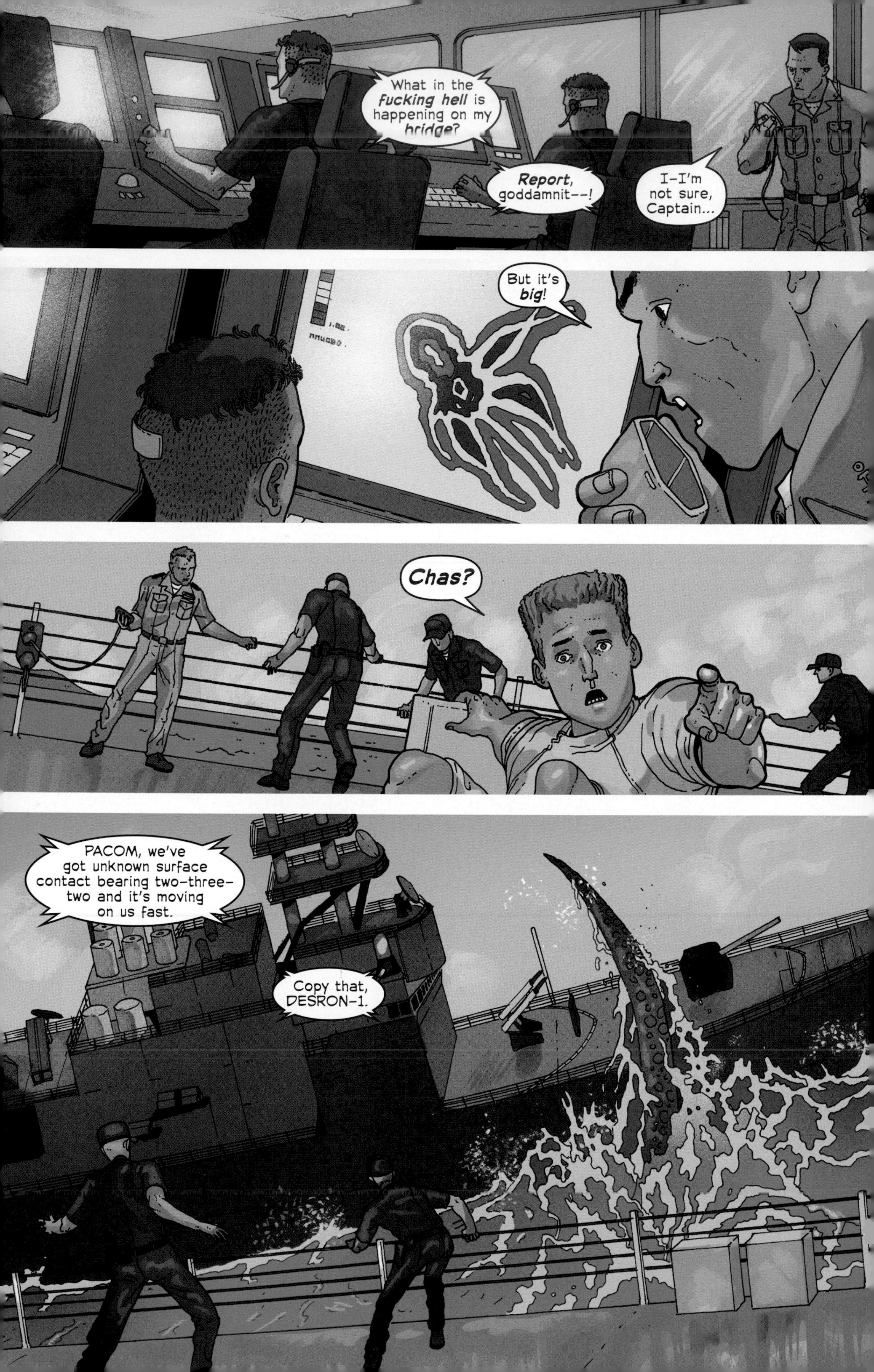
What in the *fucking hell* is happening on my *bridge*?
Report, goddamnit--!
I-I'm not sure, Captain...
But it's *big*!
Chas?
PACOM, we've got unknown surface contact bearing two-three-two and it's moving on us fast.
Copy that, DESRON-1.

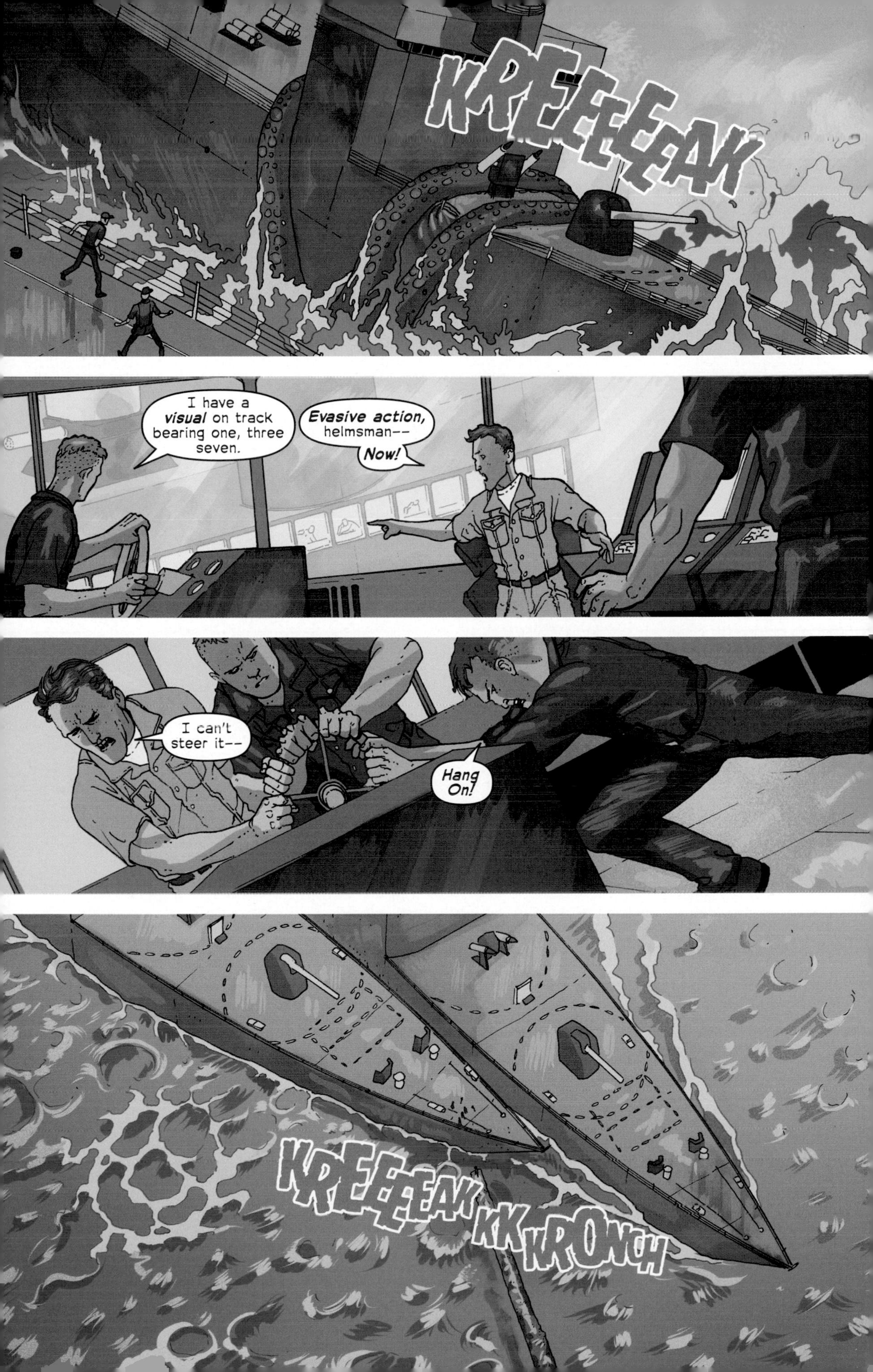
KREEEEEAK
I have a *visual* on track bearing one, three seven.
Evasive action, helmsman--
Now!
I can't steer it--
Hang On!
KREEEEEAK KK KRONCH

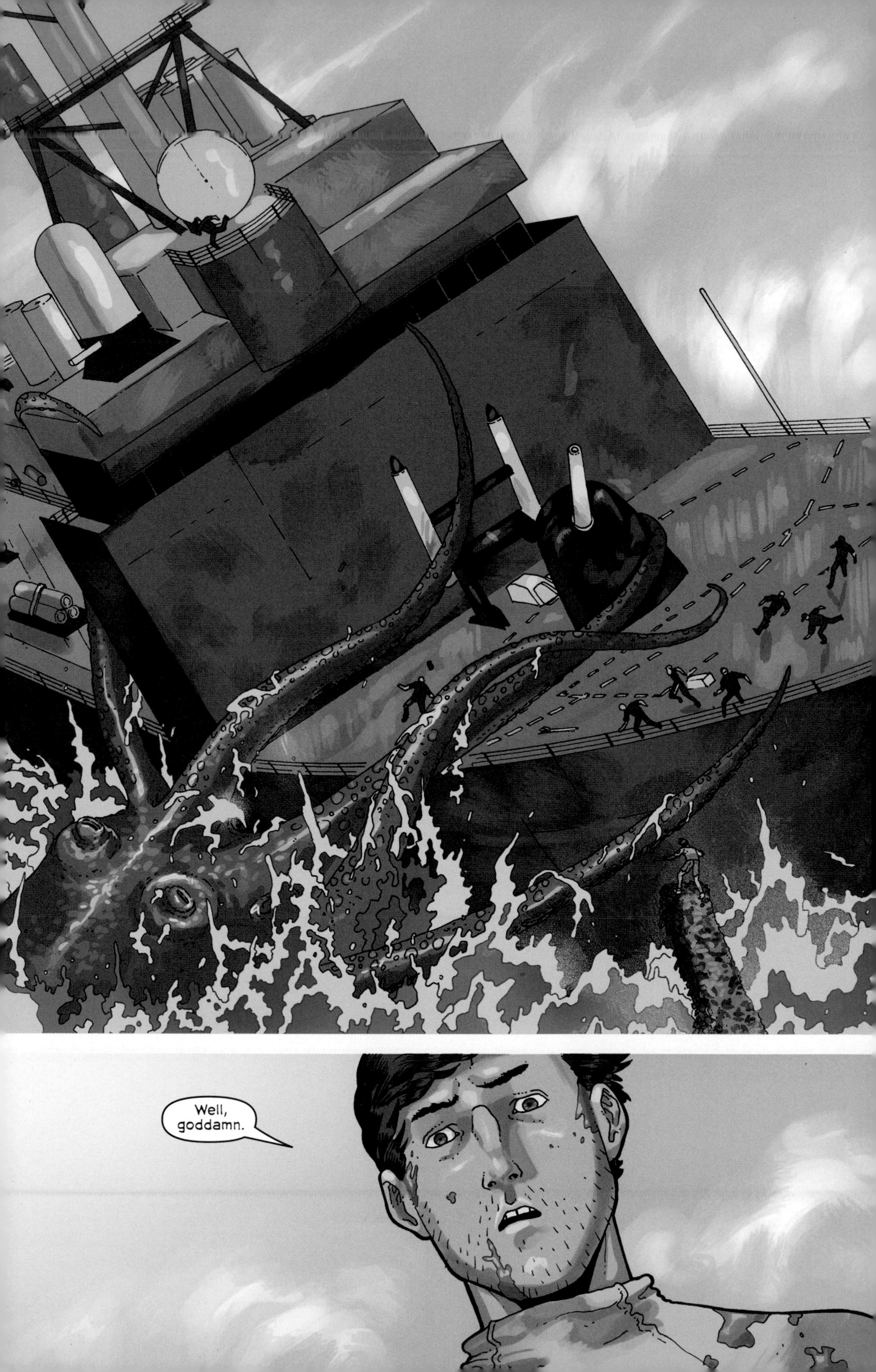
Well, goddamn.

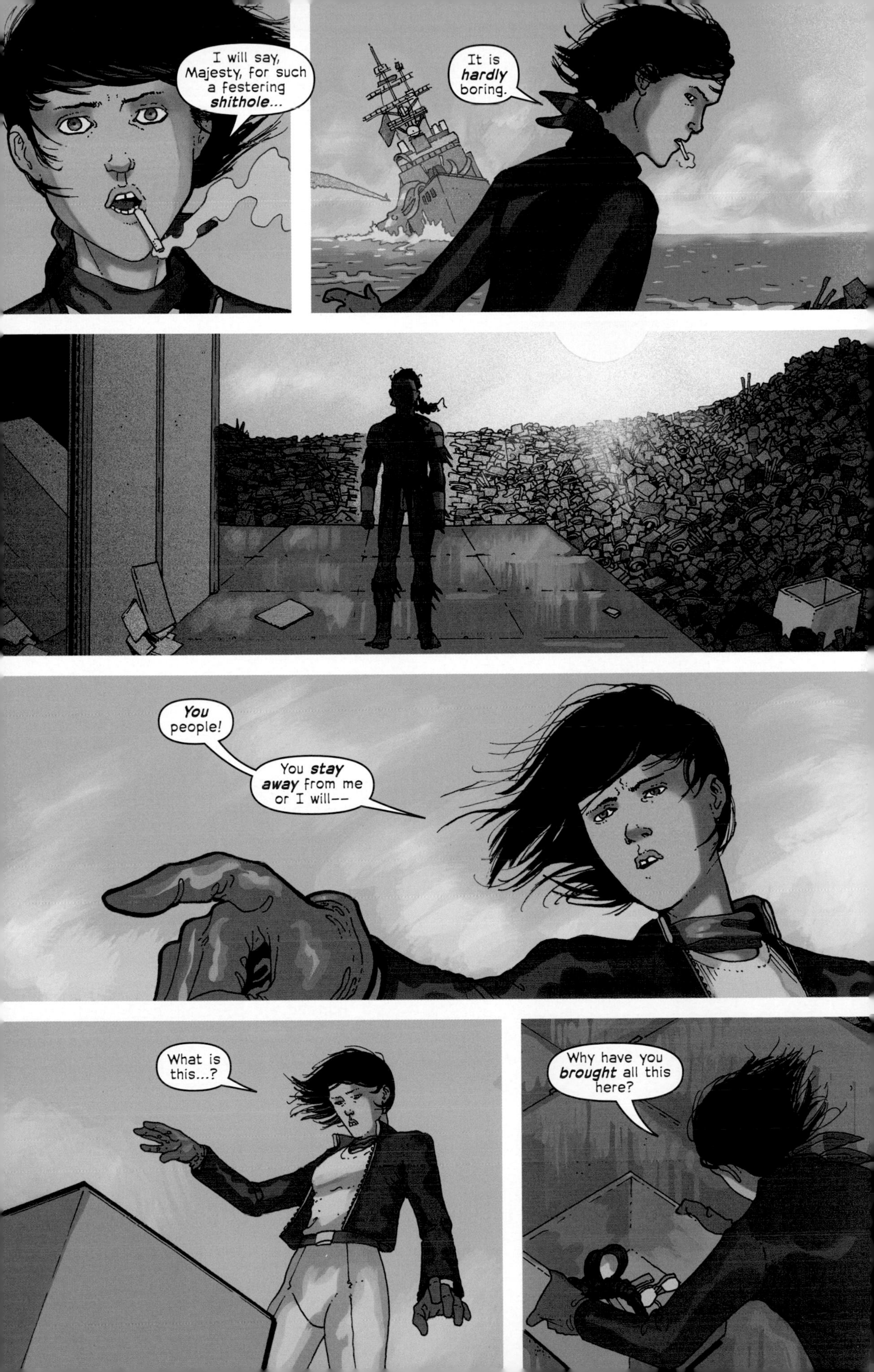

I will say, Majesty, for such a festering ***shithole...***
It is ***hardly*** boring.
You people!
You ***stay away*** from me or I will--
What is this...?
Why have you ***brought*** all this here?

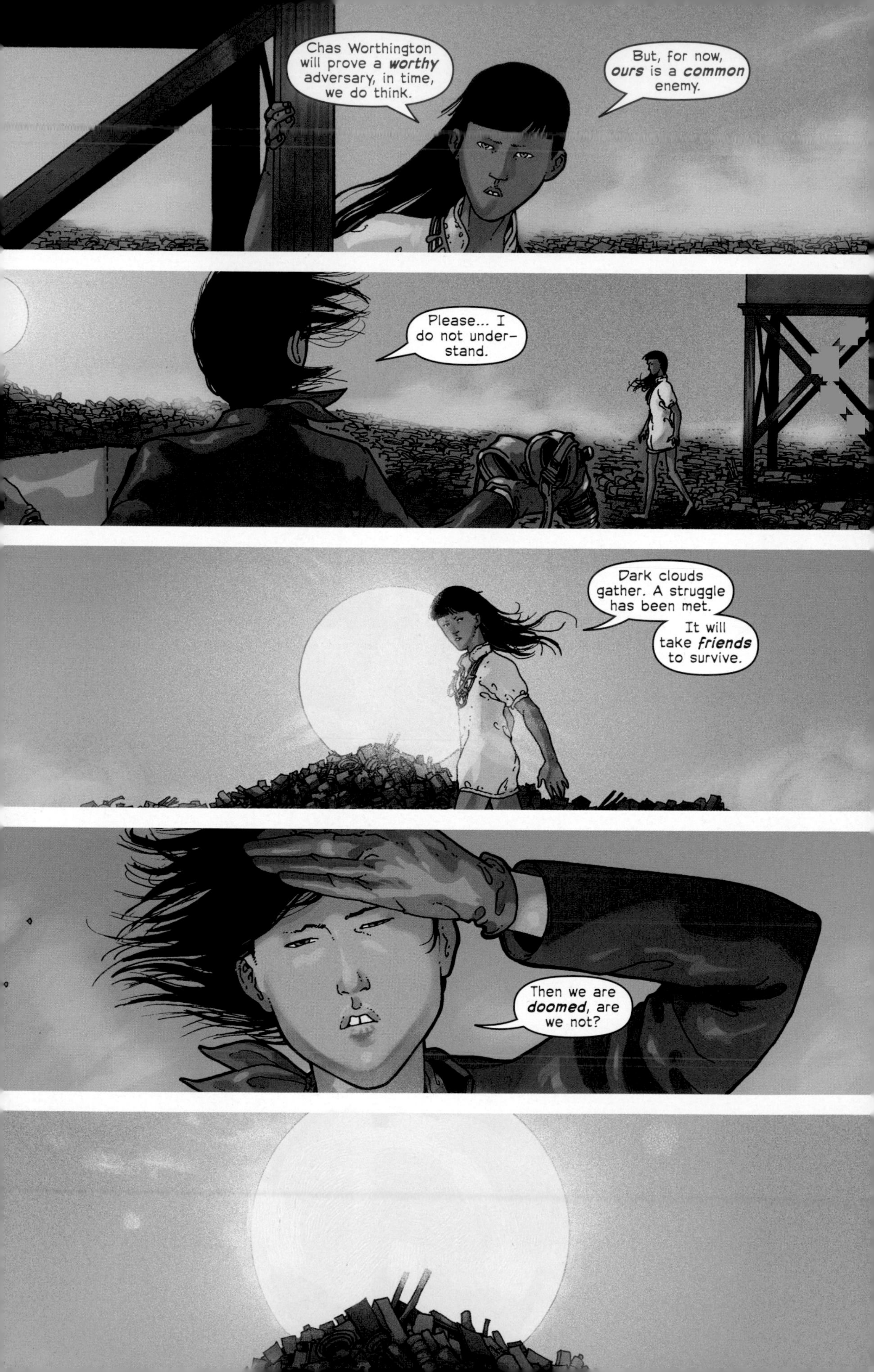
Chas Worthington will prove a *worthy* adversary, in time, we do think.
But, for now, *ours* is a *common* enemy.
Please... I do not under-stand.
Dark clouds gather. A struggle has been met.
It will take *friends* to survive.
Then we are *doomed*, are we not?

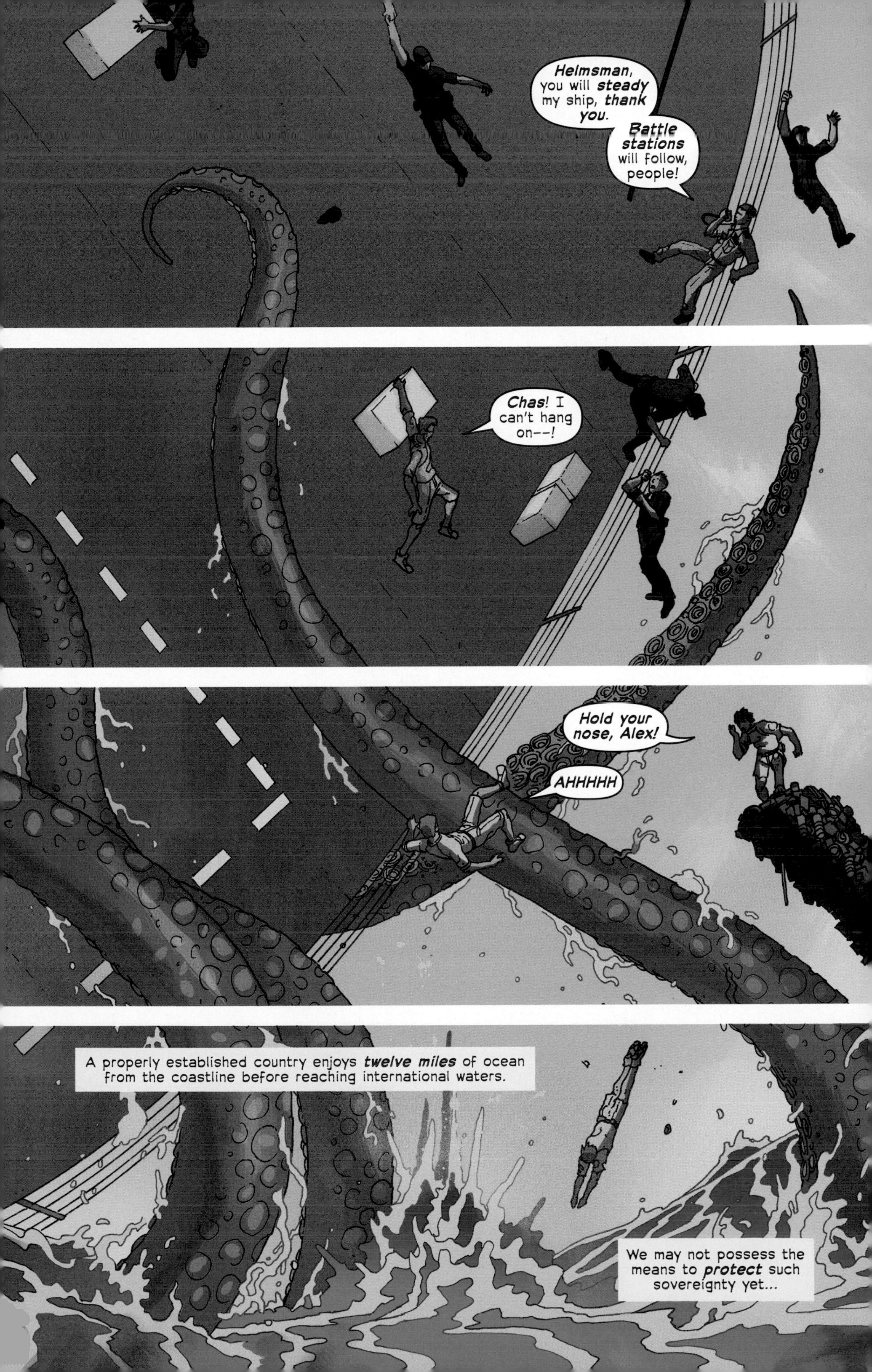
Helmsman, you will steady my ship, thank you.
Battle stations will follow, people!
Chas! I can't hang on--!
Hold your nose, Alex!
AHHHHH
A properly established country enjoys twelve miles of ocean from the coastline before reaching international waters.
We may not possess the means to protect such sovereignty yet...

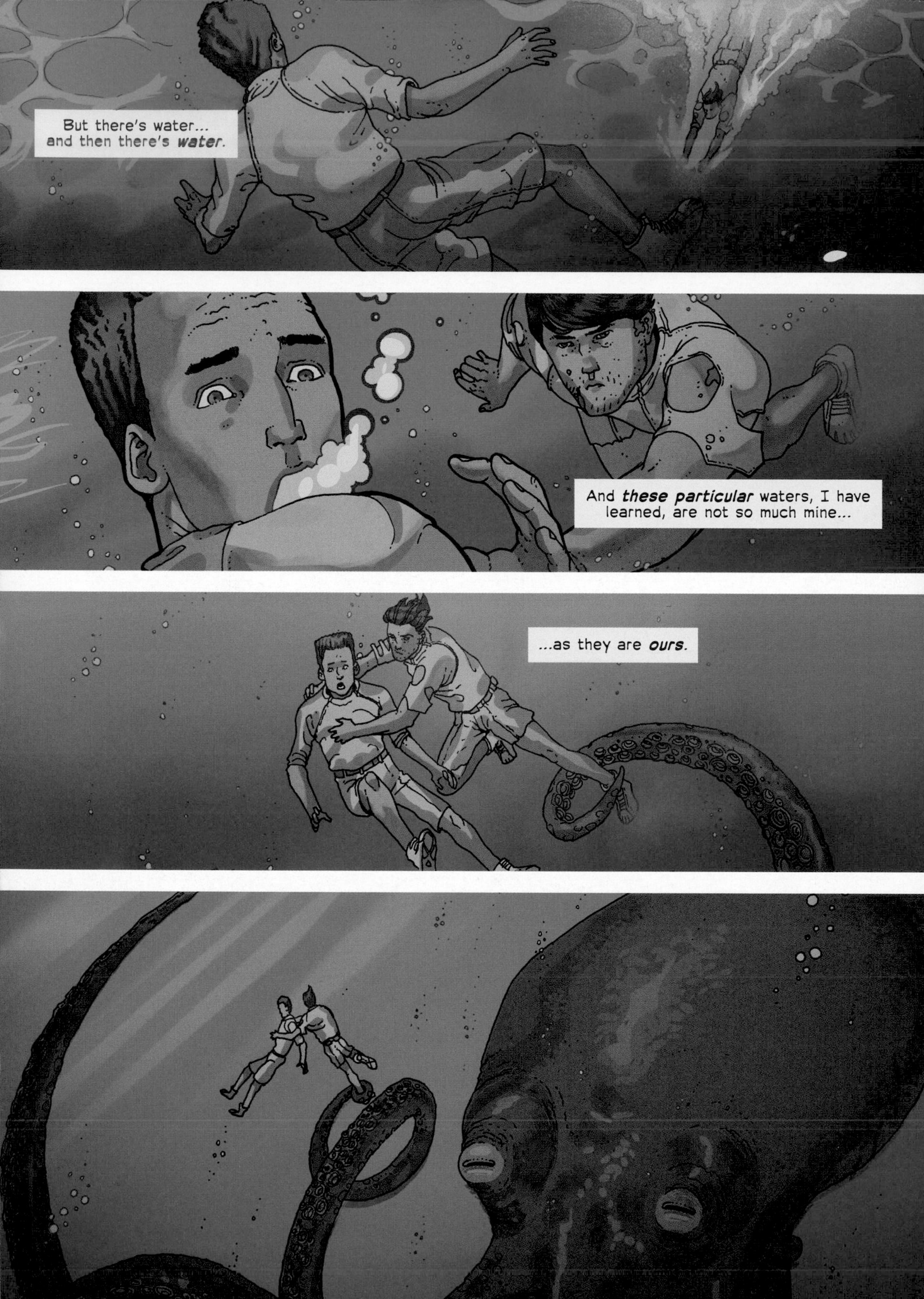
But there's water... and then there's *water*.
And *these particular* waters, I have learned, are not so much mine...
...as they are *ours*.

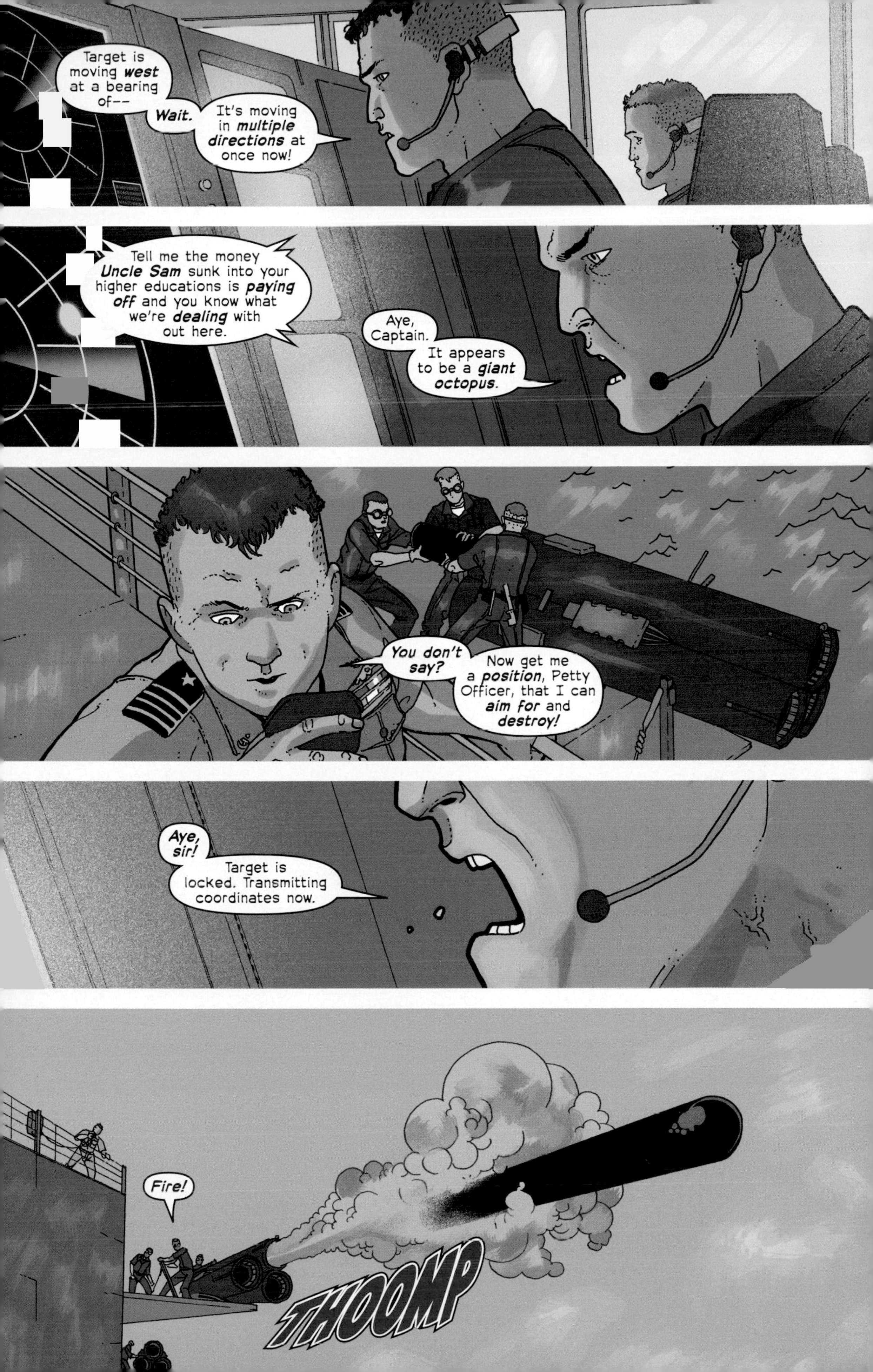
Target is moving west at a bearing of--
Wait.
It's moving in multiple directions at once now!
Tell me the money Uncle Sam sunk into your higher educations is paying off and you know what we're dealing with out here.
Aye, Captain.
It appears to be a giant octopus.
You don't say?
Now get me a position, Petty Officer, that I can aim for and destroy!
Aye, sir!
Target is locked. Transmitting coordinates now.
Fire!
THOOMP

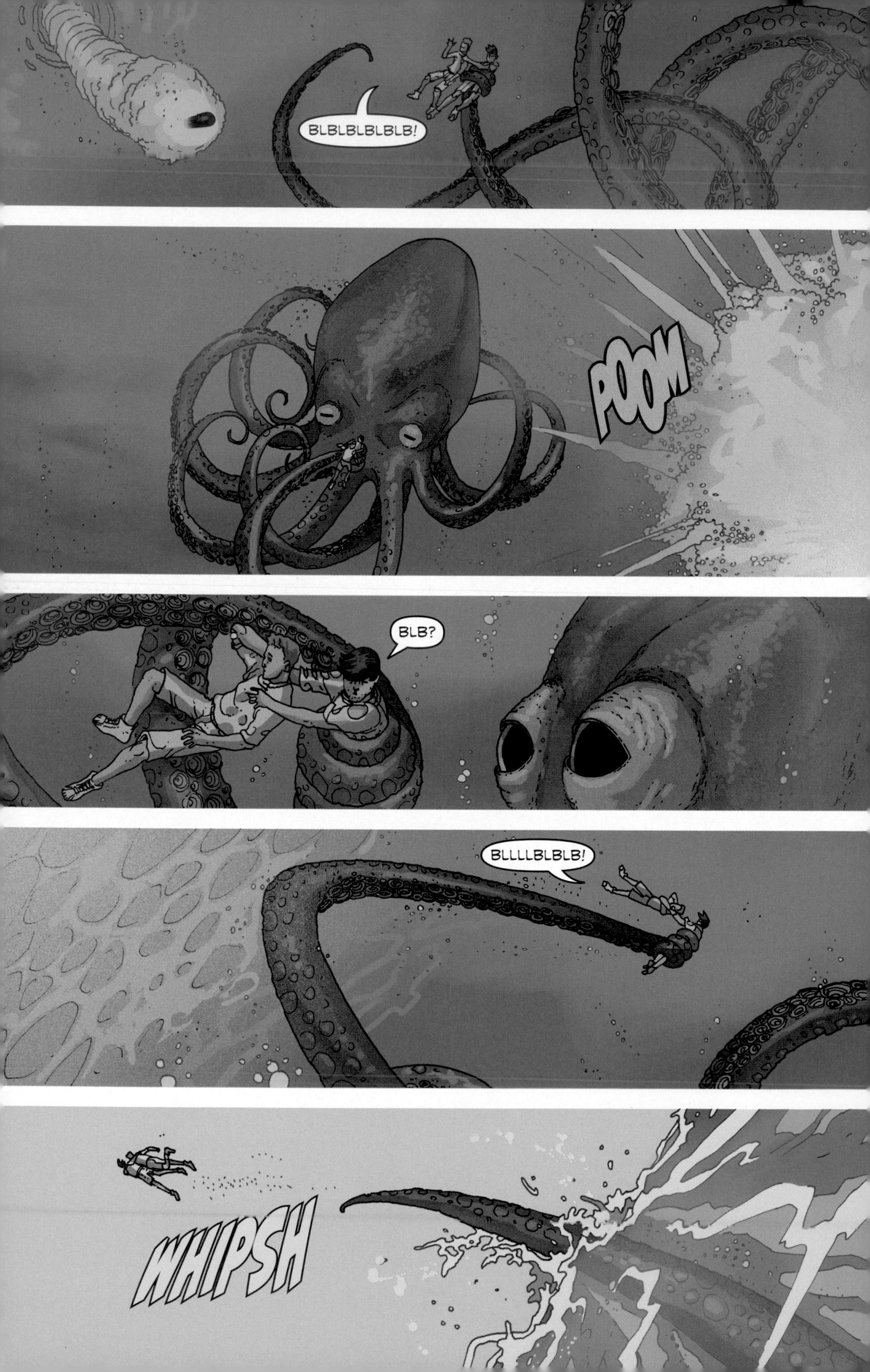
BLBLBLBLBLB!
POOM
BLB?
BLLLLBLBLB!
WHIPSH

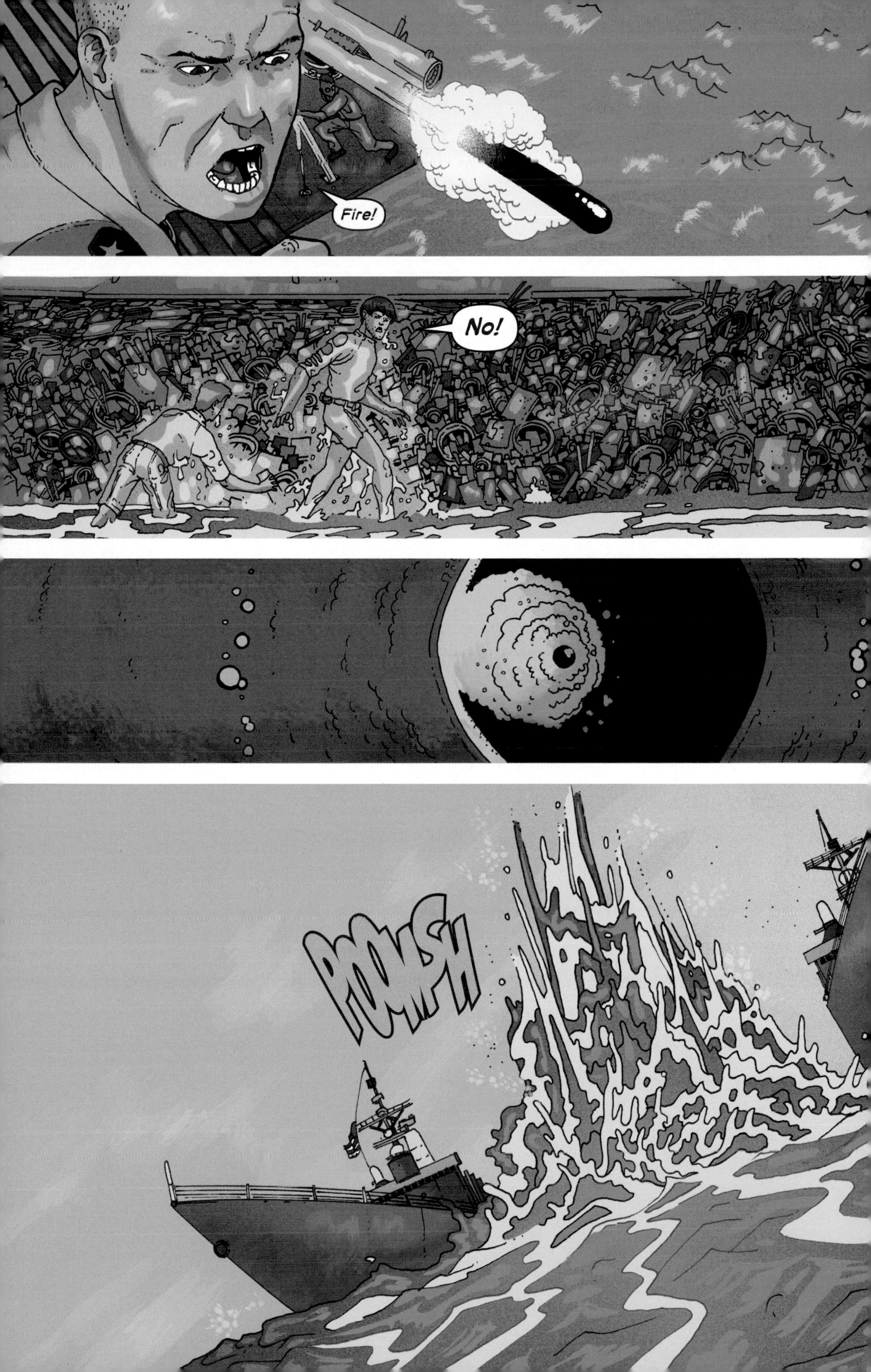

Fire!
No!
POOMSH

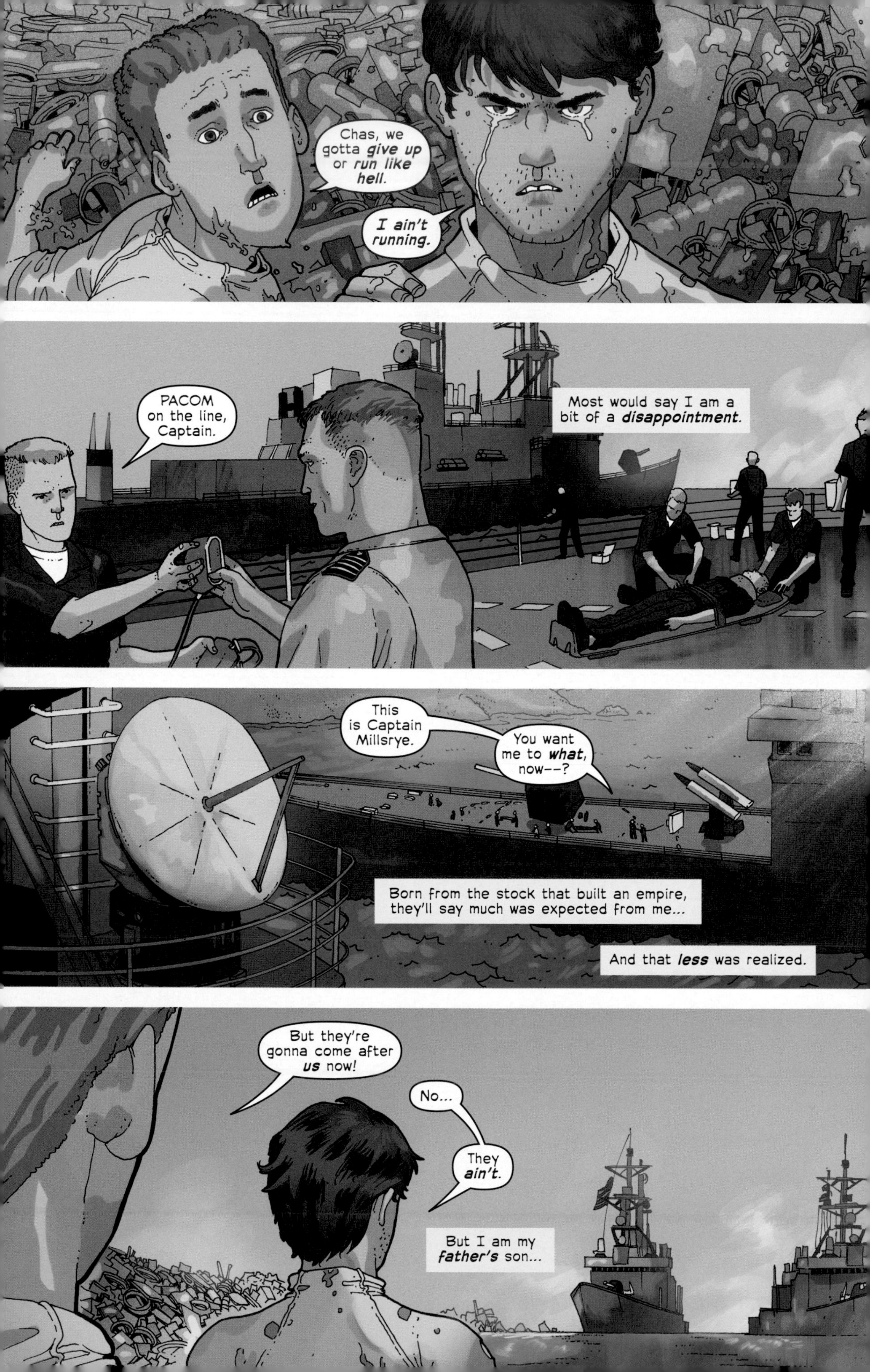

Chas, we gotta give up or run like hell.
I ain't running.
PACOM on the line, Captain.
Most would say I am a bit of a disappointment.
This is Captain Millsrye.
You want me to what, now--?
Born from the stock that built an empire, they'll say much was expected from me...
And that less was realized.
But they're gonna come after us now!
No...
They ain't.
But I am my father's son...

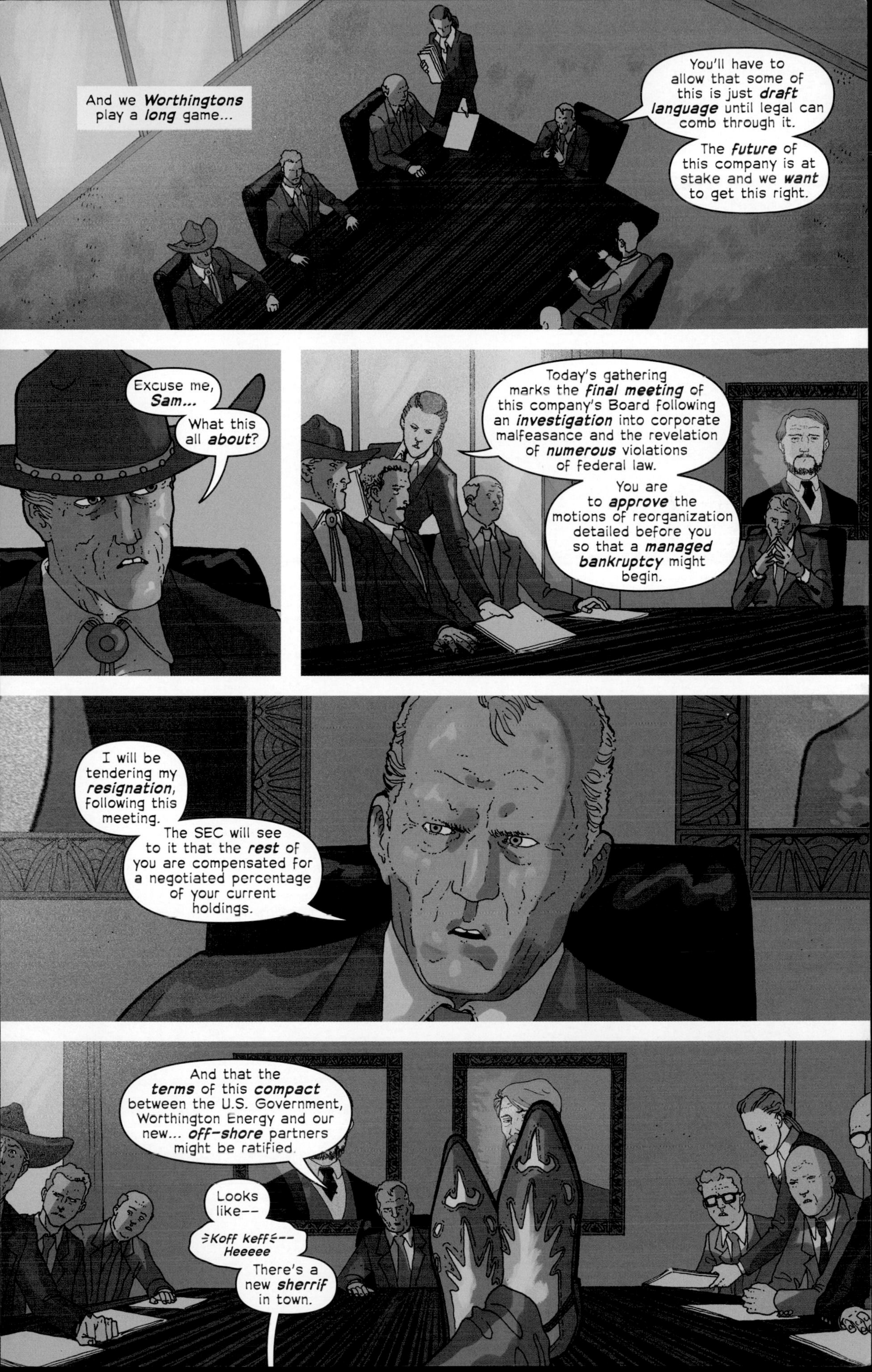

And we Worthingtons play a long game...
You'll have to allow that some of this is just draft language until legal can comb through it.
The future of this company is at stake and we want to get this right.
Excuse me, Sam...
What this all about?
Today's gathering marks the final meeting of this company's Board following an investigation into corporate malfeasance and the revelation of numerous violations of federal law.
You are to approve the motions of reorganization detailed before you so that a managed bankruptcy might begin.
I will be tendering my resignation, following this meeting.
The SEC will see to it that the rest of you are compensated for a negotiated percentage of your current holdings.
And that the terms of this compact between the U.S. Government, Worthington Energy and our new... off-shore partners might be ratified.
Looks like--
Koff keff--
Heeeee
There's a new sherrif in town.

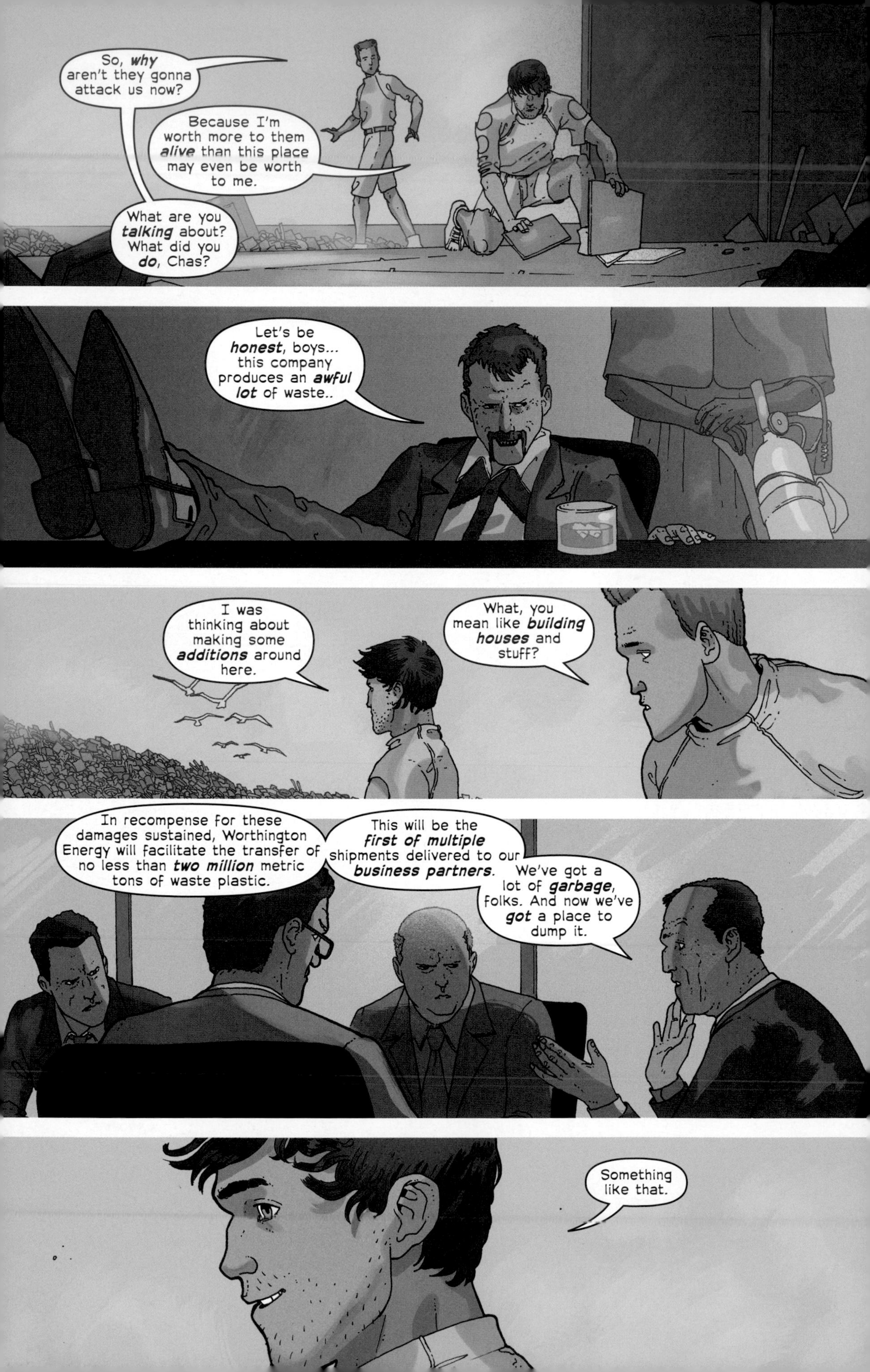
So, *why* aren't they gonna attack us now?
Because I'm worth more to them *alive* than this place may even be worth to me.
What are you *talking* about? What did you *do*, Chas?
Let's be *honest*, boys... this company produces an *awful lot* of waste..
I was thinking about making some *additions* around here.
What, you mean like *building houses* and stuff?
In recompense for these damages sustained, Worthington Energy will facilitate the transfer of no less than *two million* metric tons of waste plastic.
This will be the *first of multiple* shipments delivered to our *business partners*.
We've got a lot of *garbage*, folks. And now we've *got* a place to dump it.
Something like that.

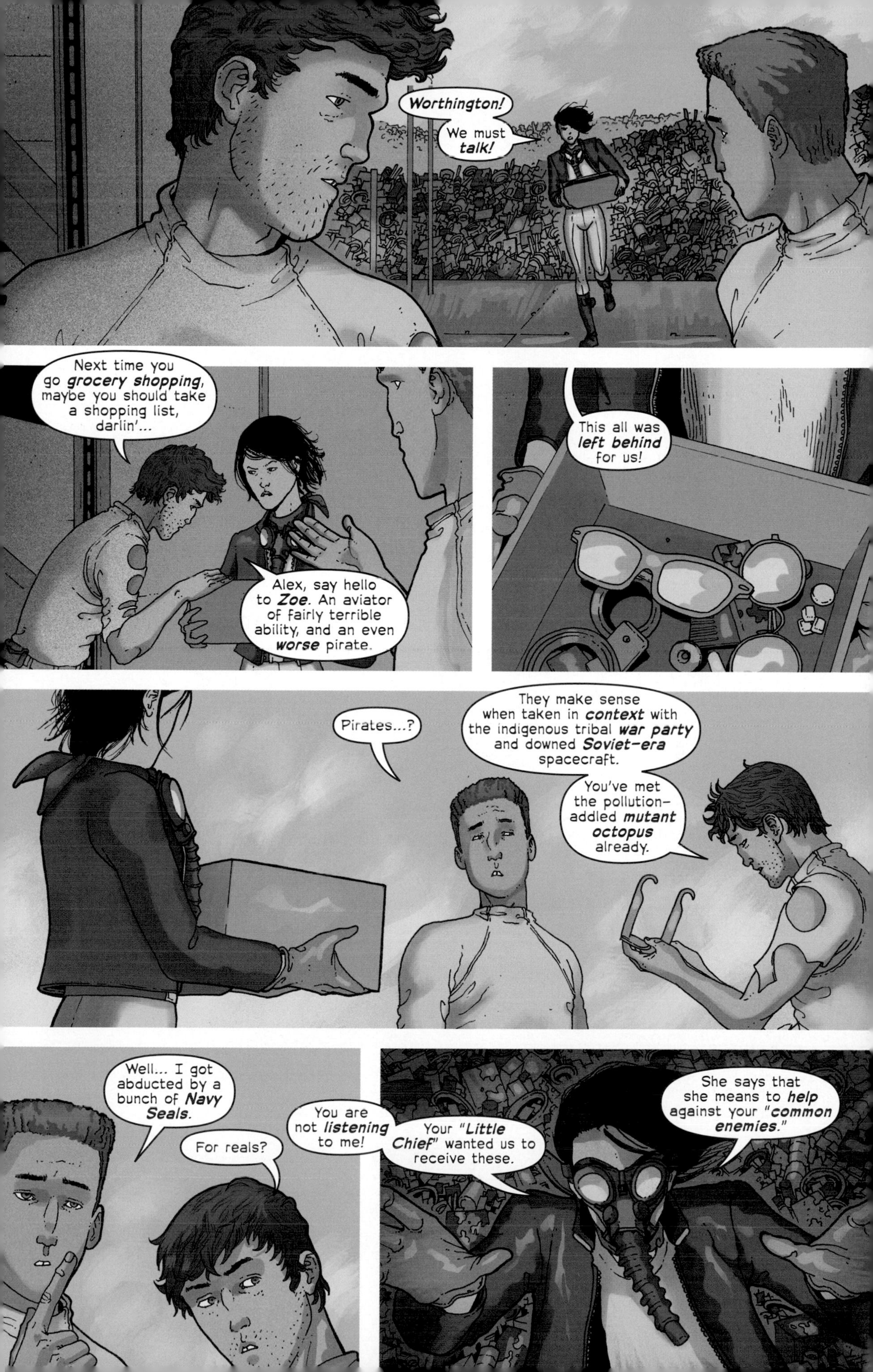

Worthington!
We must talk!
Next time you go grocery shopping, maybe you should take a shopping list, darlin'...
Alex, say hello to Zoe. An aviator of fairly terrible ability, and an even worse pirate.
This all was left behind for us!
Pirates...?
They make sense when taken in context with the indigenous tribal war party and downed Soviet-era spacecraft.
You've met the pollution-addled mutant octopus already.
Well... I got abducted by a bunch of Navy Seals.
For reals?
You are not listening to me!
Your "Little Chief" wanted us to receive these.
She says that she means to help against your "common enemies."

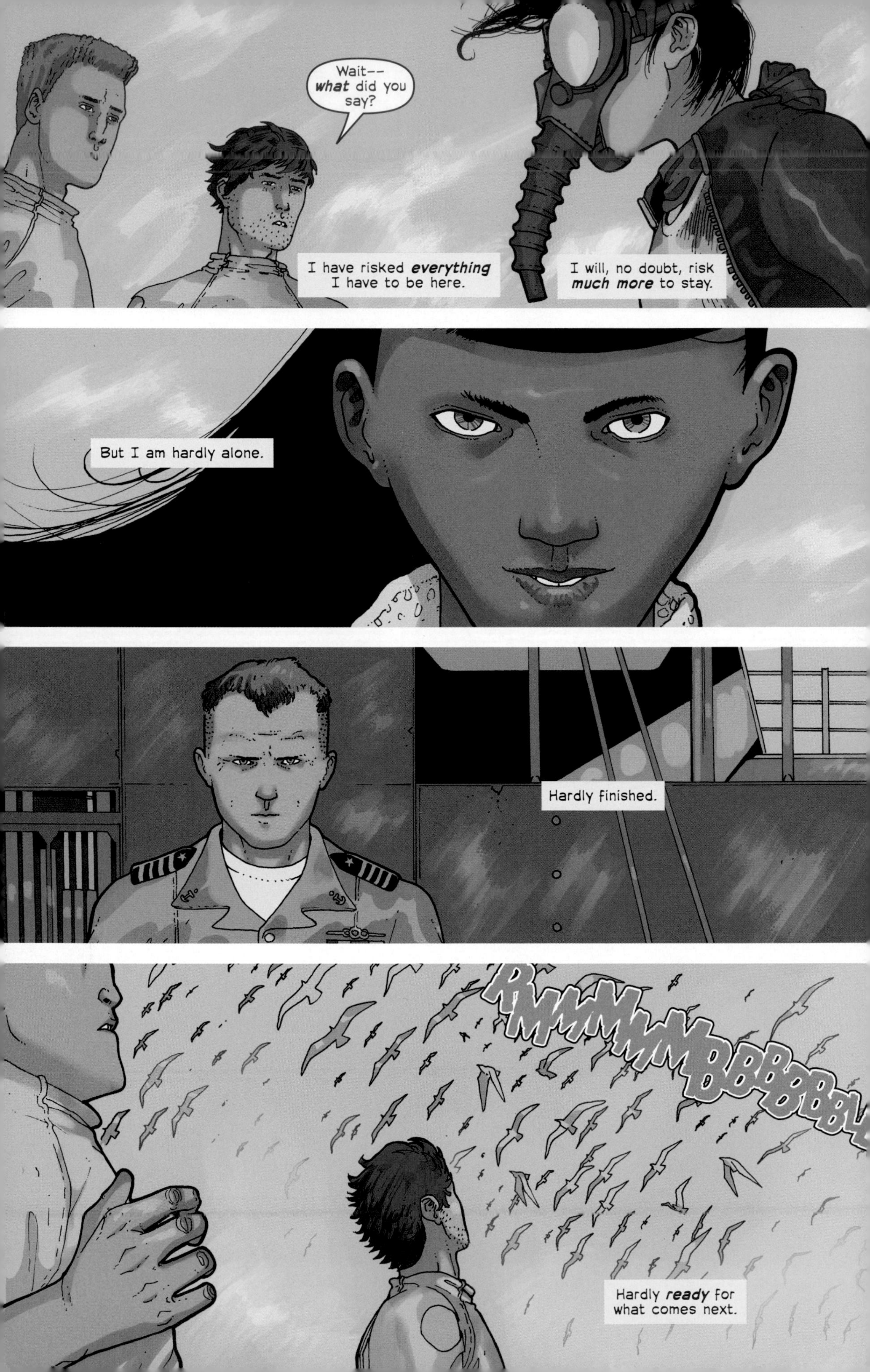
Wait-- **what** did you say?
I have risked **everything** I have to be here.
I will, no doubt, risk **much more** to stay.
But I am hardly alone.
Hardly finished.
RMMMMMBBBBBBL
Hardly **ready** for what comes next.

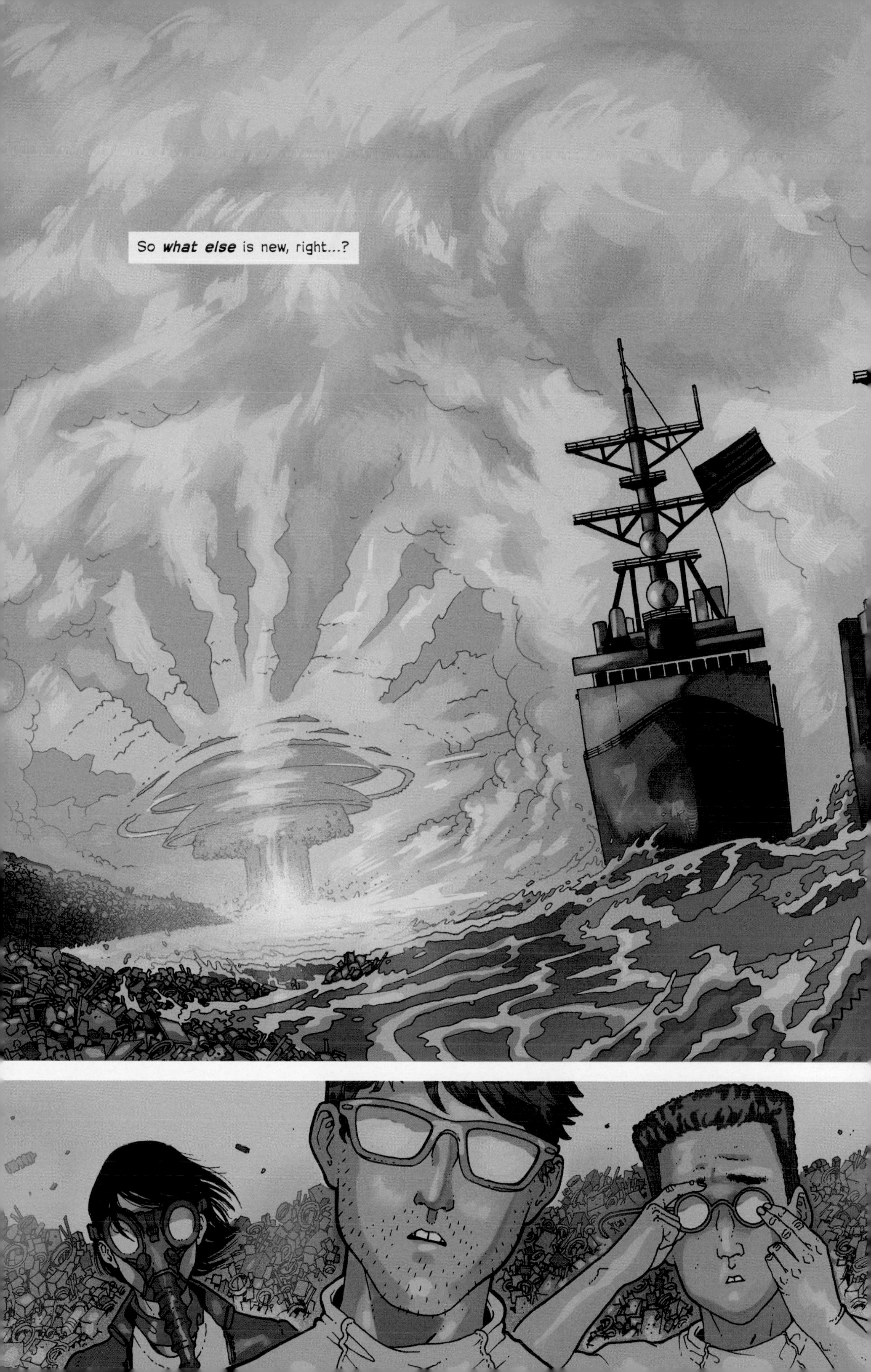
So *what else* is new, right...?

JOE HARRIS is the writer of original comics and graphic novels such as *Ghost Projekt*, *Spontaneous* and *Wars In Toyland*. He's written a bunch of books for Marvel, DC Comics and plenty of other publishers, and is presently writing *The X-Files: Season 10* for IDW.

A screenwriter (*Darkness Falls*, *The Tripper*) and filmmaker (*Witchwise*), he spent his childhood imagining the founding of his own country. While that childhood included lots of strange and exotic pets, giant octopuses were, sadly, not amongst them.

MARTIN MORAZZO is an artist based in Argentina who first came to the attention of US comics readers through his gorgeous artwork on the award-winning webcomic *Absolute Magnitude,* which was published via DC's now defunct online imprint, Zuda. Morazzo lives in Buenos Aires, and when he isn't spending every waking minute drawing *Great Pacific*, he likes to spend time at the beach with his lovely wife, Victoria and their children.

GREATPACIFIC

VOLUMETWO
"NATIONBUILDING"
COMINGSOON!